DISCOVERING SECOND

TEMPLE LITERATURE

The Jewish Publication Society expresses its gratitude for the generosity of the sponsors of this book:

Debbie Levenson and Steve Adelman, with deep gratitude to Gittel and Alan Hilibrand for all they do for כלל ישראל and for the בית נאמן of our entire family.

UNIVERSITY OF NEBRASKA PRESS
LINCOLN

DISCOVERING SECOND TEMPLE LITERATURE

THE SCRIPTURES AND STORIES THAT SHAPED EARLY JUDAISM

Malka Z. Simkovich

THE JEWISH PUBLICATION SOCIETY
PHILADELPHIA

Library of Congress Cataloging-in-Publication Data
Names: Simkovich, Malka Z., author.
Title: Discovering Second Temple literature: the scriptures
and stories that shaped early Judaism / Malka Z. Simkovich.
Description: Philadelphia: Jewish Publication Society; Lincoln:
University of Nebraska Press, [2018] | Includes
bibliographical references and index.
Identifiers: LCCN 2017053350
ISBN 9780827612655 (pbk.: alk. paper)
ISBN 9780827614284 (epub)
ISBN 9780827614291 (mobi)
ISBN 9780827614307 (web)
Subjects: LCSH: Judaism—History—Post-exilic period, 586 B.C.-
210 A.D. | Judaism—History—Talmudic period, 10-425. | Greek
literature—Jewish authors—History and criticism. | Rabbinical
literature—History and criticism. | Jews—History—586 B.C.-
70 A.D. | Jews—History—70-638. | Jews—Identity.
Classification: LCC BM176 .S516 2018 | DDC 296.09/014—dc23
LC record available at https://lccn.loc.gov/2017053350

Set in Merope by Mikala R. Kolander.
Designed by N. Putens.

Note about the cover: The image on the cover is part of a mosaic floor
discovered in Sepphoris, a town in the Galilee that flourished in the Rabbinic
period, which followed the Second Temple period. While this mosaic is
dated to the third or fourth century CE and includes scenes from the life
of Dionysus, a Greek god associated with wine, theater, and celebration,
it was discovered in a home that may have been inhabited by Jews. The
arresting images on this mosaic, and the Roman-style villa that houses
it, may testify to the ways in which some Jews admired aspects of Greek
and Roman culture to such an extent that they welcomed these features
into their own homes. Even some synagogue floors that archaeologists
have dated to the Rabbinic period incorporate images from Greek
mythology. Jewish literature of the Second Temple period paved the way
for this kind of integrative thinking, which extended well past 70 CE.

In memory of my mother,

Naomi Ruth Zeiger,

who saw the spark in

friends and strangers and

delighted in their stories

CONTENTS

ACKNOWLEDGMENTS

Both friends and colleagues read portions of this book and provided generous feedback. Professor Lawrence Schiffman pored over every page of the manuscript and offered invaluable comments, corrections, and support. His efforts have positively impacted nearly every page of this book, and my gratitude to him is immense. Professor Reuven Kimelman equipped me with key insights concerning the canonization of the Bible that lie at the core of chapter 11, and his scholarship has shaped the way that I think about all of the extracanonical books discussed in this book. Professor Steven Fine and Professor Loren Stuckenbruck responded promptly and graciously to my queries. My father and stepmother, Allen and Leah Zeiger, and my in-laws, Moshe and Laurie Simkovich, gave advice on early drafts of this book that improved it tremendously. In particular, my father read each word of the manuscript and spent hours writing detailed feedback on every section. Rabbi Etan Ehrenfeld pointed me toward texts that I would not have otherwise seen, Arn Pressner read early drafts of the book and offered helpful suggestions, and Rachel Renz provided meticulous notes on the entire manuscript that improved it tremendously. Rabbi Barry Schwartz, director of the Jewish Publication Society (JPS), gave expert recommendations that helped make this book more accessible. The time and care invested by Joy Weinberg, JPS managing editor, and the staff at the University of Nebraska Press, made the publication process efficient and pleasurable. Throughout this process, Joy remained unfailingly enthusiastic, even when discussing the most technical details of the manuscript.

My husband, Aaron, supported this project from the time that it was only an idea by helping me carve out time to research while he executed the mundane and often overlooked necessary tasks required to run a six-person household. All the while, he encouraged me to keep writing and was a sounding board whenever I needed to talk something out, playing the part of both writer and reader. This book reflects a partnership I would not give up for anything in the world. Our four children, Yonatan, Hadar, Ayelet, and Gavriel, continue to be my inspirations. Their presence reminds me of the miraculously unlikely survival of the Jewish people, and how necessary it is to provide their generation with a nuanced understanding of our history and identity, which an understanding of the Second Temple period strengthens.

The person who perhaps would have appreciated this project more than anyone else is not with us to read it. My mother, Naomi Zeiger, tragically passed away in 2005. But her unflagging energy and enthusiasm about my work has had a lasting effect, and it is to her credit that I have completed this project. My mother embraced learning about all periods of Jewish history. She taught me and my siblings to educate ourselves about subjects that interested us by exploring libraries without knowing exactly what we were looking for. She kept pictures of Israel's landscape from our recent trips in her purse and would excitedly show her friends photographs of her children and grandchildren standing on the same ground as the earliest Jews. My mother cherished the idea that her children were living on the ground where Jews had lived, or longed to live, for thousands of years. Any enthusiasm that the reader detects is to my mother's credit, and I dedicate this book to her memory.

INTRODUCTION

In Search of the Second Temple Era

The past century and a half has seen extraordinary developments in the field of Second Temple Judaism. The discoveries made at Qumran, St. Catherine's Monastery, the Cairo Genizah, and Mount Athos have been among the greatest finds in Jewish historical research, irreversibly changing our understanding of what life was like in the Second Temple period.

And yet, the study of this period is not appreciated as much as it deserves. In the early years of my doctoral program, a friend of mine who is an Orthodox rabbi remarked to me, "If I were to get a doctorate in Jewish studies, it would be in medieval Judaism. Studying Second Temple Judaism wouldn't help me as a rabbi." His dismissive attitude toward Second Temple literature is fairly typical. Over the years, other Jews have asked me questions that reflect a similar perspective: What do Second Temple texts really have to offer? If the rabbinic community is not interested in them, what value do they bring to the study of Judaism? How are they relevant to us today?

Indeed, the history and literature of the Second Temple period has been studied as its own discipline for only a few decades. A hundred years ago, if a young scholar wanted to study what Jewish life was like between the sixth century BCE and the first century CE, he or she would take courses in Bible, religion, or perhaps classics. Now, however, hundreds of specialists are experts in the field of Second Temple Judaism and its literature. The writings of Josephus and Philo, the Dead Sea Scrolls, and the many texts written in Greek with uncertain origins are all subfields to which thousands of courses, conferences, and books have been dedicated.

Still, the absence of Second Temple studies as a discipline in its own right endures today in a different educational context: the religious day school system. As in academia, students in this system are taught Bible and history as independent subjects. In these classes students might pick up some information about life in the Second Temple period, but they are primarily exposed to this period in the context of its bridging the biblical and Rabbinic eras. Because they are taught Bible studies and Oral Law as separate disciplines, their mental timeline tends to jump from the last book of the Hebrew Bible, Chronicles, to the next body of authoritative material, the Mishnah.

The tendency to not see the Second Temple period as integral to understanding the history of the Jewish and Christian people is also evident in some Christian schools. Christians also study what they call the Old Testament, which ends with Malachi, and then move on to the New Testament.

Both the Jewish and Christian timelines effect a sense of artificial continuity: In the Jewish tradition, the Hebrew Bible ends with the rebuilding of the Second Temple, and the Mishnah picks up where the Second Temple period ends by providing a guidebook on how to observe divine law in the absence of the Temple. In the Christian tradition, Malachi closes the Old Testament with a prediction of a coming savior, and the first gospel, the Gospel of Matthew, opens with a lineage that traces Jesus' ancestry back to David.

In these schemes, the literature produced during the latter half of the Second Temple period is peripheralized. Jews and Christians might acknowledge that this material is interesting, but at the same time they deny that late Second Temple literature is foundational in helping them to understand their religious roots. In Jewish communities, jumping from the end of Chronicles to the beginning of the Mishnah encourages Jewish readers to turn the latest biblical figures—primarily Daniel, Ezra, and Nehemiah—into Rabbinic-type leaders who held the same values and practices as the first generation of Rabbis who are cited in the Mishnah. According to this approach, Daniel, Ezra, and Nehemiah foresaw what normative Judaism (the Judaism that most law-observant Jews would practice) would look like by the third and fourth centuries CE. They therefore emphasized prayer, text study, and the observance of practices that would become more developed in the Rabbinic period, such as the Sabbath and dietary law.

As sensitive students of history, however, we must be careful to study the lives and teachings of these late biblical figures within their historical contexts. Few would disagree that Daniel, Ezra, and Nehemiah, who lived in the beginning of the Second Temple period under Persian rule, practiced Judaism in ways that differed from rabbis such as Akiva and Hillel, who lived at the end of the Second Temple period. These different practices were coupled with different social *realia* and challenges that had to be addressed. Ezra's top priority, for instance, was convincing his fellow Judeans that the separation of men from their foreign wives was a necessary act in order to establish a stable Judean community focused on worshipping solely the Jewish God. Biblical evidence indicates that Ezra's Judean colleagues did not necessarily feel the same way. While Ezra had to make an argument that marriage between two Jews was a core element of Jewish identity, Jews living in the Rabbinic period took this argument for granted and did not have to articulate this point explicitly.

Textual evidence attests to some of the major differences between Jewish practice in the beginning and at the end of the Second Temple period. While Jewish Law underwent major expansion and development in the late Second Temple and early Rabbinic periods, the Jews who returned from exile in the decades following 539 BCE did not know how to fully observe their own scriptural laws. Nehemiah 8, for example, recalls how the returning Judeans were unsure how to observe the holiday of Sukkot (the Tabernacles festival). Yet many of the laws and customs associated with this festival were well established by the early Rabbinic period.

The fact is, the Second Temple period contains the key to understanding how the Israelite religion of the Hebrew Bible became the normative Rabbinic religion as we now know it. In the early centuries of the Common Era, the Rabbinic community living in the Land of Israel and other Jewish communities throughout the Roman world inherited a vibrant legacy from their Jewish predecessors who lived in the Second Temple period. These Jews were themselves inheritors of a thriving tradition with which they were directly engaged. Like the Rabbis, they were working with an inherited tradition, and were in active conversation with it. Their voices are as much a part of our inherited tradition and primordial religious history as the voices of the Rabbis themselves.

Unfortunately, both Jews and Christians have had good reasons to relegate much of Second Temple Jewish literature to the sidelines. Some Christians see the Second Temple period as the era in which the Israelite religion entered into continuous decline. Rather than emphasizing the ethical behavior preached by the early prophets, Jews were ignoring the ethical aspects of their religion and becoming increasingly rigid in their legalism. To this way of thinking, by the first century CE, the decline of emphasis on ethical behavior and the increased focus on cultic ritual resulted in Judaism's becoming a shell of itself. In emphasizing the rote practices of ritual worship, some Christian theologians suggest, Judaism had lost its heart. As Judaism was flailing, and Roman imperial rule was on the rise, the road was being paved for the entry of Jesus, who would redeem the sins of humankind and offer—at least in the apostle Paul's interpretation—a new covenantal relationship between God and Israel that emphasized faith over works.

To some Christian scholars, especially those living in previous generations, Judaism was not only failing to thrive in the Second Temple period: It was barely surviving. This perspective has affected how Christians perceive Second Temple literature.

For most traditional Jews, the Second Temple period is important only in the sense that some Jews at this time preserved the chain of transmission that began with Moses' revelation at Sinai and continued through the Rabbinic period. Like Christians, these Jews relegate Jewish literature produced during this period to the sidelines. Because these texts are so unlike the "normative" Rabbinic literature written after the Second Temple's destruction in 70 CE, and because they don't seem to offer a coherent view of Jewish belief and practice, most traditionalists regard

Second Temple literature as at best irrelevant and at worst heretical. Any such literature that does not look "typically Jewish"—that does not emphasize distinctively Jewish practices such as circumcision, the Sabbath, and dietary law—is often mistakenly attributed to Jews living on the outskirts of engaged Jewish life.

The diversity of Second Temple literature, coupled with its divergence from the Rabbinic material that followed it, poses a problem for modern Christian and Jewish traditionalists. How should this literature be classified within the broader spectrum of Jewish tradition? Do any of its texts have a place in traditional Judaism? What would it mean if the texts produced at this time represented, at least for some Jews, a type of normative Judaism that correlated with full commitment to identifying as a Jew, even if this identification did not look precisely as the Rabbis depicted it in the coming centuries?

When we ignore the Second Temple period, we lose the richly diverse chorus of Jewish conversations that, together, explored how to read the scriptures, and how to express one's Jewishness. Rather than depict the Judaism of the time as either crumbling—which can lead to anti-Jewish stereotypes, or as represented by either observant proto-Rabbinic or totally Hellenized Jews, which can lead to egregious historical errors—we can approach and appreciate this period as having nurtured literary productivity by Jews who fully identified with and embraced their Jewish identities.

The Missing Link

Debate continues today regarding whether Jewish life was so diverse in the Second Temple period that it would be appropriate to refer to it as "Judaisms," or whether there was what some call a Common Judaism, a Judaism that made Jews identifiable to one another and to non-Jews. Discoveries over the past century and a half reveal just how diverse Jewish life was at the time. And yet, a common Torah; a set of practices that included circumcision, dietary law, and Sabbath observance; and a connection to a national narrative that emphasized the people's divine chosenness were common to virtually all Jewish communities.

What accounts, then, for the remarkable variety of stories, interpretations, liturgical passages, wisdom texts, novellas, and apocalyptic visions that Jews living in the Greco-Roman world produced and circulated? To answer this, we must recall that the Jewish religion did not have a single, centralized body of government to look to for guidance and legislation. The Hasmonean family, for example, controlled the region of Judea, but its oversight did not extend past Judea's borders. Likewise, the Jewish leader of Alexandrian Jewry, known as the patriarch, was responsible only for the Jews in his vicinity. Nor was there a council of regional rulers that governed all of Jewry. In the Second Temple period, it is believed that the influence of the 120-member council known as the Men of the Great Assembly did not extend beyond Judea.

The lack of centralized religious government enabled Jews to express their identities in ways that did not have to conform with normative expectations. As a result, much of the surviving Second Temple literature constitutes pure expressions of Jews' biblical interpretations. Given the vast variety of Jewish experience, fantasies about what the world was once like, or what it should be like, or what it one day would look like, abounded.

Over the following centuries, as the multicolored tapestry of Second Temple Judaism gave way to normative Judaism, the voices reflected in Second Temple Judaism continued to echo in Jewish writings. And the multivalence of the Second Temple period would be mirrored, in a narrower way, in the dialogical extrapolations of the Rabbis.

As its name indicates, the Second Temple period tends to be defined by its relation to adjacent time periods: the biblical period that preceded it and the Rabbinic period that followed it. To regard the Second Temple period as an in-between stage, however, is a mistake. The development of the Jewish religion occurred not, as is often taught, with the writing of a collection of books that represented a unified worldview, but with an explosion of literary productivity that represented diverse ideas from all over the world. The authors of these works utilized different literary genres to express a rich variety of religious beliefs. Some wrote adventure stories with romantic themes using biblical heroes as protagonists.

Some wrote wisdom texts, which instructed readers in matters of pious and proper conduct. Others wrote apocalyptic texts, which portended the events that would transition the present world into a new form of human existence following a period of divine judgment over all of the world's inhabitants.

Taken together, this material reflects an astonishing diversity of Jewish knowledge, belief, and practice during the Second Temple period. As this book demonstrates, the Jewish literature of this period also attests to the lack of correlation between where Jews lived, the language they spoke, and their level of religious piety. Some authors, such as the Jewish writer of 2 Maccabees, probably did not know any Hebrew and had never set foot in the Land of Israel. The highly stylized Greek this author employs attests to his high level of Greek education. Yet, ironically, 2 Maccabees advocates for a separation between Jewish practice and integration into Greek civic life.

Other books ignore distinguishing aspects of Judaism such as the Sabbath, circumcision, and dietary laws but have strong Jewish overtones nonetheless. The Sentences of Pseudo-Phocylides, for example, looks like a typical Greek wisdom text—comprising mainly axioms regarding how to virtuously live one's life—yet its introduction paraphrases the Decalogue (the Ten Commandments) as it appears in Exodus 20 of the Septuagint, the Greek translation of the Hebrew Bible. This author also depended on Leviticus 19, which underscores proper ethical behavior, to write his introduction.

What were these authors' true intentions in writing their books? How did their ideologies correlate with how they practiced Judaism in the Greco-Roman world? The more scholars learn about the world of Second Temple Judaism, the more they realize how complex the answers are.

The Making of the Modern Pseudepigrapha

Many of the books authored by Jews during the late Second Temple period and subsequent centuries comprise what scholars refer to as the Pseudepigrapha. This word, meaning "false writings," derives from the Greek words *pseudo*, meaning "fake," and *epigrapha*, meaning "writings." More broadly, the term refers to a common practice in which authors would intentionally conceal their identities by attributing their works to more well-known authors. Very often this "author" was a biblical hero. For instance, scholars believe that 2 Baruch and 4 Ezra, two books that are attributed to biblical figures, were actually written on the heels of the Roman destruction of the Second Temple in 70 CE. Attributing these texts to heroes who lived in the biblical period was a means to legitimize these texts by placing them in the framework of Jewish scriptural authority.

The notion of a Pseudepigrapha collection, however, did not exist until just a few centuries ago, when the German scholar Johann Albert Fabricius (1668–1736) assembled a collection of ancient books into what he called a Pseudepigrapha.

In 1913, the British scholar Robert Henry Charles (1855–1931) published a new collection, with different books. Charles' work, *The Apocrypha and Pseudepigrapha of the Old Testament*, contained two volumes. Volume 1 included the books of Judith, Tobit, 1 and 2 Maccabees, and other volumes appearing in the Apocrypha (referring to books included in the Catholic Bible, but not in the Hebrew or Protestant Bibles) and in the Septuagint (the Greek translation of the Hebrew Bible). The second volume contained only sixteen books, which he presented according to genre: History Rewritten from the Standpoint of the Law, Sacred Legends, Apocalypses, Psalms, Ethics and Wisdom Literature, and History. Accompanying each book was an introduction reflecting upon the book's content and provenance, as well as a translation and commentary.

Charles' work constituted a major turning point in the field of Second Temple Jewish literature. His books provided scholars with easier access to ancient Jewish texts. More importantly, his collection affirmed the idea that the study of nonbiblical ancient Jewish texts was a legitimate academic field, and that the texts in his collection were worthy of careful analysis.

Over the course of the twentieth century, scholars would continue to discover copies of ancient books that came to be regarded as part of the Pseudepigrapha. A cache of ancient Jewish manuscripts recovered from a synagogue storeroom, or genizah, in Cairo in the late 1890s, for example, yielded hundreds of thousands of fragments, some of which contained texts originally composed in the Second Temple period. As the contents of this cache opened to scholars over the course of the twentieth century, they realized that a vast expanse of unexplored literature dating to the Second Temple period could shed light on this formative period.

This sense came to a head with the discovery of the Dead Sea Scrolls in 1948. Found in eleven caves in Israel's Judean Desert near the northwestern edge of the Dead Sea, the scrolls were recognized almost immediately as the remains of an ancient Jewish library. As details about this library emerged, and the contents of the Cairo Genizah and the Dead Sea caves published, scholars began to appreciate the enormity of the corpus of Second Temple Jewish literature. This, in turn, revived interest in Jewish books that had been preserved for centuries in ancient synagogues and monasteries. The time had come for a new collection of Old Testament Pseudepigrapha.

In 1983, the scholar James Charlesworth, along with a highly trained team, published an expansive, two-volume edition of the Pseudepigrapha that included far more than Fabricius' and Charles' earlier collections. This work, titled *The Old Testament Pseudepigrapha*, is now regarded as the standard collection for scholars and lay readers looking to study the Jewish Pseudepigrapha. Critical editions of the books in this collection are being published independently as well. All of these editions are helping scholars to understand these books' compositional history and their place in Jewish tradition.

The notion of what can be regarded as part of the Pseudepigrapha continues to expand. In 2013, Richard Bauckham, James Davila, and Alex Panayotov edited the first of what will be a two-volume collection of texts entitled *Old Testament Pseudepigrapha: More Noncanonical Scriptures*. In addition to including material published in Charlesworth's volumes, this edition also presents passages from the writings of the early first-century CE philosopher Philo of Alexandria, the late-first-century CE historian Josephus, and documents found in the Dead Sea caves.[1] Volume 1 begins with a section, "Texts Ordered According to Biblical Chronology," comprising books that retell or expand biblical stories. A second section, "Thematic Texts," includes two texts that broadly review earlier Israelite history and offers an overview of biblical references to books lost over the centuries. Both volumes in this more recent collection comprise mainly texts that have not been included in modern collections of Pseudepigrapha.[2]

The Jewish Publication Society's monumental *Outside the Bible: Ancient Jewish Writings Related to Scripture* (OTB) was published within only a couple of weeks after the publication of *Old Testament Pseudepigrapha: More Noncanonical Scriptures*. OTB—a three-volume set comprising the most comprehensive collection of ancient Jewish writings in one publication—marked a major contribution to the study of Second Temple Judaism by presenting a far more thorough collection than the Pseudepigrapha editions of Charles and Charlesworth.

OTB collects these ancient Jewish texts in a novel way. Rather than gathering texts that could reasonably be regarded as pseudepigraphical, the editors offer a new classification system for Second Temple literature: organizing the material according to genre. Viewing Greek versions of the Bible, biblical interpretation, the writings of Philo, the writings of Josephus, sectarian texts, and so on makes it easier for readers to study late Second Temple texts alongside one another. The notion that the writings of Philo, Josephus, and the Dead Sea Scrolls should be read alongside the books preserved in the Pseudepigrapha has also enabled scholars and laypeople to study the world of the Second Temple in a more comprehensive way, with all these texts in conversation with one another and elucidating one another.

Scholars continue to debate whether many of the books preserved in the Pseudepigrapha have Jewish origins. A few books that are widely agreed to be of non-Jewish origin, such as the ancient Legend of Ahiqar, were intentionally included in Charlesworth's collection because they were well circulated in Jewish communities. And although the term "Pseudepigrapha" continues to be used, many scholars concur that the word poses difficulties. There is currently no consensus regarding what books should be included in this collection, and not all of these books are "pseudepigraphic" in the strict sense of the word.[3]

How to Use This Book

Discovering Second Temple Literature is divided into four main sections. The first section explores how the world of the Second Temple period emerged in the foreground of the field of Early Judaism over the past century and a half. The recent interest in this period is largely due to the discoveries of various caches of early Jewish manuscripts in Jewish synagogues, monasteries, and even in caves in isolated regions of the Judean Desert—regions that lay almost entirely unexplored for thousands of years. The second section discusses the vibrant Jewish communities of the Second Temple period, both in the Land of Israel and in the Diaspora. The third section delves into the lives and worldviews of the authors of some Second Temple writings. Finally, the fourth section reviews some of the books written during the Second Temple period that retell stories preserved in the Hebrew Bible and the Septuagint.

This book helps to flesh out the extensive period of time between the end of the biblical period and the beginning of the Rabbinic period in ways that will help readers appreciate the complex elements that galvanized religious change and characterized Jewish identity and practice in the Second Temple period. Teachers in college and other adult education settings that allow for time to study this period in depth can begin with chapters 4–6, which cover the history of Jewish communities in Jerusalem, Alexandria, and Antioch; move on to chapters 7–10, which explore the varied worldviews of Second Temple Jews; and close with chapters 11–13, which delve into the literature produced by Second Temple Jews. History teachers in day schools with limited time may want to focus first on Second Temple Jewish communities (chapters 4–6) and the texts produced in these communities (chapters 11–13). The book's glossary, as well as the abbreviations, bibliography, general index, and index by passage, can help readers quickly reference or learn more about a given subject.

This book can also be used as a complement to *Outside the Bible*, which supplements Second Temple documents with extensive introductions and commentaries. For delving deeply into the historical context, compositional history, and the texts of Second Temple works, this book and OTB illuminate one another. *Discovering Second Temple Literature* provides more concise analysis; OTB offers extensive material, in-depth introductions, and commentaries.

By assigning and discussing OTB selections in tandem with portions of this book, educators will take students on a rich voyage into the world of Second Temple Judaism. An instructor teaching students about how Jews in the Second Temple period interpreted the book of Genesis, for instance, could assign passages from books cited in OTB, such as Jubilees, the Genesis Apocryphon, and Joseph and Aseneth, along with passages from *Discovering Second Temple Literature* that shed light on the authors' worldviews and the communities they might have lived in. Chapter 5 of this book, which details Jewish life in Alexandria, would add new layers of understanding for readers interested in Joseph and Aseneth, a book many scholars believe was written by a Jew in Alexandria. Chapter 8, on the other hand, which examines the worldviews of sectarian Jews, would illuminate the book of Jubilees, which represents a minority perspective by advocating for a solar calendar, as well as the Genesis Apocryphon, which was likely written by a Jew living in a sectarian community at Qumran. In addition, chapter 12 studies Jubilees and the Genesis Apocryphon, among other works, and chapter 13 includes an examination of Joseph and Aseneth. These later chapters explore how the authors of these documents used—and changed—biblical stories to further their ideologies or to clarify common questions of the time. By assigning and discussing sections of chapters 8, 12, and 13 along with passages in OTB in classroom settings, educators can help students to appreciate how these works participated in the widely popular exercise of biblical interpretation by addressing questions that Jewish readers in many communities were asking.

Educators working with themes that do not correspond to chapter headings in OTB and *Discovering Second Temple Literature* can also easily incorporate these books in their curricula. An instructor teaching a course or unit on women in Judaism, for example, might assign passages from the books of Judith and 2 Maccabees in OTB. Students learning about the Second Temple period may find it striking that these Second Temple texts feature two brave women—Judith and the mother of seven sons in 2 Maccabees—who demonstrate willingness to sacrifice themselves to further the welfare of their people, were upheld as paradigms of righteousness, and stand at the center of highly pietistic stories. The instructor could then turn to chapter 4 of this book, which describes the Jews' successful rebellion against the Syrian Greeks in Judea in the second century BCE, which the author of Judith may have witnessed firsthand or heard of secondhand, and which the author of 2 Maccabees recalls with an innovative theological orientation. Chapter 13 considers the book of Judith in more detail and suggests that its author may have been satirizing stories that were circulating about the Hasmoneans who rebelled against the Syrian Greeks. Reading these books in light of chapters 4, 12, and 13 will help students understand how Jews in the late Second Temple period attributed religious meaning to the Hasmonean rebellion.

Another example of worthy collaborative review is James Kugel's excellent introduction to the book of Jubilees in OTB. His analysis of the role that Jubilees played in Christian traditions and how it was recovered in modern times provides a thoughtful read in tandem with the opening chapters of this book, which discuss the Christian preservation of ancient Jewish texts.

To help educators best utilize the resources in this book, the Jewish Publication Society has provided a complementary study and discussion guide at https://jps.org/books/discovering-second-temple-literature. The questions tied to each chapter will help students think critically, and the guide cites other scholarly sources that teachers and students will find helpful in furthering their research.

My hope is that this book will add texture to the linear way that many Jews today perceive the historical narrative of the Jewish people. As a child, I learned that the heroes of old were men who transmitted the

Oral and Written Law in an unbroken chain that effortlessly wound its way from the written Bible as we have it through the corpus of Rabbinic literature: Mishnah, Talmud, and midrash. But after immersing myself in the world of the Second Temple period, it has become evident to me that, from the very moment that they began calling themselves "Jews," Jewish authors living in Jerusalem, Alexandria, Antioch, and throughout the Greco-Roman world presumed that they were endowed with the liberty not only of being recipients of tradition but of engaging, grappling, interpreting, challenging, and sometimes even modifying their tradition.

While the Rabbis took similar liberties when engaging with the legal, or halakhic, world, the fact that Second Temple Jewish authors also actively interacted with scriptural text indicates that the Rabbis' assumption of such liberty was not an innovation but a presumption based on how Jews interacted with texts before them.

As an Orthodox Jewish woman witnessing major social and religious changes in her own community, I look to the Second Temple period as evidence that identifying as a Jew invites one to explore one's tradition and find new meanings. Such understandings can offer us an ever-rich appreciation of our past, and an impetus for effecting positive change while remaining committed to our heritage.

TIMELINE

586 BCE	The Babylonians exile much of Judea's population to Babylonia
539–538 BCE	After Cyrus II captures Babylon, he permits the Judean exiles to return to their homeland
520–515 BCE	The Second Temple is completed in Jerusalem
333–323 BCE	Alexander the Great defeats the Persian Empire; his empire is divided into three main kingdoms after his death
200 BCE	Judea transitions from being under Ptolemaic control to being under Syrian Greek control
175 BCE	High Priest Simeon II dies; conflict breaks out between supporters of his son Onias III and those of Jason
167–164 BCE	Judeans rebel against the Syrian Greeks and gain autonomy from the Greeks; Hasmonean dynasty begins
c. 76–67 BCE	Salome Alexandria rules as queen of Judea following the death of her husband, Alexander Jannaeus
63 BCE	Pompey invades Jerusalem; the Hasmonean monarchy ends and Judea is now controlled by Roman client kings
62–61 BCE	Preconsul of Asia Minor, L. Valerius Flaccus, seizes foreign funds designated by diasporan Jews to be sent to the Jerusalem Temple

59 BCE	Cicero delivers a speech defending Flaccus
37–4 BCE	Herod the Great rules Judea
c. 20 BCE	Philo of Alexandria is born
6 CE	Judea becomes a province of Rome
c. 32 CE	Jesus is crucified by the Romans
38–41 CE	Riots against the Jews in Alexandria, supported by Flaccus, the governor, and largely ignored by Gaius Caligula, the Roman emperor
c. 40 CE	Philo of Alexandria writes *Embassy to Gaius*
66–73 CE	The Jews rebel against Rome; the Jerusalem Temple is destroyed by the Romans in 70 CE; the rebellion is fully quelled three years later
115–18 CE	Jewish rebellions against Roman rule crop up throughout the empire, leaving Jewish communities, particularly those in the vicinity of Alexandria, devastated
132–135 CE	The Bar Kokhba revolt results in the Jews' expulsion from Jerusalem; Rabbinic community moves to Yavneh and the Galilee
c. 200 CE	The Mishnah, first Rabbinic code of law, is written down
fifth century CE	The Jerusalem Talmud is edited and redacted
sixth century CE	The Babylonian Talmud is edited and redacted (it will still be subject to small revisions over the next three centuries)

DISCOVERING SECOND

TEMPLE LITERATURE

PART 1

THE MODERN RECOVERY OF

SECOND TEMPLE LITERATURE

CHAPTER 1

The Cairo Genizah

In the year 1896, Scottish twin sisters embarked on a trip to Egypt from their home in Cambridge, England. It was not uncommon at the time for members of England's upper class to take luxury trips to places they regarded as exotic regions of the world, in the hopes of acquiring artifacts, ancient manuscripts, and other treasures. But these women were not ordinary explorers. After their marriages to James Young Gibson and Samuel Savage Lewis ended in their husbands' untimely deaths, the sisters, Agnes Smith Lewis (1843–1926) and Margaret Dunlop Gibson (1843–1920), found themselves widowed at the prime of their lives. Lewis and Gibson had inherited a fortune from their Scottish father, John Smith, who had encouraged them to study the Bible, world history, and ancient and modern languages. The sisters also had a passion for traveling, and so they coupled their interests in travel and academic study by journeying to Palestine, Egypt, Greece, and other regions of the Mediterranean world, hoping to find ancient manuscripts and artifacts related to the period of nascent Christianity. During their stay in the ancient city of Cairo in 1896, the sisters purchased a small fragment of a Hebrew manuscript from a local antiquities dealer.

By this time, Lewis was well regarded in Cambridge as a scholar of Early Christianity. She was especially well known for her recovery of a fourth-century CE Bible codex written in an Aramaic dialect called Syriac. A codex, a kind of book consisting of sheets of leather or papyri sewn or bound together, had replaced scrolls and papyri in about the second century CE. When Lewis had discovered this codex (which would

3

become known as the Syriac Sinaiticus) in the library of St. Catherine's Monastery in the Sinai desert, she notified other Bible scholars, who later photographed and published it.

Lewis knew enough to sense that the Hebrew manuscript fragment in her possession was very ancient, and perhaps a significant find in the field of biblical scholarship. She could read Hebrew, Syriac, and Greek, but believed the fragment needed to be examined by an expert in ancient Jewish texts. For this task, the two sisters brought the fragment to a man named Solomon Schechter.

Early Stages of Genizah Research: Solomon Schechter (1896–1915)

In selecting Solomon Schechter (1847–1915) as the person to examine their prized fragment, the sisters were making an informed decision. Raised in Romania in a family affiliated with the Chabad branch of Hasidic Judaism, Schechter was an expert in classical Rabbinic texts. He had received a formal yeshiva education in Romania that focused on the study of Talmud and other Rabbinic literature, underwent rabbinical training in Vienna, and, at age thirty-two, completed his education in Jewish studies at the University of Berlin. Three years later, in 1882, he moved to England to teach Rabbinic literature to the Jewish scholar and philanthropist Claude Montefiore. In 1890, Schechter was appointed Reader in Talmudic and Rabbinic literature at the University of Cambridge.[1] In the six years Schechter was at Cambridge before the sisters approached him with their fragment, he had made a name for himself as a learned and passionate scholar.

Upon seeing the manuscript, Schechter immediately suspected that he was looking at part of an ancient Hebrew version of the apocryphal book known as the Wisdom of Ben Sira. In Schechter's time, scholars were only aware of this text in its Greek translation. It was preserved in the Catholic Bible as part of the Apocrypha, a collection of books written by Jews in the Second Temple period that was included in the Greek translation of the Hebrew Bible, the Septuagint. Schechter had long suspected that the Greek version of Ben Sira was a translation of a Hebrew original, but he had no manuscript evidence to prove his case.

After examining the sisters' fragment, Schechter became determined to discover the rest of the manuscript. He was certain that the discovery of an ancient Hebrew manuscript of Ben Sira would make a profound impact on the academic community. On May 15, 1896, shortly after viewing the fragment, Schechter wrote a letter to his friend Judge Mayer Sulzberger, a Jewish intellectual who lived just outside of Philadelphia, saying:

> I met yesterday with a piece of good fortune of which many a Biblical scholar will be jealous. I have namely discovered among the Fragments which Mrs. Lewis (the discoverer of the Syriac Gospel) brought from her last journey in the Orient a leaf from the Hebrew Sirach (Eccliasticus). As you know [that] was the original of the Apokryph in the Hebrew and the Geonim even cite passages from it. But it is now for the first time that we have a Fragment coming from the body of the book. I am now transcribing the MS [manuscript] and shall א״ה [God willing] write a monograph on the subject which I hope you will receive soon.[2]

In his letter, Schechter divulged to Sulzberger his recent discovery of a Hebrew fragment of Ben Sira—but he did not reveal where the Ben Sira fragment had come from. Schechter only disclosed that the fragment had come into the possession of Mrs. Lewis at some point during her trip to "the Orient."

Soon thereafter, Schechter's article "A Fragment of the Original Text of Ecclesiasticus," publicizing the discovery of the Ben Sira fragment, was published in the journal *The Expositor*. He included a translation of the fragment and argued that it was not composed as a translation of an older Greek Ben Sira manuscript, but that it represented an original version of the book that was later translated into Greek.

Here, too, Schechter appeared elusive about the origin of the sisters' incredible find. He indicated that the fragment had come from Palestine, and not from Egypt:

> For this Fragment we are indebted to [Agnes Smith Lewis's and Margaret Dunlop Gibson's] last journey in Palestine and Egypt, in which countries

they have acquired various Hebrew MSS., mostly in fragments. Our Fragment was found in the Palestine bundle, among other leaves of Hebrew MSS., extending over various branches of Jewish literature, as Bible, Mishnah, Talmud, Liturgy, Grammar, etc.[3]

A few months after the article's publication, Schechter was ready to find out more. He embarked on his first trip to Cairo on December 16, 1896, to seek out additional leaves of the Ben Sira manuscript. Later that month, Schechter's wife, Mathilde, disclosed in a letter to Judge Sulzberger that her husband had traveled to Cairo specifically because he believed he would find more fragments there.

Mathilde also knew that Cairo was home to a large genizah (a Hebrew word that means "hidden," or "buried"), a site designated by the Jewish community for storing sacred texts. *Genizot* (plural of genizah) are storage areas for biblical texts, or pages that have God's name written on them. They are usually situated in synagogue basements or attics, or in Jewish cemeteries. Understanding that her husband believed that the Cairo Genizah might house more Hebrew fragments of Ben Sira, Mathilde wrote:

> Mr. Schechter left England on the 16 December for the East, Egypt, and Palestine where he was sent to by our University for purposes of research (Hebrew Mss). As it is a secret mission, the fact will be announced in the University Reporter only after the commencement of next Term about the end of January, when he will already have secured permission to work in the old Genizah, as otherwise his plans might have been defeated, caused by his discovery of the Ecclesiasticus fragment.[4]

What accounts for the discrepancy between Schechter's published article, in which he implied that the Ben Sira fragment could have come from Palestine, and Mathilde Schechter's private communication to their close friend Judge Sulzberger, in which she indicated that the fragment might have come from a genizah in Cairo? And why did Schechter choose to go to Cairo in the first place, rather than Palestine?

One possibility is that Schechter was not ready to reveal the true origin of the fragment to the public.[5] His decision would not simply have been due to a petty desire to be the first scholar to receive credit and acclaim for rediscovering a stash of ancient Hebrew documents. For Schechter, there was a great deal more at stake. He believed it was imperative that the remainder of the Ben Sira fragment, if it had indeed survived, end up in the right hands.

Schechter made the stakes clear in the opening paragraph of his article on the discovery of the fragment:

> If it could be proved that Sirach, who flourished about 200 BC, com-
> posed his work, as some believe, in the Rabbinic idiom, with which we
> are acquainted from the Talmudic literature, then between Ecclesiasticus
> and the books of the Old Testament there must lie centuries, nay, there
> must lie, in most cases, the deep waters of the Captivity, the grave of the
> Old-Hebrew and the old Israel, and the womb of the New-Hebrew and
> the new Israel. The assumption of Maccabæan Psalms, and many another
> hypothesis [sic] of Bible-Criticism would fall to the ground.[6]

This is why the Ben Sira fragment was so important to Schechter. In his opinion, the question of how to date Ben Sira's writing was part of a much greater conflict. In the 1880s and 1890s, some biblical scholars were dating parts of the Hebrew Bible to the late Second Temple period, and at the same time were characterizing Second Temple Judaism as obsessively legalistic. For these scholars, most of whom were affiliated with German Protestant schools influenced by the towering intellects of Professors Julius Wellhausen and Bernhard Duhm, the emergence of Christianity and its emphasis on universal love was a revolutionary improvement over the particularist legalism of Second Temple Judaism.

Schechter felt a personal responsibility to challenge the late dating of biblical books and their mischaracterization as negative contrasts to early Christian literature. He believed that if he could show that Ben Sira was originally written in Hebrew in the early second century BCE, he would also be able to establish that the book was stylistically different than the

Hebrew books of the Bible that Wellhausen and Duhm believed to have been written at that time. Schechter aimed to show the richness and antiquity of Jewish Scripture, in part by proving that ethical wisdom texts such as Ben Sira were integral parts of Jewish tradition.[7]

What Schechter discovered on his 1896 trip to Cairo far exceeded his greatest expectations. He had hoped to find a small cache of ancient documents, but he ended up recovering one of the world's largest and most ancient *genizot.*

Genizot were formally instituted as places to store sacred documents, but Schechter soon realized that the genizah at Cairo's Ben Ezra Synagogue contained thousands of nonreligious documents, including personal letters of correspondence and legal contracts. This genizah had been operating more broadly than its technical function, perhaps because the Jewish community in Cairo regarded the Hebrew language as so sacred that anything written in Hebrew, regardless of whether it contained God's name or religious content, could not be thrown out.[8]

When Schechter first entered the genizah in the Ben Ezra Synagogue attic, he was overwhelmed. There were hundreds of thousands of fragments, dated to different time periods, uncataloged, and lying in piles on top of one another. Some had lain untouched for centuries. Sifting through them would be an almost insurmountable job, even for an accomplished scholar like himself. In his 1908 article, "A Hoard of Hebrew Manuscripts," Schechter described the experience:

> After showing me over the place and the neighboring buildings, or rather ruins, the Rabbi [Grand Rabbi of Cairo Aaron Bensimon] introduced me to the beadles of the synagogue, who are at the same time the keepers of the Genizah, and authorized me to take from it what, and as much as, I liked. Now, as a matter of fact, I liked all. Still, some discretion was necessary. I have already indicated the mixed nature of the Genizah. But one can hardly realise the confusion in a genuine, old Genizah until one has seen it. It is a battlefield of books, and the literary production of many centuries had their share in the battle, and their *disjecta membra* are now

strewn over its area. Some of the belligerents have perished outright, and are literally ground to dust in the terrible struggle for space, whilst others, as if overtaken by a general crush, are squeezed into big, unshapely lumps, which even with the aid of chemical appliances can no longer be separated without serious damage to their constituents. In their present condition these lumps sometimes afford curiously suggestive combinations; as, for instance, when you find a piece of some rationalistic work, in which the very existence of either angels or devils is denied, clinging for its very life to an amulet in which these same beings (mostly the latter) are bound over to be on their good behavior and not interfere with Miss Jair's love for somebody. The development of the romance is obscured by the fact that the last lines of the amulet are mounted on some I. O. U., or lease, and this in turn is squeezed between the sheets of an old moralist, who treats all attention to money affairs with scorn and indignation. Again, all these contradictory matters cleave tightly to some sheets from a very old Bible.[9]

Schechter clearly recognized the formidable challenge before him. How was he to organize, catalog, and study the contents of this chaotic genizah? In his opinion, the only way to complete this massive task was to ship as many manuscripts as possible to the University of Cambridge, where he conducted his research. Indeed, one of the greatest accomplishments of Schechter's career was his success in convincing Rabbi Bensimon, the Grand Rabbi of Cairo, and the administrators of the Ben Ezra Synagogue to allow him to ship the entire contents of the genizah to Cambridge. No outsider had ever been given carte blanche to assume control of the genizah by overseeing the emptying of all its contents. At the same time, however, Schechter was not the true "discoverer" of the genizah. Many individuals had been aware of the treasures it held decades before Schechter knew of its existence, and some collectors and scholars had purchased bundles of Genizah fragments prior to Schechter's arrival.

One such individual was Rabbi Jacob Saphir (1822–1886). Authorities in Palestine had hired him to travel to Jewish communities around the world and collect money for poor Jews living in Jerusalem. In the course of his travels, between 1859 and 1864, Saphir made a number of visits to the Ben Ezra Synagogue. In his 1866 book, *Even Sapir*, Saphir wrote that during one of his trips to Cairo he was permitted to enter the Ben Ezra Synagogue Genizah but found nothing of immediate interest to him.

At this time, a Russian Crimean manuscript collector named Abraham Firkovich (1786–1874) also visited the genizah. A Karaite (a Jew who rejected the authority of Jewish traditions recorded outside of the Hebrew Bible), Firkovich had been purchasing ancient Jewish manuscripts for his private collection as early as 1864 in order to verify their Karaite origin and, by extension, the authenticity of the Karaite tradition. He would later become famous for acquiring the Leningrad Codex, the oldest complete copy of the Hebrew Bible, dated to the early eleventh century CE, under mysterious circumstances.[10]

It is very possible that Firkovich collected documents from the genizah long before Schechter first arrived in Cairo, but we cannot be certain since Firkovich did not reveal the origins of the manuscripts that he collected. We must note, however, that some fragments found in Firkovich's collection come from the same codices as fragments that are now in the genizah collection of Cambridge. One example is the Rabbinic midrashic collection called the *Mekhilta of Rabbi Shimon*. While Firkovich may have obtained his fragments of this codex from elsewhere in Cairo, it seems likely that at some point he obtained access to the contents of the Ben Ezra Synagogue's Genizah.[11]

Another visitor to the genizah around the same time was a Russian Orthodox Archimandrite, a high-ranking abbot, named Antonin Kapustin (1817–1894). A scholar of Byzantine history who had extensive interest in historical sites and their treasures (and who would become best known for purchasing the Oak of Mamre, the site where Abraham resided following his circumcision in Genesis 17), he bought more than a thousand manuscripts from the genizah.[12] Per Kapustin's will, the genizah documents were donated to the Russian Imperial Public Library after his death, where they are housed today in the Archimandrite Antonin Kapustin Collection.

By the 1880s, word had spread among elite intellectual circles in Europe regarding the existence of this special genizah. Academics in these circles worked independently from one another to gain access to the genizah and to export some of its contents to their university libraries. Reverend Greville John Chester (1830–1892), for example, purchased and exported 991 genizah manuscript fragments to the Bodleian Library at the University of Oxford, many of them ancient treasures, such as the oldest dated manuscript of the Babylonian Talmud.[13]

Elkan Adler (1861–1946), a lawyer, avid manuscript collector, and passionate Jewish intellectual—his father and brother both served as Chief Rabbis of Britain—also visited the genizah before Schechter. Over the course of multiple visits, beginning in 1888, Adler collected thousands of genizah fragments, which are housed today at the Jewish Theological Seminary in New York. Among these are Hebrew fragments of an ancient book of Ben Sira, which Adler said he acquired in January 1896—four months or so before Schechter identified the Ben Sira fragment that had come from the genizah. An article written by Adler in 1900 opens with the following statement:

> Among the numerous fragments from the Cairo Genizah which I brought away with me in January, 1896, and which I have since acquired, I have discovered a portion of the famous Hebrew Text of Eccliasticus, and hasten to publish the text and translation with fascimiles . . . the case containing the fragment was only opened on March 7 last, and the precious fragment itself identified two days later.[14]

Adler's declaration that he acquired Hebrew fragments of Ben Sira in January 1896 may reflect his desire to be recognized as the very first discoverer of the Ben Sira fragment in the Cairo Genizah. Yet Adler also admits that he did not open the box containing the precious fragment until about four years after he acquired it.

Other efforts to obtain genizah fragments have not been well documented. An Egyptologist known as Count Riamo D'Hulst (c. 1850–1916), for example, is known to have collected thousands of genizah manuscripts for the University of Oxford's Bodleian Library. In 1889, as an officer of the Egypt Exploration Fund (EEF), he was sent to Cairo, apparently to obtain ancient pottery. In its *Annual Report of the Curators of the Bodleian Library* of 1890, the EEF announced that the fund acquired numerous ancient manuscripts from Egypt that year. Years later, in 1915, d'Hulst sent a postcard to Falconer Madan, the Bodleian Library's head librarian, in which he mentioned having purchased a box of manuscripts in Egypt and sending them to "the authorities of the EEF."[15]

The opening of the genizah's doors to outside collectors marked a conscious effort on the part of Ben Ezra's leadership to raise funds for the synagogue, which was undergoing renovations during this time.[16] By discreetly opening the genizah to individual collectors who were willing to pay for fragments, these leaders were able to ensure the synagogue's financial security.

And so, by the time Schechter came on the scene in 1896, more than a few scholars were working to transport fragments in the Cairo Genizah to public and private libraries. Yet the lack of public disclosure regarding these operations suggests that these individuals wanted to secure fragments for their employers or their private collections before making the genizah's treasures known to others.

After Schechter secured the remainder of the collection, he spent years organizing, cataloging, and translating the genizah documents. Their contents, it turned out, spanned from as early as the tenth century through the nineteenth century. The overwhelming—and revealing—gleaning process would extend far beyond Schechter's own academic career, as we will see at the end of this chapter.

Cataloging the Genizah in the Mid-Twentieth Century: The Work of Shlomo Dov Goitein

Perhaps the person who contributed the most to genizah studies after Solomon Schechter was Dr. Shlomo Dov Goitein (1900–1985). Born in Burgkunstadt, Germany, and educated in Islamic studies at the University of Frankfurt, Goitein moved to Israel, where he spent the bulk of his career teaching Arabic and Islamic studies at the Hebrew University of Jerusalem.

Goitein's research focused on the social, cultural, and economic aspects of medieval Jewish life in the Mediterranean world. Culling information from thousands of genizah fragments stored in England, Russia, and the United States, Goitein's considerable effort culminated in a six-volume work that took well over two decades to publish: *A Mediterranean Society: The Jewish Communities of the Arab World as Portrayed in the Documents of the Cairo Geniza.* The first volume was published in 1967, and the last in 1993.

Goitein's work provided unprecedented access to the documents that had been stored in the Cairo Genizah: financial transactions, contracts, letters of personal correspondence, and responsa—letters written by rabbis answering legal queries sent to them by Jews living all over the world.

The responsa found in the genizah reflect the importance of case law in Jewish tradition. Since the two most authoritative Rabbinic legal codes, the Mishnah and the Talmud, did not address every possible legal scenario confronting a Jew living in medieval Europe, the responsa addressing these cases were carefully preserved by Jewish communities that relied on them for legal guidance.

More broadly, Goitein's publications unlocked centuries of Jewish writing that had a permanent impact not just on one subfield of Jewish studies, but on many: the fields of Jewish liturgy, Jewish law, and Jewish social history would be forever changed, as we will soon see.

Cataloging and Digitizing the Genizah

Great strides have been made over the past four decades in giving the public access to the Cairo Genizah's contents. Thanks primarily to the efforts of Stefan Reif (b. 1944), director of the Genizah Research Unit at the University of Cambridge, thousands of manuscripts are already online. These manuscripts come from two collections: the Taylor-Schechter Genizah Collection, consisting of more than 193,000 manuscripts, and the Mosseri Collection, comprising more than 7,000 others.[17]

Raised in Cairo, the Jewish businessman Jacques Mosseri (1884–1934) was an avid collector of ancient Jewish manuscripts. In 1909 he visited the Cairo Genizah, accompanied by the French scholar Israel Levi (1856–1939), who was seeking ancient manuscripts Schechter might have left behind. Levi was not disappointed. During this visit, and subsequent ones over the following years, Levi discovered about four thousand manuscripts remaining in the genizah. His successful career would culminate in his 1919 appointment as Chief Rabbi of France, a position he would hold for twenty years.

Mosseri, meanwhile, kept many of the literary treasures he and Levi had found in his private collection, in the hopes of someday founding a Jewish museum where he would display them. The plan, however, never materialized. In the 1930s, Mosseri moved with his family to France, where he died at age fifty.[18] By that time, Mosseri had amassed more than seven thousand ancient manuscripts, all held in his family's private collection. In 2006, they were given to the University of Cambridge as a long-term loan,[19] enabling the university to digitize them for scholars and the general public.

Today, the University of Cambridge holds the world's largest Cairo Genizah collection. Other large collection holders include the University of Oxford's Bodleian Library, which houses more than four thousand Cairo Genizah fragments, and the Russian National Library in Saint Petersburg, which contains several thousand Genizah fragments, thanks in part to Abraham Firkovich's efforts. Among the fragments stored at the Jewish Theological Seminary in New York City is an important collection that includes Elkan Adler's private repository of Cairo Genizah fragments. Other universities worldwide, such as the University of Pennsylvania and the Institut de France in Paris, have small but significant Cairo Genizah collections as well. Still others have smaller collections.

Many institutions have joined in the effort to digitize the contents of this genizah, thereby giving scholars and laypeople unprecedented access to the hundreds of thousands of Cairo Genizah fragments housed in libraries all over the world. Princeton University and the University of Pennsylvania, among others, have initiated this effort by creating websites that display digitized images of their Cairo Genizah fragments.

The largest online collection of Cairo Genizah documents is the Friedberg Genizah Project. At Genizah.org, visitors can see the Cairo Genizah holdings of dozens of public libraries and private collections around the world—from the Cambridge University Library, repository of the most esteemed collection, to tiny collections owned by laypeople and synagogues, such as Temple Israel of Hollywood, California, which preserves a single Cairo Genizah fragment of Leviticus 26. On view are high-resolution photographs of the Cairo Genizah documents as well as their identification information (including each fragment's title and genre). Photographs of the texts, rather than transcribed copies, are especially useful for scholars because many of these fragments contain marginal notes, letters and words that are crossed out, and small glosses written above, below, and beside words. These editorial details testify to the evolving interpretive traditions over the ten centuries or so that Jews were placing their sacred texts into the Cairo Genizah.

Another benefit of having access to photographs of manuscripts relates to the fact that some Genizah fragments are palimpsests, texts whose words were scratched off by a scribe, who then wrote a different text over the same parchment. With improved technology, scholars are now able to identify many of the original texts on palimpsests.

One fascinating palimpsest found in the Cairo Genizah, identified as Fragment Taylor-Schechter 12.182, preserves a poem, or *piyyut*, from the famous seventh-century CE poet Yannai, who wrote hundreds of religious poems, likely while living in the land of Israel. Beneath the text of Yannai's poem on this fragment lies what scholars believe is a seventh-century CE text of Psalm 22 from Origen's Hexapla. Origen, a Christian scholar who lived in Alexandria in the third century CE, is renowned for having written a six-column compendium of the Bible in which each column supplied a different biblical translation. The first column was in Hebrew; the second was Hebrew transliterated into Greek; the third was Aquila of Sinope's second-century CE Greek translation of the Bible; the fourth was Symmachus's second-century CE Greek translation; the fifth was the Septuagint, the Greek translation of the Hebrew Bible written in the third century BCE;

and the sixth column was Theodotion's second-century Greek translation of the Bible. The fact that a scribe had scratched out the words of Origen's Hexapla to record a Jewish poem testifies to the fluid ways in which manuscripts circulated in various religious communities. It is possible that this scribe was unaware of what text he was scratching out in order to record Yannai's poem. But it is just as possible that he was perfectly aware of what the Hexapla was, and who the famous Church Father was who had first written it. Perhaps this Jewish scribe sought to convey a subtle polemical message by repurposing this once Christian text for Jewish use.

As for the ancient Cairo Genizah manuscripts collected by Agnes Smith Lewis and Margaret Dunlop Gibson, they were deposited in Westminster College, a Presbyterian seminary that the sisters had endowed in 1899. In 2013, University of Oxford and University of Cambridge jointly purchased the 1,700 or so manuscripts from Westminster College for 1.2 million pounds. As of 2018, they are in the process of being digitized. As ancient documents are being recovered from religious libraries all over the world, new libraries are forming. These libraries exist in the virtual world, bearing contents accessible to everyone.

Genizah Texts Authored in the Second Temple Period

Of the vast repository of historical texts, personal letters, legal responsa, Rabbinic documents, and biblical manuscripts deposited in the Cairo Genizah, some manuscripts profoundly affect the way that scholars understand the world of Early Judaism.

One such text is the Wisdom of Ben Sira. As Schechter had hoped, the discovery of Hebrew fragments of Ben Sira in the genizah enabled him and the scholars who succeeded him to date the original composition of the text more accurately. This discovery also helped to place Ben Sira within a milieu of Jewish writings that influenced Rabbinic texts written centuries later in Hebrew and Aramaic. Although Ben Sira was not canonized into the Hebrew Bible, the Rabbis cite Hebrew quotations of Ben Sira, and at least some members of the Rabbinic community regarded the text as authoritative.

Schechter had hoped to show that Ben Sira was reflective of a vibrant Jewish religion that highlighted ethical behavior alongside a rich scriptural and legal tradition. In a broad sense, his aim was to rebut Christian presumptions that Second Temple Judaism was obsessively legalistic and focused mainly on the ritual technicalities of a cultic tradition.[20] Schechter's efforts were for the most part unsuccessful, and the stereotype of Judaism as a particularistic foil to the universalism of Christianity pervaded biblical scholarship through the twentieth century. Only in recent decades have scholars truly begun to replace the false binary of a particularistic Judaism versus a universalist Christianity with a more nuanced view.[21]

Later discoveries of Ben Sira fragments in the Dead Sea caves and at Masada would confirm Schechter's theory that this text was first written in Hebrew in the Second Temple period. But it would also complicate Schechter's argument for the integrity of the text and its place in Second Temple Jewish tradition,[22] because the differences between these manuscripts, called variants, indicate that copyists made small changes to the text over time.

Another Second Temple period text Schechter found in the Cairo Genizah also had a profound impact on the study of Early Judaism. It is known as the Damascus Document because of the writer's allusion to a "new covenant" that would ultimately be forged between God and His Chosen People in "the land of Damascus." This term paraphrases the biblical prophet Amos's prediction that God will bring the Jews "into exile beyond Damascus" (Amos 5:27). Since Damascus was once part of Israel's empire under King David, perhaps the writer believed in a messianic time in which God would restore Judea to its former glory.

The first half of what has survived of the Damascus Document recounts the origins and ideology of a sectarian Jewish community. It is written in the voice of a leader or teacher who exhorts his students to remain pious and committed to the sect's teachings by speaking of Israel's history and the ways in which God rewards and punishes those who observe or reject the Torah's laws. The second section of this text comprises the laws by which members of this community had to abide.

For a long time this text confounded scholars because its provenance was so difficult to determine. Some suggested the document arose in Samaritan circles—a community of people who believed they were the true Israel and followed a version of the Torah that was different than the Masoretic text of the Jews. Others thought it had been written by Sadducees—a priestly sect of Jews living in the Second Temple period who were known to reject the authority of the Jewish oral tradition.

Still others believed that the document's parallels to legal material in Rabbinic literature pointed to a Pharisaic origin.[23] The Pharisees were a sect of Jews in the Second Temple period who developed a body of Oral Law that would continue to be expanded and recorded by the Rabbis following the Second Temple period. The divergent theories regarding who authored this document led to different interpretations and assumptions regarding how it should be read.

Today, the prevailing view among most scholars is that the author of the Damascus Document was a Jew who identified with the Essenes, a sectarian group that lived in the Land of Israel and was devoted to a strict interpretation of *halakhah* (Jewish law) and yet remained separated from the Jerusalem Temple as well as the Pharisees and Sadducees associated with it.

Because of this consensus, the Damascus Document is especially significant. This text opens a new window into the highly disciplined lives of some sectarian Jews living in the late Second Temple period. It urges Jews to remain pious and committed to the sect but at the same time, it blurs the boundaries between what scholars have thought of as "traditional Judaism" and other varieties of Judaism.

Another Cairo Genizah document thought to have been written in the late Second Temple period or a century or two following it is called the Songs of David. While only four such songs survive (within the Antonin Kapustin Collection in the Russian National Library), scholars believe that these songs were part of a larger collection that perhaps contained one psalm for every day of the year.[24] Moreover, parallels with liturgical material found in the Dead Sea caves near the site of Qumran suggest that perhaps the writer had some contact with the Qumran community.[25] While this community lived in an isolated region of the Judean Desert, its members came from all over Judea and must have incorporated many of the practices and rituals that they grew up with into their sectarian lives. More scholarship will undoubtedly be produced that will shed light on how these texts fit into the larger rubric of Second Temple Judaism.

Scholars are also indebted to the discovery of fragments of the Aramaic Levi Document (ALD) in both the Cairo Genizah and the Dead Sea caves.[26] This document, likely written in the second century BCE, describes how Levi, the son of the Patriarch Jacob, conducted the priestly service, offered prayers to God, and instructed his sons regarding how to live their lives piously. Scholars once believed this text was an Aramaic version of the Testament of Levi, one of the twelve books of the Testaments of the Twelve Patriarchs preserved in the Pseudepigrapha.[27] After extensive study of the ALD fragments, however, scholars have determined that the ALD is more likely a separate work, and perhaps served as an influential source for the writer of the Testament of Levi, which scholars believe was written a century or more later, either in the first century BCE or the first century CE.[28]

The ALD fragments confirm the likelihood that the Testaments of the Twelve Patriarchs did not have exclusively Christian origins, even if its author or compiler was a Christian. Some of its sources had to be Jewish, because they were circulating as independent Jewish documents prior to the composition of the version of the Testaments of the Twelve Patriarchs that has come down to us in modern times.

This circulation, moreover, attests to a Jewish literary tradition that flourished in communities in the Land of Israel and in Egypt. The Jewish inhabitants of these communities must have greatly valued these texts, seeing as they were copied and preserved in libraries and *genizot*.

The rediscovery of the Cairo Genizah and the publication of its contents mark the greatest contribution to the field of Jewish history in the past two centuries. While the mid-twentieth-century discovery of the Dead Sea Scrolls would invite scholars and laypeople into the world of sectarian Jewish life in the Second Temple period, the 400,000 Cairo Genizah fragments opened a door into the lives of millions of Jews living in Mediterranean lands starting in the ninth century CE and onward, for the better part of a thousand years. Many of the texts preserved in the genizah were originally composed well before the genizah opened—some dating back as far as the third or second century BCE.

Even though these Second Temple texts were not canonized into Hebrew Scripture, the fact that they were copied, circulated, and preserved in the genizah attests to the importance that some Jews of the time attached to them. We have learned from these documents, moreover, that some Second Temple texts that did not find a place in Rabbinic tradition were given new life in the medieval period by Jewish writers who found religious meaning in them.

Scholars are still not certain how texts like the Damascus Document found their way into the Cairo Genizah. These mysteries add to our sense that some Jewish texts were transmitted by people who may not have believed the same things as the authors of those texts. In fact, many of the most foundational texts written in the Second Temple period were preserved not by rabbis, or even by other Jews, but by monks. The story of how ancient texts that were stored in monasteries were eventually brought into the public eye is the subject of our next chapter.

CHAPTER 2

Manuscripts and Monasteries

Many Jewish texts written in the late Second Temple period have survived thanks to Christians who carefully preserved them over many centuries. Monks, particularly those affiliated with the Eastern Orthodox Church, would painstakingly copy these texts in a room called a scriptorium and store them in their libraries. Many ancient Jewish texts thus lay untouched and preserved for centuries in monasteries. These same texts were not copied by Jews, perhaps because by the time Jews were copying their scriptural books into codices (a practice that began in the second century CE), most Second Temple texts were not regarded as scriptural, and therefore not worthy of the effort it would require to preserve them.

The story of how these ancient Jewish manuscripts came to light in the modern era is not without controversy. Beginning in the nineteenth century, some scholars and explorers visiting monastery libraries staked a claim of ownership over the monasteries' manuscripts. Many of these scholars and explorers justified this claim by arguing that the monks were careless with their ancient documents and regarded them as worthless. Disputes over ownership and accusations of carelessness created a dynamic of distrust between monks and visiting scholars. Only recently have scholars invested efforts into repairing this relationship.

St. Catherine's Monastery: Tischendorf and the Early Discovery of Codex Sinaiticus: 1844–59

In 1844, a young German scholar by the name of Constantine Tischendorf visited St. Catherine's Monastery in the Sinai desert, an isolated region that bridges the Land of Israel with Egypt, in search of precious manuscripts. Tischendorf, a talented philologist (one who studies historical records), had previously deciphered an erased palimpsest of a Greek translation of the Hebrew Bible and the New Testament, likely written in the fifth century CE.

Passionate about collecting ancient documents, Tischendorf was hoping to discover manuscripts of the New Testament at St. Catherine's Library that would help him to publish a critical edition of the Bible. This edition would cite all the differences between various New Testament manuscripts, thereby helping scholars to determine the most authentic wording of the New Testament.[1]

When Tischendorf visited St. Catherine's for the first time in 1844, he noticed some leaves of what looked to him to be a very ancient manuscript. The leaves were large sheets of vellum, a fine parchment made of calfskin. The writing on the leaves was Greek uncial script, which consists of all capital letters and does not have regular word spacing. This suggested that the sheets were very old: uncial script had fallen out of use in the eighth century. The monks, Tischendorf later reported, were just about to burn the leaves when he asked them whether he could take the incomplete parchments, 129 leaves of the Old Testament.[2] According to his account, the monks understood from Tischendorf's request that the codex had great value, and they permitted Tischendorf to depart with only 43 leaves, including passages from Jeremiah, Esther, Nehemiah, and 1 Chronicles. The monk's trash was Tischendorf's treasure: He had found part of a manuscript written in the fourth century CE, making it the oldest surviving copy of the Old and New Testaments. The leaves he secured on this first trip were later dedicated to the King of Saxony, Frederick Augustus II, and placed in the Leipzig University Library, where Tischendorf had been a doctoral student, and later became a professor.

Tischendorf returned to the monastery in 1853 and again in 1859. During this latter visit, he discovered an enormous segment of the codex.[3] According to his account, the monks showed him leaves of the Old Testament, New Testament, and early Christian books such as the Epistle of Barnabas and part of the Shepherd of Hermas.[4] Tischendorf described his reaction to seeing the codex:

> Full of joy, which this time I had the self-command to conceal from the steward and the rest of the community, I asked, as if in a careless way, for permission to take the manuscript into my sleeping chamber to look over it more at leisure. There by myself I could give way to the transport of joy which I felt. I knew that I held in my hand the most precious Biblical treasure in existence — a document whose age and importance exceeded that of all the manuscripts which I had ever examined during twenty years' study of the subject.[5]

By remarking that his "poker face" gave the monks no clue about how valuable the codex was, Tischendorf drew a compelling contrast between his own immediate appreciation of the codex and the monks' apparent ignorance. In this way, he subtly suggested that the codex was more fit to be in his own possession.

Tischendorf asked the monks if they would give him the codex for the purpose of transcribing it, but they did not want to give consent without approval from the monastery's prior, who was in Cairo attending the election of a new archbishop. Tischendorf therefore set out for Cairo, where he met with the prior, who agreed to lend Tischendorf the manuscript and dispatched Bedouin servants to retrieve the codex from St. Catherine's and bring it to him in Cairo.

Tischendorf transcribed the 110,000 lines of the codex from March through May of 1859. He described the massive effort required to complete this project in his personal account of these events, noting that "no one can say what this cost me in fatigue and exhaustion." Following his transcription, it was arranged that Tischendorf would bring the codex, on loan, to Saint Petersburg in order to compare the codex with his transcription and to ensure there were no errors. In the letter of receipt regarding this loan, signed in September of 1859, Tischendorf promised that he would return the codex to St. Catherine's upon request. Following this loan agreement, Tischendorf took the codex and presented it to the Russian czar, Alexander

II, in November of 1862, at which point the codex was transferred to the Ministry of Foreign Affairs in Saint Petersburg.[6] It is unclear whether the monks of St. Catherine's were amenable to this decision.

In 1869, the codex was transferred again, this time to Russia's Imperial Library. At this time, the newly elected archbishop of Sinai, Kallistratos, signed a letter affirming the donation of the codex to the czar.

One of the questions regarding this incident is why ten years elapsed between the time Tischendorf first obtained the codex in Cairo in order to transcribe it and the time the donation agreement between St. Catherine's and Russian authorities was signed. It seems that because Archbishop Konstantios died in 1859 and his successor was not immediately established, the monks did not have access to someone with the authority to oversee the transaction between the monastery and Tischendorf. Kyrillos (or Cyril) Byzantios was first elected to succeed Konstantios, but the patriarch of Jerusalem resisted his election, and Kyrillos soon had a falling out with his colleagues, who decided to elect a second archbishop, Kallistratos. Kallistratos signed the donation agreement between St. Catherine's and Russia in 1869, the year that the codex was brought to Russia's Imperial Library. Some scholars believe that Russian diplomats supported Kallistratos and helped him to get elected in exchange for the promise of the codex's donation.[7]

One final detail regarding this episode is noteworthy because it sheds insight into how valuable Tischendorf believed the codex to be: Just before donating the codex to the czar in 1862, Tischendorf tore off its first leaf, which he then kept in his own private collection. After his death, the Library of Cambridge purchased the first leaf.[8]

Some contemporary scholars are skeptical of Tischendorf's claim that the leaves he found in 1844 were about to be burned, since it does not seem to correlate with the degree of reverence with which the monks treated their ancient manuscripts. Moreover, Tischendorf stated that the leaves of the codex were lying in a basket waiting to be burned. Since it was common for monasteries to store books in baskets, Tischendorf may have misinterpreted what he saw and the leaves of the codex may have simply been placed in a basket used for storage.[9] Finally, it is very difficult to burn parchment, so if the monks did want to produce heat or fuel, it is doubtful they would have done so with parchment.[10] While other recent scholars have sought to restore Tischendorf's integrity by arguing that the monks eagerly lent the codex to him, or that they had indeed consigned the codex to flames, the possibility that Tischendorf discovered the codex at the moment that the monks were about to destroy it seems simply too serendipitous — especially given that the monks had preserved the codex for centuries.[11]

For years, though, the claim that the monks of St. Catherine's had little respect for their manuscripts persisted in academic circles. In 1911, Vladimir Beneshevich, a Russian scholar who sought to catalog the contents of St. Catherine's Library, wrote that he had heard three years earlier that the monks of St. Catherine's were heating their bread ovens by burning ancient books. This secondhand claim, published years after Beneshevich received this information, is unsubstantiated.[12]

In 1899, the Russian Imperial Library in Saint Petersburg lent the codex to the British Museum and, in 1933, sold it, with Joseph Stalin's approval, to the museum for 100,000 pounds — a staggering sum that would amount to about $10 million dollars today. In January 1934, *Time* magazine published a notice that the British Museum had purchased the codex from the Russian government. Explaining the manner of its discovery, the article noted that Tischendorf

> traveled through the Sinai Peninsula and up to a lonely Orthodox Greek monastery atop Mount St. Catherine. There in a wastebasket he came across a bundle of 43 stray vellum leaves which a monk had tossed aside for lighting fires. Scholar Tischendorf recognized the vellum leaves as fragments of an ancient Greek biblical text.[13]

A few weeks later, *Time* received and printed the monastery's version of events:

According to monks of the monastery, Tischendorf took the Codex to Cairo pleading that he must study it in a warm climate. He went to the Russian Consulate and, thus on Russian soil, defied the monks to get their Codex back. Tischendorf gave the manuscript to Tsar Alexander II who reimbursed the monastery with a paltry $3,500. Last week Porphyries III, Archbishop of Sinai, detailed all this in a long, indignant cablegram to the British Museum. The Archbishop demanded the Codex back, or else "substantial recognition" of its loss.[14]

Which story is true? What we know for certain is that the monks of St. Catherine's regarded the codex as having been stolen from them.[15] But the codex remains in the British Museum to this day.[16]

Although Tischendorf may have acquired ancient manuscripts under false pretenses (and possibly separated manuscripts after acquiring them), he deserves credit for recognizing the codex as being an ancient treasure. Scholars continue to date the codex to the beginning of the fourth century CE, around the same time that the Roman Empire legalized Christianity.

Agnes Smith Lewis and the Sinai Palimpsest: 1892–96

On her first visit to St. Catherine's Monastery in 1892, Agnes Smith Lewis made what would later be regarded as the greatest discovery of her career as an independent scholar — even greater than her discovery of the Ben Sira fragment that led to Solomon Schechter's trip to the Cairo Genizah. While on a visit to St. Catherine's monastery in the Sinai desert, she discovered the Syriac Sinaiticus, a fourth-century CE manuscript of the four Gospels that were canonized in the New Testament. When Lewis came across the manuscript, she immediately noticed that it was a palimpsest, and that the original text was written in Syriac, a dialect of Aramaic spoken by early Christians. In fact, Lewis could read Syriac, and she was able to discern that the passages under the later texts were from the New Testament. Realizing that she would need professional scholars to uncover this text in its entirety, Lewis left St. Catherine's and returned a year later with a team of scholars that, along with Lewis, photographed and transcribed the text. They soon discovered that it was an ancient copy of the Gospels. The original codex remained in the monastery, where it is kept to this day.

The Syriac Sinaiticus turned out to be very important in the field of Early Christianity. It provides evidence that in the early stages of Christian history, Christians were reading their Gospels, which were originally composed in Greek, in translation. Viewing the Gospels' transmission history—that is, the minor changes translators made as they rendered Greek into Syriac—provides a window into how early Christians were reading their sacred texts, and what material was important to them. This precious ancient manuscript has also brought modern readers closer to the world in which Jesus and his disciples lived and taught.

More Discoveries at St. Catherine's

In 1975, a professor of New Testament at the University of Athens named Savas Agourides embarked on a trip to St. Catherine's monastery to investigate a report that, over the course of some repair work at the monastery, workers had discovered a hidden room containing boxes of ancient manuscripts. During his one-night stay at the monastery, Agourides was shown a room containing forty-seven boxes, each filled with parchments and papyri, including some ancient documents.[17] Among these documents were twelve leaves, or twenty-four pages, that had been missing from the Codex Sinaiticus.

Discoveries at the monastery continue to emerge. In 2009, Nikolas Sarris, a doctoral student researching bookbinding practices at St. Catherine's, was examining digital manuscripts of the monastery's library when he noticed the image of a Greek fragment beneath a paper pastedown on the inside of the right board of a book bound in the early eighteenth century. The writing on the fragment was in Greek uncial type, the all-capital letter script that was used primarily between the fourth and eighth centuries CE, so Sarris immediately realized he was looking at an ancient fragment. Moreover, the columns were unusually narrow, similar to the narrow columns of the Codex Vaticanus and Codex Sinaiticus (both fourth-century

CE manuscripts of the Old and New Testament), which contained only seventeen to eighteen letters per line, as opposed to the usual twenty to thirty characters.[18] If the script on this fragment looked like these fourth-century documents, perhaps it was as ancient.

Sarris contacted Professor Nicholas Pickwoad, a professional book conservator who had been overseeing the removal of all the books at St. Catherine's in order to begin renovation of the monastery's library. Pickwoad, meanwhile, was aware that monks living at St. Catherine's had rebound many of the books brought to the monastery, sometimes even centuries later. The monks' practice of restoring and rebinding books implied a sense of guardianship and responsibility for the texts.

Sarris also contacted Father Justin, the monastery's librarian. Both Pickwoad and Father Justin confirmed that this fragment contained verses from the first chapter of Joshua and was part of the Codex Sinaiticus. Apparently, a folio of the codex had become separated, and then, like many other discarded parchments, had been used for bookbinding. The serendipitous discovery of this fragment increases the likelihood that more discoveries at St. Catherine's remain to be made.

Father Justin and the Project to Catalog and Digitize the Manuscripts: 2008–Present

The head librarian of St. Catherine's Monastery is Father Justin Sinaites, the only American monk who permanently resides there. Since joining the monastery in 1996, Father Justin has served as an integral liaison between the monks of St. Catherine's and researchers interested in gaining access to the monastery's treasures. He has also taken on the herculean task of photographing the contents of the monastery's library and making them available online.

Father Justin has collaborated with Archbishop Damianos, who oversees St. Catherine's, to make their literary treasures directly viewable by the public. Public exhibitions at New York's Metropolitan Museum of Art in 1997 and 2004 featured St. Catherine's artifacts that date from the tenth century and the thirteenth through sixteenth centuries, respectively.

In 2006, the monks helped arrange an exhibition at the Getty Museum in Los Angeles that focused on religious icons. And in 2012, artifacts belonging to St. Catherine's were again brought to New York's Metropolitan Museum of Art for their *Byzantium and Islam: Age of Transition (7th–9th Century)* exhibit. These exhibitions mark the beginning of an era of collaboration between St. Catherine's monks and scholars seeking access to the treasures they have housed over the centuries.

In 2009, Father Justin initiated a renovation and expansion of St. Catherine's Library incorporated a new reading room, a digital photography studio, and a conservation workshop. Overseeing this effort was a team of eight professional conservators as well as a librarian from Mount Athos, a small peninsula in Greece that is home to a number of monasteries whose libraries, like the one at St. Catherine's, have undergone renovations in modern times.[19] As a result, both monks and visitors now have easier access to St. Catherine's precious books.

In addition to these efforts, a special project to analyze the one hundred and thirty or so palimpsests housed at St. Catherine's is now underway, under the supervision of the Early Manuscripts Electronic Library in Los Angeles. Father Justin has recruited Michael Toth, who formerly developed satellite and imaging systems at the National Reconnaissance Office in Washington DC, to conduct hyperspectral imaging on some of St. Catherine's oldest manuscripts—thereby providing scholars with the opportunity to retrieve the original writings of St. Catherine's palimpsests.

While the entire catalog of St. Catherine's library has yet to be published, we do know that it contains a number of manuscripts authored in the Second Temple period and copied in the medieval period. These include three copies of the ancient Jewish novella Joseph and Aseneth in Greek manuscripts dated to the tenth, fifteenth or sixteenth, and seventeenth centuries; and a seventeenth-century Greek manuscript of the ancient Jewish collection of texts known as the Testaments of the Twelve Patriarchs. Although the original dates of these compositions are disputed, most scholars believe that these texts have their roots in late Second Temple Judaism, or the centuries that followed this period. These documents therefore provide rare glimpses into the worldviews of non-Rabbinic Jewish life in the ancient Greek-speaking world.

The Codex Sinaiticus has now been digitized, thanks to a collaboration between the four institutions in possession of its leaves: the British Library, which has 347 leaves; the University Library in Leipzig, Germany, which has 43 leaves; the National Library of Russia in Saint Petersburg, which has fragments of 6 leaves; and St. Catherine's Monastery, which has at least 18 leaves.[20]

Scriptures in the Monastic Libraries of Mount Athos

Other monasteries in the lands bordering the Mediterranean Sea also house ancient manuscripts. One of the largest collections of ancient Jewish texts can be found in a community of monasteries inhabiting the isolated Mount Athos peninsula, a thirty-mile-long stretch of land in northern Greece. Populated since ancient times, the peninsula is now home to some of the oldest Greek Orthodox monasteries worldwide.

The largest and oldest of these is the Great Lavra Monastery, founded by St. Athanasios (c. 920–c. 1003) in 963 CE. Over time, other monasteries were founded on the Holy Mountain, and thousands of manuscripts were collected and preserved in the monasteries' libraries. But because access to the peninsula was so restricted—both by terrain and by policy—it took until the end of the nineteenth century for most manuscripts to be cataloged. The first catalog, a Greek book entitled *Catalogue of the Greek Mss. on Mount Athos*, was published in 1895, and a second volume was published five years later.[21] Even then, however, there was no information about the manuscripts found in some of the Mount Athos libraries, such as those in the Great Lavra Monastery. Later catalogs, published in 1924 and 1925, filled in some of the gaps, but contemporary scholars do not view them as comprehensive because they exclude thousands of library titles written in Russian, Slavic, Bulgarian, and other languages.

One of Mount Athos's striking features is that it is inhabited solely by males. For about a thousand years, females have been prohibited from stepping foot on the peninsula. While the formal reason for this prohibition is that it supports the monks' vows of celibacy, the ban—enacted into law in 1953 after a woman, Maria Poimenidou, dressed up as a man and entered the island[22]—even extends to female animals (although this latter prohibition is not enforced). Women caught entering Mount Athos face up to twelve months in prison.

Some scholars who have visited the Mount Athos monasteries have been antagonistic toward the monks living on the mountain. The Belgian scholar and Catholic priest Emmanuel Amand de Mendieta (1907–76), for example, received permission from the monks to study and photograph manuscripts at the Lavra, Iviron, and Vatopedi monastery libraries, among others. In 1955 and 1971 he published declarations that the monks eschewed all learning that had no immediate relevance to them:

> Up to a hundred years ago, Western Europe thought that the monasteries of Athos were rich treasuries, crammed with unknown classical and early-Christian manuscripts, and that there were to be found unique manuscripts, lovingly copied by some monk in scriptorium or cell, of many works of which every other copy had been lost. There are still some people, so filled with Western ideas and prejudices, that they continue to believe this. If they could be induced to visit Athos, their illusions would receive a rude shock. When they reached those libraries, which are not ordinarily open to the public, they would see plain proof of the attitude towards learning of the "devout" monks. They could not fail to notice active hostility against all "profane" (non-religious) learning, or against any other form of intellectual activity, both things which cannot be fitted into the rule of life of a monk or of an ascetic. And, as monks are thus opposed to learning, it follows that they are completely uninterested in any manuscript or book on non-monastic subjects.[23]

According to de Mendieta, the monks at Mount Athos held no regard for manuscripts, or for the disciplines these manuscripts represented. The monks, he reported, used their ancient manuscripts to cover jam jars; and once, after a fire, they were so apathetic about these manuscripts that they simply let their debris lie on the floor of a monastery library, untouched, for years. In 1840, he wrote, a Greek man named Mynoides Mynas was hired by Abel-Francois Villemain (1790–1870), minister of Public Instruction in France, to retrieve manuscripts from monasteries in Europe and Asia. Mynas found ancient manuscripts on Mount Athos that were "being used to wrap stockfish."[24] De Mendieta did not cite the source of the accusation, which may have been Mynas, or, more likely, Villemain.

De Mendieta's claims echoed those of Tischendorf. And like Tischendorf, his declarations that the monks had no regard for the written word cannot be squared with the physical evidence. Each of the twenty monasteries on the Holy Mountain houses a library, and these libraries store thousands of manuscripts, including many ancient texts. Had the monks been so uninterested in their books, it seems they would have had ample opportunities to destroy them over the centuries.

De Mendieta also relied on the account of Robert Curzon (1810–73), a British intellectual who had visited Mount Athos in 1837. Curzon later stated that the monks living there were thrilled to make some extra cash by selling him an ancient book of the Gospels for twenty-two Turkish pounds. The monks were so pleased with this deal that they then volunteered to give him a copy of another book of the Gospels.

Such accounts should be read with suspicion, because they exonerate the scholar who purchased the manuscript in question for an absurdly low price. Foreign visitors who left these monasteries with treasures in hand would have had a vested stake in portraying the transactions that led to their precious acquisitions as mutually amicable.

Furthermore, the depiction of monks as eager to part with manuscripts is undermined by the mysterious manner in which texts have disappeared from Mount Athos libraries: One such manuscript, for example, vanished from the Dionysiou Monastery only to show up in the United States for sale. Had such transactions occurred amicably, the manner in which the manuscripts had left the island and later shown up on the public market would have been documented in a transparent way.

The suggestion that manuscripts disappeared from the Mount Athos libraries because monks were eager to exchange them for cash contradicts de Mendieta's own admission that there were known incidences of theft from Mount Athos. One individual purported to have executed such theft is the Russian archimandrite Porphyrius Uspensky (1804–85), whose finds from St. Catherine's Monastery and the monasteries of Mount Athos ended up in the possession of the National Library of Russia.[25]

Perhaps to bolster his own account, de Mendieta also maintained that Dr. Spyridon Lambros (1851–1919), who had authored the two-volume catalog of Mount Athos's libraries, complained that the monks were abusing manuscripts: "In a report, Dr. Lambros had spoken of the terrible losses of manuscripts during the preceding century; they had been sold for petty sums . . . and used as fuel, as covers for jam-pots and as window-panes!"[26] However, de Mendieta did not provide a citation so that one could look up Lambros's complaint directly.[27]

Recent history supports the fact that the monks of Mount Athos prize their collections of ancient manuscripts. Over the course of the past half-century, a number of monasteries have undergone major renovations, and the contents of some libraries have been transferred to new locations. The relocation of ancient documents to expensive new spaces indicates that the monks place a high value on them. Some monasteries that have moved their ancient libraries into improved facilities are also recataloging their collections, which suggests a willingness to provide the public with access to these well-guarded manuscripts.[28]

Among the manuscripts copied and preserved by the monks of Mount Athos are works first written in the Second Temple period or in the following few centuries. The library in the Koutloumos Monastery, for example, includes the Testaments of the Twelve Patriarchs, which recounts the speeches that Jacob's sons gave their children on their deathbeds regarding how to conduct themselves piously. This collection was likely written sometime between the first century BCE and the third or fourth century CE. Most scholars believe a Jewish writer (or writers) penned the original text, as this would account for the author's familiarity with Jewish law and the document's positive attitude toward the Temple and cultic worship.[29] Most believe that Christians copied and preserved the document, and at some point interpolated statements regarding the Trinity and the coming resurrection of Christ. Scholars regard the copy of this text that is in the library of the Koutloumos Monastery as an incomplete manuscript because it is missing the story of Joseph being sold to the Ishmaelites that appears in other manuscripts of this document.

Just northwest of Koutloumos, the Konstamonitou Monastery is home to a fifteenth-century manuscript of the novella Joseph and Aseneth, which recalls the story of how the Egyptian woman Aseneth came to fall in love with the biblical hero Joseph, and marry him despite a series of difficult obstacles. Some scholars believe this novella was first written as early as the second century BCE; others date it as late as the fourth century CE. Its author's identity is likewise unclear. Those who date Joseph and Aseneth early believe the author was Jewish and that Christian scribes copying the text centuries later inserted verses alluding to Christ's return. Those who date the text later maintain that a Christian writer who was well familiar with biblical stories composed the text in its entirety.[30] Regardless of its purported date of composition, scholars who study Joseph and Aseneth today rely in part on the medieval manuscripts of this story that were preserved for centuries at Mount Athos.

The precious manuscripts of Mount Athos will soon be available online to all people—male and female. In 2014, the secretary-general of Telecommunications and the Hellenic Post Office of Greece, Menelaos Daskalakis, announced that efforts are underway to digitize all the manuscripts in the Mount Athos libraries—an initiative estimated to cost 8.5 million euros. Officials estimate that once complete, more than 900,000 manuscripts will be digitized, as well as more than 146,000 pieces of art.[31]

Slavonic Libraries

Many Jewish texts that originated in the Second Temple period were translated into Slavonic languages. Russian Orthodox communities circulated these texts and stored many of them in churches and monasteries.

Some of these texts, among them 2 Enoch, the Apocalypse of Abraham, and the Ladder of Jacob, survive only in Slavonic languages. They are considered "Slavonic Pseudepigrapha," manuscripts that are preserved in Slavonic languages but originated in the Second Temple period or in the following centuries.

Many such documents are stored at the National Library of Russia in Saint Petersburg, the library that came to possess leaves of the Codex Sinaiticus. Andrei Orlov, director of the Slavonic Pseudepigrapha Project at Marquette University in Milwaukee, has dedicated his career to studying these ancient texts. Orlov and other scholars believe that although these documents do not survive in other languages, they were probably translated from Greek, which may in turn have been translated from original Hebrew versions. Scholars will continue to mine these texts for hints about the historical contexts in which they were first composed.

The Vatican

An aura of mystique clouds the question of what Jewish artifacts and manuscripts are secreted away in the libraries of the Vatican. Some treasures in the Vatican's possession have not been disclosed to the public. We do know, however, that the Vatican libraries contain hundreds of ancient Jewish manuscripts, many of which date back to the medieval period. Some manuscripts are copies of texts composed by Jews when the Second Temple stood. For instance, the Vatican houses multiple medieval manuscripts of the Letter of Aristeas, a second-century BCE text that recounts how the Hebrew Bible came to be translated into Greek; Joseph and Aseneth; and a small fragment of a Greek version of 1 Enoch, which purportedly records the visions of the biblical figure of Enoch, a person who, according to Genesis 5:21–24, did not die, but was "taken" by God. Also in the Vatican's safekeeping are texts originally written in the Rabbinic period that followed the destruction of the Second Temple, such as the Hebrew Apocalypse of Enoch (or 3 Enoch).

Despite popular myths to the contrary, no evidence exists that the Vatican is in possession of the great candelabra, or menorah, that was used in the Jerusalem Temple and that made its way to Rome after the Temple's destruction.[32] And, for the most part, scholars have been granted access to the Vatican's Jewish manuscripts, which they continue to study for clues about Second Temple life.

Ethiopia and the 1 Enoch Manuscripts

Thousands of churches and hundreds of monasteries throughout Ethiopia house ancient manuscripts. Among the many ancient religious texts in their possession, Ethiopic Christians consider the Book of 1 Enoch especially precious, for it predicts the arrival of the Son of Man, thought by some Christians to be an allusion to the coming of Jesus.[33] For many of these Christians, 1 Enoch is believed to be the earliest predictor of Jesus. The book has been preserved in the Ethiopic language, Ge'ez, in church and monastery libraries throughout Ethiopia. While Rabbinic literature does not cite Enoch, it may have influenced the authors of medieval mystical Jewish texts, who picked up on some of its themes, such as the celestial court and the throne of God. It also likely influenced Second Temple texts that were written by Jews but not canonized by the Rabbis, such as the books of Jubilees and 2 Baruch.

According to Loren Stuckenbruck, a scholar who has traveled to Ethiopia many times to find and photograph these manuscripts, at least 60 manuscripts of 1 Enoch have been counted in the country, but in all likelihood the tally is closer to 150, if one includes manuscripts that have been reported but not photographed.[34]

Manuscripts of 1 Enoch make up just a tiny part of the vast collections of ancient manuscripts preserved throughout Ethiopia's religious communities. Stuckenbruck estimates that each of the country's 800 monasteries houses an average of 100 to 125 manuscripts, and each of its 20,000 churches preserves an average of thirty manuscripts. If these estimates are correct, the number of ancient religious manuscripts in Ethiopia totals about 700,000.

To date, though, only a tiny portion of these manuscripts has been cataloged, and the guardians of Ethiopia's manuscripts have been hesitant to share them with Western scholars. Like the monks of St. Catherine's, these guardians claim that scholars visiting Ethiopian monasteries absconded with precious manuscripts without the monks' permission.

One such incident concerns the French geographer and explorer Antoine d'Abbadie (1810–97), who compiled lists of surviving manuscripts in Ethiopia that would be published as *Catalogue raisonné manuscrits éthiopiens* in 1859. During one of his visits, d'Abbadie explored the Daga Estifanos Monastery on the tiny island of Daga, in the Lake Tana region of northwestern Ethiopia. D'Abbadie left the island with ancient manuscripts of 1 Enoch in hand, precipitating visits by many other scholars who wished to learn more about the religious culture the Lake Tana monks were preserving.

According to Stuckenbruck, one of the elder monks living on Daga teaches four monks passages from Enoch every day, and the island of Daga itself is regarded as consecrated land. As at Mount Athos, women and girls are forbidden from visiting or residing on the island, and female animals may not live there either. Like other monasteries around Lake Tana, the Daga Monastery has been inhabited continuously for centuries, and monks in each generation have inherited an attitude of suspicion towards outsiders.

The Lake Tana area has an especially high concentration of monasteries where religious manuscripts have been preserved for centuries and Stuckenbruck has visited over forty monasteries in this region to examine the contents of their libraries. One library he has visited is home to a manuscript that comprises the Books of Daniel, Ezekiel, Enoch, and Jubilees. One of the holiest books in the Ethiopic Christian tradition, Jubilees has been copied and circulated in Ge'ez since ancient times, and it is considered to be canonical. While Jubilees was extremely popular in the Second Temple period—fragments of fifteen copies of the book have been found at Qumran—it survives in full only in Ge'ez.

Because Ethiopian communities have preserved their scriptures so well, scholars are interested in studying their ancient manuscripts. The Textual History of the Ethiopic Old Testament Project, headed by Dr. Steve Delamarter, an Old Testament scholar at George Fox University's Portland

Seminary, seeks to determine the Ethiopic Old Testament's textual history by comparing ancient manuscripts with one another. Delamarter and his team have also joined the Ethiopic Manuscript Imaging Project, working to digitize surviving Ethiopic codices, among them the J. Rendel Harris collection at Haverford College near Philadelphia, a corpus of eighty manuscripts dated between 1200 and 1890, and the Ethiopic Monastic Manuscript Library in Collegeville, Minnesota, a large collection of biblical manuscripts from Ethiopia.

Another individual instrumental in photographing and digitizing the manuscripts in Ethiopian churches and monasteries is Michael Knibb, a specialist in Second Temple Judaism at King's College in London. Photographers are generally not permitted to take manuscripts out of libraries or monasteries, and their lighting is therefore not always ideal. These conditions result in photographs of manuscripts that can be difficult to decipher. Knibb works with these images to improve their quality, since many of them are invaluable for scholars seeking to determine the history of ancient texts.

Many books that are now considered part of the Pseudepigrapha were copied into Ge'ez. Besides 1 Enoch and Jubilees, which survive in complete manuscripts only in this language, the Ascension of Isaiah; the Testaments of Abraham, Isaac, and Jacob; and the Lives of the Prophets also survive in Ge'ez. These manuscripts are important evidence of how religious stories were transmitted and circulated among Christians.[35]

Ongoing Discoveries: An Afghan Family Archive

In January 2012, the media outlet Reuters reported that a cache of thousands of Jewish manuscript fragments had been discovered in the secluded mountains of Afghanistan, near its Iranian border. In 2013, the National Library of Israel purchased twenty-nine of the documents, most of which have yet to be studied and published. Jewish documents may have been stored in this region of Afghanistan because of its close vicinity to a trade route linked to the Silk Road, the ancient path to China. Many Jewish merchants conducted their businesses on this route.

Scholars have identified most of the documents in this cache as belonging to a Jewish man named Abu Nassar ben Daniel, who lived with his family in the region in the eleventh century. While the documents mainly relate to Abu Nassar's family, their discovery is valuable because they include material written in a number of languages, including Hebrew, Persian, Aramaic, and Judeo-Arabic. It is hoped that these documents will no doubt shed light on the cultural, social, and economic lives of medieval Jews living at this time.

Over the centuries, both Jewish and Christian communities have gone to great lengths to preserve their precious books. This is especially true of Orthodox Christian communities, whose monasteries have preserved and protected ancient manuscripts.

One of the biggest mysteries in the story of how some of these ancient texts came to be recovered in modern times concerns Constantin Tischendorf. The monks of St. Catherine's assert that the Codex Sinaiticus was stolen, but Tischendorf never admitted to any wrongdoing. One way to shed light on the matter is to consider how the monks at St. Catherine's treated their books in the context of a broader Eastern Orthodox tradition of preserving ancient texts. There appear to be similarities between how books were copied, preserved, and cared for in monasteries located in Ethiopia, Greece, Egypt, and other Mediterranean regions. The monasteries discussed in this chapter are all relatively isolated, and the fact that generations of monks living at these monasteries designated space to store manuscripts for centuries indicates that they placed a high religious value on them.

The evidence suggests that the monks living in Ethiopia, at St. Catherine's, and on Mount Athos today likewise believe their libraries contain invaluable treasures. Over the past century, the Mount Athos libraries and the library at St. Catherine's have undergone major renovations that have upgraded the manuscripts' storage and display; meanwhile, the Enoch collections in Ethiopia remain carefully guarded. Moreover, scholars such as Nicholas Pickwoad have shown that monks living at St. Catherine's rebound books brought to them—a practice that indicates the monks felt a sense of guardianship and responsibility to preserve these texts.

The relationship between the monks of Mount Athos and eager outsiders who come to obtain precious manuscripts is similar to the relationship between monks and pilgrims at St. Catherine's; the monks appear to be far less keen on parting with ancient books than visitors to these sites have suggested. Accusing the monks of being careless with their manuscripts—maligning them as unwitting and uninterested conservators of some of the greatest literary material in Christian and Jewish tradition—seems to have been a strategy, employed especially in the nineteenth-century, to vindicate visitors who absconded with treasures. In this milieu, a scholar such as Agnes Smith Lewis can be viewed as all the more extraordinary, since she treated the owners of these treasures with courtesy and respect.

A final similarity when it comes to these stories is the aspect of secrecy. Both Schechter and Tischendorf did not initially reveal where they had found the precious manuscripts that made them famous. This silence was not simply a product of their desire to get sole credit. Both were awestruck by the magnitude of their finds and well aware that publication of their discoveries would have far-reaching impact on the study of Early Judaism and Early Christianity. Deeply religious men, both had personal stakes in ensuring that the ancient manuscripts they had found were properly preserved.

Today, many people would argue that these documents should have remained with the communities that kept them in their care for centuries. But no one would dispute both men's hunches that the publication of these manuscripts would permanently change the study of Jewish and Christian history. And while Tischendorf may not have been upfront about the monks' intentions concerning the Codex Sinaiticus, he, like Schechter, had deep respect for the treasure they had carefully protected.

CHAPTER 3

The Dead Sea Scrolls

The famous cache known as the Dead Sea Scrolls is a misnomer: The discoveries made beginning in 1947 in eleven caves near Khirbet Qumran, which lies on the northwestern corner of the Dead Sea, include not only scrolls and thousands of parchment fragments, but also pottery, phylacteries, and even a "scroll" made of copper, on which a scribe once etched information regarding the locations of sixty-four deposits of gold, silver, and other treasure throughout the region of Jerusalem. The findings in these caves were also supplemented by an extraordinary yield of artifacts—pottery, coins, sandals, pouches, even hair combs—at a nearby site. Made from clay, metals, leather, and wood, these objects were well preserved, thanks to an unusually dry climate.

On the other hand, the name is true in the sense that the scrolls are the region's greatest treasure. And the story of how the contents of these caves came to be recovered and made accessible to the public took place over the course of five decades.

The Discoveries in the Caves

Khirbet Qumran is in a mostly isolated desert. Near this site, in eleven caves, ancient manuscript fragments were discovered between 1947 and 1956. According to legend, in 1947 a Bedouin shepherd of the Ta'amireh tribe was looking for one of his goats when he stumbled into a cave and was surprised to find pottery containing ancient scrolls. The shepherd brought a few of the scrolls to an antiquities dealer in Bethlehem. From there, a dealer named Khalil Eskander Shahin, known locally as Kando, purchased four scrolls, which he then sold to Mar Athanasius Samuel, the metropolitan, or archbishop, of the Syrian Orthodox St. Mark's Monastery in Jerusalem. The four scrolls would later be identified as (1) a commentary on the Book of Habbakuk, in which Habbakuk, an Israelite prophet whose book of teachings is preserved in the Hebrew Bible, envisions the rise of a Jewish community that the author identified as his own (Pesher Habbakuk); (2.) a text that many scholars believe was written by a member of the sect in the second century BCE and that details the rules by which the members of a sectarian community must live (Rule of the Community); (3) a well-preserved scroll of the Book of Isaiah (Isaiah A); and (4) an incomplete retelling of the book of Genesis (Genesis Apocryphon).

Bedouin dealers then brought three other scrolls to an antiquities dealer named Faidi Salahi, who contacted another dealer, Nasri Ohan, who in turn reached out to an archaeologist at the Hebrew University of Jerusalem named Eliezer Sukenik (1889–1953). Because Jerusalem was under partition in 1947, Ohan and Sukenik met secretly at the Jaffa Gate in Jerusalem on two sides of the barbed wire fence that divided the Jewish and Arab sections of the city. There, through the fence, Ohan first allowed Sukenik to examine a leaf from one of the scrolls. Sukenik soon determined that it was indeed genuine and ancient, and agreed to purchase the three scrolls Salahi possessed on behalf of the university. Later, these scrolls were identified as (1) a collection of liturgical hymns (Thanksgiving Scroll); (2) a manual detailing (both militarily and liturgically) how a community of pious Jews should conduct warfare against their enemies (The War of the Sons of Light Against the Sons of Darkness); and (3) another scroll of Isaiah (Isaiah B).[1]

In 1954, Sukenik's son, the politician and archaeologist Yigael Yadin, purchased the four scrolls that had been bought by Archbishop Mar Samuel. A rocky road had preceded the transaction. For many years, Mar Samuel had been eager to sell the scrolls, but debate raged regarding their authenticity as well as their worth. Once Sukenik had heard that Mar Samuel was looking to sell the scrolls, he offered him one thousand

Jordanian pounds on behalf of the Hebrew University of Jerusalem—a higher price than Mar Samuel had anticipated. He reconsidered: Perhaps the scrolls were more valuable than he had supposed. Delaying the sale to Sukenik, Mar Samuel chose instead to bring them to the American market. He got in touch with Charles Manoog, a Syriac Christian who owned a plumbing supply company in Worcester, Massachusetts. For four years, from 1949 to 1954, the scrolls Mar Samuel owned were stored in a bedroom in the Manoog's Worcester home. Finally, in July 1954, Manoog and Mar Samuel advertised the scrolls in the *Wall Street Journal*. Their ad, which appeared under the heading "The Four Dead Sea Scrolls," read as follows:

> Biblical Manuscripts dating back to at least 200 BC, are for sale. This would be an ideal gift to an educational or religious institution by an individual or group.

Answering the ad, a representative of Chemical National Bank agreed to purchase the scrolls for $250,000, equivalent to more than two million dollars today.[2] Mar Samuel did not know that he was being played: the bank was acting on behalf of the Hebrew University of Jerusalem. The scrolls were authenticated by a "Mr. Green," a pseudonym for a Jewish studies scholar whose real name was Harry Orlinsky. Mr. Green communicated to his colleagues his view that the scrolls he had been shown were authentic by calling his Israeli contact on a pay phone and dialing the numerical values that correspond with the letters of the Hebrew word *l'chaim*, "to life."[3]

The seven scrolls that made up the initial findings from the Dead Sea Caves encouraged further investigation, but their discovery coincided with the 1948 War of Independence. After the war, the region of Qumran fell under Jordanian control, and the Jordanian Antiquities Department, in collaboration with the École Biblique et Archéologique Français of Jerusalem, organized a joint expedition to excavate the Qumran site and nearby caves. In 1952, the Palestine Archaeological Museum (later renamed the Rockefeller Museum) granted funding for the excavations.

The Early Expeditions: 1951–67

With Qumran and its nearby caves under Jordanian jurisdiction, King Hussein appointed Father Roland de Vaux, a scholar of the Dominican order who taught at the École Biblique of Jerusalem, to select a team of scholars who would excavate the ancient site and study the Dead Sea Scrolls. De Vaux appointed a team comprising Father Józef Milik, Monsignor Patrick Skehan, Father Jean Starcky, Professor Frank Moore Cross, Professor John Allegro, Professor John Strugnell, Dominique Barthélemy, and Professor Claus Hinzinger. As editor-in-chief of the project, de Vaux would oversee five archaeological excavations—from 1951 to 1956—and also oversee the publication of the scrolls.

The caves near the Qumran site yielded remarkable findings—thousands of fragments that had once belonged to about 950 scrolls. Cave 4 contained by far the most fragments—about 15,000 in all.

Yet the effort to publish these findings slowed down soon after the scrolls were recovered. Very little material from the caves was published in the late 1950s and even in the 1960s. As the original team of scholars who were assigned the massive project of organizing, deciphering, and publishing the scrolls aged out of the project, no plan was implemented to reconceive of or expand the team. When one member of the original group died, he was replaced by a close affiliate. And when Father de Vaux died, in 1971, Father Pierre Benoit, who taught at the École Biblique, took his place. Under his tenure, the team made little headway on the project. Benoit resigned in 1984 after falling ill, and John Strugnell, a professor of Christian origins at Harvard University, took over the project as chief editor.

The only member of de Vaux's original group to leave the research team well before his death was John Allegro. To his credit, Allegro had reviewed the scrolls he had been assigned, which comprised biblical interpretative texts known as *pesharim*, relatively quickly; the volume of *Discoveries in the Judaean Desert* (also known as DJD) he oversaw was published in 1968. On the other hand, the volume was slim, since Allegro had provided almost no commentary. Most problematically, there were numerous errors in the work, and John Strugnell famously wrote a critique of Allegro's edition that was longer than the edition itself. In 1970, after Allegro left the group, he published a highly controversial book entitled *The Sacred Mushroom and the Cross*, which argued that the teachings advanced by early Jesus followers were based on visions they had had after eating a certain hallucinogenic mushroom. The book's publication was the final nail in the coffin of Allegro's career.[4]

The last Israeli acquisition of a scroll found near Qumran occurred amid a dramatic political backdrop. In 1967, shortly after the end of the Six-Day War, Yigael Yadin purchased the Temple Scroll from the antiquities dealer Kando, who had apparently kept the scroll beneath some floor tiles in his home.[5]

Over the first three decades following the discoveries of the Dead Sea caves, the team of research scholars working on the scrolls did not include a single Jew. It took until 1979 for the team to bring in an Israeli scholar named Elisha Qimron, who had earned his doctorate from the Hebrew University of Jerusalem only three years earlier. Qimron would become a key figure in the debate surrounding the publication of the scrolls in the early 1990s.

John Strugnell: 1984–90

When Benoit died in 1987, John Strugnell replaced him as leader of the editorial team. Under Strugnell's leadership, though, few texts from the Dead Sea Scroll library were published, including the scrolls assigned to him directly. By this time, many scholars began to despair that the release of the full corpus of scrolls would not happen in their lifetimes.

The fate of the unpublished scrolls, however, took a surprising turn when Strugnell's leadership over the team came to an abrupt end. In 1991, he gave a bizarre interview to the Israeli newspaper *Haaretz*, during which he called Judaism a "horrible religion." He also suggested that a "mass conversion of Jews" to Christianity would help to rectify a religion that was inherently "racist."[6]

This embarrassing incident, along with rumors that Strugnell was not pushing his team to progress with their research and was an alcoholic, led the Israel Antiquities Authority to dismiss him from heading the team. Emanuel Tov, a professor of biblical studies at the Hebrew University, was soon named as his replacement.

Tov's appointment transformed the process of publishing the scrolls as he expanded the team to include more than sixty scholars from all over the world. More *Discoveries in the Judaean Desert* volumes began to appear starting in 1991, and by the early 2000s, the DJD series was finally complete.

Publishing and Copyrights: Elisha Qimron versus Hershel Shanks

In the early days of Tov's management, scholars eager to gain access to the scrolls grew increasingly apprehensive that they would not be published. Publication was taking far longer than anticipated, and scholars lamented the possibility that their careers would end without their playing a part in researching these precious manuscripts. The situation seemed to be at a standstill.

By 1991, two frustrated academics decided to take matters into their own hands. Ben Zion Wacholder, a professor of Talmud and Rabbinics at the Hebrew Union College—Jewish Institute of Religion, and his student Martin Abegg, reconstructed the texts of some scrolls by working backward and using a concordance that listed words that appeared in the scrolls in the context of short phrases. That year, the Biblical Archaeology Society (BAS) published these texts under the title *A Facsimile of the Dead Sea Scrolls: Prepared with an Introduction and Index*, which was edited by Robert Eisenman and James Robinson. The foreword, written by BAS publisher Hershel Shanks, included a transcription of a text known in English as the Halakhic Letter, or by the acronym MMT, standing for *Miqsat Ma'ase haTorah,* or "Some Precepts of the Law."

At this time, MMT had not been widely disseminated. Scholars in the Dead Sea Scrolls research community were aware that Elisha Qimron had been working on constructing a composite version of these texts for years in collaboration with John Strugnell. In fact, at a Society of

Biblical Literature conference in 1984, Qimron had intrigued and upset some audience members by presenting a paper on the text that divulged material not yet accessible to the public. Many scholars in the audience wanted direct access to the document that Qimron was discussing.[7]

In December 1990, a Polish journal called the *Qumran Chronicle*, edited by Zdzislaw Kapera, published Qimron's version of MMT, and Shanks almost immediately reprinted it. Both Kapera and Shanks had published Qimron's text without permission. In response, the Israel Antiquities Authority (IAA) sent a letter of warning to both parties. Kapera apologized to the IAA and encouraged his readership to limit the text's distribution. Shanks, on the other hand, refused to issue a retraction.[8]

Tensions came to a head in 1992, when Elisha Qimron sued Shanks, Robert Eisenman, James Robinson, and the BAS for more than $200,000, citing copyright infringement. Eisenman and Robinson argued they were unaware of Shanks's plan to publish Qimron's MMT text in full, but Judge Dalia Dorner nevertheless found the defendants jointly liable. Shanks appealed the ruling, and in 2000 the Supreme Court of Israel denied the appeal and upheld Judge Dorner's original ruling in favor of Qimron.[9] Robert Eisenman's lawyer filed a second appeal, but later withdrew it.

The publication of these texts galvanized a broader discussion regarding the scrolls. Did the scholars who had been working on the scrolls for decades own them? Did the scholars who had been waiting their entire academic careers to gain access to the scrolls lack the rights to access them? Moreover, did Qimron have a right to claim copyright over MMT on the grounds that he was the author of the text, given that he had formulated a coherent document based on six independent fragments, and was planning to publish an English translation of the text?

According to Shanks, Qimron's only contribution to MMT, which Shanks had borrowed in his reprint, were the letters Qimron had filled in wherever they were missing in the manuscripts. In other words, all he had published was Qimron's reconstructed Hebrew. From Qimron's perspective, however, the piecing together of separate fragments and the reconstruction of words that had been missing letters were acts of intellectual creativity that legitimized his claim to ownership.

As more scrolls were published, tensions continued to boil between the scholars who had access to unpublished scrolls and the broader academic community that was banned from this access. The year 1992 saw the publication of Robert Eisenman and Michael Wise's *The Dead Sea Scrolls Uncovered: The First Complete Translation and Interpretation of 50 Key Documents Withheld for Over 35 Years*, in which the authors suggested that first-century Judaism contained traces of Christian thought. The book comprised translations of fifty Dead Sea Scroll texts, including words that seemed identical to the translations members of the official team had been working on for years. Word began to spread that some of Eisenman and Wise's transcriptions looked exactly like official transcriptions: mistakes that had been made in some texts that circulated among official team members even appeared in Eisenman and Wise's book.

Upset by the suspiciously similar transcriptions that had preempted the publication of their work, nineteen scholars, including members of the official DJD editorial team, signed a public letter on December 9, 1992, condemning the book's publication in the strongest terms.[10] Wise later published a statement expressing regret for not having properly documented all of the scholars' work in his book, and the book's protestors subsequently issued a statement retracting their original letter. A tenuous resolution was thus reached.

Publicizing and Digitizing the Dead Sea Scrolls: Hebrew University and Google

Copies of the photographic proofs that Najib Albina of the Palestine Archaeological Museum took in 1948 of the Dead Sea Scrolls were initially stored in several secret locations: Hebrew Union College in Cincinnati; the Huntington Library in San Marino, California; and the Ancient Biblical Manuscript Center in Claremont, California. The IAA (then known as the Department of Antiquities) had banned everyone—including scholars who worked at these institutions—from accessing these proofs.[11] Only scholars on the official scrolls team could examine and use them. Once Emanuel Tov took the helm of leadership in 1991, this ban was lifted.

Today, the IAA possesses most of the Dead Sea Scrolls, the Israel Museum owns the first seven scrolls to be discovered, and a few others are housed in the Jordan Archaeological Museum and the Bibliothèque Nationale de France.[12]

Thanks to an IAA and Google collaboration, the Dead Sea Scrolls that are in the possession of the IAA have been digitized and are now accessible at deadseascrolls.org.il. Like the Taylor-Schechter Genizah website,[13] which allows users to comment on Genizah photographs, this site is also interactive, permitting users to comment on a given text. The website therefore marks a new stage in the history of Dead Sea Scroll scholarship. Scholars seeking to study the scrolls no longer require access to the original scrolls or to archives of the scrolls' photographs; they can examine the scrolls whenever they wish. What is more, scholars of all faiths and institutions worldwide can interact with other scholars, contributing together to the ongoing study of these ancient treasures.

Dead Sea Scroll Insights

The Dead Sea Scrolls are intriguing because there is nothing like them in the field of early Jewish history—and perhaps in the entire field of Jewish studies. To uncover a library of documents that had lain untouched for two thousand years is akin to uncovering a time capsule containing the untouched private letters of an ancient community. And once scholars came to link this library to the nearby archaeological site of Qumran—which would yield its own riches of pottery, coins, and other everyday items—the scrolls gave rise to a massive scholarly field. No other Jewish community has left behind such a large and untampered collection of evidence that attests to their beliefs and way of life.

Based on the literary and archaeological evidence at Qumran, for instance, we know that the people who lived there observed strict purity laws and studied Jewish scriptures. The community also had its own form of *halakhah* (legal observance) that bore similarities to the Rabbinic legal system, although scholars have only begun to study the legal practices that governed this community.

At the same time, it would be a mistake to draw conclusions about Second Temple Jewish beliefs and practices based solely on the Dead Sea Scrolls and the site of Qumran. This community, composing just a tiny segment of the Judean population, believed that only they were the Chosen People of God who would enjoy salvation in the end-time.

The Origins of the Dead Sea Scroll Library

The manuscripts preserved in the library near Qumran fall into three categories: texts widely accepted as scriptural and known to have been composed outside of the sectarian community, such as the biblical books of Genesis and Exodus; texts that were not regarded as scriptural but were composed outside of the sectarian community and thought to bear certain value for the sect; and texts composed within the sectarian community.

Yet the boundary lines between these categories are unclear. How do we know which texts were written by sectarians, and which other ones were written outside of the sect but preserved in the sect's library? How do we know whether books like Jubilees were regarded as scriptural and authoritative, or simply viewed as an entertaining retelling of the Genesis narratives? Scholars debate these questions and have reached different conclusions.

What we do know is that the sectarian community at Qumran preserved retellings of earlier scriptural texts, and that, given the multiple copies of these retellings found at Qumran, the sect found them to be of particular value. These texts include Jubilees and Genesis Apocryphon, which retell the stories found in Genesis, and works that are more explicitly interpretive, such as *pesher* material (interpretations of biblical prophetic texts in light of the sect's early history) on the books of Habbakuk and Nahum. Other texts, such as the Damascus Document, the Community Rule, and the War Scroll focus on details that would have been relevant only to the sect, such as everyday life among the sectarians, and how they envisioned their future would unfold.

Scholars continue to mine these documents for both particular understandings of sectarian life and broader insight into the economy, social policy, and legal practice of Judean life in the late Second Temple period.

Ongoing Discoveries: Phylacteries, Pottery, and Torah Scrolls

Questions about other discoveries at the Qumran site over the course of the site's five seasons of excavations in 1951–56 remain unresolved. Father de Vaux died before he could publish a final report detailing his conclusions regarding the excavations.[14] Work on the site was picked up in the late 1980s, when the École Biblique in Jerusalem brought in the Belgian husband-wife team Robert Donceel and Pauline Donceel-Voûte to help prepare artifacts that were recovered during de Vaux's excavations in advance of publications that would describe these finds. But the relationship between the Donceels and the IAA soured quickly. During the duration of the Donceels' work, the IAA learned that hundreds, and perhaps thousands, of artifacts originally found at the Qumran site were unaccounted for. The Donceels returned to Belgium without producing an official final report, although they did later publish some articles arguing that the Qumran site had been built as a Roman villa and was inhabited by a wealthy Jewish family.[15]

Other information pertaining to the early stages of Dead Sea Scroll research remains unpublished. Field notes and pottery housed in the Rockefeller Museum and the École Biblique, both in Jerusalem, have still not been made public.[16] And while all the documents found in the Dead Sea caves have been published, scholars still await publications providing descriptions of certain artifacts and field notes.

Nonetheless, some artifacts continue to come to light. In 2014, for example, Yonatan Adler, a young professor at Ariel University in Israel, made an important discovery after examining an intact set of phylacteries unearthed at Qumran. Adler is a specialist in ancient phylacteries, small boxes that contain scriptural passages written on parchment. Jewish men would wear these phylacteries by attaching them to strips of leather and wrapping them on their heads.

Yigael Yadin had in fact written an entire book about phylacteries found at Qumran, but the parchment inside some of the phylacteries he studied had been crushed past the point of recovering their contents.[17] Decades later, Adler revisited the collection, housed in an IAA storeroom, in hopes of salvaging and reading the damaged parchments. He experimented by putting the sets through MRI machines—and discovered that one of the crushed phylactery boxes had intact parchment within it.

The contents of the phylacteries were different than those parchments in Rabbinic phylacteries, on which Exodus 13:1–16, Deuteronomy 6:4–9, and Deuteronomy 11:13–21 are inscribed. While the Qumran phylacteries did contain these verses, some of them also contained the Decalogue from Exodus 20.

The Qumran phylacteries constitute early evidence that biblical passages were used liturgically in the Second Temple period. They also confirm that, even as the Rabbis later concretized some Jewish practices that were first established in the Second Temple period, these practices did not always look the same among the Jews who observed them.

Modern technology is also aiding the deciphering process when it comes to ancient scrolls. Until recently, scholars could not read many such scrolls because their sheets of parchment had melded together over time. One such scroll was discovered in the 1970s, at the site of an ancient synagogue in Ein Gedi, about thirty miles south of Qumran. The scroll was located near a designated niche where Torah scrolls were kept, indicating that a Jewish community had used it regularly. But its parchment was charred to the point that, had scholars tried to open it, it would have crumbled in their hands.

In 2016, two Israeli scholars, Pnina Shor and Yosef Porath, initiated a project to use high-tech imaging in order to scan the scroll's contents. Representing the IAA, Shor and Porath collaborated with David Merkel of Merkel Technologies, who provided a three-dimensional micro-CT scan, and Brent Seales of the Department of Computer Science at the University of Kentucky, who used digital imaging software to create readable images of the scroll. Amazingly, the scroll contained a version of Leviticus that is identical to the Masoretic text, the version used in the Aleppo and Leningrad codices. The scroll's age is debatable: According to carbon dating, it dates to the third or fourth century CE, but paleographical analysis, which dates texts based on how Hebrew letters are written, places the scroll earlier, in the first century CE.[18] Regardless, it is now one of the earliest known copies of the Masoretic text of Leviticus and may have been used for public readings of the Torah in synagogues. Indeed, the fact that this scroll was discovered at the site of a synagogue suggests that it was used regularly for liturgical use. This makes its contents even more fascinating, since it reveals what Jews were reading as scriptures in their synagogues.

Scholars anticipate that other scrolls that have long been discovered but never deciphered will soon divulge their contents to modern readers.

The Scrolls of St. Catherine's, Mount Athos, and Qumran

Most ancient Jewish documents appear to have been preserved by devout Jewish and Christian communities that recognized their historical and religious value. The late Second Temple period documents found to date—at places as varied as the isolated desert of St. Catherine's, the island cliffs of Mount Athos, and the caves near Qumran—do not distinguish between books that we now consider canonical or noncanonical. Some of the ancient manuscripts preserved at these sites over many centuries are texts that were canonized, that is, incorporated into Jewish or Christian scriptural tradition, while other preserved manuscripts were not regarded by most Jewish and Christian communities as being scriptural. The preservation of both canonical and noncanonical works alongside one another reflects the fluid environment in which they were originally composed. These works were copied onto scrolls, before the codex, or book, was invented in the second century CE. Scrolls were likely placed next to one another without a clear demarcation of what was scriptural and what was not. Perhaps Jews living at this time did not feel pressured to make absolute fault lines that divided texts into the categories of "holy" and "profane."

Moreover, the arrangement of scrolls on the shelves belonging to a Jew of this period, in which each scroll usually contained one text, did not demand that anyone confront the question of what was "in" and what was "out" when it came to one's list of scriptural documents. Just the opposite was the case. One could easily add a scroll to a shelf, and just as easily remove one.

The question of canon would not bear urgency until the second and third centuries, when the codex began to replace the bulky and more expensive scroll. Once scriptural books were being bound into a single codex, the question "what books are to be included in the canon?" required immediate attention. Transitioning from scrolls to codices also democratized the study of scriptures: Codices were more affordable and more easily transportable than scrolls, which meant that in the second century, more people began to have access to them. By this time, however, most Jews had agreed upon what some have called a "majority canon."[19] While the establishment of a final canon limited the Jews' sense of what "needed" to be read in order to participate in a common scriptural tradition, the Jewish canon, as it found expression in the codex, became democratized and more widespread.

The digitization of manuscripts has revolutionized the study of Early Judaism. Photographs of the Codex Sinaiticus, Dead Sea Scrolls, and some biblical manuscripts located in Ethiopia are now accessible by virtually anyone with internet access. The manuscripts in the Mount Athos libraries and even those kept in the Vatican libraries will likely be digitized and shared in the near future as well. The site digitizedmedievalmanuscripts .org, an ever-growing database comprising photographs of manuscripts worldwide, is streamlining the digitization of these texts.

A current challenge when it comes to ancient manuscripts is the proliferation of purchases by private owners through third parties or anonymous sellers on eBay. Knowing that it is more profitable to sell ancient manuscripts piecemeal, many sellers have ripped manuscripts apart in order to sell them separately. This practice makes it very difficult for scholars to locate and piece manuscript fragments together. The questions of what texts remain in the hands of private owners, and whether these texts will be made public, will continue to frustrate and intrigue scholars searching for more clues about what life was like during the years that Rabbinic Judaism and Early Christianity took form.

PART 2

JEWISH LIFE IN THE

SECOND TEMPLE PERIOD

CHAPTER 4

Jerusalem

When the Israelites settled in the land of Canaan in about the thirteenth century BCE, they did not immediately establish the city of Jerusalem as their spiritual and political epicenter. The majestic hilltop city would not gain its legendary reputation until about three centuries later, during the reign of King Solomon.

The first Israelite king, Saul, probably established his capital in a small town called Gibeah in the eleventh century BCE. But when Saul's successor, David, made Jerusalem his capital city, Jerusalem soon became the seat of Israelite leadership and religious life, where prophets came to preach and from which religious and social leadership emanated.

David's selection of Jerusalem as his capital made strategic sense. It was a central locale, close to the Spring of Gihon and to the roadways that linked it to the more populated cities of Shehem and Hebron. It was also militarily desirable. The city's elevation—it was buttressed by valleys on its western, southern, and eastern borders[1]—made it difficult to conquer.

David's son Solomon built a Temple just north of the city, thereby expanding Jerusalem's limits and concretizing Jerusalem's role as the spiritual and political nucleus of the Israelite nation. With its three adjacent valleys and looming Temple to the north, visitors approaching the city were no doubt impressed by the view. As Solomon embarked on campaigns that would expand the borders of the empire, Jerusalem remained at the center of his monarchy.

Solomon's son Rehoboam was next to rule. He imposed high taxes to offset the costs of the building projects his father had initiated. The people demanded lower taxes, and when Rehoboam refused, some of the Israelites revolted. The upshot was a split in the kingdom. The Northern Kingdom, known as Israel, encompassed the territory allotted to ten of Jacob's sons when they first entered Canaan. The Southern Kingdom, known as Judah, retained Jerusalem as its capital and comprised two tribal regions: Judah and Benjamin.

In general, the kings of the Northern Kingdom were not as loyal as the Southern kings to the Israelite God. Geography was a primary factor. The Northern Kingdom shared borders with non-Israelite, polytheistic kingdoms. To make peace with these kingdoms, the Israelites formed treaties, which sometimes involved marrying an Israelite to a foreign prince or princess. This, in turn, led to cultural integration that drew the Israelites away from their religious traditions. The Southern Kingdom, on the other hand, was more isolated, since its southern border abutted a desert.

From the tenth through eighth centuries BCE, the Northern Kingdom was in a state of almost continuous decline. According to the Hebrew Bible, prophets living at the time warned that unless the people repented and ceased to worship false gods, they would be punished and ultimately expelled from their land. These predictions were fulfilled in 722 BCE, when the Assyrian king Tiglath-Pileser III conquered and exiled the Northern Kingdom, forcibly moving the conquered Israelites to a new and unfamiliar territory.

Distanced from the land they associated with their national origins, the Israelites were prevented from becoming a cohesive nation that could unite in rebellion against the Assyrians. The Assyrians' military strategy appears to have been so effective that the Northern Israelites who were dislocated from their land assimilated into other regions of Assyria. We do not know what happened to these "ten lost tribes."

The Judean kingdom narrowly avoided Assyrian exile as well, managing to survive the entire seventh century BCE, as the Assyrian Empire waned and the Babylonian Empire waxed. But the threat of a Babylonian conquest grew more imminent beginning in the 620s BCE. Judean prophets such as Jeremiah interpreted this growing threat as evidence of God's disapproval of the people's sins.

In 586 BCE, the Babylonians destroyed the great Temple of Jerusalem and exiled much of the Judean population. This heralded an approximately seventy-year period known as the Babylonian exile.

Rather than assimilating into Babylonian culture, the Judeans living in exile found ways to practice their ancestral tradition that did not require a Temple. Scholars believe that it was in exile that Judeans first began to gather together regularly to read their scriptures—which would later give way to the formal institution of the synagogue.

Once the Jews instituted recurring meeting times to read their holy texts, the Jerusalem Temple would never play as central a role as it once did. The Judeans had developed modes of worship that would endure through the Second Temple period and beyond. Among these modes was the regular public reading of the scriptures, which enabled all Jews, regardless of where they lived, to connect to their ancestral tradition without participating in Temple ritual.

In 539 BCE, Babylonia was conquered by the Persian Empire, and Judeans who had been in exile were soon permitted to return to Judea. Jews in this region were now subjects of the Persian Empire, a status that was to last until 333 BCE. The Persians permitted the Jews to practice their ancestral tradition freely. This freedom was especially meaningful in Judea, because it allowed the Jews to rebuild their holy Temple, a project that was completed in about 515 BCE. The Jews were also permitted to oversee the Temple's administration with virtually no outside interference.

Life under the Persians was mostly peaceful, except in the last years of the Persian Empire, when the Jews suffered from persecution. According to Early Church historians, the Persian King Artaxerxes III Ochus (425–338 BCE) captured and exiled thousands of Jews living in Judea amid one of his campaigns against Egypt. Some were relocated to Hyrcania, a region lying along the Caspian Sea that Cyrus the Great (559–530 BCE) had incorporated into the Persian Empire.[2] Why Artaxerxes III initiated this persecution, particularly after a long period of seemingly peaceful relations between Jews and their Persian host government, remains unclear.[3]

Other political changes in the second half of the fourth century BCE would soon eclipse Artaxerxes III's operations. In 334 BCE, a young general named Alexander, whose father, Philip, was king of Macedonia, headed an ambitious campaign to conquer Persian territories. By the time he died in 323 BCE after a brief and sudden illness at the young age of thirty-two, Alexander had extended his empire from the Danube River to the Beas River in India—an area totaling about two million square miles.[4]

Alexander did not leave a will with instructions regarding how his massive kingdom was to be divided. His generals, known as the Diadochi (meaning "successors" in Greek), subsequently split his massive empire into four smaller empires. Seleucus I Nicator assumed control over most Near Eastern territories, Lysimachus ruled over Thrace and most of Asia Minor, Ptolemy took command over Egypt, and Cassander led Macedonia and Greece. These men would vie for additional territory for decades.

Centered in the middle of these rulers' ever-shifting borders was the land of Judea, a tiny region along the Mediterranean coast that connected Syria with the Sinai Desert. Despite its small size, Judea was coveted: It had potential as a trade route to connect the various empires that inherited Alexander's kingdom. Judea's prime location thus made it vulnerable to the territorial wars of the third century BCE.

Jewish Literature of the Time

Hardly any nonbiblical Jewish literature written during the period leading up to Alexander's conquests has survived. One notable exception regards apocalyptic stories about the biblical figure of Enoch. Many Jews found Enoch to be a fascinating figure because, according to Genesis 5:24, Enoch did not die but "walked with God; then he was no more, for God took him." In these stories, Enoch has grand visions concerning the end of days and the ultimate judgment of all creatures. Over time, different stories about Enoch were interwoven with one another. Enochic material focused on the events that would transpire as humankind moved toward a final divine judgment. Writings attributed to Enoch became increasingly relevant as more and more Jews came to believe that the end-time was imminent during the Second Temple period.

Stories about the legendary hero Daniel were also being written and circulated in the Persian period. These stories emphasized Daniel's religious piety and unparalleled cleverness. Daniel was said to have prayed regularly while facing Jerusalem, a practice not known to have become widespread until the Rabbinic period, and to have observed dietary law. He also interpreted visions that befuddled others in King Nebuchadnezzar's court. In the Greek version of the Bible known as the Septuagint, Daniel saves the innocent Susanna from false accusations of adultery and, in another episode, proves to the king that the god he has been worshiping, Bel, is in fact not a god at all. All of these stories seek to correlate Jewish piety and worldly wisdom.

The many stories about Enoch and Daniel testify to the diversity of Jewish writings being produced at this time, a diversity that would extend and grow well into the Greek period.

Judea under the Ptolemies: 333–200 BCE

Over the course of the third and early second centuries BCE, the Ptolemies, Seleucids, and Macedonians vied for territory—and sometimes their battles had devastating effects on the Judeans. In 301 BCE, Ptolemy I Soter took control of Judea at the Battle of Ipsus against the Macedonian king Antigonus I Monophthalmus and his son Demetrius Poliorcetes. Ptolemy then proceeded to deport thousands of Jews to Egypt and enslave thousands of others.[5]

Yet life for the Judeans was not always oppressive under the Ptolemies. Ptolemy II Philadelphus (283–247 BCE), for example, released some of the Jewish captives taken by Ptolemy I—an initiative regarded as a gesture of goodwill shortly before Ptolemy II began the project to translate the Hebrew Bible into Greek.[6]

The Jewish texts written in Judea under the Ptolemies span a wide spectrum of literary genres, from apocalyptic visions to wisdom texts to adventure tales. But Jews living at this time probably did not think in terms of genre, or mentally categorize their stories in the way that readers do today. Jewish authors may not even have thought of their stories as books. Many of the legends they wrote down were transmitted orally for generations before being recorded in writing. These stories, and how they were transmitted, were therefore retold with a degree of fluidity. And the fact that so many kinds of stories were being transmitted, both orally and in written record, suggests that most Jews enjoyed a high degree of creative freedom.

Judea under the Syrian Greeks: 200–164 BCE

Between around 270 and 168 BCE, the Seleucids and Ptolemies fought a series of intermittent wars, known as the Six Syrian Wars, in which they battled over regions that included Judea.[7] The Ptolemies maintained control over Judea following the first four wars, but the Seleucid king Antiochus III (also known as Antiochus the Great) conquered the area during the fifth war, at the Battle of Paneion in 200 BCE.

The Jews soon had to accustom themselves to a new political situation: They were no longer living under the Egyptian Greeks, but under the Syrian Greeks. Some Jews were no doubt optimistic that, like the Ptolemies, the Syrian Greeks would treat the Jews with tolerance. But after Antiochus III died in 187 BCE and his son Antiochus IV Epiphanes assumed control over Judea, the new ruler instituted a series of legislations that prohibited the Jews in Judea from observing their ancestral laws.[8] Violators of these prohibitions were to be killed.

Accustomed to permissive rule under the Ptolemaic Greeks, the Jews became despondent, and some were moved to take arms in rebellion. One Jew named Mattathias, a member of a family known as the Hasmoneans, encouraged his sons to resist Antiochus IV Epiphanes' harsh legislation, but died before he could oversee the rebellion. With his son Judas Maccabeus ("the Hammer") at the helm, Mattathias's five sons led a revolt against the Syrian Greeks to free the Jews from Antiochus's oppressive legislation. The books of 1 and 2 Maccabees, as well as the writings of the first-century CE historian Josephus, record this rebellion, which led to the successful establishment of a Jewish monarchy.

The social dynamics at play during this period were not simply a matter of Greek versus Jew. Intra-Jewish tensions over how to integrate Greek culture and practice into the Jewish community had been fomenting since the rise of the Greek Empire. Historical records written down just decades after the Hasmonean rebellion, especially 1 and 2 Maccabees, reveal that the conflict between Jews who advocated for Hellenization and those who resisted assimilating into the Hellenist world inflamed the conflict with Antiochus.

Both 1 and 2 Maccabees were written sometime toward the end of the second century BCE but are different in tone and content. The author of 1 Maccabees was likely a member of the Hasmonean court, as he aims to provide a historically accurate record of the Hasmonean rebellion while portraying the Hasmonean family in a positive light. This book largely focuses on the heroic deeds of the Hasmonean family.

While 2 Maccabees portrays the same events, it focuses primarily on the fate of Jerusalem and the Temple. The author argues strongly against "Hellenism," which he believes was in inherent tension with "Judaism" (and this book is the earliest Greek text to use the word "Judaism"). The book of 2 Maccabees opens with a statement by a nameless editor, noting that he had condensed a five-volume version of the book, written by a Jew named Jason, who lived in the North African city of Cyrene. Some of the historical details he includes are inaccurate or hyperbolized, since he was not an eyewitness to the events recounted in his story. In fact, the entire writing style of 2 Maccabees is more "Hellenist" than that of 1 Maccabees: 2 Maccabees uses sophisticated Greek, well-known literary techniques, and dramatic elements that would have worked well on stage. But as we will see, it is 2 Maccabees, rather than 1 Maccabees, that rails against Greek culture.

For historical reconstructions of the events of 175–164 BCE, scholars turn to 1 Maccabees and Josephus's account in *Antiquities of the Jews*. Josephus (37–c. 100 CE), however, lived two centuries after the Hasmonean rebellion, and probably relied on some historical sources lost to modern readers. Some of the details in his account may also be exaggerated. Josephus's record of one of Judah's speeches, for instance, differs from the same speech recorded in 1 Maccabees. Some scholars believe that Josephus altered this speech to make it mirror the speech that Eleazar, a leader in the Jewish rebellion against Rome, delivered to the Jews at Masada just before they committed suicide in lieu of surrendering to Rome. Parallels between Judah's and Eleazar's speeches in Josephus's works suggest that Josephus saw the 66–70 CE rebellion against Rome as another Jewish attempt to resist a political power that threatened the survival of the Jewish people.[9]

The Maccabean Dynasty: 164–63 BCE

Like many Jews living under Greek rule, Jewish leaders in Jerusalem argued with one another over the degree to which Jews should embrace the Hellenistic world. Some contended that Jews should participate in Hellenistic culture by attending events in public theaters, engaging in activities held in local gymnasiums, and observing Greek festivals. Other Jews resisted all manners of active engagement with Hellenistic culture. But most Jews took a middle stance, striking what seemed to them a natural balance between observing their ancestral traditions and participating in Greek life.

This issue came to a head in the beginning of the second century BCE, when a Jew named Jason assumed the Jerusalem Temple's high priesthood. Jason's brother Onias III, who had previously served as high priest, was known for his devotion to Jewish ancestral law. But when the Syrian-Greek king Seleucus IV died and his brother Antiochus IV Epiphanes succeeded him, Onias's brother Jason promised the new king 440 talents if he were to be instated as high priest. He also promised the king another 150 talents if he were to authorize the building of a gymnasium for the people of Judea and give the Jews of Jerusalem Greek citizenship. Jason's intentions to "buy" the high priesthood, and his interest in installing a gymnasium that would feature naked athletes, angered Jews who sought to inoculate themselves against Greek life. Tensions between Jews who advocated for integration into Hellenist culture and Jews who resisted integration began to mount.

In about 172 BCE, a Hellenized Jew named Menelaus wrested the priesthood from Jason by promising Antiochus IV Epiphanes three hundred more talents of silver than Jason had been paying Antiochus for the position. Once in office, Menelaus stole treasures from the Jerusalem Temple in order to make the pledged payments. He also had the former high priest Onias III executed for publicizing his actions.

Sometime later, a false rumor spread that Antiochus had died, and Jason seized the opportunity to amass an army and attack Menelaus. When Antiochus got wind of the chaos plaguing Jerusalem, he assumed Judea was in a state of rebellion. His consequent invasion of Jerusalem, desecration of the Temple, and decree that Jews could no longer observe their ancestral laws on pain of death provided the reasons for the Hasmonean rebellion.[10] Antiochus may not have realized that he was entering a situation already rife with internal tension. Many Jews perceived his attack as the culmination of forced Hellenization put into place decades before by the Jews themselves.

The author of 1 Maccabees opens his account by describing Mattathias's reaction to this oppressive new legislation. Mattathias tells his five sons to actively resist Antiochus. Mattathias's sons, in turn, understand that this resistance is part of a larger struggle against both the Syrian Greeks and the Hellenized Jews who support them. Mattathias's battle cry, "Let everyone who is zealous for the law and supports the covenant come out with me!" echoes Moses' cry in the Book of Exodus when he castigates the Israelites for having built a Golden Calf and calls for volunteers among the Israelites to fight against those among them who have sinned.[11] This implicit comparison indicates that the enemy was as much the Jewish apostate as the Greek foreigner.

By 164 BCE, Judas and his brothers had successfully established an independent state that would remain autonomous until Rome incorporated Judea as a province in 63 BCE. Still, as the Hasmoneans worked to secure and expand their boundaries over the next half century or so, military conflicts would continue. And as members of the Hasmonean ruling family vied for power, the family became increasingly Hellenized and fraught with internal friction.

One Hasmonean king named Alexander Jannaeus, who rose to power in 104 BCE, was notorious for his animosity toward the Pharisees, a sect of Jews who adhered to certain religious tenets, such as the authority of an Oral Law that complemented the written scriptures. Like the Rabbis who came after them, the Pharisees were credited with being teachers who disseminated information about the scriptures and oral traditions. But Alexander believed that the Pharisees threatened his political interests, which required rejecting ancestral Jewish law in favor of Hellenization. The Pharisees, in turn, regarded him with suspicion and animosity.

The Pharisees had good reason to be concerned about Alexander, who was notorious for governing his subjects with calculated ruthlessness. When Alexander conquered Gaza, for example, he slaughtered all of its residents. And like his predecessors, Alexander assumed the high priesthood, which for some Jews was as deplorable as his cruelty to his subjects. This position was meant to be inherited, not appropriated.

Over time, the Judean population, especially the Pharisees, rallied against Alexander. On the harvest festival of Tabernacles in the fall of 94 BCE, the Jews pelted him with citrons at the Temple—an act of sedition which, according to Josephus, incited Alexander to kill six thousand Jews.[12] A full-fledged rebellion broke out two years later, but in 86 BCE Alexander quashed the rebels. After reestablishing his throne, he crucified eight hundred rebels while simultaneously murdering their wives and children.[13]

Shortly before his death, Alexander commanded that control of the monarchy be passed on to his wife, Salome Alexandra, who became queen regnant in 76 BCE and remained ruler of Judea until her death in 67

BCE. During this time, Salome increased the Judean army by 50 percent and succeeded in securing the kingdom's borders, which Alexander had expanded. According to Josephus, Salome was a fearsome commander who reinforced treaties and established trade routes with neighboring countries. She engaged in military conflict when necessary but also sought to make peace with Alexander's long-standing enemies, both locally and abroad.

Salome's enduring legacy lies in her repairing the broken relationship between the Pharisees and the Hasmonean ruling family. In both *Antiquities* and *The Jewish War*, Josephus criticizes her for these efforts, arguing that Salome allowed herself to be completely controlled by the Pharisees, who took advantage of her goodwill by becoming virtually irrepressible, assassinating and arresting enemies as they saw fit.[14] At the same time, Josephus depicts Salome as being manipulative, ingratiating herself to the Pharisees to gain the goodwill of the people, who tended to look to the Pharisees for political guidance.

Salome must have appreciated the political benefits of allowing the Pharisees more power: According to Josephus, many people living in Judea did not identify as Pharisees but nevertheless regarded them as their religious and political leaders. And empowering the Pharisees would not have required great personal sacrifice if, as Josephus and Rabbinic literature indicate, she identified as one of them.

Unlike Josephus, Rabbinic sources extol Salome as a great queen. According to midrashic legend, during her time as ruler, rain came on Wednesday and Friday nights, signs of divine approval.[15] So much rain fell during this time that produce became unusually large; grains of barley, for example, were the size of olive pits. One of the talmudic legends that describes this plentiful time does not mention Salome Alexandra by name, but notes that rain fell "in the days of Simeon ben Shetaḥ," Salome's brother. In a parallel passage in the Rabbinic collection known as midrash Leviticus Rabbah, Salome is mentioned by name.[16] This same legend suggests that the Rabbis viewed Salome as one of the greatest rulers of their past — which is not surprising, since the Rabbis perceived themselves to be continuing the legacy of Torah study and teaching perpetuated by the Pharisees. Had literature about Salome written by anti-Pharisaic communities survived, we might have a very different portrait of the great queen today.

Judea under the Romans: 63 BCE–135 CE

After Salome's death, the Hasmonean kingdom descended into a period of instability as her two sons, Hyrcanus II and Aristobulus II, competed for control of the monarchy. Salome had appointed Hyrcanus II to succeed her as ruler of Judea after her death. Like his mother, Hyrcanus supported the Pharisees in adhering strictly to both written and oral Jewish tradition. Aristobulus II, however, followed his father's tendency to oppose the Pharisees and support the powerful priestly class of Sadducees, who rejected the Oral Law and the Pharisaic tenet of resurrection. While Hyrcanus was initially installed as king of Judea, Aristobulus organized a successful coup in 66 BCE to wrest the monarchy from Hyrcanus. Ultimately, the two agreed to a treaty in which Hyrcanus would surrender his position as monarch and high priest but receive the revenue of the high priest.[17] According to Josephus, an Idumean named Antipater convinced Hyrcanus that Aristobulus would never let him live, so Hyrcanus retreated to Nabataea, where he allied with the Nabataean king, Aretas III, and with his help attacked Jerusalem. Hyrcanus and Aretas besieged the Temple where Aristobulus was hiding and soon took control of the Temple.[18]

After this incident, both Hyrcanus II and Aristobulus II appealed to the Roman general Scaurus, who was traveling through Judea, for aid in fighting one another in exchange for four hundred talents. Scaurus accepted Aristobulus's offer because Scaurus assumed that Aristobulus had the money, whereas Hyrcanus did not. (It may also be that Scaurus did not want to aid Hyrcanus, who allied with Pharisees, a sect that did not generally have friendly relations with the Romans). Supported by the Romans, Aristobulus besieged and defeated Hyrcanus in battle. Yet the question of who would reign supreme remained unresolved.

When the Roman general Pompey reached Damascus some time later, both Hyrcanus and Aristobulus again pled their cases. Instructing the brothers to cease their fighting, Pompey promised to resolve the matter when he arrived in Judea. Aristobulus, however, incited the people into further rebellion against Hyrcanus, who had remained the nominal king. Infuriated by the news, Pompey amassed an army and besieged Jerusalem.[19] In 63 BCE, after a three-month siege, Pompey wrested control of the city. From this point on, Jerusalem and the rest of Judea fell under Roman control as a client state, meaning that Judea had limited independence and had to pay taxes to the Roman Empire.[20] It would take more than another half century for Judea to be fully incorporated into the Roman Empire.

Herod the Great

In the decades following Pompey's takeover, from 37–4 BCE, Antipater's son, the infamous Herod I, ruled Judea. Herod was a descendent of the Idumeans, who had been forced to convert to Judaism after the Hasmonean king Hyrcanus I conquered them in 125 BCE.[21] Julius Caesar appointed Herod's father, Antipater, as procurator of Judea in 48 BCE, and Herod as governor of Galilee one year later.[22] In 40 BCE, the Romans acknowledged Herod's rule as king of Judea, Galilee, and Perea.[23]

Herod's establishment as king of Judea began tumultuously. After the Romans declared him king, the Parthians invaded Judea and placed Hyrcanus II's nephew Antigonus on the throne. Herod escaped to Rome and returned with Roman infantry to attack and defeat Antigonus.[24]

Herod was enormously unpopular among the Jews, particularly among Pharisees who resented his allegiance to the Roman Empire. Many Jews were horrified by his treatment of his Hasmonean wife Mariamne's family. They believed that Herod's ruthlessness served as confirmation that Herod saw himself as an outsider who viewed the Hasmoneans as competitors for power. In one incident, Herod had Mariamne's seventeen-year-old brother, Aristobulus, drowned in a pool in Jericho.[25] Aristobulus was a popular member of the Hasmonean family and a newly elected high priest; Herod must have viewed him as a direct political threat who had to be eliminated. Herod later ordered the death of Mariamne herself because he believed she had been adulterous.[26] Mariamne's murder was viewed as especially egregious because she was a Hasmonean princess whom some Jews regarded as having a more legitimate claim to the throne than Herod himself. Mariamne's mother, Alexandra, testified against her own daughter, and still Herod had her killed later as well.[27] Herod even ordered his sons born to Mariamne, Alexander and Aristobulus, to be strangled to death.[28]

Herod also did not exercise restraint in response to perceived threats outside of the Hasmonean family. He killed another son, Antipater, whose mother, Doris, he had divorced when he decided to marry Mariamne. Antipater had helped Herod to carry out the murders of his half-brothers Alexander and Aristobulus, on the grounds that they had plotted against Herod.[29]

One legend about Herod's ruthlessness is recorded in the first book of the New Testament, the Gospel of Matthew. Having heard that a "king of the Jews" had been born, Herod was determined to find and kill this baby. It was due only to divine intervention, via an angel who informed Jesus' father, Joseph, to escape to Egypt, that Jesus' life was saved. Angry that Jesus had eluded him, Herod proceeded to have all children under the age of two living in the vicinity of Bethlehem murdered.[30] Whether or not this story occurred in the way the Gospel retells it, this legend reflects the first-century CE attitude toward Herod: He was so evil and ambitious that he would go so far as to murder innocent babies in order to strengthen the security of his throne.

Aware of how despised he was, Herod was concerned that when he died, the Jews would not give him an honorable burial. He commanded, therefore, that elite Jews be killed upon his death in order to ensure that the Judeans would be in a state of true mourning at the time of his funeral. Thankfully, Herod's sister Salome rescinded this edict after he died.[31]

Herod's notoriety and cruelty cast a shadow over his reign that obfuscated his accomplishments as a diplomat who maintained good relations with the Romans, and as a visionary who oversaw construction of ambitious building projects. Among his grandest building achievements were his renovation and expansion of the Jerusalem Temple, his construction of a personal summer estate known as Herodium, and his founding of the city Caesarea, which boasted a large port called Sebastos. Herod also constructed sports arenas, recreational facilities, and temples, all intended for public use, as well as private palaces for his family. In addition, he built and reinforced military fortifications, such as the famous desert fortress of Masada, later used by Jews resisting the Roman takeover of Jerusalem in the Jewish War.[32]

By the time Herod died in 4 BCE, Jerusalem was a diverse city comprising Jews and gentiles from all regions of the empire. Thousands of gentiles had moved to the city to work on Herod's building projects, and many settled in the region after the projects were completed. The New Testament book of Acts, written toward the end of the first century CE, describes Jerusalem as being as diverse as any other major city in the Roman Empire, a city where people from all over the Roman Empire gathered.[33]

After Herod died, his kingdom was split into a tetrarchy of three parts: Herod's son Archelaus was appointed tetrarch of Judea; another son, Antipas, became tetrarch of the Galilee and Berea; and a third son, Herod Philip, was elected tetrarch of Gaulonities, Trachonities, and Paneas.[34] Herod also bequeathed some regions—including Jamnia, Ashdod, and Phasaelis—to his sister Salome. Archelaus, however, who received the bulk of Herod's kingdom, was unable to maintain control over the region to Rome's satisfaction: In 6 CE he was exiled to Gaul.[35] From this point on, Judea became a Roman province. It would be ruled by prefects until Herod's grandson Agrippa I became king of Judea in 41 CE, following Caligula's death.[36]

Agrippa I ruled Judea from 41–44 CE, during the same time that Claudius ascended the throne of the Roman Empire. The two had a close connection dating from their childhoods. Agrippa was sent to Rome as a boy to escape the hands of his grandfather, Herod, who had killed his own son (and Agrippa's father) Aristobulus IV. Agrippa received a Roman education in Tiberius's court, and as a young man was appointed tutor of Tiberius's grandson. He also forged a personal relationship with Tiberius's son Drusus and Tiberius's nephew Claudius, who would later become emperor. The close relationship between Agrippa and members of the Roman government did not wane over time. Yet he also managed to maintain a positive relationship with the Pharisees. During his rule, Herod's territories were finally reunited under a single monarchy.

A story is told in the Mishnah that Agrippa observed the Pharisaic practice of publicly reading a portion of the Torah at the Temple on the last day of Tabernacles, the fall harvest holiday. On one occasion, when he reached the verse in Deuteronomy that reads "you must not set a foreigner over you" (Deut. 17:15), Agrippa began to cry. Seeing him distressed, the rabbis in the synagogue responded with words of consolation: "Agrippa, you are our brother, you are our brother!"[37] It is unclear whether this legend is referring to Agrippa I, who had close ties to the Judeans; his son, Agrippa II; or a figure representing a conflation of both Agrippa I and Agrippa II. If Agrippa I and Agrippa II had different relationships with the Pharisees, it is likely that this Mishnah, and other Rabbinic references to these men, would have made a clear distinction between them.[38] All we can say with certainty is that this legend attests to the ambiguous relationship between the last ruling members of Herod's family and the Judeans. On the one hand, Herod's grandson and great-grandson identified as Jews and on the other, they—or perhaps just Agrippa I, or just Agrippa II—worried that as descendants of Idumeans and of the notorious Herod, they would never be fully accepted as Jews, despite their sincere intentions.

While he was probably well liked in Rabbinic circles, Agrippa I, who is called Herod in Acts, did not have a good relationship with early Jewish followers of Jesus. According to Acts, he persecuted members of the Jerusalem church. He had an apostle, James, killed, and arrested another apostle, Peter, who, Acts tells us, miraculously escaped from prison.[39] The author of Acts interprets Agrippa's death in 44 CE as a divine punishment for allowing some of his subjects to treat him as a god.[40]

The Search for a Messiah in Judea

The rising numbers of Jews studying the teachings of Jesus in the middle of the first century CE was probably not of great interest to the broader Jewish population. Growing tensions with the Romans and the pockets of resistance cropping up throughout the empire were more concerning. Josephus records, for instance, that in 48 CE a Jew named Judas instigated a rebellion against the Roman Empire, along with his two sons, Jacob and Simeon. The Romans soon executed all three of them. According to Josephus, Judas was but one of many rebels who stirred sedition against Rome.[41]

In the early decades of the first century CE, many Jews believed they were living on the cusp of the end-time. Some Jews who were angered by Rome's continuous insults, which included increasingly high taxes and little or no interventions when local Roman rulers treated Jews with bias, believed that their challenging circumstances portended forward movement on the inevitable path toward messianic redemption. Many of these Jews were spurred to rebel against the empire.

Other Jews, however, believed they could help bring about the end-time by following the teachings of a messiah who would be responsible for transitioning the people into the final age. One such messianic figure was Jesus. In around 32 CE, Roman authorities crucified Jesus in Jerusalem, where a community of his Jewish followers was slowly growing. The leaders of this Jerusalem church did not want to cut off ties with the broader Jewish community. They observed certain Jewish practices, such as dietary laws, and focused on spreading the words of Jesus, whom they regarded as a great teacher. Acts 15 recalls that in about 50 CE, members of this church met at what is now called the Council of Jerusalem to discuss what Jewish practices gentile converts to their community would be required to observe. They decided that gentiles would be prohibited from practicing idolatry, violating certain sexual proscriptions, eating blood, and eating meat that contains blood.[42] All of these practices would later become cornerstones of the Rabbinic Noahide Laws.[43] In the middle of the first century, then, the followers of Jesus living in Jerusalem likely saw themselves as nothing other than devoted Jews.

The Role of the Temple

While at this time the Jewish population was scattered throughout the Roman Empire, the Jerusalem Temple remained a focal point of Jewish religious life. Many Jews in the late Second Temple period did exactly what the Torah proscribed regarding the festivals of Passover, Weeks, and Tabernacles: They offered sacrifices and worshipped the Jewish God at the Temple.[44] Thousands of Jews made the trip up to Jerusalem — "up" not in the sense that Jerusalem was topographically elevated, but, rather, they went up to a more spiritually elevated place.

While not all Jews made this trip regularly, evidence indicates that many did make the effort. The opening of the Jewish book of Tobit, preserved in the Apocrypha, describes the eponymous hero as being virtuous primarily based on his commitment to making this long pilgrimage to Jerusalem from his home in Assyria. Moreover, significant archaeological discoveries attest to this kind of pilgrimage. The father-son team Yotam Tepper and Yigal Tepper recently discovered an approximately five-and-a-half-foot-wide path with curved steps about ten miles from Jerusalem.[45] Unlike wider roads built during the Roman period, which featured mile markers and were sturdy enough to accommodate different kinds of transportation, this path would have been able to accommodate pilgrims coming to Jerusalem only by foot. Scholars believe that other paths were made as well.

The existence of paths leading to Jerusalem from multiple directions conjures an image of the influx of Jews who likely overwhelmed the city of Jerusalem on pilgrimage holidays. The mass gatherings and the thousands of sacrifices at the Temple must have been a grand sight to behold, and a pungent one. According to Josephus's account in *The Jewish War*, Roman officials counted 256,500 paschal lambs sacrificed over the course of just one Passover holiday. Given the mandate that the lamb had to be eaten communally, and assuming that about ten people gathered to eat one lamb, it can be inferred from Josephus's statement that 2,565,000 people were present in Jerusalem on Passover.[46] In another passage, Josephus comments that more than three million people would come to Jerusalem during Passover.[47]

Other historical data exist as well. A passage in a Rabbinic collection called the Tosefta states that Agrippa (here, too, it is unclear whether the Tosefta refers to Agrippa I or Agrippa II) conducted a census of Jerusalem's population during Passover by counting the hind legs of paschal lambs. This figure amounted to 1.2 million, which suggests a total presence of twelve million people.[48] This number, however, is likely exaggerated.

The Jewish Rebellion against Rome

Although Claudius (41–54 CE) regarded Agrippa I, the last Hasmonean king of Judea, as a friend and ally, some of the Roman procurators whom Claudius appointed over Judea fueled tensions between the Jewish population and Roman officials who occupied the region. One such figure was the governor of Judea, Tiberius Julius Alexander (46–48 CE). Josephus attributes the Jews' strong critique of Tiberius to his being an apostate, but Tiberius was more than simply a wayward son: During the Roman destruction of the Jerusalem Temple in 70 CE, Tiberius was the chief of Titus's army.[49]

Another Roman official blamed for fueling bitterness toward the Roman Empire was Procurator Ventidius Cumanus (48–52 CE). In one incident, a Roman soldier exposed himself indecently to a crowd of Jews who had come to the Jerusalem Temple to celebrate the Passover festival, leading to a public outcry. Asked to restore order, Cumanus responded by bringing in soldiers to forcibly remove Jews from the Temple. This, Josephus writes, led to a disastrous stampede that killed about ten thousand Jews.[50]

Gessius Florus, the Roman procurator of Jerusalem from 64 to 66 CE, also magnified Jewish yearnings for independence by antagonizing the Jews. Trouble began when some Jews complained to Florus that gentiles in Judea were harassing and stealing from the Jews, and Florus refused to intervene.[51] The relationship only continued to deteriorate. On one occasion, for example, a gentile ruffian aggravated the Jews of Caesarea by sacrificing birds on the Sabbath on an upside-down pot just outside a synagogue. When a delegation of Jews approached Florus to argue that this man's behavior was an act of mockery toward their Temple, Florus had them arrested. He then raided the Temple treasury and seized seventeen talents on the grounds that they were owed to him for imperial service. From there, he established a tribunal and demanded that Jewish leaders hand over those Jews who had protested his behavior. The Jewish leaders responded by claiming that all of the Jews in Judea were favorably disposed toward Florus. Florus, knowing this was certainly not the case, commanded his soldiers to sack the marketplace in Jerusalem and kill whomever they saw.

The enthusiasm of Florus's soldiers exceeded Florus's own expectations: According to Josephus, Florus's men killed 3,600 Jews in one day, a figure that includes women and children. Also included in this figure are men who were scourged and crucified on the cross.[52] Josephus notes that the calamities that befell the Jews under Florus played a major role in inciting the Jews to support a rebellion against the Romans.

Josephus also attributes the Jewish rebellion to members of what he calls the fourth "philosophy" of Judaism—a group that may have been associated with the Zealots, who sought to create an independent Jewish state by rebelling against Rome.[53] The members of this group were incensed by high Roman taxes, and by the antagonism of lower-level Roman officials toward the Judean populace.

Herodian client kings of the Roman Empire also agitated the population. Some Jews accused Agrippa II, who was the last member of the Herodian family to rule the Judeans, of not properly advocating on their behalves to the Roman Empire. Instead, Agrippa II supported Vespasian's military excursions to quell the Jews' rebellion, and he provided Vespasian with troops. This, too, increased unrest among the Jews.

Rebellion against the Roman Empire was further complicated by internal conflicts within the Judean population. One group of Zealots was led by a man named Eleazar bar Simeon. Eleazar achieved a surprising victory over the Romans early in the war at Beit Horon, where some six thousand Roman soldiers were killed.[54] Despite his unexpected victory, moderate Jewish leaders were concerned about Eleazar's impulsive and violent methods and refused to allow him to bear an official title in the war.[55] Eleazar therefore decided to maintain an independent operation against the Romans that did not cooperate with the main Jewish army.

Another Jewish rebel named John did likewise, encouraging thousands of Jews in his Galilean town of Gischala to join him in rebellion against the Romans. When the Romans sent troops to Judea with Titus at their helm, John pled with Titus to place a respite on the war so the Jews could properly observe their Sabbath day. Titus relented, and John escaped to Jerusalem that evening. Titus then took the city of Gischala, but he was furious that he was unable to capture John.[56]

Meanwhile, the Zealots in Jerusalem, led by Eleazar, had wrested control of the Jerusalem Temple and were being besieged by Ananus and his men. Ananus, a Sadducean who had been the Temple's high priest, opposed the Jewish rebellion against Rome.[57] When John arrived in Jerusalem, he first attempted to play both sides: He entered the Temple on the pretense of establishing a treaty with the Zealots on behalf of Ananus, but then told the Zealots that they would need outside help, since Ananus was planning to appeal to Vespasian to help defeat them.[58]

Desperate to find a way to survive the siege, the Zealots agreed to send a message to the Idumeans asking for help, and they in turn sent twenty thousand men to support the Zealots. The Idumeans broke into Jerusalem and released the Zealots from the Temple, whereupon a rampage ensued in which the Idumeans killed thousands of Jews living in the city, including Ananus.[59] After the Idumeans retreated, John once again broke off from Eleazar, and led a separate group of rebels against the Romans.

At this time, a rebel named Simon bar Giora amassed a following of forty thousand men to fight against the Romans. Simon threatened the security of both the Romans and the Zealots. Wanting to establish himself as king, he roamed Judea with his troops, plundering supplies and killing people who resisted him. In order to rein in Simon's growing power, the Zealots abducted his wife and some of her attendants. In response,

Simon killed and tortured so many Jerusalemites that the Zealots were compelled to release his wife. Soon afterward, the elders of Jerusalem invited Simon into the city to help overthrow John of Gischala, whom they regarded as a tyrant.[60] Simon took control of the upper region of Jerusalem, and John held fast over lower Jerusalem.

The infighting among Jewish rebels weakened them against their common enemy. Other factors beyond the rebels' control made the difficult situation even worse. According to Rabbinic sources, the fall of 69 CE was a sabbatical year, during which, according to biblical injunction, Jews could not plow, sow, or harvest their land. The following year yielded a smaller crop than usual, making the siege of Jerusalem even more unbearable and catastrophic than it otherwise would have been.[61]

Events came to a head in 70 CE, when Roman forces besieged Jerusalem. According to Jewish tradition, the siege ended on the ninth day of the month of Av, in the heat of summer. After the Romans breached the walls of Jerusalem, they destroyed the Temple and killed many thousands of residents—1,100,000, according to Josephus. They also took thousands of captives, which Josephus numbers at 97,000.[62]

Josephus's calculations may be too high, but it is certain that the Roman response to the Jewish rebellion devastated the Jews. The Babylonian Talmud recalls a legend in which a thousand boys and girls, taken as captives from Jerusalem to Rome, presumably to be brought into sexual slavery, committed suicide by jumping over the ship transporting them to Rome.[63]

The Romans presented the destruction of the Jerusalem Temple and the quelling of the Jewish rebellion as a major victory, and ritualized it in the same way they celebrated victories over non-Roman territories. The celebration climaxed with a triumphal procession through Rome that featured notable items plundered during the war—both precious objects and high-ranking captives. This triumph was unusual, though, in representing a victory over what had long been Roman territory. In this sense, it testified to how damaging the war in Judea had been for the Romans, and how relieved they were to have finally put the rebellion to rest. It also suggests that even when Jews were living within the boundaries of the Roman Empire, they were viewed as outsiders who had never wholly accepted Roman rule and who were never wholly accepted as Romans.

The Judean uprising tapped into the Romans' military resources, diverted their energies, and drained their finances far more than anyone could have predicted. They were determined to send the message that their quelling of the Jewish uprising was utterly final. High-quality coins were minted with the phrase "Judaea Capta" in gold, silver, and bronze, and the quantity of coins produced—more to commemorate the capture of Judea than any other triumph—is another testament to the importance with which the Romans viewed their victory.[64]

Another commemoration of the Romans' victory was the Arch of Titus. Domitian, Titus's brother who ruled from 81 to 96 CE, erected it on the western edge of the Roman Forum early on in his reign. The arch depicts the victorious Flavians carrying vessels that had been used in the Jerusalem Temple, such as the showbread table and the menorah. These objects symbolized both the Jews' worship of their God and the sacred space that housed their God. Also on the arch is Titus, who stands at a passageway above the panel depicting the Temple spoils with Victories flanking him in the spandrels (the space between the straight horizontal surface of the arch and the curve below it). The arch's message was clear: The Jewish God had been defeated at the hands of Titus, with the help of his god Jupiter, the god responsible for Roman kings' military victories. Unlike other gods, whose cults were incorporated into Roman culture after conquest, the Romans depicted the Jewish God not as being incorporated but as being defeated. In keeping with this message, Vespasian required that Jews who had previously donated money to the Jerusalem Temple now pay the same amount to the cult of Jupiter.[65]

In addition to the Arch of Titus, a second, larger arch was built in 81 CE to commemorate Titus's victory over the Jews. This arch, built in the middle of the Circus Maximus, a massive Roman arena used for sports and other entertainment, has not yet been excavated. Its enormity—over eighteen yards wide, ten yards high, and sixteen yards deep—again testifies to the seriousness with which the Romans regarded their victory over Judea.

So much loot was plundered from Judea that Vespasian was able to use the goods to fund the construction of the greatest amphitheater built in the Roman Empire. The Colosseum hosted gladiator games, theatrical entertainment, and other public events. Holes at the bottom of a stone inscription found at the site are evidence of metal letters that had once been attached to pegs and placed into the stone. Based on the location of these holes and their relationship to one another, the letters can be reconstructed to read: "The Emperor Titus Caesar Vespasian Augustus ordered the new amphitheater to be made from the (proceeds from the sale of the) booty." This booty is likely the treasure taken from Vespasian's successful war against the Jews.[66]

Rabbinic Legends about the Temple's Destruction

Rabbinic traditions recall the destruction of Jerusalem and its great Temple with emotive detail. The midrashic collection *Avot de-Rabbi Natan*, for example, describes an encounter between Rabbi Yochanan ben Zakkai and the Roman general Vespasian that occurred when Jerusalem was burning to the ground. In this account, students of Rabbi Yochanan place him in a coffin and escort it out of the city, facilitating the rabbi's escape from Jerusalem. Vespasian, standing with his cavalry just outside Jerusalem, has the coffin opened, and discovers Rabbi Yochanan alive and well inside. Vespasian asks Rabbi Yochanan, "What shall I give you?" By asking this question, Vespasian may be requesting that Rabbi Yochanan acquiesce to the Roman takeover of Jerusalem. He may also be expressing his willingness to cease fomenting antagonism between the Romans and the Jews. Rabbi Yochanan answers, "I only ask for Yavneh, where I might teach my students, and establish prayer, and keep all of the commandments."[67] Rabbi Yochanan, it seems, seeks to ensure the continuity of the Torah's transmission, and the authority to oversee the practice of Judaism without Roman intervention.

A number of Rabbinic versions of this story recount the episode with slight variations.[68] In the version preserved in the midrashic book *Eikhah Rabbah*, for example, Rabbi Yochanan does not mention Yavneh (or Jamnia in English) at all. In the Babylonian Talmud, Rabbi Yochanan asks Vespasian for "Yavneh and its sages," in addition to medical care for an ailing priest, Rabbi Zadok, and the rescue of the patriarch Rabban Gamaliel and his family. This latter version, in which Rabbi Yochanan is concerned with protecting the establishment of the priesthood, the patriarchy, and a place to conduct lay leadership, is carefully curated and probably an edited version of an older legend. Nevertheless, the fact that this account appears in multiple Rabbinic versions reflects a broad concern regarding how to ensure the survival of Rabbinic tradition in the years following the Temple's destruction.

Another Rabbinic story recalls Rabbi Akiva walking past the ruins of the Temple with Rabban Gamaliel, Rabbi Eleazar ben Azariah, and Rabbi Yehoshua. When they notice a wolf walking upon the wreckage of the Holy of Holies, Rabbi Akiva's colleagues lament, but he responds with laughter. The rabbis react incredulously to Akiva's laughter, but he explains that since the prophecy in Micah 3:12 predicting the total destruction of Jerusalem has been fulfilled, the time will soon come for the prophecy of Zechariah 8:4, which envisions the restoration of Jerusalem, to be fulfilled as well.[69] This story speaks to both the personal devastation the rabbis felt in the wake of the Temple's destruction, and also to their hope that Jerusalem would one day be restored to its former magnificence.

The legend of Rabbi Yochanan ben Zakkai's encounter with Vespasian and the story of Akiva's seeing the wolf on the Temple Mount capture the popular Jewish belief that the destruction of the Temple in 70 CE was a fulcrum in time—a moment in which the entire course of Jewish history was about to dramatically change.

The Aftermath of Destruction

One reason the Jewish rebellion lasted so long—and then was quashed with a powerful show of force—has to do with the Roman Empire's state of turmoil during this period. Nero's reign, which ended in his suicide, gave way to a period of instability that saw four men—Galba, Otho, Vitellius, and Vespasian—staking a claim to the empire in a single year. It was not until Vespasian successfully established himself on the throne that the question of how to deal with Judea was fully addressed. To distinguish himself from his capricious predecessors, Vespasian presented himself as a seasoned general interested first and foremost in the empire's security and stability. This, in turn, motivated his harsh and swift response to the Jewish rebellion.

Jewish hostility toward the Roman Empire did not soften in the years following the Temple's destruction. After the war, Vespasian imposed the Fiscus Judaicus, a high taxation imposed on Jews throughout the empire,[70] and many Jews in regions far from Jerusalem must have resented having to suffer the consequences of a rebellion that had occurred in Judea. Clashes between Jews and Romans punctuated the first century and extended into the first half of the second century. In 115 CE, Jewish riots broke out throughout the Roman Empire, and by the time they were quelled in 118 CE, thousands of Jews and Romans had lost their lives.[71] Many Jews were probably eager to reconcile with the Romans at this point, but other Jews continued to use military resistance as a means of defying Roman rule.

Aelia Capitolina and Rabbinic Settlement of the Galilee

In around 130 CE, the Roman emperor Hadrian (117–38 CE) decided that instead of rebuilding Jerusalem, which the Romans had ravaged sixty years earlier, as a Jewish city, he would build a city on the site that featured a Roman temple at its center. This city was to be called Aelia Capitolina, after Hadrian's family name, Aelia, and the god Jupiter, who was also known as Capitolinus.

For some Jews who were already distraught by the Roman presence in Judea and the destruction it had wreaked, this was the final straw. In 132 CE, a Jew named Simeon Bar Kosiba (or possibly Simeon Bar Koseba) amassed an extraordinary following of thousands of Jews who believed he was the Messiah. Bar Kosiba went by the name of Bar Kokhba, which meant "son of a star" and had typological significance, as it alluded to Numbers 24:17, which cites the gentile prophet Balaam predicting a time of salvation for Israel: "What I see for them is not yet, what I behold will not be soon, a star [*kokhav*] rises from Jacob, A scepter comes forth from Israel; It smashes the brow of Moab, the foundation of all children of Seth." While many knew him as Simeon Bar Kokhba, personal letters discovered in what scholars call the Cave of Letters in the Judean desert are signed by one Simeon Bar Kosiba, with the possible pronunciation of Koseba.

Bar Kokhba convinced his followers that the successful overthrow of Roman rule and the resulting establishment of Jewish autonomy would signal the beginning of the Messianic Era. His followers, in turn, hoped that, as an embodiment of the star mentioned in Numbers, Bar Kokhba would "smash the brow of Moab," which they interpreted to be a prediction of Rome's impending defeat.

Rabbinic passages that reference this figure deny his claim to messianic rule by calling him Bar Kosiba, which can be rendered as "son of a lie," or "bearer of deceit." Rabbis who used this appellate held Bar Kokhba responsible for the deaths of thousands of Jews who were killed by Hadrian's forces during and following the rebellion. Indeed, the destruction that occurred in the wake of Bar Kokhba's rebellion was one of the worst catastrophes in Jewish history, with perhaps as many as 250,000 Jewish casualties, and the loss of access to Jerusalem.[72] Under Hadrian's oversight, Roman legions razed Jerusalem to the ground and rebranded Judea as Syria Palestina.

The loss of life and mass destruction during these years became imprinted on Jewish memory. A legend in the Babylonian Talmud describes the slaughter of Bethar, one of the last towns in Judea to fall to the Romans. The Talmud interprets a biblical verse in light of Bethar's destruction:

> "In blazing anger He has cut down all the might of Israel" (Lam. 2.3): Rabbi Zera said in the name of Rabbi Abbahu who cited Rabbi Johanan: This refers to the eighty [thousand] battle trumpets which gathered in the city

of Bethar when it was taken. Men, women and children were killed there until their blood ran into the Great Sea. Do you think this was close? It was a whole mile away . . . the Gentiles fertilized their vineyards for seven years with Israel's blood without using manure.[73]

Even if the historical details in this legend are exaggerated, it preserves the trauma and desolation that engulfed the Jews of Judea during this time.

Economic factors also contributed to the turbulent events of the late first and early second century CE. Thousands of Judean residents were impoverished and unemployed, in part for reasons dating back to the end of the first century BCE. King Herod had initiated massive building projects throughout Judea: expanding the Temple, founding new towns, and building fortresses. To complete these immense projects swiftly, Herod had hired Jerusalem residents and thousands of foreign employees. But once the buildings were complete, the workers found themselves unemployed. Thousands of these workers stayed in the region, resulting in a large proportion of residents who became either unemployed or under-employed. Poverty plagued the region and eventually contributed to discontent with the Roman Empire that fanned the flames of rebellion.

While Jewish literature presents the Jerusalem Temple's destruction as a calamitous turning point in Jewish history, some scholars argue that it may not have had the great social and religious impact many Rabbinic texts suggest.[74] Still, there can be little doubt that the loss of the Temple led to changes in social and religious leadership for Jews living in the Land of Israel. Without the Temple to administer, the ruling priestly class of Sadducees abruptly lost the medium through which they exercised control over Jews who had looked to the Temple as a central means of worship. The Pharisees soon emerged as authoritative leaders whose competitors no longer wielded political and religious authority. And in the course of the next six or seven centuries, the heirs of the Pharisees' teachings, the Rabbis, would be instrumental in developing Rabbinic Judaism and its legal system.

The Jews who experienced the violent events of 70 and 135 CE did not reach a consensus regarding what all of these changes meant in the larger scheme of God's divine plan. Some considered their suffering at the hands of the Romans a sign of the coming end-time, when the city of Jerusalem and its Temple would finally be restored. Others, interpreting these changes through a political lens, saw the Jewish rebellion as an act of foolish resistance to the Jews' inevitable assimilation into Roman culture.

The Literature of Judea

Starting with the turn of the second century BCE, the Jews of Judea became extraordinarily prolific in their literary output. Some of the texts written during this period were soon preserved in the Apocrypha. Others were copied over the centuries and later preserved in the modern collection of ancient books known as the Pseudepigrapha. One example of a book that would be preserved in the Apocrypha is Tobit, an adventure tale about a young man who embarks on a long journey to retrieve treasure and who finds love along the way. Another example is the Wisdom of Ben Sira, a guidebook for Jewish students regarding personal conduct that was written fifteen years or so prior to the Hasmonean rebellion. Two generations later, the author's grandson translated the text from Hebrew into Greek.

Another book written in the late second century BCE, around the same time Ben Sira was being translated into Greek, is 1 Maccabees. Its Jewish author was most likely a court insider familiar with the history of the Hasmonean dynasty, and someone who had personally traveled the Land of Israel.

Jerusalem's capture by the Roman general Pompey in 63 BCE was fertile ground for Jewish writers to explore the theme of God's relationship with—and apparent abandonment—of the people. One text written at this time, the Psalms of Solomon, alludes to Pompey's invasion. Without mentioning Pompey by name, the author describes a general's invasion of Jerusalem and his murder of Judean laypeople, princes, and government officials.[75]

Similar to the Psalms of Solomon, which were written following a calamitous assault on Jerusalem in 63 BCE, the books 4 Ezra and 2 Baruch were composed following the Roman invasion of Jerusalem in 70 CE. While the Psalms of Solomon is a collection of eighteen psalms that consider how Jerusalem's fall influenced Israel's relationship with God, 4 Ezra and 2 Baruch feature apocalyptic visions and predictions of Israel's ultimate destiny: God's Chosen People will enjoy salvation and restoration, and the enemies of Israel will be destroyed.

The majority of the documents stored in the Dead Sea caves were originally composed in Judea in the second and first century BCE. These texts represent a diverse array of literary genres, including wisdom literature, novellas, poetry, apocalyptic texts, rewritten Bible texts, and biblical interpretation.

Most of the texts found in the caves, including Jubilees and Ben Sira, were written in Hebrew. While some documents, such as 1 Maccabees, have survived in Greek, most of these texts include turns of phrase that scholars believe would have looked more eloquent in Hebrew, which suggests that they were originally composed in Hebrew as well.

Jews living in the Land of Israel in the late Second Temple period wrote in Hebrew, Aramaic, and sometimes Greek. The Jews who spoke these languages did not live separately from one another. The book of Acts, for example, recalls that Paul spoke to the Jews in Hebrew while Roman authorities were arresting him outside the Jerusalem Temple—yet Paul wrote his letters to gentiles living throughout the Roman Empire in Greek.[76] Early Rabbinic texts that are preserved in Hebrew and Aramaic also show knowledge of Greek. These documents remind us that regardless of how committed Jews in the Land of Israel were to observing their ancestral tradition, and how resistant they were to integrating into a Roman way of life, they were still living in an environment in which cultural aspects of both worlds were inescapable.

The siege of Jerusalem in 69–70 CE unleashed massive death and devastation in Judea. But for Jews who wrote about the rebellion in the decades that followed, the greatest catastrophe of all was not the death toll but the destruction of the majestic Temple that had served as a centripetal force for Jews throughout the Roman Empire. The loss of this Temple would eclipse all the other effects of the war in Jewish national memory, and the meaning of this loss would occupy Jewish writing for centuries to come.

CHAPTER 5

Alexandria

In the late Second Temple period, the city of Alexandria was a center of learning, culture, and commerce. Its philosophical schools housed the greatest intellectuals of the age, and its library was renowned as one of the largest and most beautiful in the world. Alexandria's proximity to the Nile made it a fertile region where produce could be grown and exported, and so the city was also an agricultural and mercantile thoroughfare. Its streets and bustling harbor were crowded with visitors who were captivated by its beauty and liveliness.

A massive and diverse workforce thrived in Alexandria since the rural regions beyond the city produced more food than any other Roman province. During this time, the resident population included native Egyptians, Greeks who had settled there following Alexander the Great's founding of the city in the fourth century BCE, Romans, a large community of Jews, and hundreds of thousands of slaves. Overall, the city was regarded as one of the most important in the Roman Empire, a kind of modern-day New York City to which thousands of immigrants and visitors flocked from across the empire.

Alexandria boasted a grand museum where scholars worked and shared ideas. This museum housed the famous Alexandrian library, the greatest library in the Hellenist Empire. King Ptolemy I Soter, who inherited the Egyptian region of the Hellenist Empire after Alexander's death, had built the library in 306 BCE. By 262 BCE, the library held 532,800 books, and, by 47 BCE, it held about one million books.[1] This figure is staggering, given that every volume was copied by hand, and many were copied specifically to be part of the library's collection. A collection of this size was unparalleled in the Greco-Roman world. It is no wonder that the museum, and by extension the city of Alexandria itself, became a center of intellectual activity under Ptolemaic Greek rule.

Inside the museum, elite philosophers studied the writings of Homer, Aristotle, and Plato. And outside, Egyptians, Greeks, and Jews lived among one another, without establishing clear cultural and religious boundaries. Greek citizens in Egypt began to incorporate Egyptian gods, such as Isis, into their pantheon, and native Egyptians in turn took on Hellenist practices.

The Jews were not immune to these multidirectional influences. They incorporated religious and cultural aspects of the world around them into their Jewish writings and conversations, and also effected changes in the religious worship of non-Jewish Greeks. Evidence of these changes is reflected in Roman complaints that gentiles were adopting Jewish customs, such as Sabbath observance.[2] Most of these gentiles, however, probably did not convert to Judaism.

During this time, Alexandria's Jewish population was thriving and contributing to all aspects of city life.[3] The largest concentration of Egypt's Jews resided in the city. According to Josephus, Jews had settled in Alexandria at the very moment that it was founded by Alexander the Great.[4] By the late Second Temple period, there may have been some 180,000 Jews living in Alexandria, making up between 30 to 40 percent of the city's population.[5]

Perhaps the most important eyewitness to Alexandrian Jewish society in the first century is the Jewish philosopher Philo of Alexandria (c. 20 BCE–c. 50 CE), who offers fascinating details about the Jews of his city, their internal organization of limited self-leadership, and their synagogues. Philo estimates that Alexandria was home to a million Jews in his time. This figure is probably too high, based on how large scholars believe the city was in the early first century. At the same time, the Jewish population in Alexandria was large enough to draw the attention of the Romans, Greeks, and Egyptians living among them.[6] Many Greek and Roman documents that mention the Jews reference their large community in Alexandria. During the three centuries or so that Alexandria was under Ptolemaic Greek rule, this attention was not problematic, and life was relatively peaceful for Alexandria's Jewish population. Dangerous tensions between Alexandrian Jews and the non-Jewish population would arise only after Rome incorporated Alexandria into its empire.

It appears that Ptolemy I Soter (c. 367–283 BCE) was directly responsible for the initial Jewish settlement in Egypt. When he assumed control over Egypt and the Land of Israel following Alexander's death, Ptolemy took Jewish captives from Judea and Samaria and resettled them in Egypt. Some of these captives were integrated into his newly formed military garrisons, and, according to Josephus, Soter gave these men equal rights alongside the Macedonians.[7] Other Jews at this time came to Egypt of their own accord, settling throughout the region in cities such as Leontopolis, Heliopolis, and, of course, Alexandria.

Substantial literary evidence survives from other Jewish communities in Egypt besides Alexandria. About five hundred miles south of Alexandria, a cache of ancient papyri was discovered on the island of Elephantine, located on the Nile River. These papyri attest to a vibrant Jewish community, which appears to have lasted for a few hundred years. The papyri, which include records of business transactions, marriage documents, and private letters, were written in Aramaic and mostly date to the fifth century BCE, when the Persians established a military garrison of Jewish mercenary soldiers on the island.[8] Some of the papyri allude to a Jewish temple that the soldiers built on the island. One letter, for example, suggests that this temple was built as early as the late sixth century BCE, following the end of the Babylonian exile. The letter, dated to 407 BCE, petitions a Persian governor of Judea named Bagoas to aid the Jews of Elephantine in rebuilding their temple, which had been destroyed in an act of anti-Jewish violence. The letter writer says that the Jews' forefathers had built this temple during or prior to the reign of Cambyses (530–522 BCE). About three hundred ostraca (broken shards of pottery bearing inscriptional material) with Aramaic writing and dating to the fifth century BCE have also been found on Elephantine.

The discovery of papyri and ostraca indicate that Jews who were committed to observing ancestral law, including Sabbath, the holidays, dietary law, and circumcision, also saw fit to bring sacrifices to a temple outside of Jerusalem. The Rabbis would later condemn such practices, but no evidence suggests that anyone at Elephantine perceived that building a local temple and bringing sacrifices there constituted acts of impiety.[9]

The existence of a Jewish Temple at Elephantine in the early Second Temple period suggests that, before the Rabbis living in the Land of Israel and Babylonia would try to create a normative religion whose laws all Jews could observe, some Jews in the Diaspora did not believe their worship was dependent on pilgrimage to Jerusalem. These Jews may have regretted being unable to worship at the great Jerusalem Temple. Alternatively, they may have believed that their temple at Elephantine was a sufficient replacement for the Temple at Jerusalem.

While some Jews in Egypt were worshipping their God at Temples, others were building synagogues where they would gather to read the scriptures. Two entire sectors of Alexandria, for instance, eventually became inhabited primarily by Jews, and Philo says that the entire city was home to many synagogues.[10] Indeed, one of the earliest archaeological remnants of a synagogue is in Alexandria.[11]

To a certain extent, Alexandrian Jewry functioned as a single community with an internal leadership structure in the first century BCE. The Jews of the city were governed by a Jewish leader, or ethnarch, an elected Jewish official who presided over the Jews by settling local legal matters between Jews and acting as a mediator between Jews and the Roman government.[12] The Jewish community in Judea, ruled by an ethnarch in earlier times,[13] may have served as a model for the Alexandrian ethnarch. This system of leadership provided Jews with a degree of social and political independence, but, at the same time, Jews were free to interact with the many gentiles who lived throughout the city. According to the first-century BCE Roman historian Strabo, the ethnarch of the Jews was responsible for ensuring that the Jews remained loyal to Rome and, at the same time, that they lived in accordance with their ancestral laws.[14] Surely this would have been no small feat.

Following or contemporaneous with ethnarch rule, a council of elders called the *gerousia* ruled Jews in Judea and in some diasporan communities. By the first century BCE, Alexandria had its own *gerousia* to establish and enforce certain laws in keeping with ancestral Jewish practice. This council, perhaps in cooperation with the ethnarch, enabled the Jews to observe their traditions while presenting themselves to the public as being totally loyal to the Roman Empire.[15]

Philo records one particularly disturbing incident regarding the Alexandrian *gerousia*. A Roman procurator named Flaccus arrested and publicly tortured thirty-eight members of this council whom Emperor Augustus had appointed after the Jewish ethnarch died.[16] For Philo, this incident was representative of Flaccus's overt antagonism and disdain for the Jewish community. Flaccus and other Romans probably regarded the Jews as outsiders whose separate system of local governance "proved" that the Jews had no interest in integrating into Roman life. Indeed, official Roman policy and local Roman leadership were often not in sync: While Roman emperors and many of their officials granted Alexandria's Jewish community rights to conduct their internal affairs independently and enjoy a degree of religious freedom, some local leaders and laypeople felt that the Jews were undeserving of such liberties, and were unwilling to enforce them.[17]

Despite remaining a separate social entity, the Jews were deeply influenced by cultural and academic developments occurring in Alexandria, particularly under the Greeks in the third and second centuries BCE. Alexandrian Jews became extraordinarily prolific, and their works, mainly written in Greek, suggest they were aware of Greek literary techniques and styles, which they must have admired. In many of their writings, which range in genre from fictional adventure tales to scriptural interpretation, Jewish authors sought to demonstrate that their tradition and Greek culture were consonant with one another. The influence of Stoicism—a school of Greek philosophy founded in the third century BCE — on many such texts suggests that these Jewish writers had access to the philosophical schools that lay at the heart of Alexandrian life.

Jewish Life in Roman Alexandria

Many Jews living in Alexandria received Greek and Roman educations, were financially successful, and integrated well into Alexandrian society. Their integration was the result of the fact that most Greek and Roman rulers affirmed the Jews' freedom to practice their ancestral religion without intervention.[18]

Josephus states that Alexandrian Jews were given citizenship from the time that Alexander founded the city, but this claim is either inaccurate or hyperbolic since we do not have evidence that Alexandrian Jews were given citizenship. It is more likely that what Josephus took as a fact of citizenship was instead probably a special right granted to the Jews to freely practice their ancestral religion. Josephus also claims that in the middle of the first century BCE, Julius Caesar granted the Jews of Alexandria citizenship, and inscribed their rights as citizens on brass pillars, publicly displayed for all to see.[19] Again, Caesar may have given the Jews rights to practice their traditions freely and without harassment, but in all likelihood, most Jews did not have citizenship.[20]

Alexander does appear to have singled out the Jews, however, giving them certain privileges that allowed them to practice their ancestral laws, which included dietary restrictions such as abstinence from pork, and the observance of the Sabbath and holidays. Alexander may have also given the Jews formal exemption from participating in public festivals that celebrated the gods. This would have likely upset some Greeks, who felt obligated to attend such events in order to display their patriotism. It is important to recall, after all, that at this time there was no formal distinction between religious life and public civic life. If the Jews were not attending festivals that celebrated the gods, it would have been natural for some Greeks to interpret their absence as not only disrespectful to the gods but disrespectful to Hellenist authorities. Seeds of tension may thus have been sown starting from the moment Alexander granted the Jews special exemptions from participating in civic life.

After the rise of the Roman Empire in the first century BCE, the Jews and gentiles of Alexandria began to clash. It is possible that Jewish-gentile relations soured during this period because, when Alexandria was incorporated into the Roman Empire, the Greeks of the city lost their standing as an upper caste. One way to ensure their social position and establish themselves as being on par with the Romans would have been to push the Jewish community down a rung on the social ladder, so they would be regarded as lower class like the indigenous Egyptians, and thereby forced to pay the *laographia*, the census tax meant for subjects without full citizenship. In this scenario, the Greeks would have been socially superior to the Jews and closer in status to the Romans.[21]

The rising resentment against Jews in Alexandria is memorialized in *For Flaccus*, a speech the great orator Cicero delivered to the Roman senate. In 59 BCE, the Roman procurator in Alexandria, Lucius Valerius Flaccus, initiated legislation to ban gold exports from various regions to Jerusalem. Jewish communities throughout the Roman Empire, including prominent families living in Alexandria, were sending donations to Judea to support the Jews of the Land of Israel and specifically the administration of the Jerusalem Temple. So much money was being sent to this region that some Roman authorities believed the empire's economic welfare was being compromised.

In his speech, Cicero defends Flaccus's initiative, arguing that the export of gold to Judea reflects the Jews' disloyalty to Rome:

> It was the practice each year to send gold to Jerusalem on the Jews' account from Italy and all our provinces, but Flaccus issued an edict forbidding its export from Asia. Who is there, gentlemen, who cannot genuinely applaud this measure? The Senate strictly forbade the export of gold on a considerable number of previous occasions, notably during my consulship.

To oppose this outlandish superstition was an act of firmness, and to defy in the public interest the crowd of Jews that on occasion sets our public meetings ablaze was the height of responsibility.[22]

Cicero elsewhere characterizes the Jewish practice of sending gold to Jerusalem as a *superstitio*—the Latin word alluding to the practices of outsiders viewed as incompatible with the official *religio* of the Roman Empire.[23] Associating Jewish customs with *superstitio* helped Cicero to make the case that loyalty to the Jewish religion was incompatible with loyalty to the Roman Empire.

More than a century later, however, Josephus notes that Jews living throughout the Roman world continued to send sums of money to support the Jerusalem Temple: "But no one need wonder that there was so much wealth in our Temple, for all the Jews throughout the habitable world, and those who worshipped God, even those from Asia and Europe, had been contributing to it for a very long time."[24]

Cicero's speech, alongside the writings of Josephus, indicates that many Jews living in the Diaspora in the first century BCE and first century CE had no intention of moving to Judea, but nevertheless looked to the region, and to the Jerusalem Temple in particular, as a homeland to which they felt deeply connected. They expressed this connection by sending money to the Jewish community in Jerusalem, which distressed Roman authorities both in terms of the massive sums being diverted to a remote region of the empire, and in terms of the lack of patriotism that Roman authorities believed this diversion implied.

Anti-Jewish Riots in Alexandria

Philo of Alexandria confirms that the Jewish practice of sending money to support the administration of the Jerusalem Temple was popular during his lifetime, but controversial. Some Roman emperors did in fact defend the practice, arguing that as long as the Jews remained loyal to the Roman Empire, they were permitted to financially support the Jerusalem Temple.[25] In his treatise *On the Embassy to Gaius*, Philo praises the Emperor Tiberius

(14–37 CE) for allowing Jews to continue donating money to the Jerusalem Temple and contrasts Tiberius's benevolent policy with that of Tiberius's successor, Gaius Caligula (37–41 CE). While Caligula's harsh treatment of the Jews was perceived as an explicit message to gentiles that their harassment of Jews would be tolerated, Tiberius encouraged his subjects to practice tolerance when it came to the Jews. According to Philo:

> [Tiberius] knew, therefore, that [Jews] have houses of prayer and meet together in them, particularly on the sacred sabbaths when they receive as a body a training in their ancestral philosophy. He knew, too, that they collect money for sacred purposes from their first-fruits and send them to Jerusalem by persons who would offer the sacrifices. Yet, nevertheless, he neither ejected them from Rome nor deprived them of their Roman citizenship because they were careful to preserve their Jewish citizenship also, nor took any violent measures against the houses of prayer, nor prevented them from meeting to receive instructions in the laws, nor opposed their offerings of the first-fruits. Indeed, so religiously did he respect our interests that supported by wellnigh his whole household, he adorned our temple through the costliness of his dedications, and ordered that for all time continuous sacrifices of whole burnt offerings should be carried out every day at his own expense as a tribute to the most high God.[26]

While Philo defends the practice of sending money to Jerusalem, he also takes care to present the Jews living under Roman rule as entirely devoted to their host country.[27] His paramount objective was to argue that the Jews did not threaten the welfare of the Roman Empire and did not regard themselves as outsiders or dissidents. In short, his defense of Jewish contributions to the Jerusalem Temple was part of a larger goal: to defend the Jews against accusations that they were enemies of the Roman Empire.

Philo's points, however, did not change the reality on the ground: The tensions between Jews and non-Jews that had been present from the time Alexandria became Romanized were fomenting in his own city and rose to the surface during Caligula's reign. One of the most calamitous incidents of anti-Jewish violence in Alexandria occurred in 38 CE, when riots broke out on the heels of a visit from the Judean client king Agrippa I.

Agrippa I, who would rule Judea in 41–44 CE, but at this point ruled other regions of the empire, was known to be a friend of the Pharisees and committed to Jewish ancestral tradition. He had a close relationship with Claudius, who would reign as emperor from 41–54 CE; some would later credit him as influential in helping Claudius ascend the throne. But even before Claudius's tenure as emperor, many Romans resented Agrippa's close friendship with Claudius and his influence over the Roman court. They associated Agrippa with what they believed was an exclusivist and unpatriotic community of Jews living in Judea and elsewhere in the empire.

Agrippa was probably aware of his unpopularity in Egypt. He took pains, Philo tells us, to enter Alexandria in the dead of night in order to avoid public attention.[28] Yet wind of Agrippa's impending visit began to circulate throughout the city. And when Agrippa finally arrived in Alexandria en route to Judea from Rome, the people of the city gave him a mock welcome celebration, parading a town fool through the city's streets. This insulting charade instigated violent anti-Jewish riots throughout the city.[29]

The riots in 38 CE proved devastating to the Jews living in Alexandria. Thousands of Jews were killed, and many others were driven out of the city. Jewish homes and synagogues were plundered and burned. According to Philo's account, the prefect of Egypt, Aulus Avilius Flaccus (a different Flaccus than the one Cicero defended), harbored hostility toward the Jews and sanctioned the riots.[30] During the earlier reign of Tiberius, Flaccus acted as a friend to the Jews, but when Tiberius died and his nephew Caligula assumed power, an Alexandrian named Lampo promised Flaccus the support of the Alexandrian population if Flaccus would agree to turn on the Jews of Alexandria. Afterward, Flaccus began to consistently favor non-Jewish parties in legal disputes involving Jews.

When Agrippa learned that Flaccus had allowed anti-Jewish violence to break out in Alexandria, he sent a message to the emperor, Gaius Caligula, accusing Flaccus of instigating the violence and requesting that Caligula intervene on the Jews' behalf. Surprisingly, Caligula took action: Flaccus was accused of treason, arrested, and placed in exile.[31] Sometime later, Caligula had Flaccus killed.[32]

Besides the prosecution of Flaccus, however, Jewish communal leaders' continued appeals to Roman authorities were met with apathy and indifference, and the anti-Jewish violence in Alexandria continued. Having not received aid from local Roman officials, the Alexandrian Jewish community decided to send a delegation of five representatives to appeal to Caligula in Rome on behalf of the Jews.[33] Among the men was Philo, who was by this time a well-regarded leader of the Alexandrian Jewish community. In *On the Embassy to Gaius*, Philo writes about Caligula and his subordinates treating the Jewish delegation with mockery and disdain. Caligula began his interview with the delegates by asking them, "Are you the god-haters who do not believe me to be a god, a god acknowledged among all the other nations but not to be named by you?"[34]

The Jews' rejection of Caligula's status as a god was no laughing matter. Since the reign of Octavian (27 BCE–14 CE), who changed his name to Augustus (which means something like "Revered One") and claimed to have been transformed into a deity, Roman emperors were treated like gods during their lives and worshipped as gods after their deaths. While Tiberius did not enforce Augustus's practice, Caligula went a step further than Augustus by demanding that a statue of his likeness be placed in the Jerusalem Temple, which resulted in a major outcry among the Jews. The line between being treated *like* a god and being treated *as* a god was very fine indeed, and must have presented a difficult challenge to Jews throughout the empire.

Caligula's statement to the Jewish delegates, which was more accusation than question, was followed by what Philo depicts as "an invocatory address which it was a sin even to listen to, much more to reproduce in the actual words." Caligula then repeated his accusation that the Jews were guilty of not sacrificing to him as a god. At this point he rose to walk through the palace and outdoor gardens to oversee his workers and various building projects, and Philo and the rest of the Jewish delegation had to follow Caligula as he walked. As Caligula asked the delegates questions regarding why the Jews separate themselves from gentiles, the people in Caligula's palace mocked and derided the Jewish men. Philo found the entire experience, especially the delegates' subjection to Caligula's "befooling and reviling," to be exhausting and humiliating.[35] The delegation went home to Alexandria, and the turbulence in Alexandria continued.

Josephus also mentions the confrontation between Philo and Caligula. He writes that three Jewish delegates traveled to Rome to request Caligula's intervention on behalf of the Alexandrian Jews, and that three Roman delegates also visited Caligula to argue, on behalf of the Jews' opponents, that the Jews' refusal to dedicate altars and temples to Caligula proved that they were not loyal to the emperor.[36]

Caligula's successor, Claudius (41–54 CE), sought to quell the violence in Alexandria. Josephus cites an edict Claudius wrote on behalf of the Alexandrian Jews, stating that their privileges must be preserved and protected. Claudius also sent an edict to other regions of the Roman Empire, declaring that the "rights and privileges" granted to Jews living throughout the empire were to be protected, and the Jews were free to practice their customs as they pleased. Claudius decreed that this edict should be engraved on tablets and publically displayed for thirty days in cities throughout the Empire.[37]

In 41 CE, Claudius wrote a letter to the people of Alexandria that addressed, among other matters, the conflict between the Jews and gentiles in the city, which had reached a boiling point. In a papyrus document recording the letter that was discovered in Egypt in 1924, Claudius declared that the two sides must find a resolution to the conflict:[38]

> As for the question, which party was responsible for the riots and feud (or rather, if the truth be told, the war) with the Jews, although in confrontation with their opponents your ambassadors, and particularly Dionysios the son of Theon, contended with great zeal, nevertheless I was unwilling to make a strict inquiry, though guarding within me a store of immutable indignation against whichever party renews the conflict. And I tell you once and for all that unless you put a stop to this ruinous and obstinate

enmity against each other, I shall be driven to show what a benevolent Prince can be when turned to righteous indignation. . . . Wherefore, once again I conjure you that, on the one hand, the Alexandrians show themselves forebearing and kindly towards the Jews who for many years have dwelt in the same city, and dishonor none of the rites observed by them in the worship of their god, but allow them to observe their customs as in the time of the Deified Augustus, which customs I also, after hearing both sides, have sanctioned; and on the other hand, I explicitly order the Jews not to agitate for more privileges than they formerly possessed.[39]

Claudius seems to hold both Jews and gentiles responsible for the clash that had begun three years earlier. But it is striking that he refers to the Jews' antagonists as "Alexandrians," which suggests that even though the Jews had inhabited Alexandria for centuries, they were not considered Alexandrians.

There are strong similarities between this letter and the edict cited by Josephus, in which Claudius declares that the Jews are citizens (*isopoliteia*) and their rights should be protected.[40] Because Josephus presents Claudius as affirming the special status of the Jews, and Claudius comes across as more empathetic to the Jews in the edict Josephus describes than in the papyrus letter, some scholars suggest that Josephus intentionally changed the content of Claudius's letter in order to present the Jews' status as unambiguous and Claudius as being a great friend to the Alexandrian Jews. But it could also be the case that Josephus was citing a different edict. As some scholars have pointed out, there is no reason for Josephus to have changed a document from the format of a letter to the format of an edict.[41]

Claudius's efforts to achieve a lasting resolution to the tense situation in Alexandria were unsuccessful. Discussing an incident during the reign of Nero (54–68 CE), Josephus writes:

On one occasion, when the Alexandrians were holding a public meeting on the subject of an embassy which they proposed to send to Nero, a large number of Jews flocked into the amphitheater along with the Greeks;

their adversaries, the instant they caught sight of them, raised shouts of "enemies" and "spies," and then rushed forward to lay hands on them. The majority of the Jews took flight and scattered, but three of them were caught by the Alexandrians and dragged off to be burnt alive. Thereupon the whole Jewish colony rose to the rescue; first they hurled stones at the Greeks, and then snatching up torches rushed to the amphitheater, threatening to consume the assembled citizens in the flames to the last man. And this they would actually have done, had not Tiberius Alexander, the governor of the city, curbed their fury.[42]

This confrontation led to further tragedy. The governor of Alexandria, Tiberius Alexander, sent two Roman legions to stop the carnage and quell the Jews' unrest. The situation quickly grew out of control:

The troops, thereupon, rushed to the quarter of the city called "Delta," where the Jews were concentrated, and executed their orders, but not without bloodshed on their own side; for the Jews closing their ranks and putting the best armed among their number in the front offered a prolonged resistance, but when once they gave way, wholesale carnage ensued. Death in every form was theirs; some were caught in the plain, others driven into their houses, to which the Romans set fire after stripping them of their contents; there was no pity for infancy, no respect for years: all ages fell before their murderous career, until the whole district was deluged with blood and the heaps of corpses numbered fifty thousand; even the remnant would not have escaped, had they not sued for quarter. Alexander, now moved to compassion, ordered the Romans to retire. They, broken to obedience, ceased massacring at the first signal; but the Alexandrian populace in the intensity of their hate were not so easily called off and were with difficulty torn from the corpses.[43]

According to Josephus, the massacre of Jews was put to an end when the Romans, led by Tiberius Alexander, intervened and stopped the violence. And when some Alexandrians continued their assault, the Romans had to physically force them to desist. This Tiberius Alexander, then governor of Alexandria, later procurator of Judea and prefect of Egypt, was in fact Philo of Alexandria's own nephew.[44] Josephus characterizes Tiberius as not adhering to ancestral tradition, but whether he was a complete apostate or one of the many Jews who relinquished certain aspects of Jewish practice in order to integrate into Roman society is not known.[45]

The Demise of Alexandrian Jewry

After the Romans quelled the Jewish revolt in Judea in 70 CE, tensions between Jews and non-Jews remained throughout the empire. The mandatory Fiscus Judaicus tax Vespasian had levied upon all Jews living in the Roman Empire, regardless of their involvement in the rebellion, must have infuriated many Jews. The tax of two drachmae was not only a financial burden. It was also the same sum many Jews had donated annually to the Jerusalem Temple. Now it would be used to support the temple of Jupiter Capitolinus.[46]

During this time, acts of overt antagonism against Jews were becoming increasingly common in Rome. The Roman historian Suetonius (c. 69–c. 140 CE) recalls that during Domitian's reign (81–96 CE), he saw Roman authorities forcibly strip an elderly Jewish man of his clothes in a public and crowded court to see whether he was circumcised.[47] These kinds of humiliations undoubtedly incensed the Jewish population.

In 115 CE, matters came to a head when Jews throughout the empire rioted in protest against their mistreatment at the hands of Rome. These riots compelled Roman authorities to intervene, engaging in a conflict known in Jewish sources as the Kitos War. This war may have gotten its name from a corruption of the name Quintus Marcius Turbo, a military advisor to Trajan who helped quell the Jewish uprising in Egypt.[48] Alternatively, the name might refer to Lusius Quietus, a Roman general and governor of Judea, who suppressed the rebellion.[49]

The early church historian Eusebius (c. 260–c. 339 CE) describes the violent chaos of this war in his *Ecclesiastical History* and *Chronicle*. He writes that a Jew named Lucas (Lukuas in Greek) led the Jewish rebels in a campaign involving the destruction of Roman temples and other public property. Eusebius refers to Lucas as the "king" of the Jewish rebels, possibly suggesting that the Jews believed they would achieve autonomy from the Roman Empire and elect Lucas as their Jewish monarch. Lucas and his men set about attacking and plundering regions of Egypt and later fled to the Judean town of Lydda, headquarters of the Jewish rebellion.[50] When the Romans got wind of their location, they besieged and later invaded Lydda, killing thousands of Jews.[51]

Eusebius describes Emperor Trajan's policy of killing Jews beyond the Cyrene area, where the rebellion was fomenting: "The Emperor suspected that the Jews in Mesopotamia would also attack the inhabitants and ordered Lusius Quietus to clean them out of the province. He organized a force and murdered a great multitude of the Jews there, and for this reform was appointed governor of Judea by the Emperor."[52] Likewise, the Roman historian Appian (c. 95–c. 165 CE) reports that the burial plot housing the head of Pompey, who was killed in 48 BCE, was destroyed when "the Roman Emperor Trajan was exterminating the Jewish race in Egypt."[53]

Another Roman historian, Lucius Cassius Dio (155–235 CE), provides a shocking account of what happened during this war. In his *Roman History*, Cassius Dio writes that a Jew named Andrew (or Andreas) led a rebellion that began in Cyrene and quickly spread to the Greek islands. On the island of Cyprus alone, he claims, the Jews murdered 220,000 people. Because of the disastrously high number of casualties there, an edict was later issued forbidding Jews to live on or even visit the island.[54] Cassius Dio contends that among the atrocities Andrew and his men committed was eating their enemies' flesh. In addition, the fourth-century historian Paulus Orosius (c. 375–c. 418 CE) reports that so many people in North Africa were killed during the rebellion that Emperor Hadrian (117–138 CE) had to actively repopulate some North African regions.[55]

These descriptions, especially Cassius Dio's, should be taken as gross hyperbole, since there is no evidence of such devastation. But it is certain that this war had a profound impact on Jewish-gentile relations throughout the empire.

While Roman historians focused on the damage done to gentiles, the war's devastation also affected Jewish communities throughout the Diaspora and Judea. Circumstances were especially dire in Alexandria, where tens of thousands of Jews were killed and Jewish neighborhoods set on fire. With their homes in ruins, the Jews who survived the war either fled or abandoned their Jewish identities altogether, assimilating into Hellenist society for good. There is no evidence of a prominent Jewish presence in Alexandria after 118 CE.

A number of Rabbinic sources memorialize the devastation of the Alexandrian Jewish community. One moving passage that is preserved in the Talmud opens by interpreting Genesis 27:22:

> The voice is the voice of Jacob and the hands are the hands of Esau: "the voice" here refers to [the cry caused by] the Emperor Hadrian who killed in Alexandria of Egypt sixty myriads on sixty myriads, twice as many as went forth from Egypt. "The voice of Jacob": this is the cry caused by the Emperor Vespasian who killed in the city of Bethar four hundred thousand myriads, or as some say, four thousand myriads. "The hands are the hands of Esau": this is the Government of Rome which has destroyed our House and burnt our Temple and driven us out of our land.[56]

The first half of this passage recounts Hadrian's destruction of Alexandrian Jewry. While his predecessor, Trajan, also worked to quell the rebellion, Hadrian, who secured the throne after Trajan's death in 117 CE, completed the job of putting down the rebellion with violent finality. The destruction of the Alexandrian Jewish community is therefore attributed to him. The second half of this passage concerns the destruction of Bethar. While Vespasian is mentioned in surviving editions of this talmudic passage, this is probably a copyist's mistake. In all likelihood, the original version of this passage mentioned Hadrian, not Vespasian. Hadrian was emperor in 135 CE when the Roman army viciously responded to the Bar Kokhba rebellion, besieging Bethar and murdering its inhabitants.[57]

The loss of the Alexandrian Jewish community must have been devastating to Jews living in both the Diaspora and Judea. The Jews residing in Alexandria were part of a community that had not only endured, but thrived, for centuries. Its synagogues were visible testaments to a flourishing Jewish presence in Egypt, and the remarkable beauty and size of one of the city's many synagogues is even described in the Babylonian Talmud.[58] Without the presence of Alexandrian Jewry, the city's synagogues were destroyed or repurposed. The loss of these buildings signified the end of this illustrious Jewish community.

Jewish Writings in Alexandria

Some of the most popular and well-circulated Jewish books composed in the Second Temple period are thought to have been written in Alexandria. Among these is arguably the greatest Jewish literary achievement of the Second Temple period: the Septuagint, the translation of the Hebrew Bible into the Greek Bible. A number of ancient documents attest to the remarkable events surrounding this translation. Most significant among these is a second-century BCE book called the Letter of Aristeas, which retells how the Egyptian king Ptolemy II Philadelphus (281–246 BCE) invited seventy-two Jewish scholars to Alexandria in order to translate the Hebrew Bible into a Greek text that would be housed in the Royal Library of Alexandria.

The author of the Letter of Aristeas suggests that this translation was intended to be a crown jewel of the library—worthy of such attention that Ptolemy himself interviewed the Septuagint's translators to assess their philosophical acumen. According to the Letter of Aristeas, the Jewish translators of the Hebrew Bible so impressed Ptolemy that after they completed their translation, Ptolemy sent them home with lavish treasures including clothes, furnishings, gold, and other valuables.[59]

Interestingly, the Letter of Aristeas never clarifies whether the Septuagint was ultimately placed in the library, and scholars debate whether Ptolemy II really initiated this project with the idea that the Septuagint would be stored there. The book does not close with the translation's placement into the Alexandrian library, but with the king's sending the Jewish translators back to their homes with expensive gifts. It is also unclear precisely what motivated the author to compose this work. Perhaps he sought to convince other Jews that the Septuagint was equal in religious significance to the Hebrew Bible. Or perhaps he believed the Septuagint was even superior to the earlier Hebrew version. Alternatively, he might have wished to introduce this foundational text to Greeks who may not have been familiar with it. The author certainly wanted to argue for the legitimacy of the Jewish scriptures and its laws, as he includes a long passage articulating a rational explanation for Jewish dietary laws, and depicts the Jewish translators as engaging in a philosophical discussion with Ptolemy, which ultimately leaves Ptolemy with the impression that Judaism is a sophisticated religion.

Philo's *On the Life of Moses* and Josephus's *Antiquities of the Jews* also tell the story of how the Hebrew Bible was translated into Greek.[60] Like the author of the Letter of Aristeas, Philo believes the Septuagint is an extremely impressive work that merits the respect of both Jews and Greeks alike. His lengthy description of the Bible's translation from "Chaldean" to Greek includes many details from Aristeas, especially regarding the hospitable manner with which Ptolemy hosted the Judean translators.[61] Philo may have relied on a version of the Letter of Aristeas as well as another source, since some details in his account do not appear in Aristeas.

One intriguing feature of the story that appears in both the Letter of Aristeas and Philo's account is that the translation was carried out just outside of Alexandria on Pharos, a tiny island upon which the Alexandrians had built a lighthouse for incoming ships.[62] Afterward, Philo tells us, an annual festival commemorating the translation of the Bible into Greek was instituted and celebrated on this island.[63]

The story of the Hebrew Bible's translation into Greek also appears in a number of Rabbinic accounts.[64] At least some Rabbinic figures must have regarded the translation as both important and auspicious. The second-century CE rabbi Simeon ben Gamaliel, for example, ruled that the only language outside of Hebrew in which Torah scrolls may be written is Greek.[65] His statement allows for the possibility that, in the Rabbinic period, some Jews were reading the Torah in Greek on the Sabbath.[66]

Other Rabbinic traditions, however, present the Hebrew Bible's translation into the Septuagint as a catastrophe. An eighth-century CE text, for instance, refers to a fast meant to be observed on the eighth of the month of Tevet, the day the translation project supposedly concluded. A later text called *Megillat Ta'anit Batra* comments that on the eighth of Tevet, "The Torah was written in Greek and darkness descended on the world for three days."[67]

These passages attribute different symbolic meanings to the Hebrew Bible's translation. Philo and some Rabbinic authors present the production of the Septuagint as a significant milestone for non-Hebrew-speaking Jews, which enabled them to more piously practice their religion. Other Rabbinic sources, however, treat the translation as an act of unacceptable assimilation into the Greek world. For the author of the Letter of Aristeas, the Septuagint was important because positive relations with gentiles undergirded its creation, and it gave non-Hebrew-speaking Jews and gentiles valuable access to Jewish scriptures.

Many other texts surviving from the Second Temple period are also thought to have been written in the vicinity of Alexandria. For example, the novella Joseph and Aseneth, which recalls the romance between Joseph and his wife Aseneth and focuses on her "conversion" to Judaism, is set in Egypt and thought to have been written in Greek, but scholars continue to debate when and where in Egypt it was written. Some scholars believe the author was an Egyptian Jew living in the second century BCE who was influenced by Greek culture, as indicated by his allusions to other Greek texts and well-known philosophical ideas. Other scholars believe the text was written four or five centuries later, possibly by a Christian. It is probably best, however, to avoid assuming that Jewish texts that do not mention distinctively Jewish laws, such as keeping the Sabbath and dietary laws, were not written by Jews. There may have been a thriving community of Jews in Egypt who emphasized aspects of Judaism that would have appealed to the ethical sensibilities of their Egyptian, Greek, and Roman counterparts.

Another text almost certainly written in Alexandria is the wisdom book the Sentences of Pseudo-Phocylides. The writer's critique against conducting autopsies on corpses points to its Alexandrian origin, since the practice by doctors and medical students was known to be commonplace in this city.[68] Pseudo-Phocylides emphasizes ethical behavior and does not mention commandments specific to Judaism, such as the Sabbath, circumcision, and dietary law.

Because of its generic content, some scholars believe Pseudo-Phocylides was not written by a Jew, or that it was composed by a Jew hiding his identity. Yet the author's choice to open his book by paraphrasing the Decalogue in Exodus 20, among other decisions, may suggest otherwise. Most Jews would have easily recognized that the book's introduction comprised sayings adopted from Exodus 20, whereas most gentiles of the time would likely not have been familiar with Exodus or other biblical books. The author also paraphrases Deuteronomy 22:6–7 regarding not taking a mother bird along with her young from a nest, and Exodus 23:5, which discusses helping the fallen beast of an enemy to rise. These paraphrases, as well as Pseudo-Phocylides's belief in the resurrection of the dead, which was a specifically Jewish belief in the first century, indicate that the book's author may have been Jewish. If so, this author was interested in presenting Judaism as a religion whose foundational values include wisdom, self-control, and benevolent care for those in need, all of which correlate with Greco-Roman values.[69] If, on the other hand, the author of Pseudo-Phocylides was a gentile, as some suggest, this book instead reflects a Greek author's decision to draw from the Jewish scriptures because he admired some of their ethically oriented passages.

The Jewish origins of other ancient Greek documents are less contested. The Jewish poet known as Ezekiel the Tragedian, for example, rewrote the story of the Exodus in iambic trimeter, paying special attention to Moses, whom he portrayed as a great hero in the tradition of Homeric protagonists.[70] Likewise, the Jewish writer Artapanus retold the stories of Abraham, Joseph, and Moses, focusing on the theme that these men integrated successfully into Egyptian society and even made important contributions to the fields of mathematics and astronomy.

In writing these texts, Ezekiel and Artapanus were probably responding to accusations that the Israelites had been expelled from Egypt by Pharaoh, and not redeemed miraculously by their omniscient god. Other stories circulating at the time proclaimed that the Israelites who left Egypt worshipped the head of an ass, or were leprous, or suffered from other humiliating conditions and degenerate characteristics. By presenting the Jews as the very opposite of how they were portrayed in Greek literature, writers like Ezekiel and Artapanus subtly rebutted popular anti-Jewish claims.

Many books of the Apocrypha and Pseudepigrapha are presumed to have been written in Alexandria, where they are thought to have been written in Greek, the main language spoken in Egypt in the late Second Temple period. It is possible, however, that these books were written in other Jewish communities in Egypt, or were originally composed in other languages, such as Palestinian Aramaic or Hebrew.

While Alexandria has become too much of a "catch-all" location for the genesis of many Second Temple period texts, there is still good reason to believe that in the late Second Temple period, the Jews of Alexandria were producing a high volume of literature that spanned the genres of wisdom, poetry, fiction, and biblical interpretation. A number of Jewish texts written in Greek take place in Alexandria, or bear stylistic similarities to other texts that scholars believe were written in the city's vicinity. Moreover, the philosophical sophistication of some of the Jewish texts composed in this region indicates that relations between Jews and gentiles were not entirely bad at this time and that there was significant cultural interaction between Greeks and Jews.

The Jewish community of Alexandria thrived for about four centuries because its members were committed to observing foundational aspects of their tradition. They built synagogues, read from their scriptures, observed dietary laws, kept the Sabbath and holidays, and practiced circumcision. Yet, at the same time, these Jews were remarkably innovative when it came to understanding their traditions within the frameworks of Greek and, later, Roman cultures. They sought to present their religion as sophisticated and rational by justifying Jewish laws, idealizing biblical heroes, and presenting the Jewish people as ever loyal to their host empire. The result of these efforts is reflected in a body of literature that protectively embraces Judaism and yet is sensitive to the benefits enjoyed by those who were assimilated into Greek and Roman life.

CHAPTER 6

Antioch

Nestled in a narrow valley between the Orontes River to the west and majestic mountains to the east in present-day Turkey, the city of Antioch was renowned in the late Second Temple period for its lush gardens, beautiful springs, and vast array of public entertainments. First settled around 300 BCE, the city soon became a kind of corridor between the East and the West, a place where travelers conducted business and enjoyed the city's many pleasures.

By the first century CE, Antioch boasted all the amenities of a great Roman city. It had at least one theater, with a second one located in the nearby suburb of Daphne a few miles to the south. Large crowds gathered to watch horse races at the hippodrome, and both locals and visitors frequented the city's many public baths. A colonnaded boulevard was built and expanded over time until it stretched about two miles, from the northern end of the city to its southern tip. On each side of the boulevard, a covered portico protected pedestrians and extended the avenue to more than 118 feet wide. Between the pillars supporting the portico were spaces for vendors and entryways that led into houses. The boulevard intersected with grand avenues stretching from east to west, forming plazas anchored by beautiful fountains in their centers.[1]

Most of our information about the Jews of Antioch comes from Josephus, the New Testament, and the eighteen-book compendium of world history known as *Chronographia*, written by the sixth-century historian John Malalas, who lived for a time in Antioch. Malalas's account is not always reliable, but some of the details he provides have been verified by other historical sources.

Antioch's Jewish community lived mainly on the southeastern side of the city, near the amphitheater. Josephus writes that when Seleucus I Nicator founded the city in May of 300 BCE, he granted the Jews who moved there special privileges, including citizenship, which allowed them to observe their ancestral laws without harassment.[2] As their population grew, the Jews built more houses and founded synagogues.[3] By the first century CE, approximately twenty to forty thousand Jews were living in the vicinity of Antioch, making up about 5 to 10 percent of the city's population.[4]

The Political Rights of Antiochene Jews

Understanding the political status of Antiochene Jews could give us insight into how gentiles perceived Jews in the late Second Temple period, and could help illuminate how gentiles and Jews interacted with one another in this region.

Josephus discusses the civic status of Antiochene Jews in three of his works. In *Antiquities* and in *Against Apion*, Josephus writes that Seleucus I Nicator (306–281 BCE), the founder of Antioch, made the Jews of Antioch citizens.[5] In *The Jewish War*, moreover, Josephus notes that Antiochus IV Epiphanes' successors gave the Antiochene Jews "citizen rights on an equality with the Greeks."[6] And in both *The Jewish War* and *Antiquities*, Josephus reports that certain gentile Antiochenes initiated an organized effort to revoke Jews' citizenship, but were unsuccessful: Vespasian and Titus protected the Antiochene Jews' rights of citizenship, as well as the rights of Alexandrian Jews, whose neighbors also wanted their citizenship revoked.[7]

In the seventh and final book of his *The Jewish War*, Josephus comments:

It was at Antioch that [Jews] specially congregated, partly owing to the greatness of that city, but mainly because the kings after Antiochus had enabled them to live there in security. For although Antiochus surnamed

Epiphanes sacked Jerusalem and plundered the temple, his successors on the throne restored to the Jews of Antioch all such votive offerings as were made of bronze, to be laid up in their synagogue, and moreover, granted them citizen rights on an equality with the Greeks.[8]

Josephus later relates in *The Jewish War* that after Jerusalem was destroyed, Titus arrived at the outskirts of Antioch, where throngs of Antiochenes had gathered to greet him. Some called out to Titus, asking him to eject the Jews. These people had likely heard of Titus's defeat of the Jewish rebels in Judea and wanted the Jews out of Antioch before they could cause trouble. But Titus, Josephus tells us, retorted: "But their own country to which, as Jews, they ought in that case to be banished, has been destroyed, and no other place would now receive them."[9] Having failed to convince Titus to expel the Jews of Antioch, the Antiochenes then asked him to remove the brass tablets upon which the Jews' privileges were inscribed. Again, Titus refused. Josephus thus presents Titus as a pragmatist who refused to cause the Jews suffering unless it was necessary to do so to maintain the security of the empire.

The rights that Josephus speaks of in *The Jewish War, Antiquities,* and *Against Apion* may in fact not have been equivalent to citizenship. They may simply have guaranteed the Jews' protection by formally permitting them to observe Jewish traditions and abstain from attending local festivals that celebrated the Roman gods.[10] Likewise, the bronze tablets that were engraved with the Antiochene Jews' rights probably did not indicate that all Antiochene Jews were citizens, since rights were not equivalent to citizenship, and most people living in the Roman Empire did not have full Roman citizenship. Finally, Josephus's claim that the Jews of Antioch received citizenship from Seleucus I Nicator cannot be substantiated.[11]

Josephus may have sought to portray Antiochene Jews as having been granted citizenship in the early third century BCE to convince his gentile readers that the Jews had a long-standing claim to residency in the city, and that the Greeks of old had accepted the Jews as partners in helping to settle and build Antioch. Antiochene Jews, therefore, were not imposters who entered the city to take advantage of its resources but assets who exemplified patriotism toward their city and host empire. It is also possible that Josephus's report regarding when Jews came to Antioch and their status as citizens may not have been intentionally polemical but simply mistaken. Perhaps Josephus got his dates wrong, or he believed that the Jews' right to practice their religion constituted citizenship.

Some evidence does point to Antiochene Jews having citizenship in the early second century BCE, during the reign of Antiochus III (222–187 BCE).[12] According to 2 Maccabees, Jason, the Hellenized high priest of the Jerusalem Temple, attained his position by bribing Antiochus with 440 talents of silver and promising an additional 150 more if Antiochus agreed to provide the Jews of Jerusalem with citizenship, "as citizens of Antioch."[13] Whether or not the Jews of Antioch attained citizenship, they did, for the most part, enjoy freedom and security. At the same time, some gentiles of Antioch were unhappy with the increasing Jewish population and its growing political influence.

Cosmopolitan Roman Center: 64 BCE–395 CE

After the Roman Empire's rise to power in the second half of the first century BCE, Antioch became the capital of the Roman province of Syria. At this time, Antioch was the third-biggest city in the Roman Empire, after Rome and Alexandria.[14] Like these two cities, Antioch boasted a sizeable Jewish population and was reputed to offer Jews new economic opportunities: Josephus writes that one wealthy Jewish man named Zamaris moved all the way from Babylon to Antioch with a massive entourage of five hundred horsemen and one hundred relatives.[15] And because he was a well-regarded nobleman, the Romans allowed Zamaris to live on a private estate in the city.

References to numerous synagogues in Antioch also point to a thriving Jewish presence in the city. Josephus praises Antioch's great synagogue, stating that local Jews had made substantial donations to the synagogue and it was lavishly decorated.[16] According to John Malalas, a Jewish synagogue was built in Daphne as well.[17] Moreover, the Maccabean martyrs were thought by early Christians, and perhaps even by some Jews, to have been buried in Antioch near a synagogue, after Antiochus IV Epiphanes instructed that their remains be brought to the city.[18]

In the New Testament, Antioch figures as a key meeting place for members of the "Jesus movement," the community of people who believed that Jesus was a messianic figure or divine messenger of God. Some followers of Jesus settled and taught in Antioch in part because they believed that its sizeable Jewish population might be interested in their teachings. The book of Acts even specifies that the disciples of Jesus residing in Antioch preached only to the Jews of the city.[19]

But as interest in Jesus' teachings spread to gentiles, questions began to arise regarding whether these gentiles would have to take on Jewish practices before committing to a life devoted to following Jesus' teachings. Antioch soon became the site of some heated religious debates regarding this question. Although Christianity had not yet been established as a separate entity outside of Judaism, some of Jesus' disciples who lived in or frequented the city took issue with Jewish believers in Jerusalem who insisted that all of Jesus' followers adhere to strict dietary laws. Paul, along with his colleagues in Antioch, held that gentile disciples of Jesus need not take on the Jews' dietary restrictions. To them, Jesus' arrival on earth and brutal death functioned in part to abolish the Law for those gentiles who wanted to enter the newly expanded covenantal community.

Paul's Letter to the Galatians attests to the vibrant debates among Jesus' followers in Antioch. In this letter, Paul recalls one such conflict between Peter and himself: Peter (whose name means "stone" in Greek and who is sometimes referred to as Cephas, a transliteration of the Aramaic word for "stone") believed that followers of Jesus, even those coming from gentile backgrounds, should observe Jewish ancestral practices like dietary laws, while Paul believed that these practices were no longer necessary. This incident, or one like it, is also alluded to in 2 Timothy when Paul (or more likely, a writer who attributes this letter to Paul) refers to his suffering in Antioch.[20]

But when Cephas came to Antioch, I opposed him to his face, because he stood self-condemned; for until certain people came from James, he used to eat with the Gentiles. But after they came, he drew back and kept himself separate for fear of the circumcision faction. And the other Jews joined him in this hypocrisy, so that even Barnabas was led astray by their hypocrisy. But when I saw that they were not acting consistently with the truth of the gospel, I said to Cephas before them all, "If you, though a Jew, live like a Gentile and not like a Jew, how can you compel the Gentiles to live like Jews?"

As a more cosmopolitan city than Jerusalem, Antioch was fertile ground to disseminate Jesus' teachings in ways that would attract gentiles to the new faith community. Some of Jesus' disciples in Antioch believed that requiring gentiles to take on Jewish ancestral Law in order to become followers of Jesus was simply not necessary, and that doing so would make their new community seem less attractive to potential followers. Ultimately, the decision of these disciples to circumvent Jewish tradition seems to have been successful: The New Testament describes the existence of proselytes in Antioch.[21]

Yet Antioch was also home to Jews who vehemently opposed Paul's teachings. The author of Acts recalls that some Antiochene Jews were so enraged at Paul that they traveled to Lystra, where he was preaching, and tried to stone him.[22]

While Antiochene followers of Jesus engaged in lively debates about whether to practice Jewish Law, Jewish followers of Jesus in the first century probably looked more to Jerusalem than Antioch for religious leadership. According to Acts, Paul made sure to "greet the church" in Jerusalem after a long journey before proceeding on to Antioch.[23] The writer of Acts also shows deference to Jerusalem by noting that when the apostles traveled to Jerusalem, they "went up" to the city, even though Jerusalem was topographically lower than other nearby towns. Going "up" implies that the apostles viewed Jerusalem as their most revered place of worship.[24]

At the same time, members of the Jerusalem church depended on disciples in Antioch to spread the teachings of Jesus and provide them with support when necessary. According to Acts, a Jesus follower named Agabus had a prophetic vision of an impending famine "over all the world" that was soon proven correct.[25] The disciples in Antioch sent funds to Jerusalem, where the famine had hit especially hard. This chapter in Acts includes a fascinating historical nugget: The term "Christian" was first put into circulation in Antioch, after Paul and a disciple named Barnabas spent a year teaching about Jesus' life, death, and sayings in the city.[26]

As in other regions of the Roman Empire, tensions between gentiles and Jews in Antioch ebbed and flowed. Many Antiochene gentiles viewed the Jews as separatists who were disloyal to the Roman Empire. When Jewish rebellions against Roman rule began to crop up throughout the empire in 115 CE,[27] some gentiles in Antioch worried that the Jews of their city were politically allied with Jews living throughout the empire—and therefore might similarly stir up seditious activity.

As we have noted, many Greeks and Romans resented the Jews for being excused from participating in public religious life.[28] Because political activity and religious life were so intertwined, the Jews' choice to abstain from public festivals and feast days reminded their gentile neighbors that they were politically and religiously different. At the same time, the practices that some Jews fiercely adhered to—circumcision and dietary laws in particular—seemed strange and antiquated.

Some gentiles were also angered to learn that some of their brethren were actually adopting Jewish practices, and others were even converting to Judaism. To these gentiles, the growing Jewish presence in Antioch undermined the stability of "their" Greek city.[29] As resentment fomented, gentiles in Antioch and Alexandria sought to drive the Jews out of their cities by applying political pressure, requesting that officials expel the city's Jewish population, and turning to violence.[30]

Even some Jews believed that members of their community were unpatriotic to Rome. According to Josephus, a Jewish apostate named Antiochus instigated many of the Antiochene Jews' troubles. In one incident, he burst into a theater yelling that the Jews were planning to set fires in the city, causing massive destruction in retaliation for the suffering of the Judean Jews. The agitated crowd started rioting against the Jews. Antiochus himself delivered some Jews he claimed were seditious to the crowd. The people of Antioch burned them to death in the theater, and then unleashed violent attacks against other Jews throughout the city.[31]

The hysteria that Antiochus's exclamations provoked suggests that his shouts were a match in a tinderbox. Tensions were already high, and some gentiles were glad to have an excuse to seek retribution against the Jews. Matters became worse, when an actual fire spread throughout the city, and many gentiles blamed the Jews for starting it.[32] A subsequent formal investigation proved the Jews' innocence: A gentile seeking to burn public records recording his debts had set the fire. But the Jews of Antioch continued to worry about whether they would be subject to further antagonism long after the fire subsided.

We do not know if there were Jewish rebels in the region of Antioch in 115 CE, when Jewish rebellions against Roman rule began to spread throughout the empire. If such renegades existed, they may have been unable to get an insurgence off the ground because of a powerful earthquake in December of 115 CE.[33] The catastrophic destruction it wreaked was unlike any Antioch had ever seen, and it took decades for the city to recover. The houses and other buildings archaeologists have discovered at the site of ancient Antioch date primarily to the centuries following the devastation.

Unfortunately, the earthquake of 115 CE would not be ancient Antioch's last natural disaster. In 526 CE, the city experienced yet another devastating earthquake that is estimated to have killed 250,000 residents.

The Jewish Texts of Ancient Antioch

A number of surviving Jewish texts written in the Second Temple period were likely composed in Antioch. One example is the Testaments of the Twelve Patriarchs, a collection of twelve speeches recalling the final words Jacob's twelve sons spoke to their children shortly before their deaths.

These speeches may have been written separately and later compiled into a single collection.

The provenance of this work remains uncertain. If it was originally written in Aramaic, as some scholars believe, then it may have been composed in the Land of Israel. But other scholars note that these testaments presume the world power to be the Syrian Greeks, not the Ptolemaic Greeks. This would point to Syria as a more likely place of composition. Moreover, the author (or authors) did not seem to have intimate knowledge of Judea's terrain.[34]

Given the text's references to specifically Jewish customs such as mourning laws and levirate marriage, it is probable that the bulk of the Testaments of the Twelve Patriarchs was composed by a Jew. This work also contains interpretive traditions that later find expression in early Rabbinic texts. Medieval manuscripts of this book, however, include Christian interpolations that reference the universal redemption realized by Jesus' crucifixion, and his role as the Messiah. These interpolations attest to the book's importance to Christians, who saw religious value in its contents and chose to copy and circulate the book. The ease with which this text was transferred from one religious community to another is a good reminder that in big cities like Antioch, Jews and Christians exchanged cultural and religious views.[35]

The Testaments of the Twelve Patriarchs participates in a larger genre of Jewish literature that flourished in the late Second Temple period and the centuries following it: the testament genre. Books in this genre imagined what the biblical heroes of old told their loved ones as they were about to depart the physical world and enter the afterlife. Examples of such texts are the Testament of Solomon, the Testament of Job, and the Testament of Isaac. These documents have varied historical origins, but all share an interest in revealing more about the internal lives of scriptural heroes. The Testaments of the Twelve Patriarchs was likely meant to be read as part of this larger constellation of testaments.

Another first-century CE text probably written in Syria, and perhaps in Antioch, is the Gospel of Matthew. Recalling the life, teachings, and crucifixion of Jesus, the Gospel includes some of Jesus' most memorable and potent speeches, such as the Sermon on the Mount.

Scholars endorsing a Syrian provenance of Matthew's Gospel note that it specifies that Jesus' fame "spread throughout all Syria."[36] This statement does not appear in the Gospel of Mark, which scholars believe Matthew had access to when he wrote his Gospel. Matthew therefore added this phrase because he thought that his readers would find the mention of Syria meaningful. This would especially be true if Matthew believed that his readers primarily resided in Syria.

The Gospel of Matthew emphasizes Jesus' Jewishness by presenting Jesus as a Jewish messianic figure who offered salvation to a Jewish community. For this reason, Matthew links Jesus' actions and speeches with the predictions of earlier biblical prophets, such as Isaiah, in a way that suggests that Jesus fulfilled the words of these prophets. While later Christian readers of this Gospel would not identify Matthew as a Jewish text, the author of this Gospel probably had no intention of founding a religion separate from Judaism. For the writer of Matthew, Jesus is neither opposed to the teachings of earlier prophets nor to the laws they sought to uphold: In fact, the writer believes that Jesus sought to protect these laws and teachings, and that the Jews who mistook him for a rebellious miscreant made a tragic mistake in misinterpreting Jesus' role in their own destinies.

Over time, the Jewish Christians who lived in Antioch separated from other Jewish communities. And by the fourth century CE, Christianity and Judaism in Antioch and elsewhere in the Roman Empire were two entirely separate religions. Antiochene Christians were now speaking and writing religious homilies, poems, and biblical interpretations in an Aramaic dialect called Syriac, which is closely related to the Aramaic spoken by the rabbis who lived to the south in the Land of Israel. Recent studies demonstrate that Syriac-speaking Christians and Aramaic-speaking rabbis shared some interpretations of biblical scriptures, as evidenced in overlapping material found in Christian and Rabbinic biblical commentaries. Indeed, even after they no longer identified as Jews, Antiochene Christians continued to interact with Jews living in Antioch and in the northern regions of the Galilee.[37]

As the third-largest metropolis in the Roman Empire, Antioch was the crown jewel of the Levant. Jews came from all over the empire to plant roots in this great city, where they lived and thrived for centuries. Josephus's description of the city's lavishly decorated synagogue, and our knowledge of at least one other synagogue in nearby Daphne, attest to a large Jewish population in this region that was committed to its ancestral tradition.

Statements made by the fourth-century CE Antiochene bishop John Chrysostom (John "Golden Mouth") also point to the existence of a large and influential Jewish community in Antioch. Chrysostom delivered a series of homilies, now known as "Against Judaizing Christians," criticizing his Christian constituents for attending synagogue on Saturdays, which he believed signified their unwillingness to cut ties with the Jewish community.[38] By the late sixth century CE, however, Antioch and its Jewish population began to wane. Many Jews whose ancestors had made their homes in Antioch now left the city to rebuild their lives elsewhere.

The Jews who lived in Jerusalem, Alexandria, and Antioch were occupied by the challenge of how to participate in Greek and, later, Roman society while affiliating as Jews. Attempts to embrace aspects of both Judaism and Greek or Roman culture often led to total assimilation. Some Jews who strived to maintain a foothold in both communities found themselves criticized by Greeks and Romans for not properly participating in public life and also by fellow Jews for not sufficiently protecting their ancestral traditions. The special rights that allowed Jews to refrain from participating in certain public events, rights that were meant to protect Jews from being harmed by gentile neighbors who resented their absence from public events, often had the opposite effect, serving instead to foster further animosity toward the Jews. At times this animosity gave way to physical violence, and, in the case of Alexandria, it gave way to mass destruction and bloodshed. It is no surprise, then, that many Jews sought to present themselves as committed patriots whose religion correlated with Greco-Roman values.

PART 3

THE WORLDVIEWS OF

SECOND TEMPLE WRITERS

CHAPTER 7

The Wisdom Seekers

The young Macedonian who would become known as Alexander the Great achieved extraordinary and unprecedented military victories. In the span of about a decade, Alexander conquered most of Europe, Asia, and North Africa. His rule would dramatically change not only the borders of these regions but also their languages, their artistic expressions, their educational systems, and even their religious worship. Under Greek rule, Jews had to reorient themselves to a new culture that would seep into many aspects of their daily lives. Some of these Jews would begin to approach Jewish tradition as a source of wisdom that correlated with foundational ideas of the Hellenistic world in which they now lived.

As we noted in chapters 4 and 5, Alexander's vast empire was split into four smaller kingdoms following his death in 323 BCE. At the heart of one of these kingdoms, the Ptolemaic Kingdom, which included Egypt and other regions of North Africa, lay the most prestigious center of intellectual and cultural activity in the Greek world: Alexandria. Under the Ptolemaic Greeks, Alexandria's Jews enjoyed special rights that allowed them to practice their ancestral law. But Jews in this city also had opportunities to integrate into Hellenistic society by receiving Greek educations and participating in public festivals.[1]

The many opportunities for integration into Alexandrian life caused some Jews to stop practicing their ancestral traditions, which included Sabbath observance, circumcision, and adherence to dietary laws. Other Jews, however, responded to the spread of Hellenism by becoming more insular and avoiding Hellenistic activities such as public plays, festivals, and gymnasium events. Some of these Jews shunned every aspect of Hellenistic society.

Scholars have not found any relationship between where a Jew lived and the degree to which he or she remained committed to Jewish tradition. Many Jews living in Judea sought to insulate themselves from Hellenism, as did other Jews living in cosmopolitan diasporan cities such as Alexandria and Antioch.

One such individual was the writer of 2 Maccabees. The author does not identify himself by name, but does provide his readers with background information regarding the book's compositional history. In his introduction, the author writes that he is abridging a five-volume text composed by a man named Jason of Cyrene, an ancient city in present-day Libya. We do not know which elements of 2 Maccabees Jason wrote and what other material the later abridger may have inserted. In this chapter I refer to the writer of 2 Maccabees with the abridger in mind, since he was likely responsible for transmitting the book as we have inherited it.

Probably composed and abridged in the late second century BCE, 2 Maccabees is the earliest Jewish document to use the term Judaism (*Ioudaïsmos*). The writer believed that Judaism stood in opposition to the laws and customs espoused by Hellenism (*Hellenismos*). Such a binary demanded that all aspects of Hellenistic culture be rejected, including attending festivals that celebrated the gods, and events in gymnasiums that featured naked athletes. It is no small irony, then, that the author of 2 Maccabees wrote in beautiful Greek and repeatedly used popular Hellenistic literary stylistics, such as soliloquy, speeches uttered to oneself to provide the audience with a window into the speaker's thought, and encomia, speeches that praise a protagonist, usually after his or her death.[2]

As some Jewish authors presented Hellenism and Judaism as being incompatible, others sought to harmonize aspects of Jewish tradition with elements of Greek culture and thought. One such effort is the Sentences of Pseudo-Phocylides, which we explored at the end of chapter 5. This wisdom text addresses the question of how to live a virtuous life. As we have noted, the author paraphrases the Septuagint and restates the

Decalogue in his introduction. He also subscribes to the specifically Jewish idea of resurrection.[3] At the same time, the writer of Pseudo-Phocylides seeks to fuse Greek values with Jewish traditions. Sometimes this fusion doesn't quite work, such as when the author affirms the immortality of the soul and, a few lines later, envisions the resurrection of all people after their deaths.[4]

While the author of 2 Maccabees portrays Judaism and Hellenism as religions that stand in irreconcilable conflict with one another, the author of Pseudo-Phocylides ignores distinctively Jewish practices in order to merge traditions found in the Jewish scriptures with Greek culture. Yet most Jews at this time probably did not go to either of these two extremes. They likely observed at least the most fundamental aspects of their ancestral religion, such as the Sabbath and holidays, dietary laws, and circumcision, and simultaneously incorporated aspects of the Hellenistic world into their daily lives, making sure that their children received an education in such Hellenistic subjects as mathematics, astronomy, and philosophy, if they could afford it.

In the following section, we will examine the writings of two Alexandrian Jewish authors who embody this middle ground. The first author is Philo, who exemplifies the effort to balance Greek philosophical thought and Jewish tradition. The second example is the writer of the Letter of Aristeas, which retells the story of how the Hebrew Bible was translated into the Septuagint, and which we briefly discussed in chapter 5. Both Philo and the author of the Letter of Aristeas go beyond harmonizing Hellenistic culture with Jewish tradition by arguing that, in some ways, Jewish tradition is superior to Hellenistic culture.

Philo of Alexandria

Perhaps the most influential Jewish intellectual living in Alexandria toward the end of the Second Temple period was Philo of Alexandria (c. 20 BCE to 50 CE). Trained in the study of Greek philosophy and educated in Jewish scriptures and tradition, Philo believed that Greek philosophy was not in tension with Jewish values, but quite the contrary, that the study of Greek philosophy enhanced one's understanding of Judaism and its scriptures. Philo wrote treatises that interpreted sections of the Hebrew Bible (such as his three-volume work *Questions and Answers on Genesis*) as well as philosophical treatises (such as *Allegorical Interpretation* and *Every Good Man Is Free*). In other works, Philo interpreted selected passages from the Septuagint using a fusion of midrash-like homily and Hellenistic allegory (such as *On the Birth of Abel, Concerning Noah's Work as a Planter,* and *On the Life of Moses*).

Philo also wrote two treatises about historical events that he personally witnessed, *Against Flaccus* and *On the Embassy to Gaius*, which provide valuable information about Alexandrian Jewish life in the first century. Probably written in 38 CE, *Against Flaccus* recounts how anti-Jewish pogroms in Alexandria nearly devastated its Jewish population, in large part because of the complicit behavior of the Alexandrian procurator Flaccus, whose behavior we have recounted in chapter 5. *On the Embassy to Gaius*, probably completed in 41 CE, broadly describes the origins of the tensions between Jews and Gentiles in Alexandria, closing with an account of Philo's humiliating trip to Rome to appeal to Gaius Caligula on behalf of Alexandrian Jewry.

In these and other treatises, Philo addresses the common complaint among gentiles that Jews are not loyal citizens of the Roman Empire. He acknowledges that many Jews are loyal to their ancestral traditions and devoted to the city of Jerusalem and its Temple. Yet these same Jews, Philo argues, were entirely loyal to the Roman Empire and would never act to compromise its welfare. Jews are therefore no less deserving of good treatment than other people living under Roman rule.

The tension between Alexandrian Jews and their non-Jewish neighbors to which Philo was so sensitive had a long history. Since the second century BCE, Greek intellectuals had been accusing Jews of all sorts of miscreant behavior. According to some of the most sophisticated thinkers in the Hellenistic world, Jews were exclusivist and misanthropic, as evidenced by their dogged refusal to embrace the gods who were worshipped in their local communities.[5] The Jews were mutilating their sons by practicing circumcision, which was largely believed to be an antiquated and barbaric custom. Circumcision was also reflective of the Jews' misanthropy, since the practice aimed to set Jewish males apart from gentile males.[6] Furthermore, the Jews' observance of the Sabbath reflected their laziness or, alternatively, commemorated a communal plague inflicted upon the Israelites after they left Egypt.[7] Jews' origins were neither noble nor honorable; they were an ethnic group that had been expelled from Egypt.[8] They descended from beggars and were therefore concerned only with money making, and were miscreants who delighted in murdering the innocent.[9]

While some earlier Greek literature about Jews was neutral and, on occasion, even positive, by the time Philo began his career, accusations against the Jews reflected rising tensions that would reach unprecedented heights.[10] Philo's hope that the Jews of Alexandria would soon enjoy an everlasting peace with their neighbors, a hope that so deeply affected the tenor of his writing, would not be realized.

Philo is well known for his allegorical interpretation of the Torah. Influenced by Greek philosophers who believed that the allegorical meaning — that is, the nonphysical essence of a physical substance — was the true meaning of the substance itself, Philo suggests that many stories and commandments in the Torah can best be understood in light of their allegorical, symbolic meanings. For instance, when interpreting the story of God commanding Abraham to circumcise himself and his son Ishmael in Genesis 17, Philo provides the literal and also the allegorical explanation. The literal reason for circumcision concerns its physical health benefits, which, according to Philo, include the prevention of disease. The allegorical explanation, however, lies closer to the essence of the commandment itself. Philo writes:

> They say that the circumcision of the skin is a symbol, as if (to show that) it is proper to cut off superfluous and excessive desires by exercising continence and endurance in matters of the Law. For just as the skin of the foreskin is superfluous in procreation because of the burning affliction

which comes upon it, so the excess of desire is superfluous and at the same time harmful. . . . [Circumcision] indicates the cutting off not only of excessive desires but also of arrogance and great evil and such habits. [11]

For Philo, the removal of the foreskin reminded the Israelites that they must "cut away all superfluous and extravagant desires, by studying continence and religion." A circumcised male body is a perfect body, and this perfect body represents the soul that has separated itself from unnecessary desires in favor of the only meaningful pursuit in life: the pursuit of wisdom.

Philo's approach to circumcision both aligns with and departs from the Greek intellectual thinking of his day. One the one hand, the implication that the circumcised body was a perfected body, and not a mutilated body, was a radical departure from standard Greek thought. Even though Jews were not the only group of people to practice circumcision at this time, the consensus in Greek society was that it was an antiquated, and even vulgar, practice.[12] On the other hand, Philo's allegorical interpretation of circumcision as representing the shedding of all pursuits other than the pursuit of wisdom aligns with the values of his Greek contemporaries.

While Philo reads the Torah with an eye toward its allegorical meaning, he also believes that the Torah's commandments retain their literal reading. Philo therefore criticizes Jews who have abandoned practices mandated in the Torah, such as the Sabbath and circumcision. He sees these Jews as having Hellenized to the point where they no longer recognize the necessity of observing these commandments, because they consider only the commandments' symbolic interpretations to be meaningful. Such Jews, he declares, are not properly observing God's law:

There are some who, regarding laws in their literal sense in the light of symbols of matters belonging to the intellect, are overpunctilious about the latter, while treating the former with easy-going neglect. Such men I for my part should blame for handling the matter in too easy and off-hand a manner: they ought to have given careful attention to both aims, to a more full and exact investigation of what is not seen and in what is seen to be stewards without reproach. As it is, as though they were living alone by themselves in a wilderness, or as though they had become disembodied souls, and knew neither city nor village nor household nor any company of human beings at all, overlooking all that the mass of men regard, they explore reality in its naked absoluteness. These men are taught by the sacred word to have thought for good repute, and to let go nothing that is part of the customs fixed by divinely empowered men greater than those of our time. It is quite true that the Seventh Day is meant to teach the power of the Unoriginate and the non-action of created beings. But let us not for this reason abrogate the laws laid down for its observance, and light fires or till the ground or carry loads or institute proceedings in court or act as jurors or demand the restoration of deposits or recover loans, or do all else that we are permitted to do as well on days that are not festival seasons.[13]

Philo is critiquing Jews who dismiss the literal level of the Torah's commandments by interpreting its laws only symbolically. These Jews focus on the pursuit of perfecting ideas without focusing on the pursuit of perfecting one's actions by applying allegorical readings to Mosaic Law in ways that undermine traditional Jewish practice.

Philo fused Hellenistic culture with Jewish tradition by applying terms that were well known in Greek philosophical circles to Jewish concepts. His reference to the Logos is perhaps the best example of this technique. The term "Logos" had multiple meanings at this time. It could be translated as "word," "meaning," or "reason." It also referred to the essence of an object, or to a guiding principle.[14] For early Greek philosophers beginning with Heraclitus (c. 535–475 BCE), the word "Logos" referred to a body of knowledge, meaning, or truth.[15] Stoic philosophers building on these concepts interpreted the Logos as the source, or the divine force, that controls the cosmos. In this framework, the Logos was an ineffable divine essence that animated the world.[16] The Logos was particularly important for Platonic and Stoic philosophers, who sought to discern the true meaning and source that lay behind the physical world.

The Logos was of central importance to Philo's understanding of how God interacts with the universe. God created the world using the Logos, which Philo understands to be both a representation of the divine presence and a separate entity representing the divine word. This word, rather than the Creator, then interacts with the world and its inhabitants.[17]

Early Christians would build on Greek concepts of the Logos by arguing that the Logos was an entity that pre-existed creation and was later manifest in Jesus. This concept is related to what scholars call High Christology: the idea that Jesus was more divine than human. The Gospel of John contains one of the earliest articulations of High Christology. Its opening passage begins with the intriguing statement: "In the beginning was the Word (Logos), and the Word (Logos) was with God, and the Word (Logos) was God." Clearly, the translation of Logos as "word" does not do the term justice.

Another Greek concept that appears in Philo's writings is the theme of how one can achieve virtue, which is a central topic for Stoic thinkers and indicates that Philo was influenced by Stoic philosophical schools of thought. Philo maintained that one could obtain perfect virtue by practicing Judaism, just as biblical heroes achieved a state of virtue by obeying the divine will.

Philo's treatment of the Patriarchs Abraham, Isaac, and Jacob is a good example of this association. Philo knew that in Greek philosophical tradition, the three main paths to virtue were learning, perfection by nature, and perfection by practice. Philo applied one path to each of the three Patriarchs: Abraham achieved virtue through learning, Isaac through nature, and Jacob through practice.[18] According to Philo:

This then is what appears to be said of these holy men; and it is indicative of a nature more remote from our knowledge than, and much superior to, that which exists in the objects of outward sense; for the sacred word appears thoroughly to investigate and to describe the different dispositions of the soul, being all of them good, the one aiming at what is good by means of instruction, the second by nature, the last by practice; for the first, who is named Abraham, is a symbol of that virtue which is derived from instruction; the intermediate Isaac is an emblem of natural virtue; the third, Jacob, of that virtue which is devoted to and derived from practice.[19]

For Philo, then, one need not look further than the Jewish scriptures for examples attesting to the human achievement of total virtue.

Philo also borrows well-known phrases from Greek philosophical circles and contextualizes them into a Jewish framework. Philo's treatise *On the Migration of Abraham*, for instance, mentions the phrase "know thyself," a phrase from Plato's works and attributed to the great philosopher Socrates. Whereas Socrates uses the phrase to emphasize the importance of studying and perfecting one's own character, Philo employs it as an injunction to humankind to recognize its limitations and acknowledge the omnipotence of God, who created the universe.[20]

The Greek idea of the exemplum, the ideal person who is a paragon of virtue and piety, also finds its way into Philo's discussion of Abraham.[21] An important feature of some Stoics' philosophical works, the exemplum was the individual who exercised total self-control even in the face of incredible physical pain, who did not succumb to passions such as anger or jealousy, who judged others favorably and reasonably, and who behaved generously toward others. Philo applies the concept of the exemplum to Abraham and other biblical heroes to show how they had reached the highest levels of virtue, even by Greek standards.

In writing encomia, which describe the facets of a hero's virtues at length, Philo highlights how the Patriarchs and the Matriarchs exercised the qualities that exempla embodied. Philo's treatise *On Abraham*, for instance, is essentially one long encomium on the Patriarch. When retelling the biblical stories concerning Abraham, Philo teases out the qualities that make him entirely virtuous. Abraham's mourning of Sarah, for instance, underscored his total self-control:

When [Abraham] had lost his life-long partner, whose qualities have been described in our discourse and are related in the oracles, when sorrow was making itself ready to wrestle with his soul, he grappled with it, as in the arena, and prevailed. He gave strength and high courage to the natural antagonist of passion, reason, which he had taken as his counsellor throughout his life and now particularly was determined to obey, so excellent and profitable were its exhortations. The advice was that he should not grieve over-bitterly as at an utterly new and unheard-of misfortune, nor yet assume an indifference as though nothing painful had occurred, but choose the mean rather than the extremes and aim at moderation of feeling, not resent that nature should be paid the debt which is its due, but quietly and gently lighten the blow . . . as no reasonable person would chafe at repaying a debt or deposit to him who had proffered it, so too he must not fret when nature took back her own, but accept the inevitable with equanimity.[22]

Philo argues that Abraham mourned briefly for Sarah because, in his perfect wisdom, he understood that a truly wise person controls his emotions. Philo is interpreting the Septuagint based on its silences, asking why the biblical story does not provide us with the details of Abraham's mourning. Philo's answer is that Abraham's *not* mourning is, according to the Bible, a lesson in self-control and wisdom.

Philo and the Rabbis sometimes drew on common sources and traditions when writing their biblical commentaries. One interesting example of such interpretive overlap concerns their presentation of Moses as a child. Exodus 2:2 describes Moses' mother giving birth to him and seeing that "he was good." In response to this strange phrase, Philo notes that Moses' parents saw that he had an extra goodliness to him—something unusual for a baby.[23] This note parallels later Rabbinic comments on this phrase, which also presume that "he was good" indicates a special added quality that set baby Moses apart from others.[24]

Other parallels between Philo's portrayal of biblical characters and their portrayal in midrashic literature may also reflect common traditions. For instance, Philo's statement that the Patriarchs intuited divine laws because they correlate with Natural Law may derive from the same source that influenced midrashic claims that the Patriarchs observed commandments that appear only later in the Bible. Of course, it is difficult to know whether Philo and the midrashic writers were building on a common set of oral traditions, or whether they reached similar conclusions about the Patriarchs independently.

The nuanced differences between Philo and the midrash point to their different polemical interests: Philo seeks to present Jewish Law as so intuitive and rational that it correlates with Natural Law, whereas the midrashic writers seek to present the Patriarchs and Matriarchs as people whose piety rivaled and even surpassed those Israelites who would later receive the Torah from God.

As a prominent leader of Alexandria's Jewish community, Philo was aware of the high regard in which he was held by both Jews and gentiles. He considered himself personally responsible for the Alexandrian Jews' well-being and tried to foster positive relations between the Jews and their gentile neighbors. In penning voluminous treatises arguing for the integrity of the Jews' scriptures and values, and in confronting Caligula, Philo risked his own stature as a respected public intellectual for a larger goal: advancing the legitimacy of the Jews as a people loyal to the Roman Empire.

Philo would have assumed that his readership was primarily Jewish. His biblical interpretations responded to questions that he presumed Jews who read their scriptures would ask, and his philosophical treatises sought to clarify Greek philosophical ideas in light of Jewish tradition. Yet Philo's writings are not cited in Rabbinic literature. While his writings were not explicitly shunned, Philo's efforts to fuse Greek and Jewish thought did not earn him a place within Rabbinic tradition.

Ultimately, Christians would be the ones to read, copy, and circulate Philo's writings in the centuries following his death. And while he wrote mainly for a Jewish audience, Philo also made a lasting impact on gentile intellectuals who read his work. The fourth-century CE theologian Jerome refers to a once-common axiom, "Plato philonizes or Philo platonizes," which suggests that Greeks adopted Philo's ideas and, in turn, Philo adopted Greek ideas.[25] The sharing of key philosophical ideas went in both directions.

It took until the sixteenth century—when the Italian Jewish scholar and physician Azariah de Rossi (1511–78) used a Latin translation of Philo's original Greek works—for Jews to begin citing Philo in their writings. And only in the past two centuries or so have scholars begun to appreciate how deeply Jewish Philo's writings are, and to study the ways in which his biblical interpretations correlate with Jewish traditions that would find their way into Rabbinic texts.

Alexandrian Jewry in the Letter of Aristeas

As we noted in chapter 5, the Letter of Aristeas recalls the story of how the Hebrew Bible came to be translated into a Greek version known as the Septuagint. The title of this text, which indicates that it was composed as a letter, was probably established based on the opening sentence, in which the writer addresses his brother Philocrates. But the Letter of Aristeas was probably not intended to function as a private letter. Addressing or dedicating texts meant for public consumption was common in the Greco-Roman period. The Gospel of Luke, for example, opens with a dedication to someone named Theophilus.[26] This word means "lover of God," however, and thus the name might not refer to a specific individual but to any person the author thought might be interested in his message.

From this vantage point, the Letter of Aristeas may not have been written to one person, but to a Jewish audience interested in hearing about the remarkable events surrounding the Septuagint's translation. Most scholars agree that the writer was intent on convincing his readers that the Septuagint was entitled to status and authority equal (or perhaps even superior) to the Hebrew Bible itself. Readers of this document probably would have been amenable to this idea, since most Jews in the Greek-speaking world did not have a strong grasp of the Hebrew language. The author's familiarity with Ptolemy II Philadelphus's court and Greek philosophical ideas indicate that he was living in or near Egypt's cultural and intellectual hub, Alexandria.

The Letter of Aristeas opens sometime in the middle of the third century BCE when Demetrius of Phalerum, the head of the great library in Alexandria, spearheads an effort to expand the library's collection. Toward this end, he asks Ptolemy for permission to recruit Jews who can translate their Hebrew Bible into Greek. The king agrees, and seventy-two Jewish scribes are brought to Alexandria to translate the Hebrew Bible.

The climactic scene in the Letter of Aristeas involves a dinner hosted by Ptolemy that is attended by the Jewish scholars who have come to Alexandria. This dinner is modeled after a symposium, in which each guest is given a turn to demonstrate his wisdom on a particular subject. Ptolemy asks each Jewish guest a question relating to his religious philosophy. For instance, he asks one of the Jews attending the dinner, "What is the highest form of sovereignty?" and receives this answer: "Control of oneself, and not being carried away by one's impulses . . . in everyone moderation is a good thing. What therefore God gives you, take and keep; do not covet the unattainable."[27] Like the other responses provided to the king in the Letter of Aristeas, this answer demonstrates that Greek values such as wisdom and moderation lie at the core of Jewish values.[28]

The Letter of Aristeas also emphasizes the Jews' extreme loyalty to Ptolemy and his kingdom. When the Jews of Judea are asked to send seventy scribes to Egypt, the author relates that the Jewish High Priest Eleazar writes a letter to Ptolemy saying that the Jews would be glad to collaborate with him on the translation project. Eleazar emphasizes the excellent relations between the Jewish community and the Ptolemaic Empire, declaring: "[The translation of our Bible] is a sign of friendship and love. You have bestowed great unexpected benefits upon our citizens in many ways. We therefore offered sacrifices without delay for you, your sister, your children, and your friends."[29] The author's reference to the Jews bringing sacrifices at their Temple on behalf of Ptolemy underscores his view that a positive relationship between the Jews and Ptolemy's government is praiseworthy.

Although the writer likely had a Jewish audience in mind, he also endeavored to highlight commonalities between Jews and Greeks. In one passage, when Aristeas urges the king to release Jewish captives as a gesture of goodwill toward the Jewish community, the writer cites Aristeas as telling Ptolemy that all human beings worship the same God. Aristeas declares:

> Rather with a perfect and bountiful spirit release those who are afflicted in wretchedness, for the same God who has given them their law guides your kingdom also, as I have learned in my researches. God, the overseer and creator of all things, whom they worship, is he whom all men worship, and we too, Your Majesty, though we address him differently, as Zeus and Dis; by these names men of old not unsuitable signified that he through whom all creatures receive life and come into being is the guide and lord of all. Surpass all men, then, in magnanimity of spirit, and grant liberty to those oppressed in bondage.[30]

The author contends that the Jews who were taken captive share a kinship with their Hellenistic captors based on the fact that they worship the same God. Aristeas then takes this point a step further by arguing that all humankind worships the same God, although this God goes by different names. This message would have resonated with Jews, who would have appreciated the argument that Jews practice their religion with integrity, and that devotion to their ancestral tradition did not compromise their allegiance to the Roman Empire.

While the Letter of Aristeas was written two centuries or so before Philo put pen to paper, their common Alexandrian context and interest in understanding the place of Judaism in the broader scheme of Greek philosophical thought begs some comparison. Both the author of the Letter of Aristeas and Philo believed that the values inherent in Jewish tradition were well suited to ideas founded in Greek philosophical schools. Yet the author of Aristeas and Philo did not shy away from distressing realities: They understood that not all gentiles recognized Jews as worthy citizens or viewed Judaism as a legitimate religion with a strong philosophical foundation. Aristeas' opening discussion of the taking of Jewish captives, for instance, attests to a degree of tension in Jewish-gentile relations. Philo, too, made reference to anti-Jewish violence in many passages, and yet he continuously hoped for a time when all of humankind would come together in philosophical unity and religious harmony. These expressions of optimism, although recorded centuries apart, may have been characteristic of a Jewish Alexandrian outlook regarding the relationship between Jews and gentiles.

CHAPTER 8

The Sectarians

In the late Second Temple period, numerous Jewish communities were thriving in Judea. Today, these groups are referred to as sects, but scholars disagree as to how to define this term.

Some believe these groups were borne out of a concern for the Jews' increasing urbanization and the Hasmoneans' move toward Hellenization. Others attribute the sects' development to growing religious exclusivity: Sectarians staked out claims to absolute truth and God's will, which they believed nonsectarians misinterpreted. Their claims to have properly interpreted divine messages led sectarians to unite with one another, and in select cases to withdraw from society.

Lying at the heart of questions scholars debate — including what sectarianism was, exactly; which social and political circumstances allowed it to grow and thrive; and what distinguishing factors separated the sectarians in their own minds from other Jews — is the question of how many members made up each sect. If, as Josephus claims, there were 6,000 Pharisees and 4,000 Essenes in the first century CE, these sects would have made up only a very small part of the Judean population.[1] Most scholars estimate that Jerusalem alone had a population of about 60,000 to 100,000 at this time.[2] The Roman historian Tacitus reports that 600,000 Jews were living in the city when it fell to the Romans in 70 CE.[3] Josephus's casualty estimates are far larger; he writes that 1.1 million Jews were killed in the war, and 97,000 were taken as slaves.[4] But Tacitus's and Josephus's figures include the many Jews who made a pilgrimage to Jerusalem during the Passover holiday from other regions of the Roman Empire, and consequently found themselves stranded in the midst of the war.

Even if Josephus's estimates of sectarian populations consist only of adult males, and they should be enlarged to include women, children, and the aged, the estimates of Jerusalem's size at this time suggest that sectarian affiliates may not have been very representative of Jewish life in Judea. It is likely, then, that the majority of Judean Jews were not affiliated with a sectarian community but practiced what scholars call Common Judaism, which comprised a common set of practices, including the regular reading of the scriptures, observance of the Sabbath, dietary laws, and circumcision.

Josephus offers our main evidence for how these sectarian communities lived and what they believed. He describes three sectarian schools: the Pharisees, Sadducees, and Essenes.[5] The Pharisees, he says, emphasized the authority of an oral tradition that complemented the written scriptures and saw themselves as the inheritors, interpreters, and transmitters of this tradition. Since it was crucial that this oral tradition be studied and observed, the Pharisees believed that the broader Jewish population should look to them for leadership. According to Josephus, many of the Jews did just that.

The main difference between the Sadducees and the Pharisees was that the Sadducees rejected the authority of oral tradition and Oral Law.[6] As a result, the way the two sects kept the Sabbath, the holidays, and dietary laws was dramatically different. While the Pharisees and, later, the Rabbis would develop Sabbath, holiday, and dietary laws far beyond the Torah's mandates, the Sadducees observed these laws only according to what the Torah explicitly stated.

As far as we know, these sects arose sometime in the beginning of the second century BCE, since no evidence indicates that Jewish sects existed before the Maccabean uprising. The social, political, and religious changes in Judea at this time altered the landscape so dramatically that while some Jews enthusiastically embraced the Hellenistic world, other Jews, including early members of the Hasmonean dynasty, responded by delineating stronger religious and political boundaries in order to preserve the Jewish people's distinctive character. The instability of the time was so great that even the Hasmonean dynasty would become rife with corruption and insidious plotting. In this turbulent environment, it is not surprising that some Jews insulated themselves from the outside world by choosing to live among like-minded colleagues.

Josephus describes sectarian Jewish life once in his autobiography, *The Life of Flavius Josephus*, once in *The Jewish War*, and twice in *Antiquities of the Jews*.[7] In *Life*, Josephus provides a brief sketch of these groups, noting that as a youth he experimented by briefly affiliating with each of these sects:

> At about the age of sixteen I determined to gain personal experience of the several sects into which our nation is divided. These, as I have frequently mentioned, are three in number — the first that of the Pharisees, the second that of the Sadducees, and the third that of the Essenes. I thought that, after a thorough investigation, I should be in a position to select the best. So I submitted myself to hard training and laborious exercises and passed through the three courses. Not content, however, with the experience thus gained, on hearing of one named Bannus, who dwelt in the wilderness, wearing only such clothing as trees provided, feeding on such things as grew of themselves, and using frequent ablutions of cold water, by day and night, for purity's sake, I became his devoted disciple. With him I lived for three years and, having accomplished my purpose, returned to the city. Being now in my nineteenth year I began to govern my life by the rules of the Pharisees, a sect having points of resemblance to that which the Greeks call the Stoic school.[8]

Josephus presumes a fluidity between sectarian communities, implying that it was common for new members to be recruited. He does not focus here on the belief systems and lifestyles of the various sects but mentions them only as a way of describing how he came to live as a Pharisee. Perhaps Josephus wanted to communicate to his readers that his decision to live as a Pharisee was discerning, or that his accounts of these sects elsewhere are reliable, since he experimented by living among each sect.

In *Antiquities*, Josephus contrasts the attitudes of the Pharisees, Sadducees, and Essenes toward the philosophical concept of free will. While the Sadducees believe that all people have free will and can control their own fate, the Essenes maintain that fate controls the destinies of humankind, and the Pharisees assert that some, but not all, matters are controlled by fate.[9] Josephus's descriptions of these sects imply that the Sadducees and Essenes took opposing, extreme positions, and the Pharisees were the moderates.

In other passages, Josephus establishes a definitive divide between the Sadducees and the Pharisees. One example of this appears in his description of a break between the Hasmonean leader John Hyrcanus and the Pharisees. According to Josephus, the Pharisees asked John to surrender his claim to the High Priesthood after a Pharisee named Eleazar asserted that John's mother was a captive who may have been sexually violated during Antiochus's reign. Had John been conceived during or after his mother's rape, he would have been ineligible for the priesthood. The spread of this pernicious rumor resulted in John changing loyalties from the Pharisees to the Sadducees. Josephus writes that one Sadducee in particular convinced John to switch sides to the Sadducees, "who hold opinions opposed to those of the Pharisees." For Josephus, John's shift in loyalty was significant because of the ideological differences between these parties. The Sadducees' authority derived from their administrative power as Temple priests, while the Pharisees' authority derived from their positions as transmitters and interpreters of the scriptures. The Pharisees, in other words, expounded on the laws found in the Torah, while the Sadducees viewed these laws as perfect in and of themselves. As Josephus notes in his introduction to the story, "So great is [the Pharisees'] influence with the masses that even when they speak against a king or High Priest, they immediately gain credence." Josephus closes the story with more detail:

> And Jonathan in particular inflamed his anger, and so worked upon him that he brought him to join the Sadducaean party and desert the Pharisees, and to abrogate the regulations which they had established for the

people, and punish those who observed them. Out of this, of course, grew the hatred of the masses for him and his sons, but of this we shall speak hereafter. For the present I wish merely to explain that the Pharisees had passed on to the people certain regulations handed down by former generations and not recorded in the Laws of Moses, for which reason they are rejected by the Sadducaean group, who hold that only those regulations should be considered valid which were written down (in Scripture), and that those which had been handed down by former generations need not be observed. And concerning these matters the two parties came to have controversies and serious differences, the Sadducees having the confidence of the wealthy alone but no following among the populace, while the Pharisees have the support of the masses.[10]

The fact that the Sadducees and Pharisees regularly engaged with one another, and functioned as leaders alongside one another, testifies to a slow shift that Judaism was undergoing in the Second Temple period. For Jews living throughout the Greek and later Roman world, the Temple was a kind of crown jewel, though one no longer bearing the central importance it did during the First Temple period. By the late Second Temple period, most practicing Jews were regularly attending synagogues, where they gathered together to read the scriptures. As the study of the scriptures became increasingly foundational to Jewish practice and to Jewish identity, the role of teachers and scribes became increasingly central as well. Most of these teachers and scribes were associated with the Pharisees. At the same time, however, thousands of Jews from Judea and beyond continued to journey to the Temple to celebrate the annual pilgrimage festivals of Passover, Weeks, and Tabernacles. While some modern readers assume that the synagogue became a central institution only after the Temple was destroyed, it is more accurate to say that, in the Second Temple period, both support of the Temple and affiliation with one's local synagogue were part and parcel of Jewish life. This is why many Jews regarded both the Pharisees and Sadducees as communal leaders during this period.

Some passages in the New Testament also indicate that the Sadducees and Pharisees associated with one another, as they were both involved in communal administrative life, especially in Jerusalem. The Gospels and the book of Acts describe the Sadducees as being involved in the Temple's administration, and the Pharisees as being expositors and teachers of ancestral scripture and law. These sources also lump the Sadducees and Pharisees together as Jews who stood united in their opposition to Jesus and his disciples. Indeed, outside observers would most likely not have perceived the differences between these two groups.

The Pharisees

The name Pharisee might come from the Hebrew *parush*, which means "separate" or "one who separates." Why this term came to refer to this group of Jews is unclear. Perhaps the term refers to the Pharisees' efforts to separate themselves from ritual impurity. Alternatively, maybe they separated themselves from other Jews who did not accept the authority of Jewish Oral Law or who rejected the authority of the teachers who transmitted this law.

The opening Mishnah of the tractate Avot depicts the Pharisees both as inheritors of a tradition extending all the way back to Moses' receiving the Torah at Sinai and as authoritative transmitters of God's teachings to Moses. The Pharisees' authority was in turn inherited by the Rabbis:

> Moses received the Torah from Sinai, and transmitted it to Joshua, and Joshua [transmitted it] to the elders, and the elders [transmitted it] to the prophets, and the prophets transmitted it to the Men of the Great Assembly. They said three things: Be deliberate in judgment, establish many students, and make a fence for the Torah.[11]

In addition to their belief in an authoritative oral tradition that complemented the laws in their scriptures, the Pharisees believed in the resurrection of the dead[12]—a specifically Jewish doctrine that would become central to Jesus' followers when they began to disseminate it in the middle of the first century CE. While the Sadducees rejected the idea that one's body would be resurrected after death, the Pharisees' belief in resurrection would become a foundational tenet of Rabbinic theology.[13]

The New Testament makes numerous references that are specific to the Pharisees. Sometimes its authors criticize the Pharisees as hypocrites who worry about observing the letter of the law but not its spirit. One consistent trope is that the Pharisees did not have empathy for the downtrodden: It was said that they were obsessed with bringing converts into the fold of Judaism but did not attend to those within their own community who required charity and other care.[14] The Gospel of John presents the Pharisees as particularly conniving. Whereas in the first three Gospels—Matthew, Mark, and Luke—the Jews hand Jesus over to the Romans, who crucify him, the Gospel of John holds the Jews responsible for Jesus' death.[15] And because John equates the Pharisees with the Jews, all Jews, Pharisee or not, were depicted as hypocritical and legalistic. This characterization has led to false and profoundly damaging stereotypes about Jews that persist to this day.

The Pharisees were very popular among Judean Jews, in part because they helped to make the practice of Judaism relatively accessible to common people. Unlike the Sadducees, who emphasized a patrilineal, priestly hierarchy, and the Essenes, whose stringent way of life required incredible discipline, the Pharisees taught that any literate Jewish person could study the scriptures, and those who were illiterate could join a study circle and learn from a teacher about the written scriptures and the Oral Law. Of course, women were less likely to be literate than men, and were probably not permitted to formally join such study circles. Still, they would have had more access to Pharisaic teachings than priestly practices, since women were not permitted to conduct priestly service. Nor could they have joined some Essene communities, which prohibited men from marrying altogether. The idea that one could worship the Jewish God through the study of the scriptures and the observance of a set of laws outside of a Temple setting made Pharisaic life appealing to many Jews.

According to Josephus, the Pharisees had a great influence—perhaps too great an influence—on the general population of Judea. They pressured leaders such as John Hyrcanus and Salome Alexandra to make alliances with foreign kings whom they thought would support their interests and allow the Judeans to freely practice their ancestral law without intervention. And because the Pharisees had the support of the majority of Jews, the Sadducees, who oversaw the Temple's administration, were sometimes pressured to accept Pharisaic rulings in order to satisfy the broader Judean population.

At this time, Jesus was traveling in Pharisaic circles and would have been familiar with Pharisaic teachings that would later become incorporated into Rabbinic dogma. One of Jesus' most famous teachings, which concerns loving one's neighbor as oneself, is similar to a statement cited in the Talmud that is attributed to the first-century Pharisee Hillel:

> A Gentile came before Shammai and said, "I will convert if you can teach me the entire Torah while I stand on one foot." Shammai pushed the Gentile aside with the ruler that was in his hand. The Gentile came to Hillel, who converted him saying, "What is hateful to you, do not do to your neighbor. That is the entire Torah, the rest is commentary. Now go and study."[16]

The Gospel of Matthew likewise tells of the following encounter between Jesus and the Pharisees:

> When the Pharisees heard that he had silenced the Sadducees, they gathered together, and one of them, a lawyer, asked him a question to test him. '"Teacher, which commandment in the law is the greatest?" He said to him, "'You shall love the Lord your God with all your heart, and with all your soul, and with all your mind.' This is the greatest and first commandment. And a second is like it: 'You shall love your neighbour as yourself.' On these two commandments hang all the law and the prophets."[17]

Jesus' statement to the Pharisees that the most important commandments are to love God and to love one's neighbor falsely implies that these teachings stand in contrast to the Pharisees' dogma, despite the fact that the Talmud attributes a similar statement to a Pharisee. Similarly, a midrashic collection on the book of Leviticus known as *Sifra* cites the first-century CE rabbi Akiva stating that the biblical dictum to love one's neighbor as oneself is the primary principle of the Torah.[18] The implication in the New Testament that the Pharisees do not prioritize loving God or one's neighbor has given rise to centuries of accusations that, in their zeal for ritual legalities, the Jews are devoid of empathy.

The Sadducees

The name Sadducee derives from the Hebrew word *tzedukim*, which translates roughly as "righteous ones." As with the Pharisees, how this sect came to be known by their name is uncertain. The Sadducees may have regarded themselves as descendants of the priestly line of Zadok, a prominent priest mentioned in 2 Samuel. Rabbinic tradition, however, identifies the Sadducees with the second-century BCE priest Zadok, the pupil of Antigonus of Sokho.[19]

The Sadducees were associated with a priestly class that administered in the Temple and considered themselves to be part of an elite caste of Jewish society.[20] The dissolution of the Saducean sect shortly after the fall of the Second Temple was likely a result of its destruction: Once the Temple lay in ruins, the Sadducees were no longer able to fill an administrative role in Jerusalem.

Because the literature that the Sadducees wrote down is now lost, modern readers who want to learn about the Sadducees must rely on outsiders' reports. While the Mishnah and the New Testament both make reference to the Sadducees, neither gives us a full and clear picture of who the Sadducees were and what they believed. They also tend to portray the Sadducees critically. In the Mishnah, the Rabbis sometimes present the Sadducees' legal opinions as contrasting with their own rulings; yet in the New Testament, the Sadducees often stand alongside the Pharisees as opponents of Jesus and his disciples.

The Mishnah records a number of debates between the Pharisees and the Sadducees.[21] In these debates, the Pharisees are usually presented as legal victors whose opinions are followed by the people. One statement, for example, notes that the Pharisees compelled the Sadducees to follow

Pharisaic legal rulings regarding rituals performed in the Temple.[22] Given the fact that the Sadducees were the Temple administrators, this is rather striking. It also affirms Josephus's claim that since the Pharisees, and not the Sadducees, had the support of the majority of Jews, the Sadducees were sometimes pressured to accept Pharisaic rulings.[23]

An early Rabbinic commentary, or book of midrash, called *Avot de-Rabbi Natan* describes the Sadducees' origins in light of their rejection of the Oral Law. According to one account preserved in this commentary, the students of Antigonus of Sokho splintered into two groups: the Sadducees and the Boethusians. Little information is given about the Boethusians, but the Sadducees, we are told, "used gold and silver vessels all of their days." This reference to the Sadducees' wealth and their indulgence in physical pleasures may be related to their rejection of resurrection: The Sadducees had determined to live in the present world without a mind toward the future one. Both the Sadducees and the Pharisees were concerned with the here and now of the present world, but the Pharisees believed that one's actions in the present world directly influence one's experience of the world to come.[24]

While Josephus presents the Sadducees as adhering to a different belief system than the Pharisees, the Sadducees and Pharisees had more commonalities than differences. They shared the same written scriptures and some traditional practices, and they lived closely among one another. This explains why, in early Christian writings, they appear alongside one another but are not lumped into a single group.

Indeed, both the Sadducees and the Pharisees stand as foils to Jesus' teachings in the New Testament, but the Sadducees are specifically brought to the fore when their rejection of resurrection comes under scrutiny.[25] In one incident, the Sadducees confront Jesus and challenge his belief in resurrection by asking him which husband a woman would marry after her resurrection, if during her lifetime she married seven brothers. This question is conveyed antagonistically, since it is asked by Sadducees, who, the writer reminders us, "say there is no resurrection."[26] Jesus answers that when people will be resurrected, "they neither marry nor are given in marriage, but are like angels in heaven."[27] According to the New Testament, the Sadducees make no rebuttal, which suggests that they are at a loss as to how to undermine Jesus' understanding of resurrection. We would likely have a very different understanding of this and other stories about the Sadducees, however, if any of their writings had survived.

The Essenes

Most of our information about the Essenes comes from Josephus. In *The Jewish War*, Josephus spends far more time outlining their practices than he does explaining the practices of the Sadducees and Pharisees. This is probably because Josephus knew that the Essenes were lesser known to his readers, since they did not participate in civic life in the same ways that the Pharisees and Sadducees did.

Ancient sources about the Essenes contradict one another, which makes it difficult for us to know with certainty what they believed and how they lived. The reliability of Josephus's detailed descriptions of the Essenes, moreover, has been called into question.[28] While he may have lived among the Essenes as a young man, Josephus does not appear to have been an Essene at heart. No evidence remains of his having any prolonged exposure to Essene life after his brief experiment of living in their community, where he observed them firsthand. As someone with ties to Judean rulership, however, Josephus was on more familiar terms with Pharisees and Sadducees. How, then, was Josephus able to provide so many specifics regarding the Essenes? It is likely that most of what Josephus wrote about the Essenes came from a secondary source. Nonetheless, his descriptions provide most of the information that we have about the Essenes.[29]

In his discussion of the three "philosophies" among Jews in *Antiquities*, Josephus writes that the Essenes "deserve admiration in contrast to all others who claim their share of virtue because such qualities as theirs were never found before among any Greek or barbarian people, nay, not even briefly, but have been among them in constant practice and never interrupted since they adopted them from of old."[30] According to Josephus, the Essenes' piety is unparalleled not only among Jews but among all of humankind, in part because the Essenes share all of their possessions, shunning the notion of personal property. The Greeks, particularly the Stoics, greatly admired the idea of people living communally. The phrase "let all life be in common," or variants of it, appears often in Greek and Roman literature as well as in Jewish literature influenced by Stoic thought.[31]

Josephus also notes that some Essenes were granted divine revelation. According to Josephus, a young Essene named Menahem once greeted Herod as "King of the Jews" well before he was established as king of Judea. For this reason, Herod was well disposed to the Essenes during his reign.[32] For Josephus, this legend is important in that it provides information regarding Herod's relationship with sectarian communities, and it sheds light on the Essenes' apparent prophetic qualities.

For other Jewish writers of the time, the Essenes were not necessarily prophetic but were impressive nonetheless because they lived the best lifestyle one could choose. Philo in particular emphasizes the Essenes' all-encompassing virtues. He describes at length how they lived among religious brethren who shared a common belief system and immersed themselves in the study of the scriptures rather than leading mundane lives, distracted by the bustle of the city.[33] In his treatise *Hypothetica*, Philo praises the Essenes' quiet pursuit of philosophy and describes their remarkable piety and devotion to one another. He writes that the Essenes did not marry but that volunteers attracted to the integrity and piety of the Essene lifestyle continually replenished their numbers.[34]

Philo is writing from an elite position. Unlike most people living under the Roman Empire, he was independently wealthy and did not need to participate in city life. From this perspective, the peaceful life of the Essenes represented the best possible existence. In closing his description of the Essenes, Philo notes, "Such then is the life of the Essenes, a life so highly to be prized that not only commoners but also great kings look upon them with admiration and amazement, and the approbation and honors which they give add further veneration to their venerable name."[35]

Roman writers also lauded the Essenes' distinctive lifestyle. The first-century Roman historian Pliny the Elder (23–79 CE), for example, describes them as follows:

> On the west side of the Dead Sea, but out of range of the noxious exhalations of the coast, is the solitary tribe of the Essenes, which is remarkable beyond all the other tribes in the whole world, as it has no women and has renounced all sexual desire, has no money, and has only palm-trees for company. Day by day the throng of refugees is recruited to an equal number by numerous accessions of persons tired of life and driven thither by the waves of fortune to adopt their manners. Thus through thousands of ages (incredible to relate) a race in which no one is born lives on forever: so prolific for their advantage is other men's weariness of life! Lying below the Essenes was formerly the town of Engeda, second only to Jerusalem in the fertility of its land and in its grove of palm-trees, but now, like Jerusalem, a heap of ashes. Next comes Massada, a fortress on a rock, itself also not far from the Dead Sea. This is the limit of Judaea.[36]

Like Philo, Pliny focuses on the Essenes' solitary lives, which are free from the distraction of material pursuits. He asserts that the sect successfully recruits believers because so many people are "tired of life." He also believes that city life is a distraction from more noble pursuits, like the study of knowledge and piety. Pliny's description of the Essenes as living on the "west side of the Dead Sea" supports the possibility that the writers of the scrolls found in the Dead Sea caves, and the inhabitants of the ancient site of Qumran nearby, were Essenes.

On the other hand, Pliny's account of the Essenes may not be entirely reliable, since it does not line up with information found in one of Josephus's descriptions of the Essenes. Pliny writes that the Essenes did not allow women into their community, and therefore did not procreate; they relied on recruitment to maintain their numbers. And while in *Antiquities* Josephus writes that the Essenes indeed did not marry, he notes in *The Jewish War* that some Essenes did marry and have families.[37]

How are we to make sense of these discrepancies? One solution that scholars suggest is that the majority of Essenes settled throughout Judea, marrying and having children. But some Essenes, such as those living on the northwestern edge of the Dead Sea, adopted a more stringent policy that prohibited marriage.[38]

The first-century CE Greek historian and philosopher Dio Chrysostom (c. 40–c. 115 CE) also situates the Essenes near the Dead Sea. According to his biographer, Synesius, (c. 373–414 CE), Dio Chrysostom "praises the Essenes, a very blessed city situated near the Dead Water in the interior of Palestine, in the very vicinity of Sodoma."[39] Like Pliny's, Dio Chrysostom's description of the Essenes supports the widely accepted theory that it was the Essenes who occupied Qumran, and who were likely responsible for placing scrolls in its nearby caves.[40]

The Community of Qumran

Sometime in the second century BCE, a community of Judean sectarians settled in what is now known as Khirbet Qumran, a site that lies on the northwestern corner of the Dead Sea in Israel. This community was composed of devout Jews who had separated themselves from Judean society.

To determine whether the Dead Sea Scrolls that were found in nearby caves might illuminate life at Qumran, scholars had to first establish a firm connection between the scrolls and the site of Qumran. During the early stages of Dead Sea Scrolls research, some scholars argued that the scrolls did not belong to the Qumran community.[41] In the past few decades, however, archaeologists have shown that the people who lived at Qumran must have had a connection to the scrolls. Three of the caves that contained scrolls are situated within the enclosure wall that demarcates the edge of the Khirbet Qumran settlement. Also, the pottery shards unearthed at Khirbet Qumran are the same as the kind discovered in the caves.[42] Josephus's depictions of the Essenes' commitment to ritual purity also align well with the Qumran site; the ritual baths at Qumran indicate that those living there regularly immersed in natural waters.

Once scholars linked the site of Qumran to the Dead Sea Scrolls, they set about trying to determine what could be learned about the Qumran community through the literature composed specifically for them. Not all the discovered texts fell into this category. Many texts found in the caves were scriptural and well known outside the community, among them every text of the Hebrew Bible except the book of Esther. Moreover, the Qumran community would likely have regarded other texts written by outsiders as religiously valuable, if not scriptural. Copies of the book of Tobit, preserved in the Apocrypha; Enoch, a widely circulated book in the Second Temple period; and the apparently sectarian Songs of the Sabbath Sacrifice, which may also have been composed outside of the community and brought later to Qumran, were all discovered in the Dead Sea caves.[43]

The library stored in the Dead Sea caves also included texts that interpreted the Bible, stories that expand on biblical themes, blessings that served liturgical functions, documents that explain how community members should conduct themselves, and descriptions of the nature of a war between the righteous and the sinful that would herald the coming of the end-time. Most of these texts are in Hebrew, but some are in Aramaic, and a few fragments were discovered that were composed in Greek.

To this day, no scholarly consensus exists regarding precisely which texts found near Qumran were composed by sectarians living at the site and which were imported from outside the community. Still, virtually all scholars agree that the community would have regarded certain texts — the Damascus Document, the Community Rule, the War Scroll, and the *pesharim* (documents that interpret biblical prophetic literature in light of the sect's own history) — as foundational to their beliefs and practices. The authors of all of these documents believed that only those inside their community were the elect chosen ones of God. Other people, both Jews and gentiles alike, were outsiders who would one day suffer from divine retribution.

The Community Rule and the Damascus Document provide the most information about how the Qumran community lived — or at least how some members believed they *should* live. Both were likely composed by a member of the sect represented in the text. The Community Rule comprises proscriptive material that can be classified into two halves: the first describes the process of how one can become a community member, and the second lists the rules by which the community members and leaders must abide. All members of the community were expected to follow the teaching of someone referred to as "the Master," who, with the help of priests and Levites living in the community, was to guide all members in living a life of stringent religious piety. While the Community Rule advocates for a communal living style among all members, it also sets forth a social hierarchy that places priests at the top of the social ladder, followed by Levites. One rule in this document, for instance, stipulates that wherever at least ten men gather in the community, a priest must be present, and all shall sit according to rank. Other prohibitions concern general public behavior: one was not to dress sloppily or laugh foolishly, and those who violated these injunctions would incur a penalty of thirty days' penance. The document includes ethical prohibitions as well. Lying, for example, resulted in a penalty of doing penance for six months, and speaking ill of a colleague incurred a penalty of a year. If a person committed what the community considered to be one of the most egregious violations—slandering the community or the leaders of that community—that individual was not given an opportunity to do penance: he was instead to be expelled from the community. All of these rules reflect an effort to fashion a community of people who strengthened one another's pursuit of piety.

The second half of the Community Rule is a hymnic coda, written from the community leader's perspective, which focuses on his devotion to God and his commitment to guiding his people along a path of righteousness. While elements of this prayer parallel material in the Psalms, there is an added eschatological component—that is, an interest in the end of days and an expression of hope for an existence that will be far different from the one the speaker currently experiences. The focus on God's ultimate salvation of the righteous and punishment of the wicked likely offered comfort to the people who heard this prayer. It probably reminded them that while they had chosen a physical existence that deprived them of some of life's material pleasures, their choice also ensured a deeper fulfillment to be enjoyed in the end-time.

The Damascus Document, so called because the document mentions the land of Damascus as the place where a new covenant will be forged, opens with a passage that exhorts the reader to properly observe God's commandments.[44] Its introduction criticizes the majority of the people of Israel, who, the author claims, have abandoned God's instructions and have strayed from the proper path. For this reason, the Israelites have suffered at the hands of their enemies. The second half of the document lists the rules that members of the sect must abide by, which act as a kind of antidote against the divine anger described in the first half of the text. These rules include laws regarding how to make vows, keep the Sabbath, and purify oneself through water.

The many laws in the Damascus Document regarding proper physical conduct suggest that the Qumran community saw spiritual purity and physical purity as being intertwined. The community's emphasis on ritual purity is also evidenced in archaeological discoveries at Qumran. Ten *mikvaot*, or "ritual baths," excavated at the site attest to how the sect's members viewed bodily immersion as a means of spiritual cleansing.

Another text that is foundational to the sect's worldview is known today as the War Scroll. This document envisions an end-of-days battle between the righteous members of the sect, referred to as the Sons of Light, and all those foreign nations and Jews who live outside of it, referred to as the Sons of Darkness. The scroll's first section describes the details of how the Sons of Light will wage war against the Sons of Darkness in the end-time. These include the military formations to be given to the priests who will lead the army into battle, the phrases to be written on the trumpets, and descriptions of the standards to be brought into the war. The second half of the War Scroll is primarily liturgical, comprising prayers the Sons of Light will chant as they enter into battle. Most scholars read this text as a theological statement more than a historical prediction. But Yigael Yadin, the first scholar to conduct serious historical research on the War

Scroll, reads this text literally, arguing that the sectarians believed that this text would guide them when a clash between the community and those outside of it would inevitably occur.[45]

The *pesharim* are a constellation of Dead Sea texts that interpret passages of the Bible in light of the sect's history and presumed future. The Hebrew word *pesharim* is the plural form of the word *pesher*, which means "interpretation." The *pesharim* preserved at Qumran underscore the importance of certain individuals who were pivotal to the community's self-definition. *Pesher Habbakuk*, for example, interprets the biblical book of Habbakuk as a series of predictions regarding a conflict between a Wicked Priest and a Teacher of Righteousness. Although the text has not survived in its entirety and the author's details regarding the sect's early history are opaque, we learn that the Teacher of Righteousness was expelled from his community and the Wicked Priest was felled by his enemies. The Wicked Priest's downfall is presented as a divine punishment for his treatment of the Teacher of Righteousness:

> On account of human bloodshed and violence
> done to the land, the city, and all its inhabitants (Hab. 2:8b)
> Its interpretation concerns the [W]icked Priest, whom—
> because of wrong done to the Teacher of
> Righteousness and the men of his council—God gave him into the
> hand of his enemies to afflict him
> with disease for annihilation with festering wounds of the soul,
>   beca[u]se he
> had acted wickedly
> against his chosen ones.[46]

According to this passage, the prophet Habakkuk envisioned the conflict that erupted between the Wicked Priest and the Teacher of Righteousness. By retrojecting the story of the sect's origins onto Habakkuk's prophecy, the writer of this *pesher* implies that the members of the sect make up the whole community of Israel. This in turn suggests that Jews living outside of the community are not true Israelites in the eyes of Habakkuk and God.

While the Dead Sea Scrolls tell us how the people of Qumran inter-preted their scriptures and how they believed their community fit into God's plan, the material evidence found at Qumran reveals what daily life was like for this community. In particular, material anomalies specific to the Qumran site continue to intrigue scholars. Most of the ceramic clay and the style of pottery found at Qumran, for example, are different from those found at nearby archaeological sites. Also, none of the clay vessels found at Qumran have potters' stamps at the bottom, a common feature at other sites. It seems, then, that the Qumran sect made its own vessels in order to avoid the possibility of them contracting impurity between the time that they were made and the time that they were brought to Qumran. Moreover, the unusually high number of animal bone deposits that were buried in ceramic containers or found nearby suggests that animals were killed and eaten at ceremonial meals that bore religious significance. Finally, the existence of a cemetery adjacent to the site indicates that the community was so insular that its members did not want to share sacred burial spots with other communities.[47] The discovery of a few female skeletal remains on the edges of the main cemetery may indicate that the women buried at Qumran did not live there, but happened to be in the vicinity when they died.

The 1,200 intact eating and cooking vessels found in what was likely a pantry at Qumran, along with hundreds of shards of broken plates and bowls, also raise questions. Why did the community need so many dishes, and how might the answer to this question help us to understand the sect's mind-set? One answer might be found in Josephus's description of the Essenes' dining practices. According to Josephus, the Essenes did not use one plate for more than one kind of food.[48] In addition, all members of the sect received equal portions of food and ate communally. Josephus's descriptions support the prevailing theory that the inhabitants of Qumran were Essenes. As we will see, however, the matter of who the inhabitants of Qumran were and, by extension, who the authors of the Dead Sea Scrolls were, is not as straightforward as we might like.

The Identity and Origins of the Dead Sea Scroll Authors

In the early years following the discovery of the Dead Sea Scrolls, scholarly debates regarding the scrolls were complicated by their sheer diversity and obscurity. But scholars already knew something about one text, the Damascus Document, because two medieval copies of it had been discovered in the Cairo Genizah about a half century earlier. Those copies, first published by Solomon Schechter in 1910 and judged to be copied in the tenth and twelfth centuries, represented two different versions of the text. Solomon Schechter believed that the original author was a Sadducean who had connections to the same community responsible for the composition and circulation of the book of Jubilees. The author may also have had ties to a Samaritan community.[49]

When an almost identical version of the document was brought to light years later at Qumran, some scholars initially presumed that the text was of Sadducean origin, as Schechter had. But as scholars gained access to more of the scrolls, many began to question whether the community of Jews who used this library was in fact Sadducean. After all, there was no explicit evidence that the people who owned these scrolls rejected the idea of resurrection or the concept of an Oral Law, as the Sadducees did.

The presence of the Damascus Document in the Dead Sea caves does, however, support a minority position that the inhabitants of Qumran were Sadducees. Scholars such as Lawrence Schiffman have further linked the owners of the Dead Sea Scrolls to the Sadducees by connecting legal material found in the scrolls to Rabbinic statements attributed to the Sadducees. The scroll known as 4QMMT (*Miksat Ma'asei haTorah*, or "Some of the Works of the Torah"), in particular, shares striking parallels with opinions attributed to the Sadducees in the Mishnah. It states that priests who are preparing a liquid made from the ashes of a red cow that will be used to purify someone who has contracted impurity remain impure themselves from the time that they wash themselves until sundown. The Mishnah identifies this position as Sadducean, while the Pharisees maintain that the priests become pure for most purposes immediately after washing themselves.[50] Despite this and other similarities between legal content in the Dead Sea Scrolls and Sadducean opinions cited in Rabbinic literature, the scholarly consensus remains that the owners of the Dead Sea Scrolls were Essenes, for reasons that we have delineated above.

The Hasideans

The term "Hasidean" comes from the Hebrew *Hasidim*, which means "Pious Ones." The little information we have about the Hasidean sect from the Second Temple period comes from 1 and 2 Maccabees. The author of 1 Maccabees tells us that when the Syrian Greeks attacked the Jews on the Sabbath, some Jews refused to take up arms to defend themselves, believing that doing so would violate the Sabbath. As a result, the Syrian Greeks massacred them. Mattathias and his followers responded to this tragedy by implementing a policy to take up arms on the Sabbath when one's life depended on it. Following this incident, the author of 1 Maccabees tells us, the Jews' position in the war took a positive turn when a group of Jews called the Hasideans joined forces with Mattathias's men. The book of 1 Maccabees describes these Hasideans as "mighty warriors of Israel, all who offered themselves willingly for the law."[51] With Hasideans and other supporters by his side, Mattathias then went about the countryside attacking both Greeks and Hellenized Jews.

The Hasideans appear again later in 1 Maccabees, when they make a treaty with Alcimus, a Jew whose sympathy with the Syrian Greeks led to their controversial choice of installing him as the High Priest of the Jerusalem Temple. Shortly after agreeing to this treaty, however, Alcimus murdered sixty Hasideans.[52] The author of 2 Maccabees also references this incident, citing Alcimus as telling the new king of the Syrian Greeks, Demetrius, that "those of the Jews who are called Hasideans, whose leader is Judas Maccabeus, are keeping up war and stirring up sedition, and will not let the kingdom attain tranquility."[53] According to evidence in both 1 and 2 Maccabees, then, the Hasideans were fearsome soldiers who were devoted to the Maccabean cause.

The Sicarii and the Zealots

Josephus mentions two groups of Jews who actively opposed Roman rule: the Sicarii and the Zealots. There is some confusion regarding whether these groups are one and the same or whether the Sicarii constituted a subset of the Zealots. Sometimes Josephus's use of the term "Zealot" seems to refer to a specific group of Jews, whereas other times he appears to apply the term generically. The following section presumes that the two groups are distinct entities, and that the Sicarii mentioned by Josephus refer to Jews who behaved violently toward other Jews who supported the Romans.[54]

One cause of the Jewish rebellion against the Romans that began in 66 CE was the emergence of what Josephus refers to as a "fourth philosophy," which he juxtaposes with the philosophies of the Pharisees, Sadducees, and Essenes. According to Josephus:

> Here is a lesson that an innovation and reform in ancestral traditions weighs heavily in the scale in leading to the destruction of the congregation of the people. In this case certainly, Judas and Saddok started among us an intrusive fourth school of philosophy; and when they had won an abundance of devotees, they filled the body politic immediately with tumult, also planting the seeds of those troubles which subsequently overtook it, all because of the novelty of this hitherto unknown philosophy that I shall now describe. My reason for giving this brief account of it is chiefly that the zeal which Judas and Saddok inspired in the younger element meant the ruin of our cause.[55]

The leaders of this group were two men named Judas and Saddok, who began their open rebellion against the Romans by encouraging the Jews to refuse to pay a new census tax initiated by the Roman senator Cyrenius. Judas does not seem to have been involved in another sectarian community before starting his own. According to Josephus, Judas was "a sophist who founded a sect of his own, having nothing in common with the others."[56] While it seems that he operated independently, Judas must have made quite a name for himself; he is also mentioned in Acts 5, when a prominent scholar and Pharisee named Gamaliel tries to prevent the Jews from harming Jesus by warning them against zealous behavior, such as that promulgated by "Judas the Galilean," which led to his execution.[57]

Tensions between the Jews of Judea and the Romans came to a head in 66 CE, when Eleazar, a priest who served as governor, or head administrator, of the Jerusalem Temple, stopped offering the daily sacrifice on behalf of the Roman emperor. According to Josephus, this act of disloyalty signaled the real start of the war with the Romans, and Jews who affiliated with the Zealots likely took Eleazar's behavior as an encouraging sign that the rebellion was now under way.[58]

Like the Zealots, the rebels known as Sicarii were opposed to the Roman Empire. The word *Sicarii*, the plural form of the Latin word *Sicarius*, roughly translates to "dagger man." Sicarii were called this because they had a reputation for stealthily assassinating their Jewish enemies who were loyal to Rome. The leader of the Sicarii, Menahem ben Judah, claimed monarchic rights over the Jews in Judea.[59] After Menahem killed the Jewish High Priest Ananias, Ananias's son Eleazar attacked Menahem and killed most of his men.[60] Menahem's relative and supporter Eleazar ben Yair escaped with other rebels to Masada, an isolated fort in the Judean desert, where they took refuge.

Eleazar and his followers evaded Roman capture for about four years following the Jerusalem Temple's destruction. But once they realized that a Roman breaching of the fortress was inevitable, they committed suicide. Josephus attributes to Eleazar an impassioned and eloquent speech that he believes inspired Eleazar's followers to kill themselves.[61] By the time the Romans breached the fortress, the Jewish rebels that had been hiding there were dead.

It is important to note that many scholars do not take Josephus's account of what happened at Masada to be historically accurate, since there is no compelling archaeological evidence that proves that there was a mass suicide at the site.[62] It is very possible, however, that a number of Sicarii did kill themselves. And all scholars agree that there was a community of Zealots who defended themselves from the Romans at Masada during the last stage of the war. The site of Masada, moreover, is extraordinarily well preserved. One can still see the sharp cliff that deterred Roman infiltration and the caves where the Jews living there took shelter.

A number of religious documents have been discovered at Masada, including biblical texts, a copy of the Wisdom of Ben Sira, and two other documents only attested to at Qumran. The first document is a fragmentary manuscript that scholars call the Joshua Apocryphon, which retells stories found in the book of Joshua, and the second document, the Songs of the Sabbath Sacrifice, constitutes a collection of thirteen poems meant to be sung on the first thirteen Sabbaths of the year.[63] The fragment of the Joshua Apocryphon found at Masada is not identical to the fragments found at Qumran, but some scholars believe that the Qumran and Masada fragments were part of the same book.[64] The fact that both the Joshua texts and the Songs of the Sabbath Sacrifice have survived at Masada and in caves 4 and 11 of the Qumran library suggests that these documents may have been composed outside of the Qumran sect and later brought in to its community.[65]

The Babylonian Talmud also contains passages about the Zealots. The Talmud tells of a meeting between the Rabbinic sage Rabbi Yohanan ben Zakkai and his nephew, Abba Sikra, whose name may mean "Head of the Sicarii," or "Abba the Sicarius":

> Abba Sikra was the leader of the *Biryonei* in Jerusalem, and was the son of the sister of Rabban Yohanan ben Zakkai. [Rabban Yohanan ben Zakkai] sent him a message, saying, "Come secretly to me," and [Abba Sikra] came. [Rabban Yohanan ben Zakkai] said to him, "Until when are you going to act this way, and kill everyone through starvation [since you and the Biryonei won't allow Jews to leave the city]?" [Abba Sikra] answered him, "What can I do? If I say anything to them, they will kill me." [Rabban Yohanan ben Zakkai] answered, "Help me get out of the city; there may be a way to find salvation."[66]

In this talmudic account, Abba Sikra and Rabbi Yohanan ben Zakkai hatch a plan that requires Rabbi Yohanan to fake his own death in order to meet with the Emperor Vespasian and discuss the Jews' situation. Because Jews were not buried within Jerusalem's city walls, Rabbi Yohanan's "corpse" was to be carried out of Jerusalem for his burial. The Talmud notes that the "Biryonei" guarding the city wanted to stab Rabbi Yohanan in order to ensure that he was truly dead, but Abba Sikra reproved them, saying that the Romans would then believe that the great rabbi had been murdered by his own people, which would humiliate the Jews. The Biryonei tried to shove Rabbi Yohanan, but again, Abba Sikra protested. Finally, the Biryonei allowed Rabbi Yohanan's body to be carried out of the city unharmed, whereupon he was taken to Vespasian and "returned to life" to confront the newly appointed emperor.

When Vespasian asked Rabbi Yohanan why he had not paid him homage earlier, Rabbi Yohanan blamed the Biryonei, saying that they would not let the Jews of Jerusalem leave the city during the war. Vespasian retorted that the Jews should have destroyed the city's walls in order to allow the Romans to drive the Biryonei out.[67]

While the details of this story may not be historically precise, it probably contains historical kernels of truth. There may well have been a group of Jews controlling the gates of Jerusalem at the height of the Jewish War. It may also be that certain Jewish groups stood in opposition to the Rabbis, who wanted to open dialogue with the Romans, rather than prolong a painful war and endure the inevitable loss of life. The truth, however, was probably less black and white, and the lines between the Rabbinic community and the Zealots leading the rebellion were likely more blurred than this story suggests.

Philo's Therapeutae

Sectarian Jews in the first century may have found homes in regions beyond the Land of Israel. Philo of Alexandria describes a community of Jews who retreated from city life in order to focus on studying the philosophical aspects of Judaism. This community, which Philo calls the

Therapeutae, comprised both men and women and drew on the most elite Jewish circles of Alexandria. According to Philo, the Therapeutae spent six days a week in their own rooms, absorbed in their studies, but gathered together on the Sabbath to read from the scriptures:

> For six days they seek wisdom by themselves in solitude in the closets mentioned above, never passing the outside door of the house or even getting a distant view of it. But every seventh day they meet together as for a general assembly and sit in order according to their age in the proper attitude, with their hands inside the robe, the right hand between the breast and the chin and the left withdrawn along the flank. Then the senior among them who also has the fullest knowledge of the doctrines which they profess comes forward and with visage and voice alike quiet and composed gives a well-reasoned and wide discourse. He does not make an exhibition of clever rhetoric like the orators or sophists of today but follows careful examination by careful expression of the exact meaning of the thoughts, and this does not lodge just outside the ears of the audience but passes through the hearing into the soul and there stays securely. All the others sit still and listen showing their approval merely by their looks or nods. This common sanctuary in which they meet every seventh day is a double enclosure, one portion set apart for the use of the men, the other for the women.[68]

Some scholars have identified this community as Essene, perhaps because Philo references the Essenes at the beginning of his treatise *On the Contemplative Life*, which details the Therapeutae's lifestyle and beliefs. There is no compelling evidence to support this theory, however, and certain evidence disproves it. According to Josephus, at least some Essene communities did not welcome women into their communities, whereas the Therapeutae did include women. Moreover, the Therapeutae may have not been strictly a "sect." Most scholars define ancient Jewish sects as communities that believed that only they would enjoy salvation, and it is not clear that the Therapeutae held any such belief.[69] Finally, because Philo's attitude towards the Therapeutae was influenced by his own disdain for city life, the information Philo provides about these people is biased.[70] It is difficult for scholars to know what information in Philo's writings is accurate and what is conjecture, which makes it challenging for scholars to determine whether the Therapeutae identified as Essenes or aligned themselves with them.

The Jewish writings produced in the late Second Temple period attest to the presence of different groups of Jews in Judea with distinct political and religious beliefs. Some, like the Essenes, believed that by living in separate communities and adhering to a specific set of laws, they were enacting the true will of God. Others, like the Pharisees, united with one another because of their common approach to Jewish tradition and scriptural study. Yet other groups, like the Sadducees, shared a priestly heritage that they believed authorized them to act as administrators of the Jerusalem Temple.

Josephus's use of the words "philosophies" and "sects" can be misleading for modern readers. Outside of some exceptions, such as the community that lived at Qumran, these groups were integrated into broader Judean society and shared values that transcended philosophical discourse. All of these Jewish sectarians, as well as practicing Jews who did not affiliate with a sect, observed the Sabbath and holidays, dietary laws, and circumcision. Many observed complex purity laws as well. And all believed that God had elected the people of Israel to participate in a covenantal relationship that set them apart from other nations and that the sect in which they participated represented the authentic expression of this earlier covenant. Finally, sectarians shared the belief that the rules they lived by would help them enjoy salvation in the end-time. Many were certain that a cataclysmic change was on the horizon but that only their own sect would escape the wrath of God's judgment.

We have no evidence, moreover, that the Sadducees and Pharisees did not allow their children to marry one another. Nor is there evidence that all priests were Sadducees, and that all sages were Pharisees.[71] As Jesus' arguments with the Pharisees and the Sadducees indicate, outsiders perceived these two sects as making up part of a coherent, if diverse, Jewish community. The hard cultural and theological lines that Josephus describes as existing between these groups are thus probably exaggerated.

The question of why no works by the Pharisees have survived continues to intrigue scholars. One possible answer is that the Pharisees produced documents that were not preserved. It is more likely, however, that they hesitated to record legal expositions because they believed written texts would undermine the system of teacher-student transmission that required direct contact with sages. And for the Rabbis, the successors of the Pharisees, the teachings of the Torah extended far beyond legal rulings to all manners of life. One talmudic story recalls that a student lay under his teacher's bed as the teacher was having intercourse with his wife. When the teacher became aware of his student's presence and responded with shock, the student explained, "Rabbi, this too, is Torah, and I must learn it."[72] In another story, one man bet his friend that he could make Hillel lose his temper, lost, and was forced to pay his colleague four hundred *zuzim*.[73] As a community that emphasized the importance of teacher-student relationships and the experiential process of teaching and learning, it is possible that the Pharisees, followed by the early Rabbis, feared that putting Rabbinic teachings into writing would threaten the integrity of teachings that had been transmitted in their communities from generation to generation.

The Pharisees lived at a time when most information was transmitted orally. Information that needed to be written down was recorded either on papyri or on scrolls. Scrolls, however, were extremely inconvenient; in order to find a given passage, one often had to roll past many leather sheets that had been sewn together. It is perhaps no coincidence that the Mishnah was written down only after the codex, which was composed of small bound pages, came into use.

And yet, the expense and effort required to produce scrolls make the achievements of the Dead Sea Scrolls, copied primarily in the first century BCE and first century CE, all the more remarkable. Even in the Second Temple period, many Jews were developing legal and scriptural interpretations and writing them down.

CHAPTER 9

Interpreters of Israelite History

In the First Temple period (c. 960–586 BCE), Israelite worship centered around Temple service. The priests who administered in the Jerusalem Temple also served as the religious leaders of the Israelite community. When the Babylonians burned down this Temple and quashed the Judahite rebellion against Babylonia, King Nebuchadnezzar resettled much of the Judahite population in Babylonia. The fifty-year or so period following this event is known as the Babylonian exile. Without a Temple with which to worship God, the Judahites who found themselves in exile devised a form of common worship that required neither a Temple nor priests. This common worship included regular gatherings at which Jews would listen to scribes and teachers read, transmit, and explain the meaning of their sacred texts. Scribes and teachers soon established themselves as the people's religious leaders.

In 539 BCE the Persian Empire defeated the Babylonian Empire and allowed the Judahites to return to Judea to rebuild their Temple. But even after the Second Temple was completed in around 515 BCE, the religion of Judaism, as it would come to be called, emphasized the regular study of holy texts. For the Jews who remained in the Diaspora and could not easily travel to the Temple, studying the scriptures was an act that linked them to other Jews, regardless of how far away they lived. By the fifth century BCE, Jewish communities had spread throughout the Persian Empire. We will therefore refer to "Judahites" as a community of people tied to a specific region, but when discussing life during the Second Temple period in a broader sense, we will use the term "Jews."

Beginning in the early Persian period, Jews living in both the Diaspora and Judea began to compose pietistic texts that reflect a dogged commitment to a life free of outside influence. Underscoring the importance of staying faithful to Jewish tradition in a non-Jewish world, these texts explore stories of the Bible and reframe them in ways that offer new and relevant meanings. This chapter focuses on three such texts.

The Book of Chronicles

The book of Chronicles is one of the earliest surviving documents we have that revises early biblical material. It provides a genealogy of the Israelite people, starting with Adam and going all the way to King David. Most of the book focuses on the life and times of David, material that is also covered in the book of Samuel. Many scholars believe Chronicles was written in the early Second Temple period, while the Jews in Judea were living under the authority of the Persian Empire. This is in large part because Chronicles emphasizes opposition to Samaritans and support for priestly leadership, issues that engaged Judeans in the Persian period.[1] It also references the social and religious changes in Judea that concerned Jews who were establishing a second commonwealth.

While there is significant overlap between Chronicles and Samuel, there are important differences as well. Because the author of Chronicles seeks to portray David and his descendants in a positive light, he makes certain changes to older versions of the same stories. For instance, while the author of 2 Samuel 11 recounts the story of David's taking the married Bathsheba into his household and sending her husband Uriah to the front lines of war to be killed, the Chronicler omits the story of Bathsheba's abduction altogether. Yet the Chronicler's reiteration of the opening of 2 Samuel 11 indicating that David did not go off to battle, and his description of the war against the Philistines, the very war that killed Uriah, suggest that the Chronicler knows of Bathsheba's abduction, which occurs in between these two events in 2 Samuel 11. It seems, then, that the Chronicler prefers to omit a story that depicts David so negatively, deciding instead to incorporate the setting of the story into his book, without mentioning David's great sin.[2]

The author of Chronicles interprets biblical stories by using other biblical tales as inspiration. One illustration of this technique appears in a story about King David, who, against God's wishes, counts the people, and is then subjected to a choice of three punishments. The punishment David selects is a plague, and according to the author of 2 Samuel 24:

> The Lord sent a pestilence upon Israel from morning until the set time; and 70,000 of the people died, from Dan to Beer-sheba. But when the angel extended his hand against Jerusalem to destroy it, the Lord renounced further punishment and said to the angel who was destroying the people, "Enough! Stay your hand!" The angel of the Lord was then by the threshing floor of Araunah the Jebusite. When David saw the angel who was striking down the people, he said to the Lord, "I alone am guilty, I alone have done wrong; but these poor sheep, what have they done? Let Your hand fall upon me and my father's house!"[3]

The account of this plague in Chronicles, however, is markedly different. Here, a destructive angel hovers in the atmosphere with a drawn sword:

> The Lord sent a pestilence upon Israel, and 70,000 men fell in Israel. God sent an angel to Jerusalem to destroy it, but as he was about to wreak destruction, the Lord saw and renounced further punishment and said to the destroying angel, "Enough! Stay your hand!" The angel of the Lord was then standing by the threshing floor of Ornan the Jebusite. David looked up and saw the angel of the Lord standing between heaven and earth, with a drawn sword in his hand directed against Jerusalem. David and the elders, covered in sackcloth, threw themselves on their faces. David said to God, "Was it not I alone who ordered the numbering of the people? I alone am guilty, and have caused severe harm; but these sheep, what have they done? O Lord my God, let Your hand fall upon me and my father's house, and let not Your people be plagued!"[4]

The arresting image of an angel hovering in midair and holding a drawn sword adds remarkable drama to this story. This added drama extends to David and the elders, who fall to the ground in prayer upon seeing the angel. Their response, which does not appear in Samuel, heightens the story's suspense by slowing down the action of the narrative. It also amplifies David's grief and regret over his actions. This portrayal is consistent with the Chronicler's tendency to depict David as an ideal leader of the people and a pious servant of God.

But where did the Chronicler get the image of an angel hovering in midair? It appears that he was familiar with Joshua 5, which describes an almost identical scene just after the Israelites have celebrated the holiday of Passover. According to Joshua 5,

> Once, when Joshua was near Jericho, he looked up and saw a man standing before him, drawn sword in hand. Joshua went up to him and asked him, "Are you one of us or of our enemies?" He replied, "No, I am captain of the Lord's host. Now I have come!" Joshua threw himself face down to the ground and, prostrating himself, said to him, "What does my lord command his servant?" The captain of the LORD's host answered Joshua, "Remove your sandals from your feet, for the place where you stand is holy." And Joshua did so.[5]

This passage likens Joshua to Moses by depicting an angel who gives Joshua the same instructions that God gives Moses in Exodus 3:5: "Remove your sandals from your feet, for the place on which you stand is holy ground." While Joshua 5 invokes the story of the burning bush in Exodus 3, 1 Chronicles 21 invokes the story of Joshua 5. The Chronicler expands 2 Samuel 24 by drawing on elements of Joshua 5 because he wants to make a connection between these two stories. Perhaps his intended message is that, just as Joshua was a devoted servant of God, a legitimate successor to Moses, and a man who enjoyed God's care and approval, David was likewise a devoted servant of God and a legitimate successor of Moses, despite his faults.

Small differences between Chronicles and Samuel point to big differences in ideology. In describing King Saul's death, for example, the author of 1 Chronicles writes that "Saul grasped the sword and fell upon it. When the arms-bearer saw that Saul was dead, he too fell on his sword and died. Thus Saul and his three sons and his entire house died together."[6] But the account of Saul's death in 1 Samuel notes only that

> Saul grasped the sword and fell upon it. When his arms-bearer saw that Saul was dead, he too fell on his sword and died with him. Thus Saul and his three sons and his arms-bearer, as well as all his men, died together on the same day.[7]

The Chronicler makes a small change to the story in 1 Samuel: Instead of noting that Saul, his sons, his armor-bearer, and his men died, the Chronicler tells us that the entire house of Saul died together. Why was this change made? Stating that the house of Saul died was a way of saying that Saul's dynasty had come to an end. Although there were a few survivors of Saul's house who come to the fore in 2 Samuel 2, the dynasty of Saul, and its rightful claim to the monarchy, ended at the moment of his death. The end of Saul's dynasty makes room for David to emerge as the sole heir to the throne. Again, the Chronicler's aim is to position David as the legitimate ruler over the people of Israel.

This change also solves a difficulty in 1 Samuel, which states that all of Saul's men died together. Could it really have been the case that all of Saul's men died in one battle? Were there not men from Saul's army who survived, including Abner, who appoints Saul's son Ish-bosheth as king of Israel in 2 Samuel 2:8? It appears, then, that the statement in Samuel that all of Saul's men died is inaccurate. The Chronicler takes this literal statement about Saul's army and turns it into a figurative declaration of the demise of Saul's dynasty, thereby solving a difficulty in the older text and affirming that David was now in a position to assume the monarchy.

These examples illustrate that the changes that Chronicles makes to older stories about the early kings of Israel are not random or careless.

Nor can we explain these changes by suggesting that the Chronicler did not have our version of Samuel, or was working with another source. The differences between Chronicles and Samuel suggest that the Chronicler deliberately made changes to older versions of the stories about Saul and David with the purpose of presenting David as the true heir to the Israelite monarchy. While we cannot know with certainty why the book was canonized, given its overlap with material found in earlier biblical books, the Chronicler's changes to earlier material in the Bible reveal a new and distinct ideology.[8]

The Book of Jubilees

The book of Jubilees is a Hebrew document that consists of a fifty-chapter rewriting of Genesis and the beginning of Exodus. Written sometime in the second century BCE, Jubilees was one of the most popular Jewish books in circulation in the late Second Temple period: Fifteen fragments of copies of this book were found in the library of the Dead Sea Scrolls alone.

The identity of the book's author, and the manner in which the book was written, are unknown. Some scholars maintain that Jubilees is a compilation of texts composed by different authors and sewn together by a final editor, while others argue that Jubilees was written by one person whose text was later subject to small interpolations.[9] Regardless of these unresolved questions, there are common understandings concerning the book's ideology. Scholars agree, for instance, that the author of Jubilees wanted his Jewish readers to strictly observe aspects of Jewish practice that made Judaism distinct from other ancient religions, such as the Sabbath and holidays, circumcision, and dietary laws. The centrality of these laws in Jubilees is reflected in the book's emphasis that Abraham, Isaac, and Jacob kept these laws.

The author of Jubilees advocated for understanding Jewish history through the structure of jubilees, from which the book takes its name. He explains that the history of the Jewish people can be divided into units of jubilee years, with each unit lasting forty-nine years. This concept is modeled after the system of seven sets of seven years laid out in Leviticus

25, which prescribes a celebratory year every fiftieth year that includes the return of all property to its original owners and the manumission of slaves. According to Jubilees, the period between Adam and Eve's expulsion from the Garden of Eden in the eighth year of the world's creation and the Israelites' Exodus from Egypt is a span of 2,401 years, which is exactly forty-nine jubilees.

There is some confusion in Leviticus 25 as to whether a jubilee is forty-nine or fifty years long. Where Leviticus 25:8 seems to presume a forty-nine-year jubilee, Leviticus 25:11 describes a jubilee as a period of fifty years. The author of Jubilees adheres to the forty-nine-year definition but regards fifty to be a significant number as well. In his historical construction, the period from Adam and Eve's expulsion from the Garden of Eden through the Israelites' crossing the Jordan and entering the Land of Israel spans 2,450 years, which is exactly fifty jubilees.

Jubilees is not a text that would have attracted the admiration of all Jews. The author condemns Jews who disregard ancestral practices and gentiles who oppress Jews, which implies that he was living in a traditional, and perhaps sectarian, environment. An even stronger indication that the author does not adhere to a mainstream Jewish worldview is his attitude toward the calendar year. He advocates for a solar, rather than lunar, year, believing that every year is 364 days long. The ramifications for following a solar calendar are huge: Jews adhering to such a calendar would have celebrated the Sabbath and holidays such as Rosh Hashanah and Yom Kippur on different days than the majority of Jews who followed a lunar calendar.

Jubilees' solar calendar implies that the author advocates for a separatist approach from most Jews. It is likely, however, that he believed that all Jews would one day follow this calendar once they were governed by the proper Jewish leadership. In order to advocate for such a transformative change in Jewish practice, the book needed to be imbued with divine authority. It is not surprising, then, that some manuscripts of Jubilees open with an introductory statement that the book's content was imparted to the author by Moses.

Promoting a solar calendar would also have been taken as an implicit criticism of the priests administering in the Jerusalem Temple, who, from Jubilees' vantage point, were making grave errors by offering sacrifices at the wrong times. Jubilees' conviction that the priests running the Temple in Jerusalem were acting in defiance of God is expressed in the following passage:

> And there will be those who examine the moon diligently because it will corrupt the (appointed) times and it will advance from year to year ten days. Therefore, the years will come to them as they corrupt and make a day of testimony and reproach and a profane day a festival, and they will mix up everything, a holy day (as) profaned and a profane (one) for a holy day, because they will set awry the months and Sabbaths and feasts and jubilees. Therefore, I shall command you and I shall bear witness to you so that you may bear witness to them because after you have died your sons will be corrupted so that they will not make a year only three hundred and sixty-four days.[10]

Despite the author's unusual approach to the calendar cycle, he cites well-known legends that would later find their way into midrashic words such as Genesis Rabbah and Exodus Rabbah. One example of this is a legend regarding a series of tests that God gave Abraham. According to Jubilees:

> And the Lord was aware that Abraham was faithful in all of his afflictions because He tested him with his land, and with famine. And He tested him with the wealth of kings. And He tested him again his wife, when she was taken (from him), and with circumcision. And He tested him with Ishmael and with Hagar, his maidservant, when he sent them away. And in everything in which He tested him, he was found faithful.[11]

This passage lists eight tests that God administered to Abraham, although they could also be tallied to six or seven, if land and famine are lumped together, and Ishmael and Hagar as well. The tradition that God gave Abraham a series of tests endured in the early Rabbinic period. According to the Mishnah, "Ten tests were given to Abraham our father, and he endured all of them. [The purpose of these tests was] to publicize how great was our father Abraham's love [for God]."[12]

In the mishnaic tradition, God tests Abraham for almost the same reason God tests him in Jubilees: God wants to determine whether Abraham is completely faithful. The Mishnah and Jubilees, however, differ in one small detail. While in Jubilees, Abraham's choice to follow God is not known to God until Abraham passes the tests, the Mishnah implies that God knows that Abraham will pass the tests but is nevertheless proceeding with them in order to publicize Abraham's greatness. The polemical undertones of the Mishnah point to a sense of vulnerability that compels the author to present Abraham as a pious follower of God. In Jubilees, however, Abraham's piety is self-evident, and worldwide acknowledgment of Abraham's piety is not of particular concern.

Jubilees' author underscores the distinguishing aspects of Judaism, especially the practices of the Sabbath and circumcision.[13] The proper observance of the Jewish holidays is also central to the author's program. The author weaves these holidays into his narrative by recalling how the Patriarchs scrupulously observed them. We are told, for example, that Abraham, Isaac, Jacob, and Jacob's children observed the Festival of Weeks, which celebrates the giving of the Torah to the Israelites at Sinai. In a different passage, the author notes that Abraham offered sacrifices in celebration of Tebernacles, the harvest holiday that commemorates the time the Israelites spent in the wilderness, vulnerable to the elements but protected by God.[14] These comments suggest that, for the author, the Patriarchs had prophetic knowledge of events that were to come. Even more important, perhaps, is the fact that the Jewish holidays in Jubilees have a transcendent quality that places them in a realm well beyond a historical continuum of time and space.

Some content in Jubilees does not align with interpretations that would be cited in later Rabbinic midrash. One example regards the Patriarch Isaac and his wife Rebecca. In Genesis, Isaac has a minor role in comparison with his father, Abraham, and his son Jacob. Rebecca, on the other hand, has a more prominent role than Sarah, Abraham's wife, and Rachel,

Jacob's wife: She plays a pivotal part in ensuring that her younger son, Jacob, secures the firstborn rights rather than the older Esau. From the moment that Rebecca enters the scene in Genesis 24, when Abraham's servant travels to Nahor to find a wife for Isaac, Rebecca exudes self-assured confidence.

Midrashic traditions regarding Isaac and Rebecca tend to amplify Isaac's role in the Bible. On the other hand, the picture of Rebecca in midrashic literature is varied. In some traditions, Rebecca embodies a patriarchal position characterized by her control over her family, which contrasts with her husband's obliviousness.[15] Other midrashic traditions, however, portray Rebecca more conventionally, as a woman who is submissive to her husband.[16] Rather than trying to reverse Rebecca's role as these traditions do, Jubilees embraces the dynamic in Genesis by presenting Rebecca as a strong woman who takes control over her children's destinies. In Jubilees, when Jacob discovers that his grandfather Abraham has died, Jacob runs to tell Rebecca, not his father. It is Rebecca, not Isaac, who instructs Jacob not to marry a Canaanite woman. And when Jacob is in danger of physical harm, it is Rebecca, not Isaac, who prays to God asking for Jacob's protection. Rebecca even has a prophetic dream in which Esau is trying to kill Jacob. She interprets this dream correctly, and consequently saves Jacob's life by instructing him to leave her household and escape to Mesopotamia.[17] Jubilees' surprising treatment of Rebecca as a powerful woman is especially remarkable given its rigid traditionalism when it comes to observing the Sabbath, holidays, and circumcision. It may be that, for the author of Jubilees, a powerful matriarch was not a particularly untraditional notion.

Another essential element in Jubilees is the coming apocalyptic age, when God's judgment over all of creation will yield to an era of reward and punishment, followed by a period of universal peace. The author of Jubilees is especially concerned with the punishments that those who do not observe the Law will incur:

Behold, the land will be corrupted on account of all their deeds, and there will be no seed of the vine, and there will be no oil because their works are entirely faithless. And all of them will be destroyed together: beast, cattle, birds, and all of the fish of the sea on account of the sons of man. Some of these will strive with others, youths with old men and old men with youths, the poor with the rich, the lowly with the great, and the beggar with the judge concerning the Law and the Covenant because they have forgotten the commandments and covenant and festivals and months and Sabbaths and jubilees and all of the judgments. And they will stand up with bow and swords and war in order to return them to "the way," but they will not be returned until much blood is shed upon the earth by each (group). And those who escape will not be turned back from their evils to the way of righteousness because they will lift themselves up for deceit and wealth so that one shall take everything of his neighbor; and they will pollute the holy of holies with their pollution and with the corruption of their contamination.[18]

Jubilees blames the mass destruction that is to come on the many sinners who have abandoned their covenantal relationship with God. This implies that most Jews will succumb to God's wrath, since they do not observe a solar calendar, which for Jubilees means they do not properly observe the Sabbath and holidays.

Jubilees continues to fascinate scholars who study the history of biblical interpretation as well as those who study the history of the development of Jewish Law. The widespread interest in Jubilees speaks to the way in which the book transcends genre. It is neither a book of law nor a retelling of the Bible. For its author, the stories of the scriptures and the traditions of Judaism are linked together.

The Psalms of Solomon

As we noted briefly in chapter 4, the Psalms of Solomon is a collection of eighteen psalms written in the late Second Temple period. The psalms are attributed to Solomon, who was known for establishing a prosperous and secure kingdom, and for building the Jerusalem Temple. By making this attribution, the author implies that painful events of the recent past will give way to a period of restoration, and Jerusalem will soon enjoy a golden age of peace when the Jews will once again be guided by a "son of David."[19]

The psalms in this collection have been preserved in Greek manuscripts as well as in a few manuscripts written in Syriac, but they were probably first written in Hebrew. Based on the psalms' allusions to a foreign king whose entry into Jerusalem was met with resistance and who was ultimately assassinated, scholars believe that the author was a Jew from Jerusalem writing in the wake of the Roman general Pompey's invasion of Judea in 63 BCE.[20] Lamenting Jerusalem's subjugation to a gentile ruler, the writer — or writers — of these psalms predicts that one day the Jews' enemies will be subjected to God's wrathful judgment.

Before Pompey's invasion, Judea had enjoyed autonomy since about 164 BCE, when the Hasmonean family led an army against the Syrian Greeks and successfully seceded from their empire. But by the first century BCE, the Hasmonean dynasty was wracked with corruption and scandal. The divisiveness that the Hasmoneans caused by their almost constant infighting was amplified by the fact that many members of the family assimilated into Greek society. This provoked traditional Jews who had hoped that the independent Judean state would foster the development of a Jewish society that was committed to observing Jewish ancestral tradition.

The turbulent instability within the governing family of Judea made it easier for Rome to incorporate Judea into its empire by military force. Some Jews interpreted this incorporation as a reflection of God's displeasure with the Jews. These Jews believed that the autonomous Judean province of yesteryear was a lost opportunity, which, with proper governance, could have heralded the Messianic Age. Both assimilated Jews and Roman invaders were therefore responsible for the predicament in which the Jews of Judea now found themselves.

The writer of Psalms of Solomon was one such Jew. He opens his second psalm, for example, by making a correlation between the invasion of Jerusalem and the sins of the Jews:

Arrogantly the sinner broke down the strong walls with a battering ram and you did not interfere.

Gentile foreigners went up to your place of sacrifice;

They arrogantly trampled (it) with their sandals.

Because the sons of Jerusalem defiled the sanctuary of the Lord,

They were profaning the offerings of God with lawless acts; Because of these things he said, "Remove them far from me; they are not sweet-smelling."[21]

This text blames the gentile invasion of the Temple on Jews who did not treat the Temple properly but also bears a negative attitude toward non-Jews. In this sense, it is similar to Jubilees and to sectarian texts found in the Dead Sea caves, which also highlight the elected status of Israel as God's Chosen People and maintain that a new age of divine judgment is coming, when sinners will be destroyed and the righteous will be saved.

Psalm 2 provides specific information regarding the events that led to Pompey's capture of Jerusalem. In one expressive line, the writer describes the Romans taking Jewish children into captivity: "[Her] sons and the daughters were in harsh captivity, their neck in a seal, with a distinguishable mark among the nations."[22] Psalm 17 also attests to the cruel treatment of Jewish civilians: "The lawless one laid waste our land so that no one inhabited it; they destroyed young and old and children together."[23]

Despite these grim images, the writer of the Psalms of Solomon was not without hope. He despaired of Jerusalem's current position, but also envisioned a time when the Jews would worship God in the Temple, free of a subjugating enemy. In Psalm 10, for example, he predicts that all of God's people will one day worship God in peace:

Our Lord is righteous and devout in His judgments forever, and Israel shall praise the name of the Lord with joy. And the pious shall confess in the assembly of the people, and God will show mercy upon the poor to the joy of Israel. For God is eternally kind and merciful, and the congregations of Israel shall glorify the name of the Lord.[24]

Elsewhere, the author describes the eternal punishment that sinners will one day endure:

For the portion and inheritance of God is Israel. But not so are sinners and transgressors of the Law; who loved a day in the companionship of their sin. Their desire was for the briefness of corruption, and they have not remembered God. For the ways of human beings are known before Him at all times, and He knows the secret chambers of the heart before they come to pass. Therefore their inheritance is Hades and darkness and destruction, and they shall not be found in the day when the righteous obtain mercy.[25]

According to these psalms, sinners will suffer from terrible punishments in the end-time. Those who have followed God's commandments, on the other hand, will enjoy everlasting peace.

In the late Second Temple period, Jewish writers drew on past experiences to make different polemical arguments. Some reframed the stories of the Patriarchs in order to argue for the strict observance of ancestral law, while others aimed to retell stories about early Israelite kings to argue for the legitimate rule of David and his descendants. For many Jews, the hardships of the Israelites, and of Jews in their recent history, were reminders of the lasting covenantal promises made to them by their God. Despite their current sufferings, God would ultimately put an end to the Jews' hardships and usher in an era of redemptive peace.

Jewish writers seeking to highlight the importance of their ancestral tradition knew the key identifying markers of Judaism that Jews—and gentiles—would recognize: the practices of circumcision, Sabbath, and dietary laws.[26] The three pilgrimage holidays were also well known by this time. But perhaps the most central of all practices that Jews engaged in during this period was the practice of reading and interpreting the scriptures. And while there may not have been a closed biblical canon during the late Second Temple period, there were, by this time, biblical texts that were broadly regarded as authoritative. These texts were read, copied, retold, expanded upon, and interpreted by Jews living in both Judea and the Diaspora.[27] Most Jews at this time did not consider such creative expansions of the scriptures to be acts of sacrilege but rather believed them to be acts of homage. Shared ideas regarding Jewish Law and the scriptures enabled Jews to practice their religion in ways that made their Jewish identities recognizable, regardless of where they lived.

CHAPTER 10

Josephus Flavius

Josephus Flavius (37–c. 100 CE) is one of the most fascinating and influential figures of the late Second Temple period. He was raised in an aristocratic priestly family in Jerusalem, and, as we noted in chapter 8, he decided as a teenager to explore Jewish sectarian life by living among the three main Jewish sects in Judea: the Sadducees, Pharisees, and Essenes. He then spent three years living in the desert as a disciple of an ascetic to determine whether this life suited him. At the age of nineteen, Josephus returned to Jerusalem, prepared to live among the Pharisees, but the growing political turmoil in Judea catapulted him onto an unconventional path. He would later become an eyewitness, and a major player, in the Jewish revolt against the Roman Empire in 66–73 CE.

One story about Josephus is especially revealing in terms of what kind of person he was—or claimed to be. In 63 CE, just three years before the onset of the great rebellion, tensions were flaring in Judea. The Roman procurator Felix had imprisoned some Jewish priests on menial charges and ordered them to be sent to Rome. Josephus, who knew these priests, took it upon himself to obtain their release. He boarded a ship to Rome, but it was shipwrecked along the way. Grateful to have survived the wreck, Josephus found a ship the following morning that allowed him to board, and he succeeded in reaching Rome safely.

The next step was securing an audience with the emperor of the time, Nero, to request the priests' release. Josephus managed this by acquainting himself with a well-known Jewish actor named Aliturius who lived in

Rome. Aliturius knew Nero's wife, Poppea, and introduced her to Josephus. Having curried Poppea's favor, Josephus requested that she look into the matter of releasing the priests, which she did. The priests were released shortly thereafter. With Josephus's daring mission accomplished, he returned home.

This story is a kind of "tell-all" account when it comes to how Josephus sought to portray himself. Both unswervingly loyal to the Jewish people and able to cultivate the trust of the highest-level Roman officials, Josephus saw himself as a tenacious and invaluable mediator between the two parties. Yet, as we will see, there were times when both the Jews and the Romans viewed Josephus as an outsider, and even a traitor.

Returning to Judea after his trip to Rome, Josephus discovered that tensions were higher than ever. These tensions extended three ways. They flared between Jews and Romans, between Jews who were loyal to Rome and Jews who advocated for insurrection, and between Jews who advocated for insurrection but disagreed as to who should lead the cause.

When the Jewish rebellion finally broke into a full-fledged war, Josephus was assigned to lead a garrison of Jewish soldiers in Israel's northern region, despite the fact that he was not a skilled military leader. A catastrophe under his watch in 67 CE in a northern hilltop town called Jotipata (Yodfat in Hebrew) convinced Josephus that, by rebelling against Rome, the Jews were engaged in a suicide mission. They would never defeat the mighty empire. Following the fall of Jotipata and his own capture and imprisonment, Josephus defected to the Romans. In 69 CE, Vespasian released Josephus from captivity. He would remain in Rome for most of the remainder of his life.

Josephus wrote two major works: *The Jewish War*, which details the Jewish uprising against the Romans in 66–73 CE, and *Antiquities of the Jews*, which retells Jewish history, beginning with the book of Genesis. He probably composed *The Jewish War* sometime in the middle to late 70s, first in Aramaic (which he refers to as his "ancestral tongue"), and then in Greek. Josephus's comment that the Greek version was presented to Vespasian and Titus enables scholars to estimate when *The Jewish War* was written and completed. Josephus authored *Antiquities* close to the end of his life, perhaps in 93 or 94 CE.[1] We know this because Josephus states that he is writing the work in the thirteenth year of Domitian's reign, and Domitian became emperor in 81 CE.

Josephus also wrote an autobiography, *The Life of Flavius Josephus*, or *Vita*, likely soon after his completion of *Antiquities*.[2] In some manuscripts, Josephus's *Life* is appended to the end of *Antiquities*. Finally, at the very end of his life, Josephus wrote the treatise *Against Apion*, which refutes a certain Apion's numerous accusations against the Jews. Dated to after 94 CE because it cites *Antiquities*, this text is an elegant and systematic defense of the Jewish religion. And as far as we know, it was the first such defense to be written. All together, these writings paint a vivid picture of the challenges Jews faced in first-century Judea.

While it is not clear how reliable Josephus is as a historian, scholars nevertheless consider his account of the Jewish war to be vitally important to understanding this conflict. Many of the details Josephus provides also reveal information about how he perceives his own role in the war. His description of his disastrous defeat at Jotipata, for instance, which he writes resulted in the massacre of about 40,000 Jews, is a good example of how Josephus's history blends with autobiography.[3] Josephus writes that during the Roman invasion, he took refuge in a cave, where he found forty other Jews hiding. On his third day of hiding, the Romans discovered Josephus's hiding place and sent two tribunes to capture him.

Aware that capture was imminent, Josephus suggested to the other Jews in hiding that it was preferable to die by their own hands than to be given over to the Romans. Because suicide is prohibited in Jewish Law, Josephus proposed that the Jews in hiding kill one another. The Jews agreed to this plan, but when only Josephus and one other man remained alive, the two decided not to go through with their suicide pact. Shortly afterward, the Romans captured Josephus and brought him to Vespasian.[4] Josephus's account of his narrow survival at Jotipata may not have occurred exactly as he tells it, particularly since it sounds very similar to his account of a mass suicide pact at Masada in 73 CE, which most scholars agree is highly embellished.

Josephus is sympathetic toward the Romans, even when describing his capture. He praises them for their "innate generosity" in sending a Roman officer by the name of Nicanor, who had a past friendship with Josephus, to escort Josephus to Vespasian.[5] When he was presented to Vespasian, Josephus declared to him that he, and not Nero, was the true Caesar:

> You imagine, Vespasian, that in the person of Josephus you have taken a mere captive; but I come to you as a messenger of greater destinies. Had I not been sent on this errand by God, I knew the law of the Jews and how it becomes a general to die. To Nero do you send me? Why then? Think you that [Nero and] those who before your accession succeed him will continue? You will be Caesar, Vespasian, you will be emperor, you and your son here. Bind me then yet more securely in chains and keep me for yourself; for you, Caesar, are master not of me only, but of land and sea and the whole human race. For myself, I ask to be punished by stricter custody, if I have dared to trifle with the words of God.[6]

We do not know whether Josephus actually gave this speech to Vespasian. A public declaration that Vespasian was destined to inherit Nero's throne would have been extremely risky. And such a treasonous claim would have surely made Vespasian uncomfortable, especially since Nero was notorious for his capriciousness and cruelty toward his enemies. According to Josephus, Vespasian expressed his doubts in response to Josephus's prediction, but privately came to believe that he would inherit the throne. This may explain why, while Vespasian kept Josephus captive, he treated him generously.[7]

Josephus credits Vespasian's son Titus with restoring his dignity as a captive, since it was Titus who asked Vespasian to cut up Josephus's bonds rather than simply to loosen them.[8] Cutting up bonds was a symbolic gesture signifying that a prisoner was to be treated as he had been before captivity, suggesting that the reason for his captivity had never occurred in the first place. It was partly for this reason that Josephus felt warmly toward the Flavian dynasty, comprising Vespasian and his two sons, Titus and Domitian. After the war, Josephus took on their family name and called himself Titus Flavius Josephus.

After being taken to Rome, Josephus pledged his loyalty to the Romans. And when Josephus's wife died during the war, Vespasian himself arranged for Josephus to marry a Jewish woman who was also a Roman captive. But Josephus divorced her after Vespasian freed him and married another Jewish woman. He traveled with her and Titus to Jerusalem, where he was assigned to act as Titus's translator during the city's siege.[9]

Unsurprisingly, Josephus faced great difficulties in Jerusalem once word spread among the Jews that Josephus was aiding and advising Titus. Jewish leaders in the city wanted to arrest and try Josephus for defection.[10] At the same time, Josephus tells us, many Romans suspected him of collusion with the Jews when the Romans suffered military setbacks. It was Titus's trust in Josephus that helped him to maintain positive relations with the Roman army and avoid being captured by the Jews.

With his third wife, Josephus had three children, two of whom died at a young age. Josephus later divorced her and married a fourth time, this time to a Jewish woman from Crete. Together they had two sons, Justus and Simonides; the latter, Josephus tells us, was also known as Agrippa.[11]

Each member of the Flavian dynasty—Vespasian and his sons Titus and Domitian—showed Josephus kindness. Vespasian gave him Roman citizenship, an estate on which he was not required to pay land taxes, and an annual stipend. In the final passage of his autobiography, Josephus states that Vespasian even brought to justice the Jewish leaders who falsely accused Josephus of plotting against them on behalf of the Roman Empire. Titus, likewise, encouraged his father to release Josephus from captivity and treat him with dignity. He also placed Josephus in his personal employ. And when Domitian became emperor in 81 CE, he continued to recuse Josephus from paying taxes on his Judean estate.[12]

While many Jews regarded the Flavian family to be cruel tyrants who brutally quelled the Jews' rebellion and then further soured relations with the Jews by levying a tax on all Jews in the empire, Josephus's slant toward the Flavians is largely positive. Whether his portrayal reflects true feelings of friendship or a sense of pressure to portray the Flavians as kindlier than they truly were remains unclear.

While scholars disagree regarding whether Josephus's intended audience was Jewish or gentile, he likely had both in mind when writing his works. Josephus goes into great detail explaining aspects of Jewish practice and law that would have been familiar to most Jews, and he is careful not to criticize the Flavian dynasty—efforts that suggest that Josephus has a gentile audience in mind. But the fact that Josephus goes out of his way to emphasize his loyalty to the Jewish people may also indicate a Jewish readership.

Regardless of what community he was writing for, Josephus's aim was not to provide an objective history of the Jewish people. Instead, it is more likely that his goal was to retell Jewish history in a way that presented the Jews as members of an admirable religion whose values were consonant with Greek and Roman values. In both *Antiquities* and *The Jewish War*, Josephus castigates Roman accounts of the war that portray the Jews more poorly than he believes they deserve. Josephus's rebuttals of anti-Jewish claims that were made about early Israelites and contemporary Jews also suggest that Josephus felt a personal responsibility to take action against rhetoric that marginalized the Jews.

Indeed, Josephus took it upon himself to battle stereotypes commonly leveled against the Jewish people, focusing especially on those that were circulating during his own time. One of the most widespread accusations against Jews in the first century was that they were misanthropic. Derived from the Greek *misanthropía* and literally meaning something like "anti-human," this term was used in reference to the Jews' relatively insular religious world. The Jews' well-known practices of circumcision, dietary laws, and the Sabbath underscored this insularity, and were sometimes interpreted as representative of an elitism that made the Greeks critical of the Jews.

In *Against Apion*, Josephus defends these and other Jewish practices that made the Jews seem different from gentiles. Regarding the Sabbath, for example, Josephus rebuts a Greek named Agatharcides, who claims that Sabbath observance is irrational and foolish. While Agatharcides mocks the Jews' decision not to resist the invasion of Ptolemy I Soter (c. 367–c. 282 BCE) after he attacked them on the Sabbath, Josephus argues that the decision not to violate the Sabbath is a testament to the Jews' loyalty to their ancestral law and is impressive in its nobility.[13]

Josephus also presents Jewish tradition positively through his portrayal of biblical heroes. Abraham, for instance, is a great intellectual who teaches the sages of Egypt astronomical and mathematical wisdom.[14] Like Philo, Josephus adopts the Greek model of the *exemplum*, in which a hero embodies all virtuous attributes. Josephus's *exemplum* of Abraham was meant to instill in readers respect and awe of the patriarch.[15]

Josephus's assertion that there are three "philosophies" (*philosophía*) of Judaism—Pharisees, Sadducees, and Essenes—may reflect his intention to compare these groups to three known Greek philosophical schools.[16] He makes an explicit connection between the Pharisees and the Stoics in *Life*, and the Essenes and Pythagoreans in *Antiquities*. While he does not expressly link the Sadducees with the Epicureans, he would have known that both groups rejected the notions of fate and the afterlife, and may have presumed this association to be a given.[17]

Josephus's writings provide the most important evidence we have regarding Jewish life in the Second Temple period. And yet, reading Josephus is not without its challenges. Josephus has a tendency to present his life adventures in exaggerated terms. His description of his reputation as a young, brilliant scholar in his autobiography, for example, should be read delicately. The same goes for his suggestion that he had a prophetic vision when he predicted that Vespasian would become ruler over the Roman Empire.[18] When it comes to Jewish history, Josephus also takes liberties in order to underscore the integrity of the Jewish people and the valiant behavior of their heroes. These flourishes can frustrate historians who seek to elucidate the historical kernels embedded in Josephus's writings, but they are also intriguing marks of Josephus's humanity.[19]

One method of determining how to read Josephus's historical accounts is to look for outside sources that confirm, or contradict, his claims. While this method has proven useful, it is not foolproof, since Roman historians were also known to exaggerate, particularly when it came to describing conquests over their enemies.

Compounding the problem of how to read Josephus is the fact that his writings contain internal inconsistencies. In *The Jewish War*, for instance, Josephus presents himself as a skilled and devoted general who actively recruited Jewish soldiers in the Galilee. In this account, Josephus is a highly qualified leader whose military involvement in the war indicates that he initially supported the rebellion against Rome. In *Life*, however, Josephus describes himself as a novice who was sent to the Galilee only as a representative of Jewish leaders in Jerusalem who wanted him to keep the peace there. *Life* also includes details not found in *The Jewish War*, especially regarding Josephus's personal conflicts with other leaders of the rebellion, such as John of Gischala and Justus of Tiberius, who later accused Josephus of inciting the uprising. By emphasizing that he was not responsible for the rebellion against Rome and did not see eye to eye with key leaders of the rebellion, Josephus exonerates himself in *Life* from the crime of treason against Rome and preserves his status as a competent leader of the Jews.

As to which version of events is more historically reliable regarding Josephus's role in the war, the broad consensus is that *Life*, though written later than *The Jewish War*, represents a more raw and uncurated account of Josephus's experiences. It is in *Life* that Josephus focuses on his messy political relationships, which makes it a less complimentary, and likely truer, version. Perhaps Josephus did not want to present himself as embroiled in personal conflicts when writing *The Jewish War*, since he planned to formally present this work to the Flavian family. The reader should also keep in mind that while some changes Josephus made to his earlier account were intentional, others may simply have been a result of carelessness. Scholars continue to debate the degree to which Josephus was intentionally inconsistent or just sloppy.[20]

Josephus's writings were widely preserved. The Romans likely preserved them because they provide ample evidence of their military successes. And Christians would later preserve them for a number of reasons: In addition to providing information regarding Jesus' first-century context, Josephus's *Antiquities* includes a complimentary passage about Jesus known as the *Testimonium Flavianum*. Christians took this passage to be an early witness to Jesus' life, although scholars now agree that it was added by an early Christian copyist. Christians also appreciated Josephus's description of the death of John the Baptist, which appears to be authentic, and Josephus's criticism of the Pharisees, whom Jesus opposed.

The Rabbis betray no awareness of Josephus's writings. Nor do they seek to replicate Josephus's achievements by composing their own account of Jewish history. It is unclear why no histories of the Jewish people, as far as we know, were produced in the Rabbinic period. But perhaps the answer lies in the Rabbis' attitude toward Jewish history. Rather than being interested in producing a chain of facts and dates that make up Israelite history, the Rabbis wanted to cull and extract the messages conveyed in biblical retellings of this history. The twentieth-century historian Yosef Hayim Yerushalmi put it well when he wrote that "the very absence of historical writing among the rabbis may itself have been due in good measure to their total and unqualified absorption of the biblical interpretation of history."[21] Above all, the Rabbis were concerned with transmitting traditions that affirmed an ever-present covenantal relationship between God and the Jews.

Like the Rabbis, Josephus saw broad patterns in Jewish history that reflected God's concern for the Chosen People. He maintained, for example, that the Jews' catastrophic defeat in the Jewish war was not a sign of the Jewish God's defeat, as the Romans argued, but a punishment for the Jews' sins. Josephus believed that by producing a comprehensive account of Jewish history, he would be able to demonstrate that the Jews enjoyed a covenantal relationship with their God, who never fully abandoned them.

In part 3 of this book, we explored the variety of religious perspectives among Jews living in the late Second Temple period. These perspectives do not fall along geographic boundaries. While it was once assumed that the Jews of Judea were more insular than the Jews of the Diaspora, a close look at the sources and their likely provenances suggests that every major Jewish community in the late Second Temple period produced a variety of literature that reflects different modes of Jewish observance and attitudes toward the outside world.

Despite their wide range of outlooks, documents that survive from this period represent an elite population. Whether they advocated for an exclusivist or inclusivist model of Jewish living, the authors of these texts had access to the highest levels of education that their communities had to offer them. Their literacy, and their familiarity with the Septuagint, Greek culture, literary stylistics, and philosophy, indicate that these Jewish writers did not always represent the knowledge base of their readership. Even so, the fact that their works were copied and circulated indicates that many Jews believed that these texts were valuable enough to warrant preservation.

Josephus is a prime example of a profoundly influential writer who did not represent mainstream Jewish views. In addition to being born into an aristocratic family, Josephus felt obliged to walk a tightrope between gratifying (and at times critiquing) Roman and Jewish audiences in ways most Jews would not have emulated. Yet his writings were preserved and circulated more than perhaps any other Jewish writer living in the Second Temple period. Like Josephus, Philo of Alexandria wrote from a vantage point of privilege, and his writings were also not preserved by Jews. While he was widely respected by Greek and, later, Christian intellectuals, the Jews whose writings survived in the centuries following Philo's death did not cite him.

Other literary works that we examined in this section were not consciously preserved by any communities, Jewish or gentile. The writings belonging to the Dead Sea sect, for example, were carefully stored in caves but for the most part were not circulated following the sect's dissolution.

The transmission history of other texts, such as the Letter of Aristeas and the Wisdom of Solomon, is harder to trace, partly because neither assimilated nor Rabbinic Jews fully identified with these books. On the one hand, these works highlight differentiating aspects of Judaism, such as monotheism, circumcision, and the Sabbath; on the other, they demonstrate Greek stylistics and cultural influences. The precise socio-religious milieu in which these texts were written is therefore obscure. Nevertheless, scholars agree that these texts were composed primarily for Jewish audiences.

What was the unifying factor that drew these Jews, who expressed their faith in different ways and in different places, to feel a kinship with one another? How did the Jewish religion remain a single faith without splintering into multiple separate religions? The answers to these questions have to do with the common scriptural writings that Jews by this time shared. These writings were probably not canonized until after the Second Temple period, and therefore Jewish communities throughout the Greco-Roman world might have differed when it came to precisely which books they regarded as authoritative. But by the late Second Temple period, the Pentateuch, the first five books of what would later be known as the Hebrew Bible, were regarded by all Jews as scriptural.

PART 4

THE HOLY TEXTS OF

SECOND TEMPLE JUDAISM

CHAPTER 11

The Codified Bible

In the Second Temple period, documents were copied by hand, either onto sheets of parchment made of animal hide or onto papyri. Papyri were made from the papyrus plants that grew in abundance alongside the banks of the Nile River. Using papyri was a practical and inexpensive way to record documents and preserve them in the dry desert climate of Egypt. Animal hide, on the other hand, was a more durable material, but since it had to be cured and treated before a scribe could write a text on it and roll it easily into a scroll, it was a more expensive alternative. Papyri tended to be used for day-to-day documents, while scriptural texts were usually copied onto scrolls in order to ensure their endurance.

Although Jews in the Second Temple period held certain texts to be scriptural, they did not assemble all of their sacred writing into a canon. As we noted at the end of chapter 3, part of the reason for this is that sacred texts were generally written on scrolls.[1] Given the expense of purchasing even a single scroll, we can assume that most Jews living in the Second Temple period were not in possession of all the scrolls that they considered to be scriptural.[2] They would have owned a few scrolls at the most, and, if their finances allowed, would have added to their collection of scrolls over time. Since different sections of the Bible were usually written on separate scrolls, there was a degree of fluidity regarding how Jews collected sacred texts. An owner of two scrolls might have placed Judges, a text that would come to be regarded as canonical, on a shelf next to Jubilees, a document that would later be excluded from the canon, and this owner might have considered both scrolls to be equally sacred.

All of this changed in the early Rabbinic period, when scribes began to copy the Jews' scriptural texts into codices. In order to determine which documents would be included in a biblical codex, the Rabbinic community had to decide precisely which documents were considered scriptural. This decision in turn helped to canonize the Hebrew Bible. Once the Jewish scriptures were bound into a single book, they were read in light of one another, and those books that had been excluded from the collection were no longer read in conversation with the codified scriptures. The Hebrew Bible was thus solidified into a cohesive collection, and excluded books came to be viewed as marginal to normative Judaism, rather than as representative of mainstream Jewish thought.

The word "canon" is derived from the Greek word *kanon*, which refers to a straight bar the Greeks used to measure objects. The word may be connected to the Greek word *kanna*, "reed," which shares a cognate with its Hebrew counterpart, *kaneh*. The etymological connection between *kanon* and *kanna* may be due to the fact that reeds were once used as measuring tools. Just as the length of one of these reeds was considered to be a complete measurement, a collection of texts within a canon was considered to be complete and required no supplement.

This chapter examines three collections of the Bible that Jews used in the late Second Temple period: the Hebrew Bible, written in Hebrew; the Septuagint, written in Greek; and the Peshitta, written in the Aramaic dialect of Syriac.

The Hebrew Bible

The Hebrew Bible is known as the TANAKH in Hebrew, which is an acronym that refers to its three main sections: the Torah, the Nevi'im, and the Kethuvim. The Torah, its first section, contains the Five Books of Moses: Genesis, Exodus, Leviticus, Numbers, and Deuteronomy. Genesis begins with the story of the creation of the universe and then segues into a brief account of human history from Adam to Abraham. From the time that it introduces the reader to Abraham, the Torah homes in on the origins of the Israelite people. It closes with Moses' death, on the cusp of the Israelites' entry into the Land of Israel.

The second section of the Hebrew Bible, known as Nevi'im, or Prophets, consists of the books of Joshua, Judges, Samuel, Kings, Isaiah, Jeremiah, Ezekiel, and a collection of prophetic books called the Twelve Minor Prophets. Joshua, Judges, Samuel, and Kings recount Israelite history from the people's entry into the Land of Israel through the Babylonians' destruction of the Jerusalem Temple and the consequent Babylonian exile. Isaiah, Jeremiah, Ezekiel, and the Twelve Minor Prophets consist of prophetic speeches and oracles.

These books cover a period of time when the Israelites were ruled by judges and then by kings. As we mentioned in chapter 4, the Israelite monarchy split into two kingdoms following the reign of Solomon: the Northern Kingdom, called Israel, and the Southern Kingdom, called Judea. In 722 BCE, the Assyrian Empire invaded Israel and exiled the Northern Kingdom. Soon thereafter the Assyrian Empire began to decline, and the Babylonian Empire rose to power. In 587–586 BCE the Babylonians invaded Judea, destroyed the Jerusalem Temple, and exiled many of Judea's inhabitants to Babylonia.

The last accounts in the historical books of the Prophets section of the TANAKH close with the beginning of Babylonian exile. Scholars believe, however, that some of the prophecies that appear in Isaiah, Jeremiah, Ezekiel, and the Twelve Minor Prophets were actually composed during the Babylonian exile and in the decades following the Judeans' return to Judea under the Persian king Cyrus. These years are known as the Exilic and post-Exilic periods.

The final section of the Hebrew Bible, Kethuvim, or Writings, comprises Psalms, Proverbs, Job, Song of Songs, Ruth, Lamentations, Ecclesiastes, Esther, Daniel, Ezra, Nehemiah, and Chronicles. These books vary in genre, place of composition, date of composition, and, in the case of Aramaic passages in Daniel, Ezra, and Nehemiah, even in language, but most are dated to the Exilic or post-Exilic periods.

Mishnaic discussions regarding whether to include or exclude certain books from the canon suggest that, even in 200 CE, the question of precisely which books were "in" and which were "out" remained unsettled, particularly when it came to the Writings section of the TANAKH. The Mishnah recalls, for example, that some Rabbis were concerned that the Song of Songs was too erotic to be canonized, but Rabbi Akiva insisted that while other books are holy, this book is the "Holy of Holies."[3] Rabbi Akiva's argument is also clever wordplay: He matched the superlative title "Song of Songs" with the inner sanctum of the Temple, the Holy of Holies. By doing so, Rabbi Akiva correlated holy text with holy space, a strategy for which the Rabbis would become renowned. Rabbi Akiva's argument was accepted, and the Song of Songs was preserved in the TANAKH'S Writings section.

Discussions regarding the biblical canon and its authors are preserved in the Talmud. The first list of biblical books is preserved in the talmudic tractate of *Bava Batra*:

> Who wrote the Scriptures? Moses wrote his book, and the portion of Balaam and Job. Joshua wrote his book and [the last] eight verses of the Torah. Samuel wrote his book and the books of Judges and Ruth. David wrote the Book of Psalms, with the help of the elders Adam, Melchizedek, Abraham, Moses, Heman, Yedutun, Asaph, and the three sons of Korah. Jeremiah wrote his book, the book of Kings, and Lamentations. Hezekiah and his assistants wrote Isaiah, Proverbs, Song of Songs, and Ecclesiastes. The men of the Great Assembly wrote Ezekiel, the Twelve Minor Prophets, Daniel, and Esther. Ezra wrote the book that bears his name, and the genealogies of Chronicles up to his own time.[4]

This passage mentions the twenty-four books of the Hebrew Bible, and no others. That the passage opens with the question "Who wrote the Scriptures?" rather than "What *are* the Scriptures?" implies that this list was not meant to establish the biblical canon but to clarify its authors. By the time this list was written down, the Rabbinic community, or at least the community in which the Rabbinic author of this passage lived, presumed the existence of a widely accepted biblical canon.

Today, the standard text of the Hebrew Bible is based on what is called the Masoretic text, which is credited as being the "authentic" version of the Hebrew Bible. This text is based on an early eleventh-century CE manuscript called the Leningrad Codex, which is the oldest complete version of the Hebrew Bible. An older copy of the Masoretic text, the Aleppo Codex, dated to the tenth century, survives as well, but no longer in complete form.

The Masoretic text is not the only version of the Bible that the Jews used in ancient times. Many of the biblical scrolls preserved at Qumran, for instance, differ from the Masoretic text, which raises the question of whether the Masoretic text should be amended by using biblical texts preserved at Qumran. This issue is further complicated because there was not one single version of the Bible preserved at Qumran, but several. Among these versions, there is evidence for the existence of a biblical version that was extremely close to what would later become the Masoretic text. These issues will be addressed more fully in the coming decades, as scholars conduct comparative work between the biblical texts from Qumran and the Masoretic text.

The criteria used by the Rabbis to determine which books were to be canonized into the Hebrew Bible remain unclear. In some instances, there are notable similarities between biblical and nonbiblical books. Three examples, each from a different genre of literature, are especially glaring.

The first is Ben Sira and Proverbs. Both books are concerned with the question of how to achieve virtue, and both place special emphasis on religious piety and sexual chastity.[5] Perhaps Proverbs was canonized but Ben Sira was not because Proverbs was considered more authoritative, having been attributed to King Solomon. And while its date of composition is disputed, Proverbs is an earlier book than Ben Sira. These factors likely led to its canonization.

The second example is Esther and Judith. In both novellas, a beautiful Jewish woman enters into a relationship with a powerful gentile man who threatens the well-being of the Jewish people. Some might argue that the figure of Judith, and the author who tells her story, are even more pious than Esther and the author of her book. Judith observes the Sabbath and all the Jewish festivals. She also keeps Jewish dietary laws, even when she is sleeping in the tent of the Assyrian general Holofernes. God is mentioned throughout the book of Judith, and the author references Israelite history in order to highlight God's ongoing protection of the Israelite people. The book of Esther includes none of these elements. In fact, it does not make a single reference to God. Nonetheless, the Rabbis included Esther in their canon, but excluded Judith. Perhaps they did so because Esther was written in the Persian period, well before the book of Judith was composed in the Greek period. Esther may therefore have been regarded as a more well-established book in Jewish tradition.

Finally, the first half of the book of Daniel displays remarkable similarities with stories about Daniel in Greek that were not canonized. While all of these stories emphasize Daniel's impressive wisdom, religious piety, and judicial expertise, it is likely that older stories about Daniel were preserved in the Hebrew Bible because they were written in Hebrew and Aramaic, which would have signified an older or more "authentic" tradition than the stories about Daniel written in Greek.

Ben Sira, Judith, and Greek stories about Daniel would all be preserved in the Apocrypha, the collection of Greek texts that would be included in the Septuagint and are now part of the Catholic Bible, while Proverbs, Esther, and Daniel were canonized into the Writings section of the TANAKH. Discussions in the Mishnah regarding what books should be canonized in the Writings section suggest that in the Second Temple period this section was treated with more fluidity than the Torah and the Prophets sections, which by this time may have been more or less fixed. Indeed, Jesus is cited as making reference to "the law and the prophets" in the New Testament, but he makes no reference to the Writings.[6]

As we have noted, the line between scriptural and nonscriptural works was not always clear in the Second Temple period. Many Jews likely regarded some books that are now preserved in the Hebrew Bible as not scriptural, and other books that would not be canonized as scriptural. The library of the Dead Sea Scrolls illustrates this point well. The caves where the scrolls were found contained fragments of every single book of what is now the Hebrew Bible except for the Hebrew book of Esther. The caves also held fragments of fifteen manuscripts of Jubilees, a book that would not be preserved in the Hebrew Bible or in the Apocrypha. For the owners of the Dead Sea Scrolls, Jubilees may have been considered a scriptural book, whereas Esther was not.

The Septuagint

The Greek translation of the Hebrew Bible known as the Septuagint gets its name from the Latin word *septuaginta*, which means "seventy." This word refers to the number of scholars said to have been brought to Alexandria from Judea to translate the Hebrew Bible into Greek under the auspices of King Ptolemy II Philadelphus (285–246 BCE). Whether or not it happened that exactly seventy (or seventy-two, according to the Letter of Aristeas) scholars traveled to Alexandria to embark on this major scholarly effort, we know that by around 200 BCE the translation was completed, and many Jews believed that this new version of the Bible had divine approval.

Over time, the Septuagint came to include a collection of books called the Apocrypha, a word derived from the Greek adjective *apokryphos*, which means something like "hidden away," or "esoteric." This term may allude to the fact that the books of the Apocrypha were not canonized in the Hebrew Bible, although some of them were popular and well circulated among Jews in the late Second Temple period.

While no translation can perfectly capture the essence of the words it is translating, the Septuagint does more than simply select Greek words that closely resemble the original Hebrew terms: It actively interprets the Hebrew text. In its rendering of the book of Genesis, for example, the Septuagint often changes people's names and when they lived. In the list of genealogies in Genesis 11, the Septuagint adds a hundred years to the ages of some of Shem's descendants.[7] Perhaps the authors of the Septuagint were aware that Manetho, the prominent Egyptian historian of the third century BCE, did not mention a major flood in his history of the Egyptian dynasties. By increasing the ages of Shem's descendants, the authors were able to date the flood to an early period that would predate the first Egyptian dynasty.[8]

The Septuagint authors were also concerned with clarifying the meaning of names in the Hebrew Bible. While the Hebrew Bible, for instance, calls Adam's wife Hava, the Septuagint refers to her as Zoe. Both Hava and Zoe mean "life." The translators may have assumed that Jewish readers of the Septuagint did not know Hebrew and would not have understood the meaning of a Hebrew name transliterated into Greek.[9]

The Septuagint was not the only Greek translation of the Hebrew Bible circulating in the Greco-Roman period. Thanks to the efforts of the third-century CE Church Father Origen, who compiled the Hexapla, a text comprising six side-by-side versions of the Bible, we know that there were at least four other Greek versions as well. Most Greek-speaking Jewish readers of the late Second Temple period and the centuries following, however, considered only the Septuagint to be the authoritative Greek translation of the Hebrew Bible.

The Syriac Peshitta

The Syriac Peshitta, a translation of both the Hebrew Bible and the New Testament, was created by Christians who spoke Syriac, a dialect of Aramaic that was spoken during the first few centuries CE in regions to the east and to the north of Judea. The word *peshitta* means "simple" or "common" in Aramaic and indicates that this Bible was common, or widespread, among Syriac-speaking people who read the Bible. Alternatively, it may have referenced the fact that this biblical version was considered well written and easily understood.

Scholars believe that the books of the Hebrew Bible in the Peshitta were probably translated primarily from Hebrew texts, and the New Testament books were translated from Greek texts. The process of translation, however, was more complex than simply using a single Hebrew version to create a single Syriac version. Although the writers of the Peshitta seem to have relied on a Hebrew Bible that was similar to the Masoretic text, they may have used other Hebrew versions as well, and probably also used the Septuagint, or a similar Greek translation of the Bible, to aid them. Scholars continue to debate the question of what sources the authors of the Peshitta used by looking at different versions of Hebrew and Greek biblical texts that may have influenced its composition.

The Christians who authored the Peshitta had some awareness of Jewish biblical interpretations circulating at this time. Among these interpretations were Aramaic translations of the Hebrew Bible called *Targumim* (*Targum* in the singular), which first circulated orally and were later written down in order to provide Aramaic-speaking Jews with an accessible version of Scripture. The Peshitta authors were also influenced by oral legends that found their way into *Targumim* after the Peshitta was produced. When scholars discern a parallel between an interpretation in the Peshitta and the *Targumim*, therefore, they do not necessarily presume a direct connection between these two texts.

While the compositional history of the Peshitta is unclear, most scholars believe that it was in circulation by the fifth century CE. Other translations of the Bible into Syriac, such as the Syriac Sinaiticus, were also circulating at this time. By the medieval period, however, the Peshitta was the most well-known Syriac version of the Hebrew Bible and New Testament.

Like the Septuagint, the Peshitta at times expands or interprets the scriptures. Its rendering of Genesis 4's account of Adam's sons, Cain and Abel, is an interesting example of the creative license it sometimes takes. While in the Hebrew version of the story Cain's final status is unclear and God is somewhat sympathetic to Cain, the Peshitta has God unequivocally condemn Cain—and God even subtly associates him with Satan. A translation of the Hebrew account reads:

Now the man knew his wife Eve, and she conceived and bore Cain, saying, "I have gained a male child with the help of the Lord." She then bore his brother Abel. Abel became a keeper of sheep, and Cain became a tiller of the soil. In the course of time, Cain brought an offering to the Lord from the fruit of the soil; and Abel, for his part, brought the choices of the firstlings of his flock. The Lord paid heed to Abel and his offering, but to Cain and his offering He paid no heed. Cain was much distressed and his face fell. And the Lord said to Cain, "Why are you distressed, and why is your face fallen? Surely, if you do right, there is uplift. But if you do not do right sin couches at the door; its urge is toward you, yet you can be its master." . . .

And when they were in the field, Cain set upon his brother Abel and killed him. The Lord said to Cain, "Where is your brother Abel?" And he said, "I do not know. Am I my brother's keeper?" Then He said, "What have you done? Hark, your brother's blood cries out to Me from the ground! Therefore, you shall be more cursed than the ground, which opened its mouth to receive your brother's blood from your hand. If you till the soil, it shall no longer yield its strength to you. You shall become a ceaseless wanderer on earth." Cain said to the Lord, "My punishment is too great too bear! Since You have banished me this day from the soil, and I must avoid Your presence and become a restless wanderer on earth—anyone who meets me may kill me!" The Lord said to him, "I promise, if anyone kills Cain, sevenfold vengeance shall be taken on him." And the Lord put a mark on Cain, lest anyone who met him should kill him. Cain left the presence of the Lord and settled in the land of Nod, east of Eden.[10]

In this version, God condemns Cain to be a "ceaseless wanderer," and Cain despairs that his punishment is "too great to bear." The Peshitta, on the other hand, cites Cain as admitting, "My sin is too great to be forgiven." In the Hebrew Bible, moreover, God tells Cain that "[sin's] urge is toward you, yet you can be its master." But the Peshitta cites God as saying, "You shall turn to it, and he shall control you." These changes imply that Cain is not a fallible individual who can re-enter God's good graces through repentance. Instead, he is a person who is doomed to punishment because he is eternally controlled by sin.

The two versions also differ in the setting of the murder. In the Hebrew version, Cain kills Abel in a field; in the Peshitta, the field becomes a valley. The Peshitta also inserts a clause in which Cain suggests to Abel, "Let us descend into the valley." Cain's murderous activity in a valley associates him with a satanic figure who in early Christian literature is said to have dwelled in a valley.[11]

The Peshitta gives added weight to the story of Cain and Abel by depicting the brothers' conflict as a clash between the forces of good and evil. While in the Hebrew version Cain's behavior after Abel's murder could indicate his regret and sorrow, the Peshitta presents Cain as irreparably wicked. This difference, combined with allusions to Satan, led some Christians to read the Peshitta version as an allegorical account of Satan's fall from God's grace.

The Different Canons of the Hebrew and Christian Bibles

As Christianity spread and developed, Christian communities formulated lists of their holy texts, and these lists bore differences that remain today. The most well-known example is the Catholics' inclusion of the Apocrypha in the Bible, which contrasts with the Protestant Reformers' rejection of it from their canon.

The books that make up the Hebrew Bible and the Christian Bible also differ. While the Christian Bible includes the Hebrew Bible's twenty-four books, it preserves them in a different order. The Hebrew Bible closes with Chronicles, and the Christian Bible closes the Old Testament with the Twelve Minor Prophets, the last of whom is Malachi. Early Christians likely decided to conclude the Old Testament with the Twelve Minor Prophets because Malachi segues so well into the Gospel of Matthew, the first book of the New Testament. Malachi ends with the following verses:

> Lo, I will send the prophet Elijah to you before the coming of the awesome, fearful day of the Lord. He shall reconcile parents with children and children with their parents, so that, when I come, I do not strike the whole land with utter destruction.[12]

In envisioning a messianic figure acting as a harbinger of the end-time, the passage transitions well into Jesus' genealogy, chronicled in the first verses of the New Testament:

An account of the genealogy of Jesus the Messiah, the son of David, the son of Abraham.

Abraham was the father of Isaac, and Isaac the father of Jacob, and Jacob the father of Judah and his brothers, and Judah the father of Perez and Zerah by Tamar, and Perez the father of Hezron, and Hezron the father of Aram, and Aram the father of Aminadab, and Aminadab the father of Nahshon, and Nahshon the father of Salmon, and Salmon the father of Boaz by Rahab, and Boaz the father of Obed by Ruth, and Obed the father of Jesse, and Jesse the father of King David. And David was the father of Solomon by the wife of Uriah, and Solomon the father of Rehoboam, and Rehoboam the father of Abijah, and Abijah the father of Asaph, and Asaph the father of Jehoshaphat, and Jehoshaphat the father of Joram, and Joram the father of Uzziah, and Uzziah the father of Jotham, and Jotham the father of Ahaz, and Ahaz the father of Hezekiah, and Hezekiah the father of Manasseh, and Manasseh the father of Amos, and Amos the father of Josiah, and Josiah the father of Jechoniah and his brothers, at the time of the deportation to Babylon.

And after the deportation to Babylon: Jechoniah was the father of Salathiel, and Salathiel the father of Zerubbabel, and Zerubbabel the father of Abiud, and Abiud the father of Eliakim, and Eliakim the father of Azor, and Azor the father of Zadok, and Zadok the father of Achim, and Achim the father of Eliud, and Eliud the father of Eleazar, and Eleazar the father of Matthan, and Matthan the father of Jacob, and Jacob the father of Joseph the husband of Mary, of whom Jesus was born, who is called the Messiah.

So all the generations from Abraham to David are fourteen generations; and from David to the deportation to Babylon, fourteen generations; and from the deportation to Babylon to the Messiah, fourteen generations.[13]

This ordering conveys a theological argument that associates Elijah with Jesus, but also implies that Jesus was the very figure whom Malachi envisioned would come and save the people.

The Jewish Hebrew Bible and the Christian Old Testament also differ in their ordering of what is known as the Five Scrolls: The Song of Songs, Ruth, Lamentations, Ecclesiastes, and Esther. In the Hebrew Bible, these books are preserved in the TANAKH's third section, Writings, in the calendrical order in which they are read on Jewish holidays: The Song of Songs, read on Passover during Nissan, the first month of the Hebrew year, comes first, followed by Ruth, read on the Festival of Weeks, two months later. Lamentations is then read on the summer fast day of the Ninth of Av, which commemorates the destruction of the First and Second Temples. Finally, Ecclesiastes and Esther are read on the fall holiday of Tabernacles and the late winter holiday of Purim, respectively.

Christians had no pragmatic use for preserving the Five Scrolls in this order. Instead, they ordered these books according to their historical contexts. They placed the book of Ruth, for example, after the book of Judges, because Ruth's opening verse notes that the story took place when "judges judged." And they preserved Esther after Chronicles, Ezra, and Nehemiah because its events take place in the Persian period, and Chronicles, Ezra, and Nehemiah focus on events in the early Persian period.

Overall, the Catholic, Eastern Orthodox, and Protestant Bibles make a clear structural distinction between genre: Their Bibles open with historical material, segue to poetry and wisdom, and close with biblical prophetic literature. These structures enable readers to easily find the material they seek. The structuring of the Hebrew Bible is not as formulaic.

The Aramaic *Targumim*

In the early Rabbinic period, Aramaic was the lingua franca of Jews living in Persia and the Land of Israel. Aramaic was spoken in many dialects by Jews, Christians, and pagans—from Syriac, in the region north of the Land of Israel, to what scholars call Palestinian Aramaic in Judea, to the

Babylonian Aramaic spoken in Babylonia by Jews who used this dialect to compose the Talmud. Because so many Jews at this time spoke Aramaic rather than Hebrew, Jews began to produce Aramaic translations of the Hebrew Bible. As we noted above, these translations are called *Targumim*, or *Targum* in the singular, which means "translation." The earliest *Targumim* were oral rather than written; the Mishnah notes that in Babylonian synagogues, a professional translator, or *meturgeman*, would translate the Torah verse by verse from Hebrew into Aramaic, so that congregants would understand the scriptures.[14]

Some Rabbinic texts express ambivalence toward the use of *Targumim*. The following passage in the Babylonian Talmud captures this ambivalence in a discussion regarding whether one may violate the Sabbath by moving books that contain translations of holy texts in order to save them from a fire:

> If [the Scriptures] are written in a Targum or in any [other] language, they may be saved from a fire ... R. Huna answered ... If [the Scriptures] are written in Egyptian, Median, Aramaic, Elamitic, or Greek, they may be saved from a fire, but they may not be read.[15]

This passage assumes that a Hebrew Bible may be moved on the Sabbath in order to save it from being destroyed. The ruling given here is that while translations of the Hebrew Bible may likewise be saved from a fire, they are not to be read in synagogue. This ruling kills two birds with one stone: It accords *Targumim* respect by linking them to the Hebrew Bible but refrains from placing *Targumim* on the same legal level as the Hebrew Bible.

The Talmud follows this ruling with a story that purportedly occurred in the first century CE:

> R. Yose said: My father Halafta once visited R. Gamaliel in Tiberias and found him sitting at Yohanan the son of Nizuf's table reading the targum of the Book of Job. [Halafta] said to [R. Gamaliel], "I remember that your grandfather R. Gamaliel stood on the Temple Mount, when the targum of

Job was given to him. [R. Gamaliel] said to the builder, 'Bury [the targum] under the bricks.'" [R. Gamaliel's grandson, R. Gamaliel] too gave orders, and they hid it.[16]

This passage indicates that Aramaic translations of certain biblical books were in circulation as early as the first century. Indeed, such *Targumim* were preserved at Qumran, including one on the book of Job. But this passage in the Talmud notes that prominent members of the Rabbinic community critiqued these books, and wanted them hidden. The Talmud also preserves an even more incriminatory passage protesting written Aramaic translations of the Hebrew Bible:

R. Jeremiah (according to some, R. Hiyya b. Abba) said: Onkelos the prose-lyte wrote the targum of the Pentateuch under the guidance of R. Eleazar and R. Joshua. Jonathan ben Uzziel wrote the targum of the Prophets under the guidance of Haggai, Zechariah and Malachi. [When he did so,] the Land of Israel quaked over an area of four hundred parasangs by four hundred parasangs, and a Heavenly Voice proclaimed, "Who has revealed My secrets to humankind?" Jonathan b. Uzziel answered, "I have revealed Your secrets to humankind. You know that I have not done this for my honor or for the honor of my father's house. I did it for Your honor, in order that dissension may not increase in Israel. [Jonathan b. Uzziel] then tried to reveal [the Scriptures by writing] a targum of the Hagiographa [that is, the Writings], but a Heavenly Voice went forth and said, "Enough." What was the reason [that God prevented him from writing this targum]? Because the date of the Messiah is foretold in it.[17]

In this passage, God grants Onkelos permission to write a *Targum* of the Torah, but when Jonathan ben Uzziel produces a *Targum* of the Prophets, it is met with divine wrath in the form of an earthquake. God then forbids Jonathan ben Uzziel from producing a *Targum* of the Writings section of the Bible, because it would make material concerning the coming of the Messiah too accessible and prone to misinterpretation. It is also possible that, according to this account, God does not want prophecies regarding the Messiah to be made available to gentiles. Jonathan's defense of his translation is that he seeks to avoid dissention in Israel. His argument implies that Jews were producing many explanations of the Bible in multiple languages, and some of these explanations were causing rifts with other Jews who rejected them. While establishing one accepted *Targum* would have helped to resolve these rifts, this passage reveals profound anxiety about disseminating translated scriptures to communities of Jews that did not have proficiency in Hebrew.

TARGUM ONQELOS

According to Rabbinic tradition, one of the most well-known *Targumim* of the Torah was written by a Roman named Onqelos who lived in the first century CE. After converting to Judaism, he wrote an Aramaic translation of the Torah, which Rabbinic texts regard as authoritative.

Many religious Jews today study Onqelos's *Targum* by following the calendar of the weekly Torah portion that is read each Saturday in synagogues. This practice derives from the teaching in the Babylonian Talmud to read the weekly Torah portion twice, and the *Targum* once.[18]

Onqelos usually renders the Hebrew Bible into literal Aramaic, but some of his translations are subtly interpretive and possibly polemical. In one instance, Onqelos seems aware of an interpretation that he seeks to refute. In the Hebrew Bible, when Rebecca is pregnant with Jacob and Esau, God tells her: "Two nations are in your womb, two separate people shall issue from your body; One people shall be mightier than the other, And the older shall serve the younger."[19]

Some of Jesus' early followers suggested a metaphorical interpretation of the verse: Rebecca and Isaac's older son symbolizes Judaism, and their younger son symbolizes Christianity. But Onqelos translates the verse: "And God said to her, 'two nations are in your womb, and two kingdoms will emerge from them. The stronger one will be made subservient to the weaker one.'"[20]

According to Onqelos, Rebecca's prophecy is not about an older son and a younger son, but about a stronger son and a weaker son. In this context, the stronger son is probably Rome, which will one day become subjugated to the weaker son, Judea. Since Onqelos was living at the time of the Romans' destruction of Jerusalem, his rendering of the verse as a prediction that a weaker power would one day defeat a stronger power would likely have resonated with his Jewish readers. If Onqelos is indeed alluding to Rome, then he is one of the earliest interpreters to identify the figure of Esau with Rome. The association between Esau and Rome would become increasingly prominent in midrashic literature.

TARGUM PSEUDO-JONATHAN

Every translation is an interpretation, and the *Targumim* are no exception. One *Targum* on the Torah in particular enters into full midrashic mode by inserting whole sentences that do not appear in the Hebrew Bible. *Targum Pseudo-Jonathan*, written by a Jew who came to be known as Pseudo-Jonathan because of an editor's mistake associating him with the first-century BCE sage Jonathan ben Uzziel, is also known as *Targum Yerushalmi* because it is thought to have originated in the Land of Israel. We know it came to completion after the rise of Islam, since the author identifies Ishmael's wives in Genesis 21:21 as Khadijah, the name of Muhammad's first wife, and Fatima, the name of their daughter. By identifying Ishmael's wives as Khadijah and Fatima, the *Targum* portrays Ishmael as the primary ancestor of Islam and implies that Ishmael violated the prohibition in Leviticus 18:17 not to marry a woman and her daughter.[21]

By the end of the Second Temple period, most Jews were not reading the Bible in Hebrew. The Rabbis, in turn, recognized the necessity of biblical translations, but sought to maintain a separation between the Hebrew scriptures, which represented the divine word, and translations of the scriptures, which represented human interpretation.

The transmission history of Aramaic *Targumim* had stops and starts, which may be related to Rabbinic ambivalence regarding these texts. Some *Targumim* that were well known to some Rabbis were unknown to others. In response to the Talmud's reference to *Targumim* on the Hallel prayer and the book of Esther, for example, the eleventh-century talmudist Rabbi

Shlomo Itzchaki (known as Rashi) notes that the talmudic text should be emended, because no such *Targum* to the Writings exists. The Tosafists, the talmudists who commented on and often refuted Rashi, point out that he is incorrect: These *Targumim* do exist.[22] This debate is a poignant reminder that, even in post–Second Temple times, Jewish communities did not have access to the same documents.

While the notion of sacred scriptures was well in place by the end of the Second Temple period, Jews at this time enjoyed a higher degree of fluidity when it came to the notion of authoritative texts. It would not be until the Rabbinic period that Jews confronted the question of what books were to be included in or excluded from the biblical canon.

The translation of the Hebrew scriptures into other languages increased Jews' access to these books. But it also raised the question of whether the Hebrew scriptures held a unique place in Jewish tradition. As we will see in chapter 12, Jews in the late Second Temple period were not only translating biblical passages but at times even rewriting them.

CHAPTER 12

Rewriting the Bible

If the Bible was a house, then the stories written by Jews in the late Second Temple period are the house's embellishments: the landscaping, the decorative flourishes, and the fixings that resolve or distract from perceived weaknesses in the original foundation.

But how did Jews at this time perceive the relationship between the foundation and its embellishments, that is, between biblical texts and what we sometimes call "postbiblical" texts? There is no evidence that they made a formal distinction between texts that were canonized *into* Scripture, and texts that were written *about* Scripture. But as we noted in chapter 11, virtually all Jews would have agreed that the Torah contained divinely inspired retellings of Israel's earliest national history. And, sometime during the Second Temple period, Jews began to rewrite these stories about their early history. Given how many such rewritings have survived, one can only imagine how many more were composed that were not preserved for two millennia.

The term "Rewritten Bible" is controversial. Geza Vermes, a scholar of the Dead Sea Scrolls, first introduced it in 1961 in reference to texts written in the Second Temple period that were related to but not canonized into Scripture. In recent years, the term has come under criticism for two reasons. First, it falsely implies that all Second Temple writers shared a common concept of a closed twenty-four-book Bible. Second, the term suggests that all of the authors who wrote texts related to the Bible were seeking to rewrite it. The term Rewritten Bible therefore presumes motivations that Second Temple authors did not necessarily have.

One solution is to use the term "Rewritten Bible" narrowly by making it solely applicable to texts that retell biblical stories but, as far as we know, were never considered canonical. Texts that loosely relate to biblical stories, but do not seem to rewrite them, could be referred to as "parabiblical texts," a term introduced by Sidnie White Crawford.[1]

Even with these limitations, it is almost impossible to determine precisely which books Jews considered to be canonical, and in which communities. If there was a deliberate method of categorizing books at this time, the criteria for determining the status of each book could have differed from community to community.

Why Did Jews Rewrite Biblical Stories?

A number of factors motivated Jews to compose or rewrite stories related to the Bible in the Second Temple period. First, challenging questions arose when the Jews read their scriptures. Many stories seemed to be unnecessarily detailed, while others provided minimal information that left the reader with more questions than answers. Sometimes one narrative directly conflicted with another. Other times, stories were ethically problematic. To address these discrepancies, extraneous details, contradictions, and ethically concerning material, Jews composed stories that supplemented or revised the ones they already had.

Second, Jews who wanted to engage with the outside world sought to present their biblical heroes as individuals who embodied Greco-Roman values. To this end, they depicted figures such as Abraham as a wise philosopher, astrologer, or mathematician. These portrayals, and others like them, rebutted Greek and Roman writers who challenged the integrity of the Jewish people by circulating legends that suggested that the ancient Israelites, and the Jews of the present, were not contributors to society but threats to its well-being.

The Legacy of Abraham

Abraham's family was a favorite subject for Jews writing in the late Second Temple period. Many authors perceived Abraham and his family as the first "Jews," and were intrigued by the adventures, conflicts, and divine encounters they experienced. Readers must have wondered how the Abrahamic family worshiped their God, and whether that worship looked similar to Jewish practices in their own day. In many retellings of the Patriarchal narratives, Abraham and his descendants observe the Jewish holidays, reject idolatry, scrupulously practice circumcision, and separate themselves from pagan life. Other Jewish texts present Abraham in more universal terms, as the father of all humankind.

THE BOOK OF JUBILEES

While we already discussed Jubilees in chapter 9, we will briefly return to it in this chapter to consider how Jubilees expands the stories about Abraham and his family. Jubilees emphasizes that the Patriarchs observed all of God's commandments, including holidays that commemorate events in Israelite history that occurred *after* the Patriarchs lived. The author tells us, for example, that Abraham observed the Festival of Weeks and the Festival of Tabernacles by offering sacrifices, even though there is no evidence in the Hebrew Bible that the Patriarchs were aware of these holidays. Jubilees clarifies that the Patriarchs were aware of the Israelites' destiny because God appeared to them in prophetic visions and informed them of what was to come. In Jubilees' retelling of Abraham's circumcision, for example, God reveals to Abraham that in the future the Israelites will neglect this law. Jubilees condemns these Israelites to permanent excommunication and exile:

> And now I shall announce to you that the sons of Israel will deny this ordinance and they will not circumcise their sons according to all of this law because some of the flesh of their circumcision they will leave in the circumcision of their sons. And all of the sons of Beliar will leave their sons without circumcising just as they were born. And great wrath from the LORD will be upon the sons of Israel because they have left His covenant and have turned aside from His words. And they have provoked and blasphemed inasmuch as they have not done the ordinance of this law

because they have made themselves like the Gentiles to be removed and be uprooted from the land. And there is therefore for them no forgiveness or pardon so that they might be pardoned and forgiven from all of the sins of this eternal error.[2]

Jubilees predicts that there will come a time when the "sons of Beliar" will not circumcise their sons. Beliar is a satanic figure who appears in late Second Temple literature as part of God's divine retinue and who seeks to cause the downfall of God's Chosen People. Jubilees' condemnation of Jews who do not practice circumcision is part of a larger debate occurring at this time between Jews who favored integrating into Hellenistic society by either not practicing circumcision or concealing it, and Jews who believed that circumcision must be observed. The author expresses his disapproval toward Jews who neglect circumcision by depicting God as warning Abraham that these Jews would not receive divine forgiveness.

Jubilees seeks to clarify the moral standing of figures who are portrayed ambiguously in the Patriarchal narratives. The author views Esau, for example, as a sympathetic character. In the Bible, when Jacob receives word that his estranged brother Esau is coming to meet him, he assumes that Esau is planning to instigate a war. While the two brothers reconcile, Esau's original intention remains ambiguous. In Jubilees, however, Esau has good intentions toward Jacob from the outset. Only Esau's sons bear ill will toward Jacob on account of his having wrested the birthright from their father.[3]

As we have noted, Jubilees follows the biblical account by presenting the Matriarch Rebecca in powerful terms. In both the Bible and Jubilees, Rebecca functions almost as a Patriarch by taking personal responsibility for overseeing the welfare of her children and the continuity of her family dynasty. Jubilees even expands on Rebecca's role by citing a lengthy last will and testament that Rebecca delivers to her sons just before her death that instructs them in proper conduct.[4] Since Abraham and Jacob give similar speeches, this addition suggests that the author perceives

Rebecca, and not her husband, Isaac, as the parent whom God tasks with preserving the Abrahamic dynasty.

Jubilees' portrayals of Esau and Rebecca indicate that the author's motivation was not to turn biblical characters into one-dimensional heroes in order to present the Patriarchs and Matriarchs in the best light but to skillfully resolve problems that readers may have encountered in the biblical text. In the cases of Esau and Rebecca, these questions may have been, "How could Esau have had murderous enmity toward Jacob, if Isaac believed Esau to be righteous?" (Answer: Esau's sons were responsible for this enmity), and "Why was Rebecca successful in ensuring that Jacob received Isaac's blessing, even though he was not the eldest and therefore not entitled to a blessing?" (Answer: Rebecca was a prophetess who was fulfilling God's will by making sure that Isaac gave Jacob, rather than Esau, a firstborn blessing.)

While the author of Jubilees picks up on small details in the biblical text, he also wants his readers to perceive Israelite history as consisting of patterns that reflect a larger divine plan for God's elect people. The fifty-jubilee duration between Adam's creation and the Israelites' entry into the Land of Israel is a good example of such a pattern.[5] Noting that exactly fifty jubilees elapsed between these periods would have offered readers in the Second Temple period hope for better times, since, as James Kugel notes, "the apparent disorder of a few hundred years disappears when you consider these larger patterns."[6]

THE GENESIS APOCRYPHON

The Aramaic text known today as the Genesis Apocryphon was written in Judea in the late Second Temple period. Its surviving segments, discovered in one of the Dead Sea caves near Qumran, begin with the illicit relationship between angels and human women in Genesis 6:1, and close with God's promise in Genesis 15 to provide Abram with continuity by giving him both land and children.

Many of the Genesis Apocryphon's retellings diverge from the scriptural account by inserting information where there are narrative gaps.

In Genesis 12, for example, when Abram and Sarai (their names become Abraham and Sarah in Genesis 17) are about to enter Egypt, Abram tells Sarai to inform the Egyptians that she is Abram's sister, explaining that if Pharaoh discovers that they are married, he will kill Abram. After obeying Abram, Sarai is abducted by Pharaoh's officials and brought to Pharaoh, whereupon God brings a plague on Pharaoh and his household. The plague leads Pharaoh to understand that Abram's God disapproves of his taking Sarai, and he subsequently releases her to Abram. In the biblical account, Abram expresses no concern over Sarai's welfare. In the Genesis Apocryphon, however, Abram is overwhelmed with distress following her abduction. The author also adds dramatic elements that underscore Abram's philanthropy and wisdom, as well as Sarai's beauty. The account opens with Abram having a dream on the eve of his entry into Egypt:

> And I, Abram, dreamt a dream on the night that I entered the land of Egypt. I saw in my dream a cedar tree and a palm tree . . . together from [one] roo[t]. People came, seeking to chop down and to uproot the [ce]dar tree and to spare only the palm tree. Now the palm tree cried out and said, "Don't cut down the [c]edar, for both of us have [sprouted] from one root," and the cedar tree was spared for the sake of the palm tree and was not chopped down. I awoke in the night from my sleep and said to Sarai, my wife, "I dreamt a dream . . . [I] am afraid [because of] this dream." She said to me, "Tell me your dream that I may know (it)." So I began to tell her my dream and said to [her] ". . . dream . . . that they will seek to kill me and to spare you. But this is all the favour that [you can/must do for me]: every[where] that [we go say] of me, 'He is my brother,' that I may live for your sake and my life will be spared on your account . . . to ta[ke] you away from me and to kill me." And Sarai cried at my words on that night.[7]

Abram dreams that men who intend to cut down a certain cedar tree abandon their plan when a palm tree begs them to spare the cedar. Upon waking, Abram understands that the cedar tree is a stand-in for him, and the palm tree symbolizes Sarai. The cedar, known for being durable and valuable, is used to build homes and other structures; Abram is likewise a strong leader whose influence makes him a valuable commodity. His survival is necessary in order to build the Israelite nation. The palm tree, known for being beautiful, delicate, and bearing delicious fruit, symbolizes Sarai, whose fertility is potentially important to the development of the Israelite nation, but whose survival is not as foundational to the Israelite people. Abram understands that as the "cedar," he must prioritize his survival over Sarai's survival upon their entry into Egypt. And just as the palm tree saves the cedar tree from danger, Abram recognizes that Sarai must save him by claiming to be his sister rather than his wife.

Whereas in the biblical version, Abram decides on his own that Sarai should conceal her marriage from Pharaoh, the Genesis Apocryphon indicates that this strategy is divinely ordained through a prophetic dream, which absolves Abram of responsibility for endangering Sarai. When Sarai cries upon hearing Abram's interpretation of the dream in the Genesis Apocryphon, Abram is empathetic toward her. And after she is abducted, Abram also cries:

> That night I prayed, entreated and asked for mercy, and I said in sorrow— with my tears running down— "Blessed are you, Lord Most High, Lord for all eternities. For you are Lord and Sovereign over all. You are empowered over all the kings of the earth to mete out justice. Now, I place my complaint before you, regarding Pharaoh Zoan, king of Egypt, because my wife has been taken away from me by force. Mete out justice to him for me, and show your great hand against him and all his household; let him not be allowed this night to defile my wife for me! Then they will all know you my Lord, that you are the Lord of all the kings of the earth." I cried and fell silent. That night God Most High sent a spirit of affliction to afflict him and all the people of his household—an evil spirit—and it afflicted [Pharaoh] and all the people of his household, so that he was unable to touch her, nor did he have intercourse with her, though she was with him for two years.[8]

The Genesis Apocryphon's retelling of Genesis 12 features two popular motifs that appear often in Second Temple literature: divinely sent dreams or visions, and prayers uttered by a hero in a time of crisis. These tropes appear together in texts such as 2 Maccabees, when the Jews pray for salvation from Antiochus IV Epiphanes, and God consequently sends two "remarkably strong, gloriously beautiful, and splendidly dressed" angelic messengers to attack the Greek general Heliodorus.[9] They also appear together in the Greek version of Esther, when Mordecai dreams of a major conflict between the Jews and the foreign nations. After Mordecai interprets his dream in detail, he declares that the prayers of the Jews have led to their salvation.[10] While 2 Maccabees and Greek Esther were written in Greek, and the Genesis Apocryphon was written in Aramaic, it is possible that all three texts participate in a common interpretive tradition that transcends language and shares key themes.

ARTAPANUS

Aware that some Greek writers described the Jews' early history in decidedly uncomplimentary ways,many Jewish intellectuals tried to restore the integrity of the Jewish religion by portraying the Jewish Patriarchs as the greatest of heroes.[11] One such figure was Artapanus, who lived sometime between the middle of the third century BCE and the early first century BCE.[12]

In his rewriting of select portions of the scriptures, Artapanus portrays biblical figures such as Abraham and Moses as mastering scientific disciplines and embodying virtues that were valued by the Greeks and Romans of his day. He also actively engages in an ongoing debate among Second Temple interpreters regarding whether Abraham studied astrology. While some, such as Philo and the author of Jubilees, praise Abraham for his rejection of astrology, Artapanus's Abraham is an expert in astrology who teaches this discipline to the Egyptians.[13] Josephus would later make the same claim about Abraham. As we will see later in this chapter, Artapanus likewise presents Moses as a great intellectual and formidable warrior.

THE TESTAMENT OF ABRAHAM

This intriguing novella probably originated in the first century CE from the intellectual hub of Alexandria or Antioch. Scholars see the work as a humorous parody of what is known as the testament genre, a genre in which a biblical hero imparts his last words of wisdom to his children. Many medieval manuscripts of such testaments have been preserved, among them the Testament of Jacob, the Testament of Isaac, and the Testaments of the Twelve Patriarchs. The Testament of Abraham, however, is different from all of these books. Instead of portraying Abraham as a wise sage serenely providing his descendants with advice on the cusp of his death, the author writes what one might call an "untestament." In this story God sends the archangel Michael to retrieve Abraham from earth and to bring him into the afterlife, but Abraham resists Michael at every turn, prompting a despairing Michael to request that God choose someone else to carry out this task. God then sends the Angel of Death to retrieve Abraham. While he is initially unsuccessful, the Angel of Death ultimately tricks Abraham into dying by having Abraham touch him.

The Testament of Abraham features entertaining twists and turns. At times, the tone is humorous, as when Michael shows up in God's heavenly court once again without Abraham. At other times, the tone is serious, as when Isaac learns in a dream of Abraham's imminent death. The story comes to a climax after Abraham tells Michael that he will not willingly follow him into the afterlife unless he is shown two visions: one of all humanity, and one of how souls are divinely judged after they depart from their bodies. Michael acquiesces, and leads Abraham into a chariot that flies over the earth so that Abraham can observe all humanity. In this vision, Abraham sees people below him committing murder, theft, and sexual impropriety. He commands that these sinners be killed, and God obliges by striking them dead. After Abraham makes three such commands, God abruptly ends the trip, explaining that, unlike Abraham, God leaves sinners alive in the hopes that they may repent:

And he saw in another place people digging into a house and stealing other people's possessions, and he said, "Lord, Lord, command that fire may come down from heaven and consume them." Even as he spoke, fire came down from heaven and consumed them. Straightway, there came a voice from heaven to the commander-in-chief, saying thus, "Commander-in-chief Michael, command the chariot to stop! Turn Abraham away so that he may not see all the earth, for if he beheld all who live in wickedness, he would destroy all creation! For behold, Abraham has not sinned and has no pity on sinners."[14]

After their chariot ride, Michael takes Abraham to the place where souls are judged upon departing from their bodies. Abraham watches as sinful souls are brought to hell and righteous souls are brought to heaven. He then observes a soul who has an equal number of good and bad deeds. When Abraham and Michael pray to God on its behalf, this soul is saved and brought to heaven.

The figure of Abraham in the Testament of Abraham is clearly incongruous with the biblical image of Abraham. In fact, he is the foil of his biblical counterpart. Rather than asking God to save a city on account of a few people's good deeds, as he does in Genesis 18, Abraham insists that God should kill sinners before giving them a chance to repent. And rather than serving God's messengers in diffident obedience, as he does when three messengers visit him in Genesis 18 following his circumcision, Abraham makes a mockery of divine messengers by repeatedly defying their orders to accompany them into the afterlife.

On the other hand, Abraham's generosity and eagerness to accommodate guests are present in both the Bible and the Testament of Abraham. It is possible that the author of the Testament of Abraham preserved these attributes to link his story with the biblical account, and to impress Hellenized Jewish (and perhaps also gentile) readers who valued these qualities. Abraham's piety in this book also underscores the ironic parody of his disobedient behavior.

Many scholars believe that the author of the Testament of Abraham was a Jew who penned a clever satire that other Jews would have found entertaining. At the same time, the author may have been targeting a gentile audience who would have found the book's humorous qualities appealing as well. Since the author makes no mention of distinctively Jewish practices but instead emphasizes Abraham's virtues (or lack thereof), this text could have been easily enjoyed by a variety of audiences.

THE TESTAMENTS OF THE TWELVE PATRIARCHS

As we noted in chapter 6, the collection of twelve books written in Greek and known as the Testaments of the Twelve Patriarchs builds on Abraham's legacy by recalling the parting messages that his great-grandchildren, Jacob's sons, leave for their progeny on their deathbeds. Its references to levirate marriage and Jewish laws of mourning, as well as positive references to the Temple and the priesthood, suggest that at least in an early stage, the collection was authored by a Jew, or by a number of Jews, perhaps in the first century CE.[15] A fragment known as the Aramaic Levi Document, as well as a Hebrew fragment that looks similar to the Testament of Naphtali preserved in Greek, have been discovered in the Dead Sea caves and suggest that the author of the Testaments of the Twelve Patriarchs relied on older sources that were written in Hebrew and Aramaic.[16]

The testaments in this collection offer interpretive insights on biblical stories about Jacob's sons. In the Testament of Reuben, for example, which underscores the importance of sexual purity, Reuben recalls how he slept with his father's concubine Bilhah but expands on the biblical version by asserting that Bilhah was innocent of wrongdoing.[17] In doing so, Reuben takes full responsibility for his sin while presenting himself as pious at the same time. The Testament of Levi also supplements the Patriarchal narratives with added detail by maintaining that Levi, rather than his descendent Aaron, is assigned the first Israelite priesthood. By arguing that priestly leadership derives from the early period of the Patriarchs, the author effectively highlights the centrality of priestly service in Israelite tradition.

The author (or authors) of the Testaments of the Twelve Patriarchs had specific ideas about the hierarchical structure of the twelve tribes and about each tribe's role in the future restoration of Israel. This restoration was to be led by descendants of Judah and Levi, who would become kings and priests over Israel in the end-time. The Testament of Naphtali offers a clear articulation of these roles:

> And in the fortieth year of my life, I had a vision on the Mount of Olives, to the east of Jerusalem, that the sun and the moon were standing still. And behold, Isaac, my father's father, said to us: Run and [try to] seize, each of you as best he can, and the sun and the moon will belong to whoever manages to take hold of them. And we all ran together and Levi got the sun, and then Judah was the first to seize the moon, and both of them were lifted up with them. And Levi was like the sun, and a certain young man gave him twelve palm branches; and Judah was shining like the moon and beneath his feet were twelve rays [of light]. And Levi and Judah ran toward each other and took hold of each other.[18]

Levi's outrunning his brothers and seizing the sun symbolizes his destiny to become the priestly leader over the Israelites. Judah, depicted as "luminous like the moon," is to act as second-in-command to Levi. While Judah was traditionally known as the progenitor of the monarchy, this testament suggests that the monarchs who descend from Judah will be subject to the Temple priests' authority.

The Testament of Reuben also presents Judah as subordinate to Levi. This testament even portrays Levi in a monarchic role, as Reuben instructs his sons to "approach Levi in humbleness of heart, so that you may receive a blessing from his mouth. He shall bless Israel and Judah; for the Lord has chosen him to be king over all peoples. Bow down to his descendants, for they have died on our behalf in visible and invisible battles, and they will be king[s] in you forever."[19] Perhaps most surprising of all is that Judah himself declares Levi to be superior to him. In the Testament of Judah, Judah declares that "to me the Lord gave kingship, and to Levi the priesthood, and he put kingship beneath the priesthood."[20] Some testaments, however, do present Levi and Judah on equal terms. This discrepancy is one of many clues that indicate that one author was unlikely to have composed all twelve of these testaments.[21]

Joseph also plays a key role in the Testaments of the Twelve Patriarchs.

Unlike Levi and Judah, who are regarded as religious and political leaders, Joseph functions as an embodiment of ethical perfection. The Testament of Joseph, the Testament of Reuben, and the Testament of Simeon in particular highlight Joseph's virtuous behavior and emphasize his total self-control. Joseph's reputation derives from his resistance to the sexual overtures of Potiphar's wife in Genesis 39. Furthermore, his ability to thrive in Pharaoh's court while displaying unwavering loyalty to his ancestral tradition no doubt contributed to the fact that in this collection and elsewhere in Second Temple literature, Joseph is the model of devotional commitment and self-restraint.

One example of Joseph's function as a paragon of virtue appears in the Testament of Reuben. Contrasting his own sexual promiscuity with Joseph's ability to control his sexual desires, Reuben tells his sons:

Licentiousness has brought many [people] to ruin; even if someone is old or of noble birth, it brings upon him the reproof of the sons of men and is a stumbling block of Beliar. It was because Joseph guarded himself from a woman and purified his thoughts from any licentiousness that he found favor in the sight of God and men. For the Egyptian woman did many things to him, and called out magicians and brought him love potions, yet the disposition of his soul did not accept any evil desire. That is why the God of our fathers saved him from any visible or hidden death. For if licentiousness cannot overcome your mind, Beliar cannot overcome you.[22]

Joseph's mastery over his physical desires thus serves as the author's basis for presenting Joseph as the embodiment of total virtue.

In the Testament of Simeon, moreover, Simeon emphasizes Joseph's ability to forgive those who wronged him: "And Joseph was a good man and he had the spirit of God in him, merciful and compassionate, and he did not bear a grudge against me but even loved me, as he did all the other brothers."[23] While the authors of this collection view Levi and Judah as priestly and kingly rulers over Israel, the universally admirable traits attributed to Joseph in the Testaments of the Twelve Patriarchs point to the fact that it is Joseph who is meant to be emulated.[24]

Moses and the Nation of Israel

The figure of Moses and his role in the formation of the Israelite people were important to Jewish authors in the Second Temple period, who were aware of Greek and Roman legends suggesting that the origins of the Jewish people were ignominious. In seeking to counter these claims, Jewish authors presented Moses as embodying virtues that Greeks and Romans admired, such as bravery, integrity, patriotism, and intellect.

ARTAPANUS

Based on Artapanus's description of Abraham, which we discussed earlier in this chapter, it will come as no surprise that Artapanus also presents Moses in a way that would have impressed readers familiar with Greek and Roman ideals of virtue. In Artapanus's account, Moses is a philosopher and a warrior who unites Egypt and assists a local ruler named Chenephres in taking control over Egypt. Chenephres grows jealous of Moses' popularity and amasses an army to wage war against him, but Moses defeats him. Chenephres' antipathy toward Moses compels Moses to escape to Arabia, where he encounters God in a fiery vision. In this vision, God tells Moses to return to Egypt to lead the Israelites out of the land. Artapanus's introduction to this story is typical of his embellished style:

> When [Moses] became a man, he was called Mousaios by the Greeks. This Moses became the teacher of Orpheus. When he reached manhood, he bestowed on humanity many useful contributions, for he invented ships, machines for lifting stones, Egyptian weapons, devices for drawing water and fighting, and philosophy. He also divided the state into thirty-six nomes, and to each of the nomes he assigned the god to be worshipped; in addition, he assigned the sacred writing to the priests. . . . He did all these things for the sake of keeping the monarchy stable for Chenephres, for prior to this time the masses were disorganized and they would sometimes depose, sometimes install rulers, often the same persons, but sometime others. Thus, for these reasons Moses was loved by the masses, and being

deemed worthy of divine honor by the priests, he was called Hermes because of his ability to interpret the sacred writings.[25]

By underscoring Moses' contributions to Egyptian society and his loyalty to Chenephres, Artapanus presents Moses as a model citizen who contributes to society, has no ambitions for social advancement, and never poses a threat to his host empire. Like the Israelites of ancient times, Artapanus implies, Jews living in the Greco-Roman world who admire such heroes must also be model subjects who want only to improve the welfare of their host empire.

Artapanus's association of Moses with Hermes, the Greek messenger god, is also significant. Hermes was known to travel between the earthly physical world and the world of the gods, and Moses, who had more access to God than anyone else in human history, appears to travel between the physical world and the celestial world, appealing to God to forgive the Israelites' sins, and entreating the Israelites to obey God's will. Artapanus's association of Moses with Hermes cleverly reminds his readers that the Jewish tradition boasts heroes whose abilities rival those of the Greek gods.

PSEUDO-PHILO

Scholars refer to the author of *Liber Antiquitatum Biblicarum* (*LAB*), or the "Book of Biblical Antiquities," as Pseudo-Philo, or "False Philo," because in the medieval period his work was transmitted in Latin alongside Latin translations of Philo's treatises.[26] Yet Pseudo-Philo's work is entirely unlike the material that Philo produced. For one thing, the two authors wrote in different languages; *LAB* was probably composed in Hebrew, while Philo wrote in Greek. Philo also uses a philosophical vocabulary when writing about the scriptures and focuses on the allegorical meanings of biblical stories or philosophical aspects of biblical laws.

Pseudo-Philo, on the other hand, is unconcerned with philosophical ideas. His intention is to retell biblical stories from the time of Adam through the time of King Saul's death, and, in doing so, he redistributes the amount of attention given to some of these stories. Pseudo-Philo condenses the Bible's fifteen chapters detailing the Exodus from Egypt into just seven verses, but devotes twenty-five verses to the revelation at Sinai and the story of the Golden Calf. By emphasizing these latter two stories, the author presents Moses as a conveyor of God's law rather than an independent leader and an antagonist of the Egyptians. Perhaps the author wanted to make it unambiguously clear that the Israelite God is the one and only agent responsible for the Exodus, and that God, not Moses, should be credited for the Israelites' leaving Egypt. This may be why Pseudo-Philo inserts phrases that highlight divine providence. When Moses strikes the sea and causes it to split, for example, Pseudo-Philo adds that it was God who split it, and not Moses:

> And God said, "Since you have cried out to me, lift up your rod and strike the sea, and it will be dried up." Moses did all this and God raged at the sea and dried it up. The streams of water stood up and the depths of the earth became visible, and the foundations of the world were laid bare by the fearful roar of God and by the breath of the anger of the Lord.[27]

The account in the Hebrew Bible is markedly different:

> Then the Lord said to Moses, "Why do you cry out to Me? Tell the Israelites to go forward. And you lift up your rod and hold out your arm over the sea and split it, so that the Israelites may march into the sea on dry ground. And I will stiffen the hearts of the Egyptians so that they go in after them; and I will gain glory through Pharaoh and all his warriors, his chariots and his horsemen. Let the Egyptians know that I am Lord, when I gain glory through Pharaoh, his chariots, and his horsemen." The angel of God, who had been going ahead of the Israelite army, now moved and followed behind them; and the pillar of cloud shifted from in front of them and took up a place behind them, and it came between the army of the Egyptians and the army of Israel. Thus there was the cloud with the darkness, and it cast a spell upon the night, so that the one could not come near the other all through the night. Then Moses held out his arm

over the sea and the Lord drove back the sea with a strong east wind all that night, and turned the sea into dry ground. The waters were split, and the Israelites went into the sea on dry ground, the water forming a wall for them on their right and on their left.[28]

The Bible credits three figures for saving the Israelites: God, Moses, and the angel of God. Moses holds his rod over the sea, and when he does, an easterly wind splits the sea. The angel of God leads the Israelites out of Egypt, first from the front and later from behind. While God executes the actual miracle, Moses and the angel of God are nonetheless agents in the miracle, guiding the Israelites to freedom. In Pseudo-Philo's version, however, God controls all the action, intervening to save the Israelites both out of mercy for them and out of wrath toward their enemies.

This shift in perspective is evident in other details of the story. In the biblical version, the Israelites call out to God in fear as the Egyptians advance toward them, and God responds to their cries with a question: "Why do you cry out to Me?" Pseudo-Philo, on the other hand, changes the question to a statement: "Since you have cried out to me." God's question in the Bible implies that the Israelites' cries have little effect on God, who expects the Israelites to stop wailing and move toward the Red Sea. In Pseudo-Philo's account, however, God responds directly to the Israelites' prayers by acting mercifully. Pseudo-Philo thus portrays God as the sole unyielding advocate for the Israelite people.

Pseudo-Philo paints Moses as a zealous leader devoted to God and God's Law. His retelling of the Golden Calf incident is a good example of this portrayal. When God tells Moses that the Israelites have built a Golden Calf and have been worshiping it in Moses' absence, Moses hurries down the mountain and, after catching sight of the scene below, breaks the tablets that God has given him. In Pseudo-Philo's account:

Moses descended in haste and saw the calf. He looked at the tablets and saw that they were not written upon, and agitated, he smashed them. He stretched out his hands; and he became like a woman in labor with her first child who, when she is seized by pains, her hands are upon her chest and she has no strength to aid her delivery. After one hour he said to himself, "Does bitterness persist always, and does evil prevail forever? Now I will rise up and gird my loins, because even if they have sinned, what was declared to me on high will not be in vain." He arose and smashed the calf and cast it into the water and made the people drink of it. Whoever had it in his will and mind that the calf be made, his tongue was cut off; but whoever had consented under compulsion of fear, his face shone.[29]

Pseudo-Philo follows the account in Exodus 32 regarding why Moses broke the tablets. The biblical account reads: "As soon as Moses came near the camp and saw the calf and the dancing, he became enraged; and he hurled the tablets from his hands and shattered them at the foot of the mountain."[30]

In both Exodus 32 and Pseudo-Philo's account, Moses watches the Israelites dancing around the calf at the foot of the mountain and seems intent on punishing the Israelites by breaking the tablets. But Pseudo-Philo's version of this incident differs slightly—and significantly. In Exodus, God tells Moses in advance of his descent from the mountain that the Israelites have built a Golden Calf, but it is only when Moses sees them worshiping the calf that he responds by spontaneously, impulsively—and perhaps vindictively—breaking the tablets. In Pseudo-Philo's account, however, Moses notices that the writing on the tablets has disappeared, and realizes that God no longer approves of the Israelites receiving such a great gift. He consequently breaks the tablets. In this scene, Moses makes a more calculated decision to deprive the people of a gift that he recognizes they no longer deserve.

Pseudo-Philo notes, moreover, that during this ordeal, Moses loses all of his strength, as if he were a woman in labor. Comparing Moses' pain to the pain of a woman in labor, an image that is absent from the biblical account of this story, elegantly underscores Moses' nurturing relationship with the Israelites.

In Pseudo-Philo's retelling, Moses is a deliberate and wise leader who cares deeply for the Israelites. Yet his position as leader is only significant in that he functions as a mediator between God and the people. Moses' achievements go only as far as the Israelites' own commitment to observe God's Law.

EZEKIEL THE TRAGEDIAN

The second-century BCE poet Ezekiel the Tragedian is known for his poem, entitled *Exagogue*, the Greek word for Exodus, in which he retells the story of Exodus 1–15. Ezekiel must have been familiar with the Greek literary traditions of his day, since the poem is composed in iambic trimeter, a popular meter in contemporaneous Greek poetry.

Ezekiel embellishes aspects of Moses' upbringing, adolescence, and tenure as leader of the Israelites. In his account of Moses' time in Midian, for example, Moses tells his father-in-law, Raguel, of a vision he has had:

> I had a vision of a great throne on the top of Mount Sinai
> and it reached till the folds of heaven.
> A noble man was sitting on it,
> with a crown and a large scepter in his
> left hand. He beckoned to me with his right hand,
> so I approached and stood before the throne.
> He gave me the scepter and instructed me to sit
> on the great throne. Then he gave me the royal crown
> and got up from the throne.
> I beheld the whole earth all around and saw
> beneath the earth and above the heavens.
> A multitude of stars fell beneath my knees
> and I counted them all.
> They paraded past me like a battalion of men.
> Then I awoke from my sleep in fear.[31]

In this vision, Moses approaches God's throne and is then taken on a trip through the heavens during which he looks out over the entire earth. From there he traverses the celestial spheres. This two-part trip is reminiscent of Abraham's adventures in the Testament of Abraham, in which Abraham observes human activity from a chariot that travels through the heavens and afterward witnesses the divine judgment of souls in the afterlife. The theme of a pious individual being divinely selected to observe mysterious heavenly images appears in other Second Temple books as well, such as Daniel and 1 Enoch. Ezekiel may have been influenced by a popular narrative framework in which God chooses a biblical hero to witness a celestial or apocalyptic vision.

Prophetic dreams are also frequently featured in the Hebrew Bible and in late Second Temple literature. In Genesis 37 and 40–41, for example, Joseph interprets his dreams to mean that his brothers will become subservient to him, and later interprets the dreams of his prison mates and Pharaoh. In the Septuagint's Greek version of Esther, Mordecai dreams of two dragons battling one another, which signifies a future conflict between Haman and Mordecai. And as we noted above, the Genesis Apocryphon describes Abram's dream that indicates that Sarai is to risk her well-being in order to save Abram's life.[32] Moses' vision in *Exagogue* is emblematic of a tendency among Jewish writers working in the Second Temple period to insert divinely sent visions and dreams into retellings of biblical stories. They likely saw themselves as building on a precedent in the Scriptures, which feature dreams and visions that are central to the stories in which they appear.

Unfortunately, *Exagogue* does not survive as an independent text. We have only fragmented quotations of it in the writings of the third-century CE church historian Eusebius of Caesarea, the late second-century to early third-century CE Church Father Clement of Alexandria, and Pseudo-Eustathius, who probably lived sometime in the fourth century CE.

Israelite History

Jewish writers in the late Second Temple period were intrigued by early Israelite history. They sought to make connections between their own experiences of suffering and the experiences of the early Israelites. By retelling or reimagining life in early Israel, these writers constructed a continuum of history that implied that the Jewish people had always faced challenges but were never entirely abandoned by their God.

THE BOOKS OF 2 BARUCH AND 4 EZRA

Written in the wake of the destruction of the Jerusalem Temple in 70 CE, 2 Baruch and 4 Ezra are considered pseudepigraphic, that is, falsely attributed to authors who did not write them.[33] These books were written in Greek, a language that Baruch, the scribe of Jeremiah the Prophet, who warned the Judeans of the Babylonian invasion, and Ezra, who helped to restore the Jewish community in the Land of Israel after the Babylonian exile, would not have known. By attributing their books to Baruch and Ezra, the authors (or later copyists) drew effective parallels between the destructions of the First and Second Temples.

Drawing these parallels would have conveyed important messages to Jewish readers. First, just as many Jews in the Second Temple period regarded the Babylonian exile to be a divine punishment for the Judeans' sins, so too the destruction of the Second Temple was a divine punishment for the Jews' sins. This segued well into the next inference: Just as the First Temple's destruction did not signal God's permanent abandonment of the Israelites but was a punishment meant to encourage them to repent, so too the Second Temple's destruction did not signal God's permanent abandonment of the Jews. The attribution of 4 Ezra to the biblical Ezra would have invited a third comparison as well: Just as God terminated the Babylonian exile with a restorative period, so too would the Jews soon enter another restorative period, and this one would permanently put an end to the suffering of all pious Jews.

The book of 2 Baruch asserts that the sinners among Israel are responsible for the people's suffering, and that righteous people will soon enjoy salvation. The book opens with a divine promise that in the upcoming end-time, sinners will endure terrible punishment:

> For the aspect of those who now act wickedly shall become worse than it is, as they shall suffer torment. Also as for the glory of those who have now

been justified in my law, who have had understanding in their life, and who have planted in their heart the root of wisdom, then their splendor shall be glorified in changes, and the form of their face shall be turned into the light of their beauty, that they may be able to acquire and receive the world which does not die, which is then promised to them. For over this above all shall those who come then lament, that they rejected my law, and stopped their ears that they might not hear wisdom or receive understanding. When therefore they see those, over whom they are now exalted, but who shall then be exalted and glorified more than they, they shall respectively be transformed, the latter into the splendor of angels, and the former shall yet more waste away in wonder at the visions and in the beholding of the forms. For they shall first behold and afterward depart to be tormented.[34]

The author of 4 Ezra also believes that the righteous will one day get their due but struggles with the question of why the elect people of God experience great suffering in the present time. In one vision, Ezra learns that in the end-time the majority of humankind will perish as punishment for their sins. According to an angel who speaks to Ezra:

The Most High made this world for the sake of many, but the world to come for the sake of only a few. But I tell you a parable, Ezra. Just as, when you ask the earth, it will tell you that it provides a large amount of clay from which earthenware is made, but only a little dust from which gold comes, so is the course of the present world. Many have been created, but only a few shall be saved.[35]

The authors of 2 Baruch and 4 Ezra may have been thinking of Jews who had assimilated into Roman life or had defected to the Romans when they declared that sinners would not be saved in the end-time. Both authors were struggling to understand Israel's relationship with God on the heels of the Second Temple's destruction. The conviction that the Jews had caused their own suffering would have enabled them to continue believing that God had not abandoned the people, and that the covenantal relationship that God had established with them at Sinai was still in effect. In such a relationship, God would punish the Jews for their sins but would never permanently abandon them.

Biblical Heroes of the Diaspora

As Jews settled throughout the Diaspora in the Second Temple period, they sought inspiration from characters in the Bible who did not live in the Land of Israel and yet were paradigms of piety and leadership. Daniel and Esther were two such figures. Second Temple writers expanded the biblical stories about Daniel and Esther to demonstrate that one could successfully practice the Jewish religion in the Diaspora and be a model citizen at the same time. As we will see, the Greek version of Esther seems even more pious than the Hebrew original.

DANIEL

Daniel was a popular hero in ancient Jewish folklore who was renowned for the respect he garnered in the Persian king's court and his commitment to his Jewish faith. The Septuagint preserves a number of stories about him: the tale of Susanna, the Prayer of Azariah and the Song of the Three Jews, and Bel and the Dragon.

The story of Susanna recalls a crisis endured by the beautiful and virtuous Susanna (*Shoshana* means "rose" in Hebrew), who is married to a wealthy man named Joakim in Babylon. One day, two wicked elders corner Susanna in her garden, threatening to accuse her of committing adultery if she refuses to have sex with them. Susanna rebuffs the elders, who then publicly claim that Susanna has committed adultery. The local Jewish magistrate is convened, and the elders convince those present that Susanna must be executed.

At this point, when the reader cannot help but wonder how Susanna's life can be spared, Daniel comes to the rescue. The author dramatically declares: "Just as she was being led off to execution, God stirred up the holy spirit of a young lad named Daniel, and he shouted with a loud voice, 'I want no part in shedding this woman's blood!'"[36] Demanding that

Susanna receive a trial, Daniel separates the elders from one another and interrogates them individually. When discrepancies in their accounts of the alleged adultery emerge, it becomes clear that Susanna is innocent of wrongdoing.

This story highlights two aspects of Daniel's personality that are also central to the first half of the biblical book of Daniel: his legal prowess and his religious piety. Daniel's piety is evident in his concern for others' well-being, especially for those who are vulnerable and powerless. While Susanna's story includes the titillating themes of sexuality and power, its message is that true piety lies in one's loyalty to the Jewish God. The author thus takes license in employing entertaining, and perhaps not entirely virtuous, themes, while advancing a pious worldview.

The Prayer of Azariah and the Song of the Three Jews similarly attests to Daniel's piety. This addition is embedded in the Septuagint between Daniel 3:23 and 3:24, within a tale about how Daniel and his three Jewish comrades, Azariah, Hananiah, and Mishael, are cast into a fiery furnace for refusing to worship idols, and miraculously survive.

Azariah sings the first song of prayer. Lamenting that the Jews' sufferings are a result of their sins, Azariah recalls the covenant that God made with the Patriarchs and emphasizes God's commitment to them and their descendants. By referencing the Patriarchal narratives, the author situates his story into the spectrum of Jewish national history. Azariah, Hananiah, and Mishael sing the second song, which is a hymn exhorting all elements of life to bless God. They open by directing the monumental elements of the universe that seem out of reach—the heavens, the angels, the waters, and the celestial spheres—to bless God. The companions then narrow their scope to more accessible elements, exhorting rain, wind, fire, and other natural elements on earth to bless God. Finally, the speakers address humankind, urging Israel, priests, and those who are righteous to bless God. The song opens with the following exhortation:

Bless the Lord, you heavens;
Sing praise to Him and highly exalt him forever.

Bless the Lord, you angels of the Lord, sing praise to him and highly
 exalt him forever.
Bless the Lord, all you waters above the heavens,
Sing praise to him and highly exalt him forever.
Bless the Lord, all you powers of the Lord;
Sing praise to him and highly exalt him forever.
Bless the Lord, sun and moon;
Sing praise to him and highly exalt him forever.
Bless the Lord, stars of heaven;
Sing praise to him and highly exalt him forever.[37]

This song is reminiscent of material preserved in Psalms 148–50,
especially Psalm 148, which opens by calling upon celestial elements to
praise God:

Hallelujah.
Praise the Lord from the heavens;
Praise Him on high.
Praise Him, all His angels,
Praise Him, all His hosts.
Praise Him, sun and moon,
Praise Him, all bright stars.
Praise Him, highest heavens,
And you waters that are above the heavens.[38]

The similarities between this text and the beginning of Daniel's companions' song are striking. If the author of this text in Daniel did not
have the exact passage of Psalm 148 before him, he certainly drew on a
shared tradition.

The Prayer of Azariah and the Song of the Three Jews is typical of Jewish poetic prayers written in the late Second Temple period. The Greek
additions to the book of Esther, for example, also include such prayers,
which are uttered by Esther and Mordecai. The book of 2 Maccabees
likewise includes numerous short prayers to God, often in the form of

soliloquies and similar in style to speeches featured in Greek plays. All of these texts use prayer as a means of highlighting the religious piety of Jewish heroes. They also use it as a strategy to increase tension in their stories by slowing down the pace of action before a crisis is resolved.

The addition known as Bel and the Dragon also testifies to Daniel's extraordinary faith and piety. This narrative is divisible into three stories. In the first, Daniel convinces King Cyrus that Cyrus' god, Bel, is a powerless idol. He does so by proving that it is not Bel who consumes the food and drink left for him by supplicants in his temple, but the seventy priests who administer this temple, along with their families. Daniel spreads ashes on the temple floor, and, on the following day, he shows King Cyrus the footsteps left by the priests and their families who ate the offering intended for Bel the previous night. Cyrus then kills the priests and their families and allows Daniel to destroy the idol of Bel and the temple.

In the second story, Daniel announces that he will slay a certain dragon whom the people worship as a god, and that he will do so without a weapon. He feeds this dragon a combination of pitch, fat, and hair, which causes its stomach to explode. While the king lauds Daniel for his success, other Persians accuse the king of "becoming a Jew" and demand that he hand Daniel over to them. The king agrees to do so out of fear for his life.

This incident segues into the third and final story, in which Daniel is thrown into a lions' den to perish. While the lions miraculously leave Daniel alone, the prophet Habakkuk, who resides in far-away Judea, receives a prophecy that he must bring Daniel food. When the Persian king comes to retrieve Daniel's body seven days after tossing Daniel into the den and finds him alive and well, Cyrus declares: "You are great, O Lord, the God of Daniel, and there is no other besides you!"[39]

In all of these stories, foreign leaders acknowledge Daniel's superior intellect and the superiority of his God as well. Rather than being drastically different from the biblical stories about Daniel preserved in Hebrew and Aramaic, these tales build on biblical themes about Daniel's time in the Babylonian court and incorporate narrative elements that Jews living in the Greco-Roman world would have recognized from both Jewish and

Hellenistic sources: prayer, contests to determine which god or human is most powerful, a divine messenger intervening to help a hero in crisis, and the theme of sacred space.

GREEK ESTHER

The Greek translation of Esther that is preserved in the Septuagint portrays Esther as being considerably more pious and sensitive to her Jewish identity than her character in the biblical version.

Both Hebrew and Greek Esther center on four characters: King Ahasuerus, who rules Persia; Esther, the pious and beautiful Jewess who is brought into the Persian court to marry Ahasuerus; Mordecai, the wise and righteous Jew; and Haman, who plots to destroy all of the Jews in the empire when Mordecai refuses to bow down to him. Both accounts also portray the king as a pawn: At certain times he is manipulated into supporting Haman, and at others he is maneuvered into supporting Esther.

The two books differ, however, when it comes to God's role in the story. In Hebrew Esther, Mordecai and Esther never pray to God in their time of crisis. In fact, God is never mentioned at all. The closest that the text comes to acknowledging divine activity is in chapter 4, when Mordecai tries to convince Esther to intervene with Ahasuerus on the Jews' behalf. Mordecai tells Esther, "Do not imagine that you, of all the Jews, will escape with your life by being in the king's palace. On the contrary, if you keep silent in this crisis, relief and deliverance will come to the Jews from another quarter, while you and your father's house will perish."[40] Mordecai informs Esther that it is the Jews' destiny to be saved, implying that God will ensure that this salvation will happen with or without her.

Greek Esther, on the other hand, highlights God's total control over the story's events from the start. The story opens with a prophetic dream:

> In the second year of the reign of Artaxerxes the Great, on the first day of Nisan, Mordecai son of Jair son of Shimei son of Kish, of the tribe of Benjamin, had a dream. He was a Jew living in the city of Susa, a great man, serving in the court of the king. He was one of the captives whom

King Nebuchadnezzar of Babylon had brought from Jerusalem with King Jeconiah of Judea. And this was his dream: Noises and confusion, thunders and earthquake, tumult on the earth! Then two great dragons came forward, both ready to fight, and they roared terribly. At their roaring every nation prepared for war, to fight against the righteous nation. It was a day of darkness and gloom, of tribulation and distress, affliction and great tumult on the earth! And the whole righteous nation was troubled; they feared the evils that threatened them, and were ready to perish. Then they cried out to God; and at their outcry, as though from a tiny spring, there came a great river, with abundant water; light came, and the sun rose, and the lowly were exalted and devoured those held in honor. Mordecai saw in this dream what God had determined to do, and after he awoke he had it on his mind, seeking all day to understand it in every detail.[41]

Mordecai's dream begins with two dragons battling one another, and segues into a scene in which the nations of the earth prepare to fight against a single virtuous nation. Mordecai realizes that the dream contains the key to what "God had determined to do," but, like the reader, he does not exactly understand what events are to come. As the story progresses, it becomes clear that the Jewish people are being pitted against the biggest empire of its day, an empire that, for the author, embodies the gentile world. Mordecai's dream is thus clarified.

This "nations versus nation" dynamic is subtler in Hebrew Esther. After Ahasuerus issues an edict declaring that all the nations should kill the Jews, the reader is told that "the city of Shushan was dumbfounded,"[42] which implies that both Jews and non-Jews were shocked by the king's decree. On the other hand, the fact that Jews kill gentiles in self-defense at the end of the book suggests that some Persians harbor anti-Jewish feeling in the story.

God's control comes to a head in Greek Ester toward the end of the book, when the Jews cry out to God for salvation and are consequently saved, and Mordecai recognizes that his dream was a divinely sent message meant to guide him through the crisis.

Greek Esther features five other additions to Hebrew Esther that add elements of adventure and divine provenance. In Addition C, for example, Mordecai and Esther utter prayers in response to the edict against the Jews. In her prayer, Esther laments the Jews' predicament and affirms her loyalty to Judaism:

> Then Queen Esther, seized with deadly anxiety, fled to the Lord. She took off her splendid apparel and put on the garments of distress and mourning, and instead of costly perfumes she covered her head with ashes and dung.... She prayed to the Lord God of Israel, and said: "O my Lord, you are our only king; help me, who am alone and have no helper but you.... You have knowledge of all things, and you know that I hate the splendor of the wicked and abhor the bed of the uncircumcised and of any alien. You know my necessity—that I abhor the sign of my proud position, which is upon my head on days when I appear in public. I abhor it like a filthy rag, and I do not wear it on the days when I am at leisure. And your servant has not eaten at Haman's table, and I have not honored the king's feast or drunk the wine of libations. Your servant has had no joy since the day that I was brought here until now, except in you, O Lord God of Abraham."[43]

Esther's prayer adds pathos to the story, increases drama by slowing down the action, and also addresses possible questions that readers of Hebrew Esther might have had. In the Hebrew version, Esther does not take action on behalf of the Jews until Mordecai convinces her to approach Ahasuerus on their behalf. Nor does Esther seem disturbed by the fact that she is sleeping with Ahasuerus, a gentile, and eating the food in his palace, which would not have been kosher. Greek Esther addresses these issues by presenting Esther as being completely devoted to the laws of her faith.

The author of Greek Esther wanted to supplement Hebrew Esther by adding information that is lacking in the Hebrew version, particularly regarding the centrality of divine providence and the protagonists' religious piety. Other details, such as Mordecai's dream about the dueling dragons, were inserted to make Esther's story more suspenseful and dramatic, and therefore more appealing to a Greek-speaking Jewish audience familiar with Hellenistic adventure stories.

The changes in Greek Esther support the theory that "Rewritten Bible" texts were motivated by questions that arose when reading the scriptures. But they also suggest that many added details in these texts were reflections of an influential host culture.

Jews in the late Second Temple period paid homage to their scriptural texts by rewriting them in ways that added entirely new dimensions. These dimensions often situated biblical characters within the world of Greco-Roman life by attributing to them Hellenistic soliloquys and Homeric bravado. And while in one sense Jewish authors drew their early history closer to their own lives by modernizing these characters, in another sense these same authors created distance between Jews of their day and the biblical characters they wrote about, whom they fashioned as more perfect, more intellectual, more courageous, and less relatable than they are in the biblical account. In these rewritten versions, biblical heroes were meant to prove that Judaism was a religion to be admired, and Jews were people to be welcomed as they continued to spread and build communities throughout the Greco-Roman world. The texts that scholars refer to as Rewritten Bible helped to instill pride in Jews who wanted to preserve, rather than abandon, their religious heritage as they engaged daily with the outside world.

CHAPTER 13

The Expanded Bible

Many writers in the Second Temple period expanded on biblical stories by exploring the lives of unknown biblical characters. Some of these characters, like Aseneth, are mentioned in passing in biblical literature. Others, like Judith, are depicted as living in biblical times but do not appear in earlier biblical stories. Some figures are folkloric and legendary, such as the magicians Jannes and Jambres and the wise sage Ahikar, who all appear in a cross-section of many ancient texts.[1] Among these figures are characters like Ahiqar, whose origins are rooted in older Near Eastern literature. Some legendary figures aren't even human, but divine or semi-divine.

Folkloric Heroes

ASENETH

As we have noted, Jewish writers were fascinated by the biblical figure of Joseph and his meteoric rise in fortune. A Hebrew sold into slavery by his jealous brothers, Joseph became a servant in the house of Potiphar, was falsely accused and imprisoned for sexual assault, accurately interpreted the dreams of Pharaoh's butler and baker and subsequently the dreams of Pharaoh himself, joined Pharaoh's council, and eventually rose up the ranks to become Pharaoh's closest advisor. What would it have been like to live Joseph's life as an important member of Pharaoh's court in the aftermath of these experiences?

One product of this question is a book called Joseph and Aseneth, which embellishes the details of Joseph's life in Egypt that the Hebrew

Bible does not provide. The work is divisible into two separate sections, which can each stand on its own as an independent novella. The first tells the story of Aseneth, the beautiful daughter of the wealthy priest Pentephres, who falls in love with Joseph after seeing him for the first time. When Joseph rebuffs Aseneth's advances because she is not an Israelite, Aseneth undergoes a major transformation in which she rejects her idols and embraces the God of Joseph. Aseneth then returns to Joseph and the two get married. This section ends "happily ever after," with the happy couple bound together in love and shared worship of the same God.

The second novella focuses on four of Joseph's brothers, Dan, Naphtali, Gad, and Asher, who envy Joseph's success in Pharaoh's court and his marriage to Aseneth. They conspire with Pharaoh's son, who is in love with Aseneth, to kill Pharaoh, which would enable Pharaoh's son to seize the throne, marry Aseneth, and kill Joseph, and would rid the brothers of their fraternal rival. What happens, however, is not according to plan. The brothers' army ambushes Aseneth in a field, but the six hundred men accompanying her stave them off. Benjamin, meanwhile, who is traveling alongside Aseneth, hurls a rock at Pharaoh's son, injuring him. Dan, Naphtali, Gad, and Asher continue to pursue Aseneth, this time to kill her in revenge for injuring Pharaoh's son. But after their swords miraculously turn to ashes and they become defenseless, Aseneth begs the other brothers to have mercy on these wicked brigands. While she succeeds in appeasing them, Benjamin approaches Pharaoh's son to fatally strike him. Levi convinces Benjamin to retreat and brings Pharaoh's son to Pharaoh, after which Pharaoh bows to Levi, and a reconciliation ensues. Pharaoh's son, however, dies from his wounds three days later. The enemy is thus defeated, and Joseph and Aseneth are left to live their lives in peace. After Pharaoh's death, Joseph becomes king of Egypt and later hands the monarchy over to Pharaoh's grandson. The story thus ends harmoniously.

The portrayal of Joseph in Joseph and Aseneth is broadly consistent with the scriptural account. In both works, Joseph is a principled Israelite beloved by Jews and gentiles, and his devotion to God enables him to control his sexual desires. Joseph and Aseneth adds many details, however, which address some of the troubling questions that arise when reading the biblical account of Joseph's life. How could Joseph have married an Egyptian woman, who presumably kept pagan customs, which would have been incongruous with living as an Israelite? And was Joseph really as arrogant as his behavior in Genesis 37 implies, when he reports his brothers' behavior to their father Jacob? The author of Joseph and Aseneth clarifies these questions: Joseph would never have married a woman who had not accepted the one true God of Israel; Aseneth accepted the Israelite God as her own while Joseph remained wholly committed to his ancestral traditions; and Joseph was not arrogant, but simply superior in virtue to some of his brothers, who were consumed with petty jealousy.

The author also suggests that children of Israelites are superior to children of gentiles by vindicating Reuben, Simeon, Levi, Judah, Issachar, and Zebulon, the sons of Jacob's wives Leah and Rachel. Leah and Rachel are kin of Abraham and Sarah, and presumably accepted the Abrahamic God as soon as they married Jacob. On the other hand, the author demonizes Dan, Naphtali, Gad, and Asher, the sons of Jacob's concubines Bilhah and Zilpah, who are of non-Abrahamic origin and are relegated by biblical and Rabbinic literature to the sidelines of history. The author goes even further than the biblical account by depicting Bilhah's and Zilpah's sons as outsiders who embody the role of "rejected sons": Just as Isaac inherits the Abrahamic covenant while God rejects Ishmael, and Jacob inherits the covenant while his brother Esau is rejected, the sons of Rachel and Leah are chosen, while the sons of Bilhah and Zilpah are rejected.

Scholars continue to debate who authored Joseph and Aseneth. Some believe that Christians authored the book, but its emphases on entering into the Israelite religion, adhering to religious piety, and employing ethical behavior, along with its condemnation of paganism and extensive liturgical material, all have parallels with other early Jewish literature. On the other hand, Joseph and Aseneth omits distinctively Jewish practices such as circumcision, dietary laws, and the Sabbath. Perhaps the author observed a kind of distilled practice of Judaism that underscored its ethical values rather than its ritual traditions. Other contemporaneous Jewish books, such as the Testaments of the Twelve Patriarchs and the Testament of Abraham, likewise emphasize the ethical aspects of Judaism while downplaying Jewish rituals.

Like many other books of the Pseudepigrapha, Joseph and Aseneth was copied and edited by Christians, and ultimately the book attained an important place in Christian tradition.[2] In the Second Temple period and the centuries that followed, however, the book likely appealed to both Jews and Christians, since it valorizes a brave and handsome hero who puts his faith above all else—even true love.

JANNES AND JAMBRES

Numerous late Second Temple, early Christian, and early Rabbinic texts refer to two brothers named Jannes and Jambres, who work as magicians for Pharaoh during the time of Moses. These brothers usually act as troublesome antagonists to both Moses and God.[3] In the New Testament epistle of 2 Timothy, for example, sinful people who reject truthful teachings are compared to Jannes and Jambres, who rejected the teachings of Moses.[4] In midrashic literature, Jannes and Jambres ridicule Moses and Aaron for attempting to conduct magical feats against the Egyptians, who have mastered the art of magic.[5] The Roman historian Pliny the Elder, moreover, cites the brothers in his discussion about how Jews conduct magic.[6] These are only a few examples of about forty separate traditions circulating about Jannes and Jambres in antiquity.[7]

In one surviving story about the brothers that is usually dated to the late Second Temple period, Jannes and Jambres stand in opposition to Moses and Aaron. Jannes soon dies, but, by practicing necromancy, Jambres brings his brother back from the dead. Once summoned, Jannes informs his brother that idolatry is wicked and that his condemnation to suffering in Hades is justifiable. This account closes with Jannes warning Jambres that evil behavior will result in eternal suffering in the afterlife:

Jambres opened the magical books of his brother Jannes; he performed necromancy and brought up from the netherworld his brother's shade. The soul of Jannes said in response, I your brother did not die unjustly, and the judgment will go against me, since I was more clever than all clever magicians, and opposed the two brothers, Moses and Aaron, who performed great signs and wonders. As a result I died and was brought from among (the living) to the netherworld where there is great burning and the pit of perdition, whence no ascent is possible.[8]

Elsewhere in the story Jannes tells Jambres: "[We who w]orshiped ido[ls and carved images until we came [to destruction together with [our] idols, [for neither the idols nor their worship[ers does God the King [of the earth love(?)]."[9] From surviving fragments such as this one, it is clear that the author of this legend believed that idol worship was reprehensible. This attitude, coupled with dependence on the biblical story of Moses confronting magicians in Pharaoh's court, indicates that the author of this document was probably Jewish.

The stories circulating about Jannes and Jambres are consistent with the importance some Jews ascribed to the practice of magic. Indeed, Jewish incantations inscribed on bowls and amulets have been discovered by archaeologists at many ancient Jewish sites.[10]

JUDITH

The book of Judith, which recalls the story of a beautiful and pious Jewish woman who saves the Jews of her town from destruction at the hands of a ruthless enemy, was probably written by a Jew living in Judea in the second century BCE.

The story begins when the Assyrians besiege the residents of Judith's town, Bethulia, after the people of Bethulia refuse to join them in a military campaign. While the town elders despair that they will soon be destroyed, Judith devises a plan. She sneaks out of Bethulia with her handmaiden, seduces the Assyrian general Holofernes over the course of a few days, and one evening, after he has fallen into a drunken sleep, she beheads him. Judith and her handmaiden then return to Bethulia with Holofernes' severed head, and Judith declares to the town's residents that their trials are over. In the morning, the residents of Bethulia are ready for battle, but the Assyrians, having lost their general, are not. They attempt to flee, but the Israelites overcome and defeat them.

The author's portrayal of Judith as the perfect heroine—beautiful, astute, and righteous—is modeled after earlier portrayals of biblical heroines, especially the depictions of Deborah and Jael in Judges 4–5. In this biblical story, Deborah is ruling the Israelites as a judge when the Canaanites send a general named Sisera to attack the Israelites. Deborah responds by summoning a warrior named Barak, whom she instructs to lead the Israelites into battle. Barak, however, refuses to lead the troops without Deborah, so she joins him in the fight and leads the Israelites to victory. Sisera, meanwhile, escapes on foot, and Jael leaves her tent to intercept him. She offers him a place to eat and rest, and when he falls asleep, she assassinates him, finalizing the Israelite victory.

Judith embodies the figures of both Deborah and Jael. Like Deborah, Judith leads the Israelites when the local male leaders are incapable of ruling, and she takes the initiative to engage with the enemy general. And like Jael, Judith initiates a rendezvous with the enemy general in a tent, where she seduces and kills him. By likening his heroine to Deborah and Jael, the only two women in the Bible who work together to achieve an Israelite victory over an enemy without assistance from male leaders, the author fashions Judith into a kind of superwoman. The larger-than-life Judith possesses abilities that most Jews thought could only be contained within two separate women.

Although there might have existed a woman named Judith who was a highly respected leader of her Jewish community, there are many indications that Judith, as this author describes her, is not a historical character. Neither Josephus nor Philo mention her in their writings. Nor does she appear in the Mishnah or the Talmud. The figure of Judith did, however, become prominent in medieval Christian literature and art, and also in Jewish medieval texts regarding Hanukkah. In some of these texts, Judith becomes a key player in the Hanukkah story. Perhaps Jews in medieval times knew that the book of Judith was written during the Hasmonean period.

It is also possible that Judith was linked to Hanukkah because its "partner holiday," Purim, also featured a heroine, Esther. Hanukkah and Purim are "minor" holidays that are not mentioned in the Pentatesch, and both have their historical origins in the Second Temple period. As we noted in chapter 11, moreover, the stories of Esther and Judith that are associated with these holidays are strikingly similar to one another. Both recall a dangerous crisis that the Jews faced, and miraculously avoided, thanks to the intervention of a brave heroine and the implicit hand of God. Given that the story of Esther recalls Mordecai and Esther working together to save the Jews, it may be that some Jews saw Judah the Maccabee and Judith working in similar partnership to save the Jews from the Syrian Greeks.

The author of Judith is purposely ahistorical. Judith lives in Bethulia, which roughly translates into "Virgin Town." No evidence indicates that such a town existed in ancient Israel, but the name enforces other elements of the story that highlight Judith's sexuality. Moreover, the enemies seeking to destroy Bethulia are Assyrians, whose empire fell to the Babylonians in the seventh century BCE. In Judith, however, the Assyrian king Nebuchadnezzar has a Babylonian name, and his general, whom Judith kills, has a Greek-sounding name, Holofernes.

While the author's motivation for writing this book is unclear, it may be that he wanted to compose a satirical version of the Hasmonean victory against the Syrian Greeks. The books 1 and 2 Maccabees tell the story of a valiant hero named Judah who leads the Jews to an unexpected victory against a powerful enemy, and Judith tells the story of a woman (whose name is the feminized version of Judah) who likewise helps her people to defeat a powerful enemy. Both Judah and Judith possess bravery that is contrasted with the fear and cowardice exhibited by other Jewish leaders, and both end up saving their people by acting independently of the Jews' political and religious leadership. Retelling the story of Judith, then, may have been a safe way for Jews to memorialize Judah, his family, and the Hasmonean rebellion in the framework of an ahistorical narrative that would not have been perceived as being disloyal to the Greeks.

Devils

In the Second Temple period, many people believed that the world was inhabited not only by human beings and animals but also by divine and semi-divine creatures whose behaviors had an impact on human destinies. Even monotheistic Jews presumed that God was accompanied by a body of celestial beings. Some of these celestial beings were satanic figures, others were angels, and still others were half humans. The appearance of a devil figure in late Second Temple literature especially corresponds with the emergence of a dualistic view that a benevolent God was engaged in an ongoing conflict with a being that aimed to bring evil into the world. This kind of dualism in Jewish literature might have been a result of exposure to the Zoroastrian religion of the Persian Empire, since Zoroastrians held that divine forces were continually at odds with one another.

As Second Temple writers developed ideas about God's celestial cohorts, the figure of an evil angel in charge of a community of "fallen angels" began to emerge. This figure, who is held responsible for human sin, went by many names. Some authors describe him as a *daimonos*, the Greek word for "demon." Other authors refer to an angel named Samael, or Satan, who seeks to cause the downfall of virtuous humans and angels. In other texts, a figure called Beliar, Belial, or Mastema is cited as the head of a community of evil angels. Yet other legends mention a demonic figure named Azael, sometimes referred to as Azazel, who proliferates evil upon the earth. Many descriptions of these figures are rooted in scriptural passages that were interpreted as cryptic references to the celestial world.

SATAN

In the Hebrew Bible, the word *satan* usually refers to a divinely sent stumbling block that is meant to test or punish a biblical character. The exception to this appears in the book of Job, in which a figure called "the satan" is a member of God's heavenly court who believes that Job is not as righteous as God believes him to be, and who therefore suggests that God test Job's virtue by stripping him of his wealth and family. While the satan's plan in Job can be interpreted as sinister, it is a far cry from the evil character that appears in later material. Moreover, the fact that the satan in the book of Job is referred to as "the satan" rather than "Satan" allows for the possibility that the word "satan" in Job is not an angelic name but rather a prosecutorial role that one of God's angels fills. Nevertheless, the satan's role in Job may have been the precedent that later Jewish authors built upon, since nowhere else in the Hebrew Bible is a satan depicted as part of the divine retinue who tries to test the limits of human goodness.[11] This trait would become central to the depiction of the devilish figure who goes by many names in late Second Temple literature.

In the Testament of Dan, for example, Dan tells his sons that one day they will forge an alliance with Satan in order to induce Levi's sons to stray, but an angel of peace will deflect Satan's efforts:[12]

> For I have read in the book of the righteous Enoch that your guardian angel is Satan and that all the Spirits of licentiousness and arrogance will [sometime in the future] turn their attention to Levi, and keep a close watch on Levi's sons and will sin with them in all things, while Judah's sons will lust after gain and will snatch up the wealth of others like lions. . . . And now, my children, fear the Lord and guard yourselves against Satan and his Spirits. Come close to God and to the angel who intercedes for you, for he is an intermediary between God and men for the peace of Israel, and he will stand up against the enemy's kingdom. That is why the enemy is eager to trip up all those who call upon the name of the Lord. For he knows that on the day that Israel believes, the enemy's kingdom will be brought to an end. The angel of peace will strengthen Israel, so that it will not fall into the worst of evils.[13]

This passage opens with Dan warning his sons not to follow Satan on his crusade to cause Levi to sin. Instead, his sons must follow both God and God's good angel who intercedes on their behalf. This angel is not named, but may be the angel Michael, who in other Second Temple texts functions as an intermediary who communicates God's will to human beings. Dan predicts that, in the end-time, it is this peaceful angel who will save God's people from Satan's evil designs.

Satan also plays a prominent role in the Testament of Job, a book written in the first century BCE or first century CE in Greek. While in the biblical book of Job Satan is a member of God's celestial court who suggests that Job's righteousness must be tested, the Testament of Job presents Satan as the archangel over evil angels. At one point, Satan, who is also referred to as "the devil," disguises himself as a Persian king, gathers an angry mob against Job, and makes false accusations against him.[14] In another passage, Job attributes his wife's complaints to the fact that the devil is standing behind her and muddling her reasoning.[15] By depicting Satan as Job's enemy, the author of the Testament of Job absolves God from being responsible for Job's suffering.

BELIAR AND BELIAL

The satanic figures Beliar and Belial appear often in Second Temple literature. Belial is related to the biblical *beliya'al*, which usually refers to an impious person who stirs up trouble in the Israelite community.[16] Belial appears in a number of fragments preserved in the Dead Sea Scrolls. In the War Scroll, for example, Belial leads the Sons of Darkness against the Sons of Light in an apocalyptic war that will mark the defeat of all sinners. He fills a similar role in the Damascus Document, which portrays him as an adversary of the righteous people of Israel, whom he will attack in the end-time.[17] In this text, Belial aids the Egyptian magicians in their confrontation with Moses and Aaron.

Beliar, whom we briefly mentioned in chapter 12, appears in Greek texts, and is probably the equivalent of Belial, who is mentioned in Hebrew texts. Beliar appears prominently in the Testaments of the Twelve Patriarchs as a figure who is in charge of evil angels and who tries to provoke humans to sin.[18] While Beliar and other devil figures are almost never identified with real people in Second Temple literature, one intriguing exception is in a document called the Third Sibylline Oracle, which associates Beliar with the Roman emperor Nero. The passage reads:

> Then Beliar will come from the *Sebastenoi* and he will raise up the height of the mountains, he will raise up the sea, the great fiery sun and shining moon, and he will raise up the dead, and perform many signs for men. But they will not be effective in him. But he will indeed, also lead men astray, and he will lead astray many faithful, chosen Hebrews, and also other lawless men who have not yet listened to the word of God. But whenever the threats of the great God draws [sic] nigh and a burning power comes through the sea to land it will also burn Beliar and all overbearing men, as many as put faith in him.[19]

Although enigmatic, most scholars believe that this passage alludes to the reign of Nero. *Sebastenoi* is the Greek word for the Latin *Augusti*, and Nero was a descendent of the emperor Augustus.[20] Known as a capricious and often violent ruler, Nero was particularly unpopular with the Jews living in Judea because he dispatched General Vespasian to quell the Jewish rebellion against Rome in 66 CE. The unusual link between a legendary being, Beliar, and a historical figure, Nero, might reflect the author's belief that since Beliar-Nero had brought great destruction upon the Earth, the messiah would soon follow.

MASTEMA

Mastema is an evil angel who is mentioned often in the book of Jubilees, and who seeks to cause the downfall of humanity, particularly of Israel. Jubilees attributes the proliferation of idolatry and sin following the death of Noah to Mastema's evil designs.[21] Mastema also suggests to God that Abraham be tested by commanding him to sacrifice his son, which parallels the satan's function in the book of Job.[22] He has a particularly prominent role as the instigator of all of Israel's troubles in Jubilees' retelling of the Israelites' exodus from Egypt. When Moses departs from Midian with the intention of saving the Israelites from slavery, for example, he is confronted and attacked by Mastema on the way. Mastema wants to kill Moses so that the Israelites will remain in a state of suffering, but God intervenes to save Moses. Mastema later aids the Egyptian sorcerers in producing magic that harms the Israelites, and after God kills these magicians, it is Mastema who hardens the Egyptians' hearts and causes them to refuse to release the Israelites. According to Jubilees, God allows Mastema to harden the Egyptians' hearts so that the Egyptians would pursue the Israelites to the Red Sea, where God would destroy them.[23] For Jubilees, then, the story about God saving the Israelites from the Egyptians is at its core a story about God saving the Israelites from an evil angel.

On the other hand, Mastema is not simply an advocate for the Egyptians in Jubilees. He represents evil and death in a broader sense. This explains why Jubilees attributes the deaths of the Egyptians' firstborn children to Mastema's destructive powers. Mastema is the adversary of Israel, but also the source of all pain and death. Mastema appears in the Damascus Document as well, where he seems to be referenced interchangeably with Belial.[24] Given that Belial aids the Egyptian magicians in this document, and Mastema aids them in Jubilees, it could certainly be that Belial/Beliar and Mastema were used interchangeably and regarded as one and the same among some Jewish authors.

DAIMONOS

Another evil angel in Second Temple literature is Daimonos, whose name is related to the English word "demon." Daimonos is mentioned in the Sentences of Pseudo-Phocylides and the Third Sibylline Oracle, but appears most prominently in the Testament of Solomon. In this text, Solomon battles and defeats dozens of demonic creatures.[25] Solomon is assisted by the archangel Michael, who gives Solomon a magical ring that enables him to imprison the demons. The head demon in this text is called Beelzeboul and is the product of a human mother and an angelic father. Beelzeboul's unusual genealogy is an allusion to Genesis 6:1–4, in which divine beings have sexual intercourse with human women. Second

Temple authors often used these verses as a springboard to understand the nature of fallen angels who strove to corrupt righteous humans.[26]

DIABOLOS

Two texts composed in the Second Temple period or shortly thereafter, the Life of Adam and Eve and the Testament of Job, feature yet another satanic figure, Diabolos.[27] This Greek word means "hurl across" or "slanderer" and is the etymological root of the English word "devil." In the Life of Adam and Eve, Diabolos is an evil angel who convinces the serpent in the Garden of Eden to allow him to speak to Adam and the woman (who is unnamed until the end of the story) through the serpent's mouth. Eve tells her sons the details of this exchange:

> When the Devil came to your father's portion the Devil summoned the serpent and told him, "Arise and come to me, and I will teach you a useful word." Then, the serpent came and the Devil told the serpent, "I [hear] that you are wiser than all the animals and I have come to test your knowledge, for Adam gives food to all the animals, and thus also to you. When then all the animals come to bow down before Adam from day to day and from morning to morning, every day, you also come to bow down. You were created before him, as old (as you) are, and you bow down before this younger one! And why do you eat (food) inferior [to Adam's and his spouse's] and not the good fruit of the Garden? But come and hearken to me so that we may have Adam expelled from the wall of the Garden just as we are outside. Perhaps we can somehow reenter the Garden." And the serpent told him, "How can we have them excluded?" The Devil replied and told the serpent, "Be a sheath for me and I will speak to the woman through your mouth a word by which we will trick them."[28]

While in the biblical story the serpent corrupts Adam and the woman by encouraging them to sin against God, this account implies that Adam and the woman were controlled by more powerful forces of evil that were operating behind the scenes. Such a dynamic serves to help exonerate both Adam and the woman.

AZAEL/AZAZEL

In 1 Enoch we meet yet another satanic figure, Azael, an evil angel depicted as overseeing "all forms of oppression upon the earth."[29] Azael's name probably derives from the Hebrew word *azazel*, which is mentioned in Leviticus 16, when the Israelites are instructed to assign an emissary who will bring a goat into the desert wilderness on the Day of Atonement, where it will reach *azazel*. This ritual symbolically cleansed the Israelites of their sins (and serves as the origin for the English term "scapegoat").[30] The term as it is used in Leviticus 16 seems to be a place in the wilderness, but later Jewish and Christian interpreters who believed that demons lived in the desert came to associate Azazel, or Azael, with a demonic figure.[31] Even today, the Hebrew phrase *Lech La'Azazel*, "Go to Azazel," means "Go to Hell."

SAMAEL

The book 3 Baruch is a document that was written in Greek, probably sometime during the first three centuries of the Common Era. The text features an unnamed good angel who accompanies Baruch through a series of otherworldly visions. When Baruch requests that the angel show him the Tree of Knowledge of Good and Evil, the good angel describes this tree as a vine that an evil angel named Samael once planted in the Garden of Eden. Explaining to Baruch that God was angered at Samael for interfering with the Garden, the angel recalls the consequences that followed:

> And I said, "I pray you, show me which is the tree which caused Adam to stray." And the angel said, "It is the vine which the angel Samael planted by which the Lord God became angered, and he cursed him and his planting. For this reason he did not permit Adam to touch it. And because of this the devil became envious and tricked him by means of his vine."[32]

God curses Samael for planting a vine in the Garden of Eden. In revenge, Samael decides to manipulate Adam and the woman into touching this vine, an act that constitutes a sin against God. The angel then explains to Baruch the connection between Samael and the serpent:

> And again I asked, "Why does [the moon] sometimes grow larger and sometimes grow smaller?" "Listen, O Baruch: This which you see was designed by God to be beautiful without peer. And during the transgression of the first Adam, she gave light to Samael when he took the serpent as a garment, and did not hide, but, on the contrary, waxed. And God was angered with her, and diminished her and shortened her days."[33]

According to the angel, the moon provided light to Samael as he disguised himself within the body of the serpent. The waning of the moon is thus a divine punishment for giving Samael light. Samael's responsibility for Adam and the woman's sin is similar to that of Diabolos in the Life of Adam and Eve. Both evil angels seek to bring about humankind's fall from God's favor. The authors of these texts use Diabolos and Samael to explain why humans are repeatedly tempted into sin and cause one another harm, even against their better judgment.

Samael rarely appears in Second Temple texts but comes to the foreground in Rabbinic literature. In one Rabbinic tradition, Michael and Samael stand alongside one another as defender and prosecutor of the Israelites as God decides whether the Israelites are deserving of being taken out of Egypt.[34] The juxtaposition of Samael with Michael indicates that Samael was considered to be a significant angelic adversary in the Rabbinic period, as extreme in his evil as Michael is extreme in his goodness.[35]

As Christianity developed in the early centuries of the Common Era, the concept of divine dual forces that were locked in opposition would find expression in early Christian texts known as Gnostic literature. Some of these texts assert the existence of a divine Creator, who is not involved in human affairs, and a less supreme deity, who is responsible for introducing evil into the human world.[36]

A good versus evil paradigm helped Jewish and Christian writers to understand the most difficult theological problem of all: With so much pain and suffering in the world, how could God possibly be good? The prospect that the Creator of the World was not responsible for the pain of humankind would have brought many readers relief and comfort.

Angels

Just as Greeks believed that the behavior of the gods affected human destiny, many Jews believed that their God was buttressed by angelic forces that fought against evil demons who were trying to wreak havoc among humankind. Jews were also intrigued by the idea of a messiah, a semi-angelic figure who would come to earth as a harbinger of the final age.

MICHAEL THE ARCHANGEL

The second half of the book of Daniel makes three references to an angelic figure named Michael.[37] One such reference appears in Daniel 10, when Daniel has a vision of a man who tells him what "is inscribed in the book of truth."[38] The man predicts that the "prince of the kingdom of Persia" will oppose Daniel, but that Michael will come to his rescue:

> Then a hand touched me, and shook me onto my hands and knees. He said to me, "O Daniel, precious man, mark what I say to you and stand up, for I have been sent to you." After he said this to me, I stood up, trembling. He then said to me, "Have no fear, Daniel, for from the first day that you set your mind to get understanding, practicing abstinence before your God, your prayer was heard, and I have come because of your prayer. However, the prince of the Persian kingdom opposed me for twenty-one days; now Michael, a prince of the first rank, has come to my aid, after I was detained there with the kings of Persia."[39]

Later in Daniel's vision, this man foretells that in the end-time, Michael's appearance will mark a new period during which the dead will be resurrected and the righteous will be saved:

> At that time, the great prince, Michael, who stands beside the sons of your people, will appear. It will be a time of trouble, the like of which has

never been since the nation came into being. At that time, your people will be rescued, all who are found inscribed in the book. Many of those that sleep in the dust of the earth will awake, some to eternal life, others to reproaches, to everlasting abhorrence.[40]

Over the course of the Second Temple period, Michael would become an increasingly important figure. As the "right-hand man" of God, he acts as a liaison between God and the Jewish people, is in charge of the entire body of angelic beings, and provides righteous people with special access to the celestial world. In 3 Baruch, for example, a divine messenger escorts Baruch through five heavenly realms. Upon his entry into the fifth realm, Baruch sees the archangel Michael, who is serenely described as the "holder of the keys of the kingdom of heaven," because he oversees the angels who bring tidings of good and bad human behavior.[41] Likewise, in 1 Enoch, Michael, along with his comrades Gabriel, Suriel, and Uriel, bemoans the wicked behavior of humankind, especially the sexual relationships between angels and human women that have brought evil into the world.[42] And in Daniel and the War Scroll, Michael is depicted as personally overseeing the destiny of Israel.[43]

All of these sources indicate that Michael's primary job is to somehow act as mediator between the celestial and human worlds. The humorous elements in the Testament of Abraham, moreover, which highlight Michael's professional failures, only work because Jewish readers would have known him to be the divine messenger par excellence.[44]

In the Assumption of Moses and the New Testament epistle of Jude, which are both dated to roughly the first century CE, Michael engages in direct conflict with the devil.[45] These sources share a common tradition about the devil confronting Michael while he is burying Moses. The devil argues that Moses is not entitled to an honorable burial because he is a murderer. In both accounts, Michael rebukes the devil by quoting the prophet Zechariah 3:2: "May the Lord rebuke you!" This legend addresses two questions readers may have had when studying the beginning and end of Moses' life: Could Moses have been the perfect servant of God if he killed an Egyptian man in Exodus 2? And does the lack of information regarding Moses' burial indicate that he was given a dishonorable burial as a divine punishment for an earlier sin? The legend regarding Michael burying Moses addresses these questions by pinning the devil against the greatest angel known to Jews. Of course, it is no surprise that Michael has the last word. By the end of the first century CE, Michael's role as head of the angels was solidified.[46]

THE MESSIAH

Jewish apocalyptic texts such as 1 Enoch, 2 Baruch, and 4 Ezra envision a dramatic clash between the righteous followers of God and wicked sinners. According to these books, sinners will be destroyed or subjugated, and God's Chosen People, a category that sometimes excludes not only the foreign nations but also sinful Jews, will emerge victorious. This clash will be followed by a utopian period in which all people will live among one another in peace and acknowledge the Jewish God. The belief that one individual would oversee this clash and lead the victors to salvation is expressed in many late Second Temple texts.

Some books written at this time envision not one, but two messianic figures. As we noted in chapter 12, for example, the Testaments of the Twelve Patriarchs predict that both Levi and Judah will govern the Jews in the messianic age.[47] Some of the Dead Sea Scrolls also attest to the coming of two messiahs: one that will descend from King David and represent monarchic leadership, and another that will descend from priestly lineage and govern from the Temple. Still, since most texts from Qumran do not mention two messiahs, but either one or the other, the question of whether Jews living at Qumran believed that two messianic figures would rule Israel together remains a matter of debate.[48]

Other Jewish works written at this time also envision the coming of just one messiah. Among these is the Psalms of Solomon, which predicts that a messiah will come down to earth from the heavens to usher in the end-time as the foreign nations stream to Jerusalem:

And he shall have the peoples of the nations to serve him under his yoke, and he shall glorify the Lord in the center of all the earth, and he shall purify Jerusalem in holiness as it was at the beginning, so that nations may come from the end of the earth to see his glory, bringing as gifts her sons who are exhausted, and to see the glory of the Lord with which God has glorified her.[49]

This passage echoes Isaiah 66:18–24, in which God calls upon delegates among the foreign nations to gather the dispersed members of Israel and bring them back to Jerusalem. But rather than focusing on the actions of humanity, this psalm focuses on the actions of the messiah, whose arrival will be witnessed by the foreign nations upon their entry into Zion.

The books of 2 Baruch and 4 Ezra also predict that the arrival of a messianic figure will signal the coming end-time. In 2 Baruch, Baruch learns that the messiah's arrival will be accompanied by the resurrection of the righteous and the eternal punishment of the wicked.[50] Baruch is later informed that not all of humanity can be saved: "After the signs have come, which were previously told to you, when the nations become turbulent, and the time of my messiah has come, he shall both summon all the nations, and some of them he shall let live, and some of them he shall kill."[51] In 4 Ezra, on the other hand, the messiah's death, along with the death of all of humankind, is to be followed by a worldwide resurrection and final judgment.[52] After his own death and resurrection, the messiah will administer rewards to the righteous and punishments to the wicked.[53]

The Jewish writers who predicted that a semi-divine individual would lead Israel into a period of redemption may have thought that God would not directly intervene in the Jews' affairs. Perhaps Jews writing such texts after 70 CE believed that, in the absence of a Temple, God was no longer in direct communication with the people. The end-time, moreover, would not come through the Jews' own merit, since they had brought suffering upon themselves with their sinful behavior. A Jewish redemption could only occur through the merit of a perfect individual who bore a special relationship with God.

Conclusion

The books that Jews composed during the Second Temple period and shortly afterward fill in narrative gaps and solve contradictions in the scriptures. They also feature heroes who possess the same qualities that characterize the heroes of the great Greek epics. And while many Jewish writers looked to well-known biblical heroes for sources of inspiration, other authors developed new characters to admire. Some of these characters are briefly referenced in the Bible, and others are only loosely fashioned in the image of biblical heroes. Jewish writers at this time also introduced angels, devils, and other nonhuman characters into their literature. These figures enjoy special access to the cosmic world of divine activity, and their adventures helped readers to understand why human suffering was so proliferate. The idea that God was entirely good and cared for all of humankind, but that other celestial beings sought to wreak harm and havoc on humankind, offered Jews comfort by acknowledging the intense suffering that some of them had experienced. It also affirmed the lasting nature of the covenantal relationship between God and the Jews.

For the most part, the stories discussed in this book were probably not meant to "prove something" to the gentiles. They were mainly written for a Jewish audience that would have been familiar with the stories in the Jewish scriptures, but that was also integrated, in varying degrees, into the Hellenistic world.[1]

One remarkable aspect of Second Temple literature is that no portion of its literary corpus dominates any other. But this unique quality also poses particular challenges for modern readers. It is difficult, if not impossible, to argue that one text written in the first century BCE reflects a more normative view of Judaism than another. Even texts that later authorities regarded as authoritative, and ultimately scriptural, were not necessarily representative of the thinking of an "average" Jew at the time. Certainly a concept of "Common Judaism" existed in the sense that people who identified as Jewish generally read the scriptures, observed the Sabbath, practiced circumcision, and kept dietary laws. But the absence of a formal system that guided Jewish practice granted the Jews who lived in Antioch, Rome, Alexandria, and elsewhere in the Greco-Roman world the freedom to express their ideas in ways that appealed to their cultural tastes.

In the period that followed the Second Temple's destruction, early Christian and early Rabbinic communities separated into distinct religious bodies with systematized leadership that evaluated which practices and texts were acceptable and which were not. The kind of literature that their communities consequently produced became more monolithic. At the same time, Christians and Jews began to reclaim texts dated to the Second Temple period as their own. For Christians, this often meant copying Second Temple books and interpolating statements about Jesus and the Trinity into these works. For the Rabbis, this meant incorporating exegetical traditions from the Second Temple period into their midrashic collections.

In the Second Temple period, Jews were free to express pride in their tradition using a remarkable variety of languages, genres, and perspectives. The majority of these Jews admired the cultural gifts that the Greco-Roman world offered. Jews living in cities such as Antioch, Rome, Alexandria, and even Jerusalem allowed themselves the agency and the freedom to pay homage to their tradition in ways that embraced, rather than rejected, Persian, Greek, and Roman culture. Other Jews sought to eschew all foreign influence.

Conceptualizing this period as a time when Jews were either fully "Jewish" or entirely "Hellenized," however, is a false characterization. Second Temple literature reveals that most Jews did not believe that they had to subdue their admiration for their host culture in order to commit to their Jewish heritage. Curious about the world around them, these Jews sought to take the best of what their host cultures had to offer as they wrote, rewrote, and transmitted their stories.

The literature written in the Second Temple period constitutes the link that reveals how the Israelite religion of the Bible became the more normative Jewish religion fashioned by the Rabbis. But the Jews of the Second Temple period were neither biblical Israelites nor Rabbinic Jews, and while some were intrigued by their origins and others consumed with a future restoration, they would not have thought of themselves as working to build a bridge between the biblical world and the future Rabbinic Judaism that was to come. Instead, Jews at this time considered different ways to practice their religion and interpret their scriptures in light of a cultural setting that was unlike that of their Israelite forefathers. Like many Jews today, Jews in the Second Temple period navigated this challenge by forging remarkably creative ways to make an ancient religion meaningful in an ever-changing world.

GLOSSARY OF KEY NAMES, PLACES, AND BOOKS

Agrippa I: The grandson of Herod and a confidant of Emperor Claudius. Agrippa ruled northern regions of the Levant before he was appointed king of Judea following Gaius Caligula's death in 41 CE. His visit to Alexandria in 38 CE set off violent anti-Jewish riots in the city.

Agrippa II: The son of Agrippa I, and the last descendent of the Hasmonean and Herodian families to rule Judea. Agrippa ruled regions of his father's kingdom along with his sister, Berenice. The New Testament depicts the siblings as oppressing Jesus' earliest followers.

Alexandria: A thriving port city on the northern coast of Egypt that boasted a large Jewish population in the late Second Temple period. While many Jews of Alexandria enjoyed the privilege of being allowed to freely practice their ancestral law and integrated into Greco-Roman society, they also encountered resistance, and sometimes violent harassment, from their Greek and Roman counterparts.

Antioch: Lying along the Orontes River in modern-day Turkey, Antioch was the third-largest city in the Roman Empire, after Rome and Alexandria. The city's lush springs and lovely plazas made it a popular attraction for traders and other travelers. In the first century, Antioch was also an important place of gathering for Jesus' followers.

Antiochus IV Epiphanes: Seleucid king who implemented oppressive legislation against the Judeans in the early second century BCE. Judah Maccabee and his four brothers led a successful uprising against him in 167 BCE.

Apocrypha: Books that are excluded from the Hebrew Bible but included in the Septuagint, the Greek translation of the Hebrew Bible. The books of the Apocrypha are included in the Catholic Old Testament, but not in the

Protestant Old Testament. Many of the Apocrypha's books were written in the late Second Temple period.

Cairo Genizah Collection: About a quarter of a million fragments and documents discovered in an upper-level storeroom of the Ben Ezra Synagogue in Fustat, an old Cairo neighborhood. Dating from the early medieval period, the documents are one of the most important surviving caches of Jewish manuscripts, revealing how medieval Jews conducted business, wrote personal correspondence, interpreted Rabbinic law, and read their scriptures.

Constantin Tischendorf: The nineteenth-century scholar and antiquities collector credited with recovering the Codex Sinaiticus, a fourth-century CE Bible written in Greek. Tischendorf remains a controversial figure. Some scholars believe he was given permission to remove the Bible from St. Catherine's Monastery and present it to the Russian czar, Alexander II, who then transferred it to the Ministry of Foreign Affairs and later the Imperial Library. Other scholars accuse Tischendorf of absconding with a treasure that was lent to him temporarily.

Daniel: A popular figure in Second Temple literature whose eponymous book was canonized in the Hebrew Bible. The Septuagint contains legends about Daniel that circulated in the Second Temple period, which, like the book of Daniel in the Hebrew Bible, emphasized his success as a clever courtier in the Persian court.

Dead Sea Scrolls: Scrolls, mostly in fragments, found in caves near the northwestern corner of the Dead Sea between 1947 and 1956. Most scholars connect the authors of these texts with a late Second Temple community that lived at nearby Qumran. Members of this community were probably Essenes.

Enoch: A biblical figure cited in Genesis 5:22 who "walked with God." Second Temple writers circulated legends regarding his visions, which sometimes involved mysterious symbolic images that foretold the future destiny of the Jewish people.

Essenes: A sect of Jews living in the late Second Temple period that adhered to a strict interpretation of Jewish law, which included a communal lifestyle and an emphasis on ritual purity. The Essenes lived in different areas of Judea, and many scholars believe this included Qumran, an isolated community on the northwestern corner of the Dead Sea, close to the site of the Dead Sea Scrolls.

Flaccus: A prefect in Alexandria during the anti-Jewish riots in 38 CE. According to Philo, Flaccus condoned the anti-Jewish violence and refused to help the Jews.

Gaius Caligula: Emperor of Rome from 37 to 41 CE. According to Philo, Caligula refused to intervene on behalf of the Alexandrian Jewish community when violent anti-Jewish riots spread throughout Alexandria in 38 CE.

Hadrian: The Roman emperor during the time of Simeon Bar Kokhba's revolt against Rome. Hadrian's program to rename Jerusalem Aelia Capitolina instigated a major Jewish rebellion that eventually resulted in the deaths of tens of thousands of Jews.

Herod: Ruled Judea as a client king of Rome from 37 to 4 BCE. Herod was notorious for his ruthless scheming to eliminate potential competitors for the throne; victims of his assassination plots include his Hasmonean wife, Mariamne, and members of her family. Herod also undertook major building projects, including renovating the Temple and founding the city of Caesarea.

Joseph and Aseneth: An adventure story composed in the late Second Temple period or the centuries that followed that tells the story of how the biblical Joseph came to marry Aseneth, an Egyptian woman who enthusiastically accepts Joseph's God.

Josephus: A late first-century CE Jewish historian who was an eyewitness to the Great Revolt against Rome (66 CE–73 CE). While leading a military garrison against the Romans in the Galilee, Josephus was captured by the Romans and ultimately defected to them. Josephus is known for *The Jewish War*, his account of the Jewish rebellion; *Antiquities of the Jews*, which retells biblical and postbiblical Jewish history; *The Life of Flavius Josephus*, his autobiography; and *Against Apion*, his defense of the Jewish religion.

Jubilees: A retelling of the book of Genesis and the beginning of the book of Exodus that includes legends about the Patriarchs that are not found in the Hebrew Bible or Septuagint. Dating to the second century BCE and written in Hebrew, Jubilees advocates for a solar calendar and condemns Jews who do not properly observe ancestral law.

Letter of Aristeas: A text that details how the Hebrew Bible came to be translated into the Septuagint. Likely composed in the second century BCE in Alexandria, this text recalls how Ptolemy II Philadelphus, king of Ptolemaic

Egypt, commissioned seventy-two Jewish scholars to translate the Bible. The Letter of Aristeas emphasizes Ptolemy's good relationships with the Jewish community and the rational elements of Jewish Law and Scripture.

1 Maccabees: A formal account of the Hasmonean rebellion against Antiochus IV Epiphanes that is preserved in the Apocrypha. A court insider likely composed this pro-Hasmonean document in Hebrew.

2 Maccabees: Like 1 Maccabees, this book recounts the Hasmonean rebellion against Antiochus and the decades that followed. It was originally a five-volume work before it was condensed. This theologically oriented text uses Greek stylistics to convey a broad conflict between two clashing cultures. It is the first book we know of to use the Greek word for "Judaism."

Mount Athos: A Greek peninsula that since antiquity has been home to monastic communities that have preserved ancient manuscripts. Some of these manuscripts are copies of Jewish books that were originally composed in the Second Temple period. An up-to-date catalog of all the books contained in the Mount Athos libraries has not been published.

Peshitta: A translation of the Hebrew Bible and New Testament into Syriac, a dialect of Aramaic with a distinct alphabet spoken primarily by Christians. Syriac-speaking Christians began using this Bible in the early centuries of the Common Era.

Pharisees: A sect of Jews that emphasized the study and interpretation of the scriptures and developed an oral tradition that complemented the Written Law. The Pharisees thrived in the late Second Temple period in Judea. Many scholars believe that they are precursors of the Rabbinic community that developed following the Temple's destruction.

Philo of Alexandria: A Jewish philosopher living in Alexandria who wrote voluminously about the Jewish religion and its scriptures, as well as about the anti-Jewish violence that plagued Alexandria in 38 CE. His work testifies to the existence of a thriving but embattled Jewish community in Alexandria. Philo believed that the Jewish religion embodied values that were upheld by Hellenistic culture, and he applied allegorical methods that were well known in Alexandrian intellectual circles to his interpretation of the Jewish scriptures.

Pseudepigrapha: Ancient writings that have not been canonized, but that are broadly regarded as being of Jewish, Second Temple, or post–Second

Temple origin. The texts that have been collected in the Pseudepigrapha vary in genre and ideology. The term Pseudepigrapha derives from the Greek words *pseudo*, which means "false," and *epigrapha*, which means "writings," and alludes to the fact that many books in this collection were attributed to biblical characters who lived long before they were composed.

Qumran: A site on the northwestern corner of the Dead Sea, close to the caves where the Dead Sea Scrolls were discovered. It has yielded thousands of artifacts that attest to a Jewish community dating from the first century BCE to the first century CE. The question of what kind of community lived at Qumran remains open, but most scholars identify Qumran with the owners of the Dead Sea Scrolls library and believe that the Jews who settled there were Essene.

Rewritten Bible: A loosely defined term for literature written in the Second Temple period that either expands biblical stories, retells biblical stories, or uses biblical stories as platforms to write new texts.

Sadducees: A priestly Jewish sect in the late Second Temple period that rejected a system of Oral Law that complemented Written Law. While the Mishnah cites the Sadducees as opposing the Pharisees' legal opinions, the New Testament lumps the Sadducees and Pharisees together as Jesus' interlocutors, which suggests that these groups may have been more closely associated than Rabbinic texts indicate.

Septuagint: The Greek translation of the Hebrew Bible. According to the *Letter of Aristeas* and Rabbinic tradition, Ptolemy II Philadelphus, king of Ptolemaic Egypt from 283 to 246 BCE, commissioned this translation.

Salome Alexandra: The queen regnant of Judea from 76 to 67 BCE, following the death of her husband, Alexander Jannaeus. Unlike her husband, Salome Alexandra was known to sympathize with the Pharisees. Josephus criticizes Salome for allowing the Pharisees to manipulate her.

Simeon Bar Kokhba: Initiated a Jewish rebellion against the Roman Empire in 132–135 CE, which culminated in one of the biggest catastrophes in all of Jewish history. With Emperor Hadrian at the helm, the Romans severely quashed the revolt and killed as many as 250,000 Jews in Judea.

Solomon Schechter: A Jewish Romanian scholar of Rabbinic literature at Cambridge University who gained access to the Cairo Genizah and helped initiate the process of publicizing and publishing its cache of hundreds of thousands of Hebrew fragments. The eventual publication of these documents dramatically changed our understanding of Jewish life in medieval times. Some of the genizah's documents were first composed in the Second Temple period.

St. Catherine's Monastery: A monastery founded in the sixth century in the Sinai desert. Many devout Christians believe it was built on the site where God appeared to Moses in a burning bush. Its vast library is home to rare and ancient books, including the Syriac Sinaiticus, a fourth-century manuscript of the Gospels written in Syriac.

Testament of Abraham: A satirical book, dating to the late Second Temple period or shortly afterward, which tells the humorous story of the Patriarch Abraham refusing to accompany the Archangel Michael into paradise.

Testaments of the Twelve Patriarchs: A collection of twelve testaments that recall the last sayings of Jacob's twelve sons. Written over time and by multiple authors, this collection emphasizes Judaism's ethical aspects—piety, moderation, chastity, and self-control—values that would have appealed to Jews living in the Hellenistic world.

NOTES

Translations of the Hebrew Bible in this book adhere to the New Jewish Publication Society (NJPS) version. Translations of the Deuterocanonical Books and the New Testament adhere to the New Revised Standard Version (NRSV). Unless otherwise noted, translations of other texts are my own.

ABBREVIATIONS

Abbreviations of ancient sources follow those provided in the *Chicago Manual of Style*.

ACCSOT	Ancient Christian Commentary on Scripture: Old Testament
AJAJ	*American Jewish Archives Journal*
AJEC	Studies in Ancient Judaism and Early Christianity
ASOR	American Schools of Oriental Research
ATR	*Anglican Theological Review*
BA	*The Biblical Archaeologist*
BAR	*Biblical Archaeology Review*
BAS	Biblical Archaeology Society
BBR	*Bulletin for Biblical Research*
BJS	Brown Judaic Studies
BRLJ	Brill Reference Library of Judaism
CEJL	Commentaries on Early Jewish Literature
CPJ	*Corpus Papyrorum Judaicarum*
CTL	Crown Theological Library Series
DJD	*Discoveries in the Judaean Desert*
DSD	*Dead Sea Discoveries*

EEMT	Explorations in Early and Medieval Theology
EJL	Early Judaism and Its Literature
FOTC	Fathers of the Church
HTR	*Harvard Theological Review*
IEJ	*Israel Excavation Journal*
ISACR	Interdisciplinary Studies in Ancient Culture and Religion
JBL	*Journal of Biblical Literature*
JJS	*Journal of Jewish Studies*
JPS	Jewish Publication Society
JQR	*Jewish Quarterly Review*
JS	*Jewish Studies*
JSJ	*Journal for the Study of Judaism in the Persian, Hellenistic, and Roman Periods*
JSJSup	*Journal for the Study of Judaism in the Persian, Hellenistic, and Roman Periods: Supplement Series*
JSPSup	*Journal for the Study of the Pseudepigrapha: Supplement Series*
JSS	*Jewish Social Studies*
JTS	*Journal of Theological Studies*
LA	*Liber Annus*
LCL	Loeb Classical Library
LXX	Septuagint
MMT	*Miqsat Ma'aseh haTorah*
NJPS	New Jewish Publication Society TANAKH
NRSV	New Revised Standard Version
NT	*Novum Testamentum*
NTOASA	Novum Testamentum et Orbis Antiquus Series Archaeologica
OTB	*Outside the Bible*
PG	Patrologia Graeca
RevQ	*Revue de Qumran*
SOAS	School of Oriental and African Studies
SVF	*Stoicorum Veterum Fragmenta*
SVTP	Studia in Veteris Testamenti Pseudepigrapha
VT	*Vetus Testamentum*
WUNT	Wissenschaftliche Untersuchungen zum Neuen Testament

INTRODUCTION

1. Bauckham, Davila, and Panayotov, *Old Testament Pseudepigrapha*.
2. The documents that will be published in volume 2 of this collection, many of which survive only in later Christian quotations, include Horarium of Adam, Oracle of Hystaspes, and Words of Gad the Seer.
3. De Jonge, *Pseudepigrapha of the Old Testament*, 9–17; Donaldson, *Judaism and the Gentiles*, 77.

1. THE CAIRO GENIZAH

1. Bentwich, *Solomon Schechter*, 81.
2. Ben-Horin, "Solomon Schechter to Judge Mayer Sulzberger," 257.
3. Schechter, "Fragment of the Original Text of Ecclesiasticus," 4.
4. Ben-Horin, "Solomon Schechter to Judge Mayer Sulzberger," 259.
5. Other accounts of Schechter's decision to go to Cairo differ. According to Mark Glickman, Schechter was not ready to publicly announce that the Ben Sira manuscript came from the Cairo Genizah because he was not certain of its origins prior to his 1896 trip to Cairo. See Glickman, *Sacred Treasure*, 95. But in the second volume of Schechter's *Studies in Judaism*, published in 1908, Schechter writes that he knew from the beginning that the fragment had come from the Cairo Genizah.
6. Schechter, "Fragment of the Original Text of Ecclesiasticus," 1.
7. Hoffman and Cole, *Sacred Trash*, 46–52. Emphases on the particularism of Judaism in negative contrast to Christianity is especially evident in the work of Bousset, Jeremias, Harnack, Bultmann, and Baur. See Bousset, *Die Bedeutung der Person Jesu für den Glauben*, 14–17; Bultmann, *Primitive Christianity in Its Contemporary Setting*, 74–75; Jeremias, *Jesus and the Message of the New Testament*, 10, 19; Von Harnack, *New Testament Studies*, 14; Baur, *Der Gegensatz des Katholicismus und Protestantismus*. Jeremias's unnuanced point that "the attitude of late Judaism towards non-Jews was uncompromisingly severe" and that Jesus rectified this narrowness by universalizing God's covenant is, sadly, representative of these scholars' underlying thought. Jeremias, *Jesus' Promise to the Nations*, 40.
8. For more on the unique nature of the Cairo Genizah, listen to the interview with Dr. Moshe Lavee at http://tlv1.fm/the-tel-aviv-review/2014/11/14/bottomless -pit-the-cairo-geniza-and-the-untold-history-of-medieval-jewry/.
9. Schechter, *Studies in Judaism*, 2:6–7.
10. Firkovich was not simply a bibliophile, but more of a "bibliomaniac." Harviainen, "Abraham Firkovich," 883. His guiding belief was that some greatly respected Jewish texts were Karaite in origin, and he wanted to restore these texts to their

rightful owners. Firkovich believed that the inscription of the tenth-century Aleppo Codex, for example, proved its Karaite origin. After he was shown the codex during a visit to Aleppo in 1863 and suggested to community leaders that the codex was Karaite, it was decided that they would not show him the codex again. Harviainen, "Abraham Firkovich, the Aleppo Codex, and its Dedication," 132–36. Firkovich became notorious for acquiring precious texts through shady means and aggressive tactics. He used the financial support he received from Karaite communities to pressure individuals into selling him their ancient documents. Firkovich's most prized acquisition was the Leningrad Codex, and he provided virtually no explanation as to how it came into his hands. In his work *Avnei Zikkaron*, Firkovich makes only two allusions to the codex:

> On Thursday, We-Adar 21st, I took all the books and the ancient volumes which I had found and also the very valuable book of 24 which was written in 4770 in Egypt/Cairo and which was brought from Damascus—and this happened on the order of R. Simhah Babovich, the Head of the Sages of blessed memory. In the evening I went from Gözlävä and came to Akmejis. The next morning I went to the Governor. Firkovich, *Avnei Zikkaron*, 32, cited in Harviainen, "Abraham Firkovich," 887–88.

> On Tuesday, April 2, 1840 . . . I collected all the books and volumes which I had found in Kale, Kaffa, and Karasub and the Book of the Bible which was brought from Egypt/Cairo, and with the permission of the Governor I placed them in the best safekeeping in the archive of the Governor. Firkovich, *Avnei Zikkaron*, 35, cited in Harviainen, "Abraham Firkovich," 888.

After Firkovich died, a longtime rival named Albert Harkavy accused Firkovich of forging the dates that were written on thousands of texts and tombstone inscriptions. This accusation would tarnish Firkovich's reputation for over a century. Some scholars have recently argued that Firkovich was not, in fact, a con man. Harviainen, "Abraham Firkovich," 892.

11. Kahana, "Tannaitic Midrashim," 63.
12. Reif, *A Jewish Archive from Old Cairo*, 15–16.
13. Jefferson, "Cairo Genizah Unearthed," 175.
14. Adler, "Some Missing Chapters of Ben Sira," 466.
15. Jefferson, "Cairo Genizah Unearthed," 173.
16. Reif, *Jewish Archive from Old Cairo*, 15.
17. The Taylor-Schechter Genizah site is accessible at http://www.lib.cam.ac.uk /collections/departments/taylor-schechter-genizah-research-unit. The Mosseri Collection is available at http://www.lib.cam.ac.uk/collections/departments /taylor-schechter-genizah-research-unit/jacques-mosseri-genizah-collection.

18. On Mosseri's collection, see Glickman, *Sacred Treasure*, 186–92.
19. Outhwaite, "Hebrew Manuscript Collection of Cambridge University Library," 37.
20. Hoffman and Cole, *Sacred Trash*, 46–52.
21. On this topic, see Simkovich, *Making of Jewish Universalism*.
22. Note Schiffman's point that "the finding of manuscripts of Ben Sira in the Cairo Genizah was the beginning of the recovery of the original Hebrew of this text, a process which culminated with the discovery of the Ben Sira manuscripts from Qumran and Masada. But comparison of these manuscripts indicates that Ben Sira had a complex textual history in rabbinic and medieval times that has yet to be fully analyzed or appreciated." Schiffman, "Second Temple Literature and the Cairo Genizah," 146.
23. Ginzberg, *An Unknown Jewish Sect*, 124–30.
24. Lorein and van Staalduine-Sulman, "A Song of David for Each Day," 58–59.
25. Bauckham, Davila, and Panayotiv, *Old Testament Pseudepigrapha*, 257–60.
26. These Cairo Genizah fragments are known as T-S 16.94, housed in Cambridge University, and MS Heb c 27 f 56, housed in Oxford University's Bodleian Library. The Dead Sea texts are 1Q21, 4Q213, 213a, 214, 214a, and 214b. See Kugel, "How Old Is the 'Aramaic Levi Document?'" 291.
27. See, for instance, Arendzen and Pass, "Fragment of an Aramaic Text of the Testament of Levi," 652.
28. Kugel, "How Old Is the 'Aramaic Levi Document?'" 292–93.

2. MANUSCRIPTS AND MONASTERIES

1. Peterson, "Tischendorf and the *Codex Sinaiticus*: The Saga Continues," 75.
2. Tischendorf, *Codex Sinaiticus*, 23.
3. Pattie, "The Codex Sinaiticus," 2.
4. Milne and Skeat, *Scribes and Correctors*.
5. Tischendorf, *Codex Sinaiticus*, 27.
6. Tischendorf, *Codex Sinaiticus*, 29.
7. According to James Charlesworth, there is a pillar in St. Catherine's Library upon which hangs a letter written by Tischendorf to the monks that contains the phrase, "this manuscript I promise to return safely." Charlesworth, "St. Catherine's Monastery," 178.
8. Parker, *Codex Sinaiticus*; Porter, *Constantine Tischendorf*.
9. Parker, *Codex Sinaiticus*, 130.
10. Parker, *Codex Sinaiticus*, 132.
11. A more generous interpretation of these events can be found in Porter, "Hero or Thief?" 45–53; cf. Böttrich, *Bibliographie Konstantin von Tischendorf*.
12. Pattie, "The Codex Sinaiticus," 6; Beneshevich, *Opisanie grecheskikh*, vxi.

13. *Time*, January 1, 1934.

14. *Time*, February 5, 1934.

15. Ševĉenko, "New Documents on Constantine Tischendorf," 80.

16. Brooke and McLean, "On a Petersburg MS of the Septuagint," 209–11.

17. Agourides and Charlesworth, "New Discovery of Old Manuscripts," 29–31.

18. Sarris, "Discovery of a New Fragment," 1.

19. *Sinaiticus: The Bulletin of the Saint Catherine Foundation* 11 (2012): 1.

20. Photographs of the codex are accessible at http://codexsinaiticus.org/en/codex /history.aspx.

21. De Mendieta, *Mount Athos*, 245.

22. On this prohibition, see http://www.bbc.com/news/magazine-36378690.

23. De Mendieta, *Mount Athos*, 243.

24. De Mendieta, *Mount Athos*, 249.

25. De Mendieta, *Mount Athos*, 249. Uspensky's first name is sometimes spelled Porphyre or Porphry, and his last name can be spelled Uspenskij, Uspensky, or Uspenski. On the ancient treasures that have come under National Library of Russia ownership, see http://www.nlr.ru/eng/coll/manuscripts/eastscripts.html.

26. De Mendieta, *Mount Athos*, 244.

27. I could not find any indication of this claim in Spyridon Lambros' work *Catalogue of the Greek Manuscripts on Mount Athos*.

28. Speake, *Mount Athos*, 199.

29. H. C. Kee, "Testaments of the Twelve Patriarchs," in Charlesworth, *Old Testament Pseudepigrapha*, 1:778. De Jonge, "Christian Influence in the Testaments of the Twelve Patriarchs," 182–235; De Jonge, *Testaments of the Twelve Patriarchs*, 128.

30. James Davila has recently argued that most pseudepigraphic texts were written by gentiles in the centuries following the Second Temple period. Davila, *The Provenance of the Pseudepigrapha*, 229–30. His opinion is supported by some scholars who have focused on individual cases. Ross Kraemer, for instance, attributes Joseph and Aseneth to Christian writers. Kraemer dates the long version of this text to the fourth century and the short version to the third century. Kraemer, *When Aseneth Met Joseph*, 296.

31. On the manuscript digitization project, see https://archaeologynewsnetwork .blogspot.com/2014/11/byzantine-treasures-of-mount-athos-to.html #l7pdUvUSBP7YImA1.97.

32. Fine, *Art, History and the Historiography of Judaism*, 169–80; Sophia Hollander, "Yeshiva Students Challenge Myths of the Menorah," *Wall Street Journal*, August 14, 2014.

33. For references to "the Son of Man," see 1 Enoch 46:1–5; 48:1–4.

34. The details here were related by Stuckenbruck during a presentation at the Enoch Seminar (McGill University, Montreal, Canada, May 22, 2014).
35. Erho, "New Ethiopic Witnesses," 75–97.

3. THE DEAD SEA SCROLLS

1. Sukenik, *Dead Sea Scrolls of the Hebrew University*, 7.
2. The amount $250,000 in the summer of 1954 would be equivalent to $2,388,143 on January 1, 2019, based on an annual inflation rate of 3.62 percent.
3. Kalman, "Optimistic, Even with the Negatives," 23.
4. Trever, *The Dead Sea Scrolls—A Personal Account*.
5. For details regarding Yadin's acquisition of the Temple Scroll, see the Israel Museum's description of this account at http://www.imj.org.il/shrine_center /Temple_article.html.
6. The English translation of the interview was published in an article by the journalist who interviewed Strugnell, Avi Katzman. Katzman, "Chief Dead Sea Scroll Editor Denounces Judaism, Israel," 64–65, 70–72. According to Katzman's account,

   [Strugnell] was, he said, an "anti-Judaist." "Judaism," he said, "is originally racist . . . it's a folk religion; it's not a higher religion. An anti-Judaist, that's what I am. There, I plead guilty. I plead guilty in the way the Church has pleaded guilty all along, because we're not guilty; we're right. Christianity presents itself as a religion which replaces the Jewish religion. The correct answer of Jews to Christianity is to become Christian. I agree that there have been monstrosities in the past—the Inquisition, things like that. We should certainly behave ourselves like Christian gentlemen. But the basic judgment on the Jewish religion is, for me, a negative one."

7. Bernstein, "Miqsat Ma'ase Ha-torah," 68.
8. Shanks, "Intellectual Property Law and the Scholar," 64.
9. Lim, "Intellectual Property and the Dead Sea Scrolls," 187–98.
10. VanderKam and Flint, *Meaning of the Dead Sea Scrolls*, 395.
11. Kalman, *Hebrew Union College and the Dead Sea Scrolls*, 70–79.
12. See http://dss.collections.imj.org.il/discovery.
13. See http://www.lib.cam.ac.uk/collections/departments/taylor-schechter-genizah -research-unit.
14. It took decades for de Vaux's field notes to be published, first in French in 1994 and then with some added material in English in 2003. See Humbert and Chambon, *Excavations of Khirbet Qumran*.

15. Magness, *Archaeology of Qumran and the Dead Sea Scrolls*, 2.
16. Schiffman, "Short History of the Dead Sea Scrolls," 44–53.
17. See Milik, "Tefillin, Mezuzot et Targums," 33–85; Yadin, "Tefillin (Phylacteries) from Qumran," 60–83; Yadin, *Tefillin from Qumran*; cf. Yadin, *Excavations of Masada, 1964/64*. For a broad survey on this subject, see Cohn, *Tangled Up in Text*.
18. Segal et al., "Early Leviticus Scroll from En-Gedi," 1–30; see also Marc Brettler's article "The Ein Gedi Torah Scroll?" at http://thetorah.com/the-ein-gedi-torah -scroll/.
19. Most Jews did not accept some books, such as Ecclesiastes and Song of Songs, as canonical until the Rabbinic period. Lim, *Formation of the Jewish Canon*, 16.

4. JERUSALEM

1. Mazar, "Jerusalem in the Biblical Period," 2–5.
2. The Christian scholar Jerome (347–420 CE) cites a now-lost account of this exile written by Eusebius in Jerome, *Chronicon*, Olympiad 105, in Donalson, *Translation of Jerome's Chronicon*. See also Orosius, *Seven Books of History against the Pagans*, 3.7.
3. Heinrich Graetz suggests that the final chapter of Zechariah alludes to the Persian persecution. Graetz, "Last Chapter of Zechariah," 208–19.
4. Waterfield, *Dividing the Spoils*, 6.
5. Plutarch, *Life of Demetrius*, 28–29. According to Josephus, Ptolemy I deported 100,000 people to Egypt, and, of those, 30,000 men were taken as soldiers. These numbers may be exaggerated. See Josephus, *Antiquities*, 13.12.1.
6. Wright, *Letter of Aristeas* 4–8, 14–20.
7. Campbell and Tritle, *Oxford Handbook of Warfare*, ix; Green, *Alexander to Actium*, 499.
8. 1 Macc. 1:20–41; 2 Macc. 6:1–6; Josephus, *Antiquities* 12.5.4.
9. Compare 1 Maccabees 3:58 with Josephus, *Antiquities* 12.7.3. On the ways in which Josephus makes adjustments to 1 Maccabees, see Gafni, "Josephus and 1 Maccabees," 116–31.
10. 1 Macc. 1:43–49; 2 Macc. 6:1.
11. 1 Macc. 2:27; cf. "Whoever is for the Lord, come here!" Exod. 32:26.
12. Josephus, *Antiquities* 13.13.5.
13. Josephus, *Antiquities* 13.14.2.
14. For more on Salome, see Josephus *Antiquities*, 13.16.1–6; *War* 1.5.1–2.
15. B. Ta'an. 23a.
16. Leviticus Rabbah 35.10.
17. Josephus, *Antiquities* 14.1.2.
18. Josephus, *Antiquities* 14.1.4.
19. Josephus, *Antiquities* 14.3.4.
20. Josephus, *Antiquities* 14.4–13; *War* 1.8–13.

21. Josephus, *Antiquities*, 13.9.1.

22. Josephus, *Antiquities* 14.9.2.

23. Josephus, *Antiquities* 14.13–14; *War* 1.14.4.

24. Josephus, *Antiquities* 14.16.1–4.

25. Josephus, *War* 1.22.2.

26. Josephus, *War* 1.22.3–5; cf. *Antiquities* 15.7.4.

27. Josephus, *Antiquities* 15.7.8.

28. Josephus, *War* 1.27.5.

29. Josephus, *Antiquities* 17.7.1.

30. Matt. 2:16–18.

31. Josephus, *Antiquities* 17.6.5.

32. Netzer, *Architecture of Herod*, 303.

33. "Now there were devout Jews from every nation under heaven living in Jerusalem. And at this sound the crowd gathered and was bewildered, because each one heard them speaking in the native language of each. Amazed and astonished, they asked, 'Are not all these who are speaking Galileans? And how is it that we hear, each of us, in our own native language? Parthians, Medes, Elamites, and residents of Mesopotamia, Judea and Cappadocia, Pontus and Asia, Phrygia and Pamphylia, Egypt and the parts of Libya belonging to Cyrene, and visitors from Rome, both Jews and proselytes, Cretans and Arabs—in our own languages we hear them speaking about God's deeds of power.'" Acts 2:5–11.

34. Josephus, *Antiquities* 17.8.1.

35. Josephus, *Antiquities* 17.13.2; *War* 2.7.3.

36. Josephus, *War* 2.8.1.

37. M. Sot. 7:8.

38. Schwartz, *Agrippa I*, 162.

39. Acts 12:1–11.

40. Acts 12:22–23.

41. Josephus, *Antiquities* 17.10.4–7.

42. Acts 15:20.

43. See T. Avod. Zar. 8:4; B. Sanh. 52b; Genesis Rabbah 16:6. It is possible that the observances that gentiles must keep listed in Jubilees 7:20 is an early articulation of the Noahide Laws, but this list is not identical to the later one provided by the Rabbis.

44. On the biblical mandate to make such pilgrimages, see Exod. 23:17, 34:22–23; Deut. 16:16.

45. Tepper and Tepper, "Archaeological Views," 20, 62.

46. Josephus, *War* 6.9.3.

47. Josephus, *War* 2.14.3.

48. Tos. Pes. 4.64b.

49. Josephus, *War* 5.1.6.

50. In Josephus's account in *Antiquities*, the crowd of Jews at the Temple ran from Cumanus's soldiers in fear, which led to a stampede, while in *The Jewish War*, Josephus gives the impression that the Jews were forced out of the area. Josephus, *War* 2.12.1; *Antiquities* 20.5.3.

51. Josephus, *Antiquities* 20.11.1.

52. Josephus, *War* 2.14.

53. Josephus, *Antiquities* 18.1.6.

54. Josephus, *War* 2.19.9.

55. Josephus, *War* 2.20.2.

56. Josephus, *War* 4.2.1–2.

57. According to Josephus, Agrippa II deposed Ananus from the high priesthood because he killed James the Just. Josephus, *Antiquities* 20.9.1.

58. Josephus, *War* 4.3.13–14.

59. Josephus, *War* 4.4.5.

60. Josephus, *War* 4.9.11.

61. B. Taʿan. 29a; B. Arak. 11b; T. Taʿan. 3:9.

62. Josephus, *War* 6.9.3.

63. B. Git. 57b.

64. Deutsch, "Roman Coins Boast," 51–53.

65. Magness, "Arch of Titus," 207.

66. Feldman, "Financing the Colosseum," 20–31, 60–61.

67. *Avot de-Rabbi Nathan* A 4.22–23, in Schechter, 12.

68. *Avot de-Rabbi Nathan* B 8.19, in Schechter, 12; B. Git. 56b; Eikhah Rabbah 1:31.

69. B. Mak. 24b.

70. Josephus, *War* 7.6.6; Cassius Dio, *Roman History* 65.7.2.

71. While there is little evidence that the Jews of Judea were involved in the uprising of 115–118 CE, E. Mary Smallwood has made a compelling case that there was unrest in Judea at this time, and although they did not suffer as much destruction as the diaspora Jews who were involved in this war, at least some Jews in Judea regarded themselves as partaking in this uprising. Smallwood, "Palestine c. A. D. 115–118," 500–10.

72. Cassius Dio writes that 580,000 people were killed by the time the revolt was quelled, but these numbers are likely exaggerated. See Cassius Dio, *Roman History* 69.12–14.

73. B. Git. 56b–57a.

74. For a compendium of essays on this question, see Schwartz, *Was 70 CE a Watershed in Jewish History*.

75. Psalms of Solomon 8:21–24; Josephus, *Antiquities* 14.4.1–4.

76. Acts 21:37–40.

5. ALEXANDRIA

1. Ellens, *Ancient Library of Alexandria*, 2–4.

2. Juvenal, *Satires* 14.96–106, in *Juvenal and Persius*; Valerius Maximus writes that the Jews are responsible for trying to "infect Roman manners with the cult of Jupiter Sabazius." See Maximus, *Memorable Doings and Sayings* 1.3.3; Tacitus, *Histories* 5.1–13; Epictetus, *Discourses* 2.9.19–21; Josephus, *Against Apion* 2.282.

3. Feldman, *Jew and Gentile in the Ancient World*, 108.

4. Josephus, *Antiquities* 19.5.2.

5. Feldman, *Jew and Gentile in the Ancient World*, 108.

6. Philo, *Against Flaccus* 43. Dorothy Sly suggests that when it comes to the population of Jews living in Alexandria, the figure of 180,000, mentioned in the Acts of the Alexandrians, may be close to the correct figure, presuming a population size of 500,000 to 600,000 and the likelihood that about a third of the city's population was Jewish. Sly, *Philo's Alexandria*, 46.

7. Josephus relies on a historian named Agatharchides of Cnidus in Josephus, *Antiquities* 12.1.8.

8. Some of these were found in the Zenon Papyri, a cache of archives belonging to one Zeno, the secretary of an Egyptian official. This cache, found on the site of ancient Philadelphia, dates to the third century BCE and includes documents with Jewish names. For a study of Jewish life in Egypt during this period, see Kasher, *Jews in Hellenistic and Roman Egypt*; Moore, *With Walls of Iron*.

9. M. Menah. 13:10; b. Menah. 109a.

10. Philo says that the city was divided into five sections, and of these five, two were predominantly Jewish. Each section was named according to a letter of the Greek alphabet. During the rule of the Alexandrian procurator Flaccus, the Jews of Alexandria were forcibly moved out of their homes and crammed into one portion of one section. Philo, *Flaccus* 55. This was regarded as an insulting act of antagonism, since at least some Jews believed that Alexander's successors gave the Jews a section of Alexandria to live in (Josephus, *War* 2.18.7). In *Against Apion*, Josephus says that it was Alexander himself who allotted land for Jewish settlement, but since *Against Apion* is a more polemical book than *The Jewish War*, the latter version should be taken as more likely. Josephus, *Against Apion* 2.42–64.

11. A number of ancient inscriptions and papyri found in or near Alexandria speak of prayer halls (*proseuche*), or make references to the ruler of the synagogue (*archisynagogos*). Runesson, Binder, and Olsson, *Ancient Synagogue*, 185–86; Horbury and Noy, *Jewish Inscriptions of Graeco-Roman Egypt*, 9, 13, 18, 20. See also Tcherikover and Fuks, *Corpus Papyrorum Judaicarum*, 1.128. Cf. Levine, "Second Temple Synagogue," 7–32.

12. See, for example, 2 Cor. 11:32. Josephus quotes the historian Strabo, who mentions the Jewish ethnarch. Josephus, *Antiquities*, 14.7.2.

13. 1 Macc. 14:47, 15:1–2.

14. Josephus, *Antiquities* 14.7.1.

15. Toward the end of the Second Temple period, the *gerousia* in Judea developed into what became known as the Sanhedrin and comprised seventy-one members. On the Sanhedrin in the first century CE, see M. Mid. 5:4; Mark 14:53–55.

16. Philo, *Flaccus* 10.

17. Schwartz, "Philo, His Life and Times," 16.

18. Marcus, commentary, in Josephus, *Antiquities*, vol. 5, bks. 12–13, 467–72.

19. Josephus, *Antiquities* 14.10.1; *Against Apion* 2.4–5.

20. Sly, *Philo's Alexandria*, 7–8, 178–80; Pucci Ben Zeev, *Jewish Rights in the Roman World*, 386–87.

21. Schwartz, "Philo, His Life and Times," 21.

22. Cicero, *For Flaccus* 28.66–67.

23. Mucznik and Ovadiah, "*Deisidaimonia, Superstitio*, and *Religio*," 420.

24. Josephus, *Antiquities* 14.7.2.

25. Josephus, *War* 2.17.2; Cicero, *For Flaccus* 28.66–69.

26. Philo, *Embassy to Gaius* 22.156–57.

27. Philo, *Flaccus* 7.46–47; Philo, *On the Confusion of Tongues* 17.77–78.

28. Philo, *Flaccus* 5.27.

29. Philo, *Flaccus* 6.36–40.

30. Philo, *Flaccus* 6.40.

31. Philo, *Flaccus* 14.116, 21.185.

32. Philo, *Flaccus* 21.185–91.

33. Josephus says that just three delegates were sent. *Antiquities* 18.8.1–2.

34. Philo, *Embassy to Gaius* 352–53.

35. Philo, *Embassy to Gaius* 363.

36. Josephus, *Antiquities* 18.8.1–2. The fact that Josephus states that there were three Jewish and three gentile delegates, while Philo states that there were five delegates of each group, suggests that Josephus did not read Philo's account of this incident.

37. Josephus, *Antiquities* 19.5.1–2.

38. Pucci Ben Zeev, *Jewish Rights*, 311.

39. P. London 1912, CPJ I 151, in Edgar and Hunt, *Select Papyri*, 2:78–79; see also Bell, *Jews and Christians in Egypt*; Tcherikover and Fuks, *Corpus Papyrorum Judaicarum*, no. 153.

40. Josephus, *Antiquities* 19.5.3.

41. Pucci Ben Zeev, *Jewish Rights*, 310.

42. Josephus, *War* 2.18.7.

43. Josephus, *War* 2.18.7–8.

44. Josephus identifies Philo as the brother of Alexander the Jewish alabarch, a wealthy customs official who was Tiberius's father. Josephus, *Antiquities* 18.8.1. Alexander had strong ties to both the Roman imperial family and the Herodian family ruling Judea. See Josephus, *Antiquities* 18.6.1–4. Alexander's son Marcus married Agrippa I's daughter, Berenice. Josephus, *Antiquities* 19.5.1.

45. Josephus, *Antiquities* 20.5.2. See also Kraft, "Tiberius Julius Alexander," 175–84.

46. Josephus, *War* 7.6.6; Dio Cassius, *Roman History* 65.7.2.

47. Suetonius, *Life of Domitian*, 12.

48. Horbury, *Jewish War under Trajan and Hadrian*, 258.

49. Smallwood, "Palestine c. A. D. 115–118," 500–510.

50. Eusebius, *Ecclesiastical History* 4.2; Eusebius, *Chronicle* 2.164.

51. B. Pesah. 50a; b. B. Bat. 10b.

52. Eusebius, *Ecclesiastical History* 4.2.

53. Appian, *Civil Wars* 2.90, in *Roman History*, vol. 3.

54. Cassius Dio's description of the Jewish rebellion is startlingly gory. According to his account, "The Jews in the region of Cyrene had put a certain Andreas at their head, and were destroying both the Romans and the Greeks. They would eat the flesh of their victims, make belts for themselves of their entrails, anoint themselves with their blood and wear their skins for clothing; many they sawed in two, from the head downwards; others they gave to wild beasts, and still others they forced to fight as gladiators. In all two hundred and twenty thousand persons perished. In Egypt, too, they perpetrated many similar outrages, and in Cyprus, under the leadership of a certain Artemion. There, also, two hundred and forty thousand perished, and for this reason no Jew may set foot on that island, but even if one of them is driven upon its shores by a storm he is put to death." Cassius Dio, *Roman History* 68.32.

55. "Then, all at once, the Jews in different parts of the world, as if enraged with madness, burst forth in an incredible revolution. For throughout all Libya, they carried on most violent wars against the inhabitants, and Libya was, then, so

forsaken by the killing of the cultivators of the soil that, unless Hadrian afterwards had not gathered colonists from without and brought them there, the land would have remained completely destitute and without an inhabitant. Indeed, they threw into confusion all Egypt, Cyrene, and the Thebaid with bloody seditions. But in Alexandria, in a pitched battle, they were conquered and crushed. In Mesopotamia also, when they rebelled, by order of the emperor, war was introduced against them. And thus many thousands of them were destroyed in a vast slaughter. Indeed, they did destroy Salamis, a city of Cyprus, after killing all the inhabitants." Orosius, *Seven Books of History against the Pagans* 7.12.

56. B. Git. 57b (Soncino).

57. Y. Ta'an. 4.8, 68d–69a; b. Git. 57a–b.

58. Philo, *Embassy to Gaius* 20; B. Sukkah 51b.

59. Letter of Aristeas, in *OTB*, 319–21.

60. Philo, *On the Life of Moses* 2.25–44; Josephus, *Antiquities* 12.2.1–12.2.15. Josephus is likely using the Letter of Aristeas, although he may have had a different version than the text that survives today. On the differences between Josephus's account and the Letter of Aristeas, see Wright, *Letter of Aristeas*.

61. Philo, *On the Life of Moses* 2.43.

62. Aristeas also says that the Septuagint was written on Pharos. See Letter of Aristeas, 301.

63. Philo, *On the Life of Moses* 2.41.

64. B. Meg. 9a; Megillat Taanit, although this text may not be Rabbinic; Leiman, "Scroll of Fasts," 194; Wasserstein and Wasserstein, *Legend of the Septuagint*, 81–82.

65. M. Meg. 1:8.

66. This practice seems more likely if we take into account that the Torah was translated into Aramaic in synagogues whose members spoke Aramaic as their first language. On *tannaitic* references to the *meturgeman*, see Levine, *Ancient Synagogue*, 442–58.

67. Translation by Moshe Simon-Shoshan in Simon-Shoshan, "Tasks of the Translators," 28.

68. The knowledge of the human body reflected in the Egyptian medical treatises known as the Edwin Smith Surgical Papyrus and the Ebers Papyrus suggests that human autopsies were conducted by medical students. See Breasted, *Edwin Smith Surgical Papyrus*. See also Finkbeiner, Ursell, and Davis, *Autopsy Pathology*, 1–2.

69. Pseudo-Phocylides 102, in Charlesworth, *Old Testament Pseudepigrapha*; Van der Horst, *Sentences of Pseudo-Phocylides*, 183–84.

70. These quotations are preserved in Eusebius, *Praeparatio Evangelica*, 9.28–29; Clement of Alexandria, *Stromateis* 1.23.155f; Pseudo-Eustathius, *Commentarius in Hexaemeron*, PG 18.729. See R. G. Robertson, "Ezekiel the Tragedian," in Charlesworth, *Old Testament Pseudepigrapha*, 2:803.

6. ANTIOCH

1. Kondoleon, "City of Antioch," 9.
2. Josephus, *Antiquities* 12.3.1; *Against Apion* 2.39.
3. According to Josephus, after the Jerusalem Temple was restored following the Hasmonean rebellion, Antiochus IV Epiphanes' successors donated beautiful brass ornaments to the synagogue at Antioch. Josephus, *War* 7.3.3.
4. Zetterholm, "Antioch," 336.
5. Josephus, *Against Apion* 2.39.
6. Josephus, *War* 7.3.3.
7. Josephus, *War* 7.5.2; *Antiquities* 12.3.1.
8. Josephus, *War* 7.3.3.
9. Josephus, *War* 7.5.2.
10. Josephus, *War* 7.5.2.
11. Josephus, *Antiquities* 12.3.1.
12. Marcus, commentary, in Josephus, *Jewish Antiquities*, vol. 5, 472.
13. 2 Macc. 4:9.
14. Josephus, *War* 3.2.3.
15. Josephus, *Antiquities* 17.2.1–3.
16. "For, although Antiochus surnamed Epiphanes sacked Jerusalem and plundered the temple, his successors on the throne restored to the Jews of Antioch all such votive offerings as were made of brass to be laid up in their synagogue, and, moreover, granted them citizen rights on an equality with the Greeks. Continuing to receive similar treatment from later monarchs, the Jewish colony grew . in numbers, and their richly designed and costly offerings formed a splendid ornament to the temple." Because Josephus uses the term "synagogue" in the above passage, scholars take his reference to a temple in Antioch as a reference to the city's great synagogue. Josephus, *Jewish War* 7.3.3; Levine, *Ancient Synagogue*, 125–26.
17. Malalas, *Chronicle*, 10.261. Daphne's Jewish population must have gone back to at least the early second century BCE, when Onias, the ousted anti-Hellenistic high priest, chose to flee to Daphne in attempt to escape the assassination plot of the corrupt High Priest Menelaus (2 Macc. 4:33). Even if the author of 2 Maccabees is wrong on this detail, the fact that he inserted it suggests that his readers would have found Onias's retirement at Daphne plausible.

18. Malalas, *Chronicle*, 8.206–7; see Levine, *Ancient Synagogue*, 126; Joslyn-Siemiatkoski, *Christian Memories of the Maccabean Martyrs*, 42–50.

19. Acts 11:19. See also Acts 14:21–22, 15:35, 18:22.

20. Gal. 2:11–14; 2 Tim. 3:11.

21. Acts 6:5.

22. Acts 14:19.

23. Acts 18:22.

24. Acts 11:2, 11:27, 18:22, 24:11, 25:1, 25:6.

25. Acts 11:28.

26. The term appears in the New Testament in only two other places, and it is not clear when it caught on with the larger population.

27. Paulus Orosius says that Jews rebelled throughout the world, but specifies the regions of Libya, Egypt, Cyrene, Thebais in Upper Egypt, and Salamis in Cyprus. He does not mention Antioch. Orosius, *Against the Pagans*, 7.12.

28. Downey, *Ancient Antioch*, 91.

29. Josephus, *War* 7.3.3.

30. Josephus, *War* 7.5.2.

31. Josephus, *War* 7.3.3.

32. Josephus, *War* 7.3.4.

33. Cassius Dio describes the wreckage as follows:

> First there came, on a sudden, a great bellowing roar, and this was followed by a tremendous quaking. The whole earth was upheaved, and buildings leaped into the air; some were carried aloft only to collapse and be broken in pieces, while others were tossed this way and that as if by the surge of the sea, and overturned, and the wreckage spread out over a great extent even of the open country. The crash of grinding and breaking timbers together with tiles and stones was most frightful; and an inconceivable amount of dust arose, so that it was impossible for one to see anything or to speak or hear a word.

Cassius Dio, *Roman History*, Epitome of Book 68.24.

34. H. C. Kee, "Testaments of the Twelve Patriarchs," in Charlesworth, *Old Testament Pseudepigrapha*, 1:778.

35. See James L. Kugel's introduction to the Testaments of the Twelve Patriarchs in OTB, 1697–1703. Kugel underscores how difficult it is to pin down the historical context and providence of this collection but makes a compelling case for its Jewish authorship.

36. Matt. 4:24.

37. For parallels between the Syriac Christian exegetical tradition and Jewish exegetical tradition, see Narinskaya, *Ephrem, a 'Jewish' Sage*. See also Frishman, "'And Abraham had Faith,'" 164; Amar, *St. Ephrem the Syrian*.

38. Chrysostom, *Discourses* 11–12. For more on the Jewish community during this period, see Brooten, "Jews of Ancient Antioch," 33.

7. THE WISDOM SEEKERS

1. While Josephus claims that the Jews of Alexandria were granted the rights of full citizenship, he was probably exaggerating the equity between Jews and Greeks in Alexandria, or he had misinformation. Josephus, *Antiquities* 19.5.2. For a discussion of the question of whether Josephus should be taken as a reliable source, see Ritter, *Judeans in the Greek Cities of the Roman Empire*, 4–11.

2. See Simkovich, "Greek Influence," 293–310.

3. Pseudo-Phocylides 103.

4. Pseudo-Phocylides 115.

5. See Katell Berthelot's extensive study of the writings of Lysimachus, Posidonius, Apollonius Molon, Apion, and Philostratus on this subject in her *Philanthrôpia Judaica*, 79–171. See also Feldman and Reinhold, *Jewish Life and Thought among Greeks and Romans*, 350–96; Josephus on anti-Jewish historians in Stern, *Greek and Latin Authors on Jews and Judaism*, 62–83.

6. Josephus defends circumcision against Apion's critique of the practice in *Against Apion* 2.13. Circumcision is also mocked in Petronius, *Satyricon* 102, and Martial, *Epigrams* 7.30.

7. As for the Sabbath reflecting laziness, see Seneca, cited in Augustine's *City of God* 6.11; Juvenal, *Satire* 14.105–6; Tacitus, *Histories* 5.4. In *Against Apion*, Josephus recounts Apion's claims that six days after leaving Egypt, the Jews developed a pain in their groin, which is called *sabbatosis* in Egyptian. Because they needed to rest before recovering, the Jews instituted a practice of resting every seven days. According to this account, the Jews' observance of the Sabbath is both trivial and shameful. Josephus, *Against Apion* 2.2.

8. The third-century BCE priest Manetho is refuted in Josephus's *Against Apion* 1.26–32. See also Josephus's refutation of Lysimachus in *Against Apion* 1.34.

9. Apollonius Molon, cited by Josephus in *Against Apion* 2.7–8. See also Juvenal, *Satires* 3.10–16.

10. See, for example, Hecataeus, *Aegyptiaca*, cited in Diodorus Sicilus, *Library of History* 40.3; Stern, *Greek and Latin Authors on Jews and Judaism*, 1:28, 50; and *De Somno 180*, in Josephus, *Against Apion* 1.176–83.

11. Philo, *Questions and Answers on Genesis* 3.48.

12. Tacitus, *Histories* 5.5.2; Petronius, *Satyricon* 102:14.

13. Philo, *On the Migration of Abraham* 88–91.
14. Vladimir de Beer has traced the development of how the word "Logos" was used from Heraclitus through the time of John Scottus Eriugena. De Beer, "Cosmic Role of the Logos," 39.
15. The many ways in which scholars have interpreted the meaning of Logos in the writings of Heraclitus is reviewed in Robinson, "Heraclitus and Plato," 481–90.
16. See, among many others, Allred, "Divine *Logos*," 1–18; Mansfeld, "Zeno on the Unity of Philosophy," 120; Boyarin, "Gospel of the Memra," 248.
17. Boyarin, "Gospel of the Memra," 248–50.
18. Birnbaum, "Exegetical Building Blocks," 78.
19. Philo, *On Abraham* 52.
20. Philo, *On the Migration of Abraham* 136–37.
21. Yoshiko Reed, "Construction and Subversion of Patriarchal Perfection," 192.
22. Philo, *On Abraham* 255–59.
23. Philo, *On the Life of Moses* 1.8–9.
24. B. Sotah 12a.
25. Schäfer, *Origins of Jewish Mysticism*, 155.
26. "Since many have undertaken to set down an orderly account of the events that have been fulfilled among us, just as they were handed on to us by those who from the beginning were eyewitnesses and servants of the word, I too decided, after investigating everything carefully from the very first, to write an orderly account for you, most excellent Theophilus, so that you may know the truth concerning the things about which you have been instructed." Luke 1:1–4.
27. Letter of Aristeas, 222–24.
28. On the importance of wisdom and moderation in Greek literature, see Laertius, *Lives of the Eminent Philosophers* 7.92; on moderation in Seneca, *Epistles* 66.29–30, 85.2–3; Cicero, *On Duties* 1.15–16, 46; Stobaeus, *Eclogues* II.97.15, in SVF, 3.22–23.
29. Letter of Aristeas, 44–45.
30. Letter of Aristeas, 15–16, in *OTB*, 2719.

8. THE SECTARIANS

1. Josephus, *Antiquities* 17.2.4, 18.1.2–4.
2. Levine, *Jerusalem*, 340–43; Broshi, "Estimating the Population," 10–15.
3. Tacitus, *Histories*, 5.12.3.
4. Josephus, *War* 6.9.3.
5. Not all scholars view Josephus as completely reliable. Steve Mason argues that Josephus takes many liberties and that it is difficult to discern what historical kernels lie in his descriptions, and Shaye Cohen reads Josephus as a largely undependable witness to history. Mason, "Will the Real Josephus Please Stand

Up?" 58–68; Mason, "Essenes and Lurking Spartans in Josephus' *Judean War*," 219–61; Cohen, *Josephus in Galilee and Rome*, 181. But Jonathan Klawans leans toward treating Josephus as largely reliable, particularly when it comes to his descriptions of the varieties of Jewish theological positions in the first century. Klawans, *Josephus and Theologies of Ancient Judaism*, 42–44. Likewise, Albert Baumgarten defends Josephus as a reliable historical source in Baumgarten, "Josephus on Ancient Jewish Groups," 1–13. Daniel Schwartz argues for a middle ground in his *Reading the First Century*.

6. Josephus, *Antiquities* 13.10.6, 18.1.4; *War* 2.8.2.

7. Josephus, *Antiquities* 13.10.6, 13.5.9; 18.1.2–4; *War* 2.8.2–14; *Life* 2.

8. Josephus, *Life* 2.

9. Josephus, *Antiquities* 13.5.9.

10. Josephus, *Antiquities* 13.10.6.

11. M. Avot 1:1.

12. Josephus, *War* 2.8.14, 3.8.5; *Antiquities* 18:1.3–4. See also Vermes, *Resurrection*, 44–49.

13. Josephus, *Antiquities* 13.10.6; *War* 2.8.14.

14. This is articulated clearly when Jesus says in Matthew 23:23: "Woe to you, scribes and Pharisees, hypocrites! For you tithe mint, dill, and cumin, and have neglected the weightier matters of the law: justice and mercy and faith." See also Luke 11:42.

15. John 5:18, 7:1, 10:31, 18:31, 19:3–12.

16. B. Shab. 31a.

17. Matt. 22:34–40.

18. Sifra Kedoshim 2.4.

19. *Avot de-Rabbi Nathan* A 5.2.

20. Acts 4:1, 5:17; Josephus, *Antiquities* 18.1.4.

21. M. Yad. 4:6–7; M. Mak. 1:6.

22. M. Parah 3:7. The tradition that the Sadducees were compelled to follow the practices of the Pharisees is repeated later in the Babylonian Talmud. B. Yoma 19b; B. Nid. 33b.

23. Josephus, *Antiquities* 18.1.4.

24. *Avot de-Rabbi Nathan* A 5.6; *Avot de-Rabbi Nathan* B 10.5, in Schechter, 26.

25. Jesus calls the Pharisees and Sadducees a "brood of vipers" (Matt. 3:7); both the Pharisees and Sadducees come "to test [Jesus]") (Matt. 16:1); Jesus warns of the "yeast of the Pharisees and Sadducees" (Matt. 16:6, 16:11). The Sadducees' rejection of the doctrine of resurrection is mentioned in Mark 12:18–27; Matt. 22:23–33; Luke 20:27–38; and also in Acts 4:2 and 23:8.

26. Mark 12:18.

27. Mark 12:25.

28. Josephus, *Antiquities*, 13.5.9, 18.1.2–4; *War*, 2.8.2–14.

29. Despite some scholars' warnings against studying Qumran documents through the lens of Josephus, Kenneth Atkinson and Jodi Magness have compellingly shown that Josephus's writings correlate with information about the sect provided in a Qumran document called the Community Rule. Atkinson and Magness, "Josephus's Essenes and the Qumran Community," 318. See also Mason, "Essenes and Lurking Spartans in Josephus' *Judean War*," 219–26.

30. Josephus, *Antiquities* 18.1.5.

31. Plutarch quotes Zeno, the founder of Stoic thought, as saying, "We should have a common life and an order common to us all." Plutarch, *On the Fortune or the Virtue of Alexander* 329A–B, in *Moralia*, vol. 4. The first-century BCE Roman statesman Cicero develops this idea in Cicero, *On Ends* 3.19.62–63, 5.23.65; cf. Cicero, *On Duties* 1.53–58. Likewise, see Seneca's Epistle 47. For Jewish texts that praise the idea of people living in common with one another, see Pseudo-Phocylides 27–30; Sibylline Oracle 3.247, 3.261, 8.208, 14.354, in Charlesworth, *Old Testament Pseudepigrapha*. See also Pseudo-Phocylides 112; Sibylline Oracle 2.87–90, 131, 247, 321–24, 3.494, 757, 8.121, 208, 14.354; Testament of Abraham Recension A 1.3; and 3 Macc 4:4.

32. Josephus, *Antiquities* 15.10.5.

33. Philo, *Contemplative Life* 1.1–3.

34. Philo, *Hypothetica* 11.1.

35. Philo, *Hypothetica* 11.18.

36. Pliny, *Natural History* 5.73.

37. Josephus, *Antiquities* 18.1.5; *War* 2.8.2, 2.8.13.

38. The problem with this theory, however, is that the bodies of women and children have been found in a side cemetery adjacent to Khirbet Qumran. It is possible that these women and children were not living at Qumran. Indeed, Magness finds little evidence of female life at Qumran based on what she calls "'gendered' objects." Magness, *Debating Qumran*, 113–50.

39. Stern, *Greek and Latin Authors on Jews and Judaism*, 539.

40. For other possible references to the Essenes, see Schofield, *From Qumran to the Yaḥad*.

41. One such scholar was Professor Solomon Zeitlin, who taught Rabbinic literature at Dropsie College. Zeitlin believed that Jews wrote the scrolls sometime in the medieval period. At a public lecture in 1956 he rhetorically asked, "If one assigned to Shakespeare the authorship of a newly-found manuscript wherein there were words like . . . 'telephone,' 'automobile,' 'New Deal,' and reference was made to laws which were enacted in the Victorian age, would any student of English literature regard the manuscript as that of Shakespeare?" See

http://www.jta.org/1956/02/22/archive/prof-zeitlin-disputes-value-of-dead
-sea-scrolls-for-judaism. More recently, Norman Golb has rejected the idea
that the owners of the Dead Sea Scrolls lived at Qumran. Golb, "Who Hid the
Dead Sea Scrolls?" 68–82.

42. Atkinson and Magness, "Josephus's Essenes and the Qumran Community," 325.

43. Newsom, "Sectually Explicit Literature from Qumran," 188.

44. Damascus Document 8.23, in Vermes, *Complete Dead Sea Scrolls*.

45. Yadin, *The Scroll of the War of the Sons of Light Against the Sons of Darkness*.

46. *Pesher Habbakuk*, trans. Bilhah Nitzan, in OTB, 653–54.

47. Atkinson and Magness, "Josephus's Essenes and the Qumran Community," 324.

48. Josephus, *War* 2.8.4.

49. Schechter, *Fragments of a Zadokite Work*, xv–xviii.

50. M. Parah 3:7; Schiffman, "The Place of 4QMMT in the Corpus of Qumran,"
81–88.

51. 1 Macc. 2:42.

52. 1 Macc. 7:12–18.

53. 2 Macc. 14:6.

54. Brighton, *Sicarii in Josephus's Judean War*, 141.

55. Josephus, *Antiquities* 18:1.1.

56. Josephus, *War* 2.8.1.

57. Acts 5:37.

58. Josephus, *War* 2.17.8.

59. Josephus, *War* 2.17.4.

60. Josephus, *War* 2.17.9.

61. Josephus, *War*, 7.8.6–7.

62. Cohen, "Masada: Literary Tradition, Archaeological Remains, and the Credibility
of Josephus," 385–405.

63. *DJD*, vol. 11, contains photographs of the Songs of the Sabbath Sacrifices manuscripts found at both Qumran and Masada. The Masada manuscript uses a
Herodian script dating to the middle of the first century CE. Newsom and Schuller
et al., *DJD*, 11:239.

64. See Talmon, *Masada*, 6:105–16; Emanuel Tov, "The Rewritten Book of Joshua
as Found at Qumran and Masada," http://orion.mscc.huji.ac.il/symposiums/1st
/papers/tov.html. For the Joshua Apocryphon found at Qumran, see Newsom
et al., *DJD*, 22:237–88.

65. An alternative explanation is that some members of the Essene sect later joined
the Sicarii at Masada. See Trever, *Dead Sea Scrolls*, 174.

66. B. Git. 56a.

67. B. Git. 56b.

68. Philo, *On the Contemplative Life*, 24–33.

69. Josephus, *Antiquities* 17.2.4, 18.1.2–4.

70. Sandmel, *Philo of Alexandria*, 39; Taylor and Davies, "So-Called Therapeutae," 24.

71. On this topic, see Regev, "Were the Priests All the Same?" 158–88.

72. B. Ber. 62a.

73. B. Shab. 31a.

9. INTERPRETERS OF ISRAELITE HISTORY

1. Japhet, *Ideology of the Book of Chronicles*, 5.

2. 1 Chron. 20.1.

3. 2 Sam. 24:15–17.

4. 1 Chron. 21:14–17.

5. Josh. 5:13–15.

6. 1 Chron. 10:4–6.

7. 1 Sam. 31:4–6.

8. Japhet, *Chronicles*, 444–45.

9. Michael Segal advances the first theory; see Segal, *Book of Jubilees*. For the second position, see Kugel, "On the Interpolations," 215–72.

10. Jubilees 6:36–37, in *OTB*, 317.

11. Jubilees 17:17–18, in *OTB*, 357.

12. M. Avot 5:3.

13. Sabbath (see opening of the book); circumcision (15:25–32). Strangely, the book of Jubilees does not make reference to dietary laws.

14. Jubilees 6:18–31 (Festival of Weeks); 16:20–31 (Tabernacles); 22:1–9 (Festival of Weeks).

15. Genesis Rabbah 65:14.

16. Genesis Rabbah 65:4.

17. Jubilees 25:1–3, 11–23, 27:1–12.

18. Jubilees 23:18–21, in *OTB*, 377.

19. Psalms of Solomon 17:21.

20. Josephus, *Antiquities* 14.4.1–5.

21. Psalms of Solomon 2.1–4. For the English rendering of this text, I use Kenneth Atkinson's translation in *OTB*, 1903–23.

22. Psalms of Solomon 2.6, in *OTB*, 1905.

23. Psalms of Solomon 17.11, in *OTB*, 1918.

24. Psalms of Solomon 10.5–7, in *OTB*, 1913.

25. Psalms of Solomon 14.5–9, in *OTB*, 1915.

26. In fact, the practices of dietary laws, Sabbath, and circumcision were so well known in the Greco-Roman world that some gentiles expressed their admiration

of or interest in affiliating with Judaism by observing any combination of these practices.

27. Thanks in part to the Church Fathers and historians who cited these interpreters, such as Eusebius of Caesarea (c. 260–c. 340 CE), we have fragments attributed to Jews like Demetrius the Chronographer and Aristeas the Exegete who rewrote and expanded the Jewish scriptures.

10. JOSEPHUS FLAVIUS

1. Josephus, *Antiquities* 20.11.3.
2. At the end of his conclusion to *Antiquities*, Josephus writes that his autobiography is to be a kind of addendum to *Antiquities*, but his autobiography mentions the death of Agrippa, whom Photius says died in 100 CE. The exact date of Josephus's *Life*, therefore, is unclear. *The Jewish War*, Josephus's first major work, was written between 75 and 79 CE. Cohen, *Josephus in Galilee and Rome*, 84, 170; Mason, *Life of Josephus*, ix.
3. Josephus, *War* 3.7.3.
4. Josephus, *War* 3.8.7.
5. Josephus, *War* 3.8.8.
6. Josephus, *War* 3.8.9. Suetonius also attests to this legend in *Lives of the Caesars*, Vespasian 5.
7. Josephus, *War* 3.8.9.
8. Josephus, *War* 4.10.7; cf. *Life* 74.
9. Josephus, *Life* 75.
10. Josephus, *Life* 75.
11. Josephus, *Life* 76.
12. Josephus, *Life* 76.
13. Josephus, *Against Apion* 1.22.
14. Josephus, *Antiquities* 1.8.2.
15. Yoshiko Reed, "Construction and Subversion of Patriarchal Perfection," 196.
16. Josephus, *War* 2.8.2.
17. Josephus, *Life* 2; *Antiquities* 15.10.4; Goodman, *Rome and Jerusalem*, 16.
18. Josephus, *War* 3.8.9.
19. Cohen, *Josephus in Galilee and Rome*, 181.
20. Cohen, *Josephus in Galilee and Rome*, 7, 233.
21. Yerushalmi, *Zakhor*, 22.

11. THE CODIFIED BIBLE

1. Scholars who disagree regarding when the scriptures were canonized also disagree about why they were canonized. Philip Davies, for instance, suggests that the

process began in the early Second Temple period, and, by the Hasmonean period, a canon was essentially in place, with occasional minor variations depending on community. According to Marc Brettler, however, the canonization of the Hebrew Bible happened in the late Second Temple period in response to the various "Judaisms" being practiced in the Greco-Roman world. See Davies, *Scribes and Schools*, 70–72. Cf. Halbertal, *People of the Book*; Leiman, *Canonization of Hebrew Literature*; Haran, "Book-Scrolls," 111–22; Brettler, *How to Read the Bible*.

2. The list of the twenty-four books in the Hebrew Bible appears in b. B. Bat. 14b–15a.
3. M. Yad. 3:5.
4. M. B. Bat. 14b–15a.
5. The Greek version of Ben Sira was a translation made of an original Hebrew text. This Hebrew text was composed in around 180 BCE, and the translation was made by the author's grandson in about 130 BCE. Benjamin G. Wright III, in *OTB*, 2208.
6. Matt. 5:17, 7:12, 22:40; Luke 16:16.
7. Emmanuel Tov, in *OTB*, 34.
8. Larsson, "Chronology of the Pentateuch," 403–4.
9. Louth, Conti, and Oden, *Genesis 1–11*, xlv.
10. Gen. 4:1–16.
11. Levine, "Syriac Version of Genesis," 70–78. The link between Cain and Satan was an emerging motif that appears in both Christian and Rabbinic sources.
12. Mal. 3:23–24.
13. Matt. 1:1–17.
14. M. Meg. 4:4–6.
15. B. Shab. 115a.
16. B. Shab. 115a.
17. B. Meg. 3a.
18. B. Ber. 8a–b.
19. Gen 25:23.
20. Targum Onqelos on Gen. 25:23.
21. Flesher and Chilton, *Targums*, 162.
22. B. Meg. 21b.

12. REWRITING THE BIBLE

1. Crawford, "The 'Rewritten' Bible at Qumran," 1–8.
2. Jubilees 15:33–34, in *OTB*, 348.
3. Jubilees 37:1–38:14.
4. Jubilees 35:18–27.
5. Orval S. Wintermute, in Charlesworth, *Old Testament Pseudepigrapha*, 2:39.

6. James L. Kugel, in *OTB*, 277.
7. Genesis Apocryphon 19.13–22, in *OTB*, 250–51.
8. Genesis Apocryphon 20.12–17, in *OTB*, 253.
9. 2 Macc. 3:26. Another juxtaposition of a divine vision and prayer occurs in 2 Macc. 10:26–31.
10. Greek Esther 10:4–11:1 (Addition F).
11. One popular legend was that the Israelites worshiped the head of an ass. Josephus, *Against Apion* 2.80, 148. The idea that the Jews worshiped an ass is also found in the writings of other Greek thinkers, such as Mnaseas of Patara and Apion, and may be connected with the belief that the Jews were unhygienic and unclean. Josephus, *Against Apion*, 2.114. Similarly, according to the third-century BCE historian Manetho, the Jews were not led out of Egypt because their God miraculously freed them from slavery but were expelled from Egypt because they were leprous. Josephus, *Against Apion* 1.229. And, according to the Greek writer Lysimachus, the Jews were a diseased people who survived by plundering other people's lands. Lysimachus probably lived in the second or first century BCE. Josephus, *Against Apion* 1.308–9.
12. Artapanus is cited by the first-century BCE historian Alexander Polyhistor, so he must have lived before or during Polyhistor's time. Given the heavy Hellenistic influence on his work, it is unlikely that Artapanus lived before the rise of Alexander the Great and the founding of the Greek Empire. See Erich Gruen's introduction to Artapanus, in *OTB*, 676.
13. Josephus, *Antiquities of the Jews* 1.7.1; Philo, *On Abraham* 15.68–80; Jubilees 12:16–21, in *OTB*, 338; Artapanus Fragment 1 in Eusebius, *Praeparatio Evangelica* 9:18:1, in *OTB*, 677.
14. Testament of Abraham Recension A 10:10–13, in *OTB*, 1683.
15. H. C. Kee, "Testaments of the Twelve Patriarchs," in Charlesworth, *Old Testament Pseudepigrapha*, 1:778.
16. James L. Kugel, in *OTB*, 1698.
17. Testament of Reuben 3:11–15. For more on this subject, see Kugel, "Reuben's Sin," 525–54.
18. Testament of Naphtali 5:1–5, in *OTB*, 1798–99.
19. Testament of Reuben 6:10–12, in *OTB*, 1715. Also see a similar statement in the Testament of Simeon that Levi will lead the Israelites in a series of apocalyptic wars. Simeon tells his sons:

> For I have seen it written in the writings of Enoch that your sons after you will be destroyed by licentiousness and will [seek to] harm Levi by the sword. But they will not prevail against Levi, for he will wage the war of the Lord

and will overcome all your [descendants'] battle lines, and they will become few in number and will be divided in Levi and Judah, and there will be no one from you for sovereignty, just as my father foretold as well in his blessings.

Testament of Simeon 5:4-6, in OTB, 1720. Later in the testament, Simeon instructs his children to "listen to Levi, and through Judah you will be redeemed; and do not rise up against these two tribes." Testament of Simeon 7:1, in OTB, 1722.

20. Testament of Judah 21:2, in OTB, 1766.

21. In the Testament of Naphtali, for example, Naphtali tells his children to "order your sons to be united with Levi and Judah." Testament of Naphtali 8:1 in OTB, 1801.

22. Testament of Reuben 4:7-11, in OTB, 1712.

23. Testament of Simeon 4:4, in OTB, 1718-19.

24. Hollander, *Joseph as an Ethical Model*, 50-64.

25. Artapanus Fragment 3 in Eusebius, *Praeparatio Evangelica* 9:27.1-37, in OTB, 679.

26. Murphy, *Pseudo-Philo*, 3.

27. Pseudo-Philo 10:5, in OTB, 494.

28. Exod. 14:15-22.

29. Pseudo-Philo 12:5-7, in OTB, 499.

30. Exod. 32:19.

31. *Exagogue* 68-82, in OTB, 734.

32. Genesis Apocryphon 19.14-17, in OTB, 251.

33. On 2 Baruch, see Adam H. Becker, in OTB, 1565; on 4 Ezra, see Karina Martin Hogan, in OTB, 1607.

34. 2 Baruch 51:2-6 in OTB, 1578.

35. 4 Ezra 8:1-3, in OTB, 1638.

36. Susanna 45-46.

37. The Prayer of Azariah and the Song of the Three Jews 36-41.

38. Ps. 148:1-4.

39. Bel and the Dragon 41.

40. Esther 4:13-14.

41. Greek Esther Addition A.

42. Esther 3:15.

43. Greek Esther Addition C, 12-15, 2-29, in OTB, 103-5.

13. THE EXPANDED BIBLE

1. The figure of Ahikar originates in ancient Near Eastern literature. Although he appears in Jewish writings of the Second Temple period, he is not an invention of Jewish writers. See Lindenberger, *Aramaic Proverbs*; Kottsieper, "'Look, Son, What Nadab Did to Ahikaros," 145-67.

2. Medieval manuscripts of this book have been preserved until modern times in St. Catherine's Monastery, the Vatican Library, and the monasteries of Vatopedi and Konstamonitou on Mount Athos, among other places. Charlesworth, *Old Testament Pseudepigrapha*, 2:178–79.

3. Pseudo-Jonathan on Exod. 1:15, 7:11–12; Damascus Document; Sefer haYashar 70:1–31; Yalkut Shimoni Exodus 168; Sefer haYashar 70–73; Genesis Rabbah 86:5; Exodus Rabbah 9:7; B. Men. 85a.

4. 2 Tim. 3:8.

5. Exodus Rabbah 9:7; see also B. Men. 85a; Pseudo-Jonathan on Exod. 7:11–12.

6. Pliny, *Natural History* 30.2.11.

7. On these traditions, see Pietersma, *Apocryphon of Jannes and Jambres*.

8. Jannes and Jambres, Brit. Lib., Cotton, Tiberius B.V., fol. 87, in Charlesworth, *Old Testament Pseudepigrapha*, 2:440.

9. Jannes and Jambres, Pap. Chester Beatty XVI.22av, in Charlesworth, *Old Testament Pseudepigrapha*, 2:442.

10. On the practice of magic in early Judaism, see Bohak, *Ancient Jewish Magic*.

11. In the Hebrew Bible, Satan is mentioned in Num. 22:22, 22:32; 1 Sam. 29:4, 2 Sam. 19:22; 1 Kings 5:4, 11:14, 11:23, 11:25; Zech. 3:1–2; Ps. 38:20, 71:13, 109:4, 109:6, 109:20, 109:29; Job 1:6–12, 2:1–7; Dan. 3:6, 5:6, 6:1; and 1 Chron. 21:1.

12. Satan is also mentioned in the Testament of Gad 4:7; Testament of Job 3:6, 4:4, 6:4, 7:6, 7:12, 16:2, 20:1, 23:1–3, 23:11, 27:1, 27:6, 41:5; Life of Adam and Eve 17:1; History of Rechabites 7:8, 19:1–2.

13. Testament of Dan 5:6, 6:1–5, in *OTB*, 1788–90.

14. In the biblical book of Job, the Satan is mentioned in 1:6–12, 2:1–4, and 2:6–7. In the Testament of Job, Satan is mentioned in 3:3–6 and is referred to as the devil in 17:1.

15. Testament of Job 26.6.

16. Deut. 13:14, 15:9; Judges 19:22, 20:13; 1 Sam. 1:16, 2:12, 10:27, 25:17, 25:25, 30:22; 2 Sam. 16:7, 20:1, 22:5, 23:6; 1 Kings 21:10, 21:13; Nah. 1:11, 1:15; Ps. 18:4, 41:8, 101:3; Job 34:18; Prov. 6:12, 16:27, 19:28; 2 Chron. 13:7.

17. Damascus Document 6:9–11.

18. Testament of Reuben 2:2, 3:3–3:7. See also Testament of Reuben 4:7, 4:11, 6:3; Testament of Simeon 5:3; Testament of Levi 3:3, 18:12, 19:1; Testament of Judah 25:3; Testament of Issachar, 6:1, 7:7; Testament of Zebulon 9:8; Testament of Asher 1:8–10, 6:4; Testament of Dan 1:7, 4:7, 5:1, 5:10–11; Testament of Naphtali 2:6; Testament of Asher 1:8, 3:2; Testament of Joseph 7:4, 20:2; Testament of Benjamin 3:3, 3:8, 6:1, 6:7, 7:1–2. Beliar is also mentioned as the head of the evil angels who cause good men to sin in the Lives of the Prophets 4:7, 4:21, 17:2.

19. Sibylline Oracle 3.63–74, in Charlesworth, *Old Testament Pseudepigrapha*, 1:363.

20. These verses are believed to be among the latest verses to be added to this text, which probably underwent three major stages of composition. This passage was likely added soon after the Second Temple's destruction in 70 CE. John J. Collins, in Charlesworth, *Old Testament Pseudepigrapha*, 1:360.

21. Jubilees 11:4–6.

22. Jubilees 17:16.

23. Jubilees 48:2, 9–12, 15–19; 49:2.

24. Damascus Document 16:5.

25. Pseudo-Phocylides 101; Sibylline Oracle 3:331; Testament of Solomon Recension A 1:2, 1:5, 1:9–14, 2:1–2, 2:8, 3:6, 4:1, 5:1, 5:7, 5:9, 5:12, 7:1, 7:4, 7:8, 8:1, 9:1–3, 10:1, 10:5, 11:5–6, 12:1, 12:5–6, 13:1, 14:1, 14:6–7, 16:1, 17:5, 18:1, 20:6, 20:8, 20:18, 20:21, 22:2, 22:11–14, 22:18–19, 23:2, 24:1, 25:1–3.

26. Testament of Solomon 6:1–11.

27. For other references to Diabolos, see Apocalypse of Sedrach 4:5, 5:3; Testament of Naphtali 3:1, 8:4, 8:6, Testament of Solomon Recension A 15:11; Jubilees 10:8; Joseph and Aseneth 12:9; History of the Rechabites 20:1, 21:1, 21:4, 22:2; and Assumption of Moses 2, 8–10.

28. Life of Adam and Eve 16:1–4, in *OTB*, 1348–49.

29. 1 Enoch 9:6. See also Enoch 8:1, 10:4, 10:8, 13:1. Azael is also referred to as the head of fallen angels in the Testament of Solomon. See Testament of Solomon Recension A 7:7.

30. Lev. 16:7–10; see also Lev. 16:18, 26.

31. This possibility is suggested by D. C. Duling, in Charlesworth, *Old Testament Pseudepigrapha*, 1:969. See Isa. 31:21, 34:11; Tob. 8:3, Matt. 12:43; 1 Enoch 9:6; 10.

32. 3 Baruch 4:8–9, in *OTB*, 1593.

33. 3 Baruch 9:5–7, in *OTB*, 1598.

34. Exodus Rabbah 18:5.

35. Exodus Rabbah 21:7, B. Sotah 10b; Tanhuma Vayishlach 8; Song of Songs Rabbah 3:6; Targum Yonatan to Genesis 3:6; Deuteronomy Rabbah 11; Targum Job 28:7.

36. Some examples of dualist religions are Manichaeism and Mandaeanism. The term "Gnostic" is falling out of use, largely because it refers to texts that were regarded as heretical and antithetical to the teachings of the Church, but as Karen King points out, these texts do not share inherent relationships with one another. King, *What Is Gnosticism?*

37. Dan. 10:13, 10:21, 12:1. The name Michael appears in other biblical passages, but in these verses, the name appears to be unassociated with a princely or angelic figure. See Num. 13:13; 1 Chron. 5:13–14; 6:40, 7:3, 8:16, 12:20, 27:18; 2 Chron. 21:2; and Ezra 8:8.

38. Dan. 10:21.

39. Dan. 10:10–13.

40. Dan. 12:1–2.

41. 3 Baruch 11:2; 3 Baruch 11:2–8, 12:1, 12:7–8, 13:2–5, 14:1–2, 15:1.

42. 1 Enoch 9:1–11. See also 1 Enoch 10:11, 20:5, 24:6–25:6. The theme of angels having sexual intercourse with human women in Enoch is derived from the enigmatic passage in Genesis 6, which reads,

> When men began to increase on earth and daughters were born to them, the divine beings saw how beautiful the daughters of men were and took wives from among those that pleased them. The Lord said, "My breath shall not abide in man forever, since he too is flesh; let the days allowed him be one hundred and twenty years." It was then, and later too, that the Nephilim appeared on earth when the divine beings cohabited with the daughters of men, who bore them offspring. They were the heroes of old, the men of renown. The Lord saw how great was man's wickedness on earth, and how every plan devised by his mind was nothing but evil all the time.

Gen. 6:1–5. The fact that the story of divine beings having sexual intercourse with human women flows directly into the story of people being so evil that God chooses to destroy all of humankind indicated to Jewish writers in the Second Temple period that the sort of evil behavior that compelled God to make this decision related to the sexual relationships of the angels and human women.

43. Dan. 10:21, 12:1; War Scroll (1QM) 17:6–7; cf. *OTB*, 1382.

44. Michael is mentioned in the Testament of Abraham Recension A 1:4, 2:2, 3:9, 4:4, 4:7, 7:11, 8:4, 8:8, 8:11, 9:8, 10:1, 10:12, 11:1, 12:15, 14:5, 14:12, 15:1, 16:2, 16:7, 19:4, 20:10; and the Testament of Abraham Recension B 1:1, 2:1–2, 2:4, 2:7, 2:10, 2:13, 3:10, 4:4–5, 4:7–8, 4:14, 5:1, 6:3, 6:6, 7:1–2, 7:15, 7:18–19, 8:1–3, 8:7–8, 8:10, 9:4, 9:6–7, 9:10–11, 10:2, 11:1–2, 11:16, 12:3, 12:5, 12:10, 12:12, 12:14, 13:1, 13:3, 14:7.

45. Assumption of Moses 2, 8–10; Jude 9.

46. Jude 9; Rev. 12:7.

47. Testament of Simeon 7:1–2; Testament of Issachar 5:7; Testament of Dan 5:7; and Testament of Naphtali 8:2–3. Yet many other sections in the Testaments of the Twelve Patriarchs state explicitly that Levi will take the primary role of leadership. See Testament of Reuben 6:5–7, 10–12; Testament of Simeon 5:4–6; Testament of Judah 21:1–2, 25:1–2; and Testament of Naphtali 5:1–5.

48. Texts that mention the Davidic Messiah are 4Q252; Pesher Isaiah[a] (4Q161, 4QpIsa[a] 8–10 iii 18–25); Messianic Apocalypse (4Q521); Pesher Genesis (4QpGen). See also 4Q504; 1Q28b; 4Q252; 4Q174; 4Q161; 4Q285; 4Q246. Martin Abegg suggests

that since there are far more allusions to a Davidic Messiah than to a priestly Messiah in the Qumran texts, scholars should rethink their assumptions about the belief in a dual Messiah at Qumran. See Abegg, "Messiah at Qumran," 143–44; see also Hurst, "Did Qumran Expect Two Messiahs?" 157–80.

49. Psalms of Solomon 17:30–31, in *OTB*, 1920. The eighteenth psalm also depicts a messianic figure in detail. In particular, see Psalms of Solomon 18:0 [heading], 18:5, 18:7.

50. 2 Baruch 29–30.

51. 2 Baruch 72:2, in *OTB*, 1582.

52. 4 Ezra 7:26–44.

53. 4 Ezra 12:29–36. See also 13:25–58. In 1 Enoch, Enoch is the messianic figure who is to lead the righteous as they enter a final redemptive stage of history. 1 Enoch 71:14–17. See Knohl, *The Messiah before Jesus*; Stuckenbruck, "Messianic Ideas," 90–113. Because of the many Christian interpolations found in manuscripts that were originally written by Jews, some scholars have incorrectly rendered the Greek word *christos* as Jesus Christ. In actuality, however, this word may have referred to a generic figure, and should be translated as "Messiah" or "Anointed One." See, for example, Robert B. Wright's refutation of the possibility that *christos* in Psalms of Solomon 17 is a Christian interpolation in Wright, *Psalms of Solomon*, in Charlesworth, *Old Testament Pseudepigrapha*, 2:668n.z.

CONCLUSION

1. Tcherikover, "Jewish Apologetic," 169–93.

BIBLIOGRAPHY

Abegg, Martin. "The Messiah at Qumran: Are We Still Seeing Double?" *DSD* 2 (1995): 125–44.

Adler, Elkan Nathan. "Some Missing Chapters of Ben Sira." *JQR* 12, no. 3 (1900): 466–80.

Agourides, Savas, and James H. Charlesworth. "A New Discovery of Old Manuscripts on Mt. Sinai: A Preliminary Project." *BA* 41, no. 1 (1978): 29–31.

Allred, Ammon. "The Divine *Logos*: Plato, Heraclitus, and Heidegger in the *Sophist*." *Epoché: A Journal for the History of Philosophy* 14, no. 1 (2009): 1–18.

Amar, Joseph. *St. Ephrem the Syrian: Selected Prose Works*. FOC 91. Washington DC: Catholic University of America Press, 1994.

Appian. *Roman History*. Vol. 3. Translated by Horace White. LCL 4. Cambridge MA: Harvard University Press, 1913.

Arendzen, J., and H. Leonard Pass. "Fragment of an Aramaic Text of the Testament of Levi." *JQR* 12, no. 4 (1900): 651–61.

Atkinson, Kenneth, and Jodi Magness. "Josephus's Essenes and the Qumran Community." *JBL* 129, no. 2 (2010): 317–42.

Augustin, Nikitin. "The Baptism of Kievan Russia and the Manuscript Heritage of Mount Athos." *Greek Orthodox Theological Review* 33, no. 2 (1988): 201–20.

Augustine. *City of God*. Vol. 2, bks. 4–7. Translated by William M. Green. LCL 412. Cambridge MA: Harvard University Press, 1963.

Bauckham, Richard, James R. Davila, and Alexander Panayotov, eds. *Old Testament Pseudepigrapha: More Noncanonical Scriptures*. Vol. 1. Grand Rapids MI: Eerdmans, 2013.

Baumgarten, Albert I. *The Flourishing of Jewish Sects in the Maccabean Era: An Interpretation:* Leiden, Netherlands: Brill, 1997.

———. "Josephus on Ancient Jewish Groups from a Social Scientific Perspective." In *Studies in Josephus and the Varieties of Ancient Judaism: Louis H. Feldman Jubilee Volume*, edited by Shaye J. D. Cohen and Joshua J. Schwartz, 1–13. AJEC 67. Leiden, Netherlands: Brill, 2007.

Baur, Ferdinand Christian. *Der Gegensatz des Katholicismus und Prostestantismus nach den Principien und Hauptogmen der Beiden Lehrbegriff.* Tübingen, Germany: L. F. Fues, 1836.

Bell, Idris H. *Jews and Christians in Egypt: The Jewish Troubles in Alexandria and the Athanasian Controversy.* London: Oxford University Press, 1924.

———. "Scribes and Correctors of the Codex Sinaiticus: A Reply." *Classical Philology* 37, no. 4 (1942): 429–31.

Beneshevich, V. N. *Opisanie grecheskikh rukopisei monastyria Sviatoi Ekateriny na Sinaie.* Hildesheim, Germany: Olms, 1965.

Ben-Horin, Meir. "Solomon Schechter to Judge Mayer Sulzberger: Part I. Letters from the Pre-Seminary Period (1895–1901)." *JSS* 25, no. 4 (1963): 249–86.

———. "Solomon Schechter to Judge Mayer Sulzberger: Part II. Letters from the Pre-Seminary Period (1902–1915)." *JSS* 27, no. 2 (1965): 75–102.

———. "Solomon Schechter to Judge Mayer Sulzberger: Supplement to Parts I and II (Notes, Letters, and Corrections)." *JSS* 30, no. 4 (1968): 262–71.

Bentwich, Norman De Mattos. *Solomon Schechter: A Biography.* Philadelphia: Jewish Publication Society, 1938.

Bernstein, Moshe. Review of *Miqsat Ma'ase Ha-torah* from Qumran Cave 4.V. *JS* 36 (1996): 53–65.

Berthelot, Katell. *Philanthrôpia Judaica: Le débat autour de la "misanthrope" des lois juices dans l'Antiquité.* Leiden, Netherlands: Brill, 2003.

Birnbaum, Ellen. "Exegetical Building Blocks in Philo's Interpretation of the Patriarchs." In *From Judaism to Christianity: Tradition and Transition: A Festschrift for Thomas H. Tobin S. J., on the Occasion of his Sixty-Fifth Birthday,* edited by Patricia Walters, 69–92. Leiden, Netherlands: Brill, 2010.

Bohak, Gideon. *Ancient Jewish Magic: A History.* Cambridge: Cambridge University Press, 2008.

Böttrich, Christfried. *Bibliographie Konstantin von Tischendorf (1815–1874).* Leipzig: Leipziger Universitätsverlag, 1999.

Bousset, Willhelm. *Die Bedeutung der Person Jesu für den Glauben: Historische und Rationale Grundlagen des Glaubens.* Berlin: Proestantischer Schriftenbertrieb, 1910.

Boyarin, Daniel. "The Gospel of the Memra: Jewish Binitarianism and the Prologue to John." *HTR* 94, no. 3 (2001): 243–84.

Breasted, James Henry, ed. *The Edwin Smith Surgical Papyrus.* 2 vols. Chicago: University of Chicago Press, 1930.

Brettler, Marc Z. *How to Read the Bible.* Philadelphia: Jewish Publication Society, 2005.

Brighton, Mark Andrew. *The Sicarii in Josephus's Judean War: Rhetorical Analysis and Historical Observations.* EJL 27. Leiden, Netherlands: Brill, 2009.

Brooke, A. E., and N. McLean, "On a Petersburg MS of the Septuagint." *Classical Review* 13, no. 4 (1899): 209–11.

Brooke, George, and John Collins, Peter Flint, Jonas Greenfield, Erik Larson, Carol A Newsom, Emile Puech, Lawrence H. Schiffman, Michael Stone, and Julio Trebolle Barrera. *DJD*. Vol. 22, *Qumran Cave 4, vol. 17: Parabiblical Texts, part 3*. Oxford: Clarendon, 1996.

Brooten, Bernadette J. "The Jews of Ancient Antioch." In *Antioch: The Lost Ancient City*, edited by Christine Kondoleon, 29–37. Princeton NJ: Princeton University Press, 2000.

Broshi, Magen. "Estimating the Population of Ancient Jerusalem." *BAR* 4, no. 2 (1978): 10–15.

Bultmann, Rudolf. *Primitive Christianity in Its Contemporary Setting*. Trans. R. H. Fuller; London: Thames and Hudson, 1956.

Campbell, Brian, and Lawrence A. Tritle, eds. *The Oxford Handbook of Warfare in the Classical World*. Oxford: Oxford University Press, 2013.

Cassius Dio. *Roman History*. Vol. 8. Trans. Earnest Cary and Herbert B. Foster. LCL 176. Cambridge MA: Harvard University Press, 1925.

Chambon, A., and H.-B. Humbert. *Fouilles de Khirbet Qumran et de Ain Feshka I Album de photographies, Reportoire du fonds photographique, Synthese des notes de chantier du Pere Roland de Vaux OP*. NTOASA 1. Fribourg: Editions Universitaires, 1994.

Charles, Robert H. *The Apocrypha and Pseudepigrapha of the Old Testament in English*. 2 vols. Oxford: Clarendon Press, 1913.

Charlesworth, James H. "The Dead Sea Scrolls: Fifty Years of Discovery and Controversy." In *Hebrew Bible and Qumran*, edited by James H. Charlesworth, 1–27. Richland Hills TX: Bibal Press, 2000.

——. "A History of Pseudepigrapha Research: The Re-emerging Importance of the Pseudepigrapha." *Principat* 19, no. 1 (1979): 54–88.

——. "The Manuscripts of St. Catherine's Monastery." *BA* 43, no. 1 (1980): 26–34.

——. *The New Discoveries in St. Catherine's Monastery: A Preliminary Report on the Manuscripts*. Cambridge MA: American Schools of Oriental Research, 1981.

——. *The Old Testament Pseudepigrapha*. 2 vols. Peabody MA: Hendrickson, 1983.

——. "St. Catherine's Monastery: Myths and Mysteries." *BA* 42, no. 3 (1979): 174–79.

Cheesman, R. E. "Lake Tana and Its Islands." *Geographical Journal* 85, no. 6 (1935): 489–502.

Chrysostom, John. *Discourses against Judaizing Christians*. FOTC 68. Washington DC: Catholic University of America Press, 1979.

Cicero. *In Catilinam 1–4; Pro Murena; Pro Sulla; Pro Flacco*. Translated by C. MacDonald. LCL 324. Cambridge MA: Harvard University Press, 1976.

———. *On Duties*. Translated by Walter Miller. LCL 30. Cambridge MA: Harvard University Press, 1913.

———. *On Ends*. Translated by H. Rackham. LCL 40. Cambridge MA: Harvard University Press, 1914.

Clark, Kenneth W., ed. *Checklist of Manuscripts in St. Catherine's Monastery, Mount Sinai*. Washington DC: Library of Congress, 1953.

Cohen, Shaye J. D. *The Beginnings of Jewishness: Boundaries, Varieties, Uncertainties*. Berkeley: University of California Press, 1999.

———. *From the Maccabees to the Mishnah*. 3rd ed. Louisville KY: Westminster John Knox Press, 2014.

———. *Josephus in Galilee and Rome: His Vita and Development as a Historian*. Leiden, Netherlands: Brill, 1979.

———. "Masada: Literary Tradition, Archaeological Remains, and the Credibility of Josephus." *Journal of Jewish Studies* 33, no. 1–2 (1982): 385–405.

Cohn, Yehudah B. *Tangled Up in Text: Tefillin and the Ancient World*. BJS 351. Providence RI: Brown University Press, 2008.

Collins, John J. *Between Athens and Jerusalem: Jewish Identity in the Hellenistic Diaspora*. New York: Crossroad, 1983.

Collins, John J., and Daniel C. Harlow. *Early Judaism: A Comprehensive Overview*. Grand Rapids MI: Eerdmans, 2012.

Coogan, Michael D., ed. *The New Oxford Annotated Bible*. 3rd ed. Oxford: Oxford University Press, 2001.

Crawford, Sidnie White. "The 'Rewritten' Bible at Qumran: A Look at Three Texts." *Eretz-Israel* 26 (1999): 1–8.

Davies, Philip R. *Scribes and Schools: The Canonization of Hebrew Scriptures*. Louisville KY: Westminster John Knox Press, 1998.

Davila, James R. *The Provenance of the Pseudepigrapha*. Leiden, Netherlands: Brill, 2005.

Davis, Malcolm C., and Ben Outhwaite. *Hebrew Bible Manuscripts in the Cambridge Genizah Collections*. 4 vols. Cambridge: Cambridge University Library, 1978–2003.

De Beer, Vladimir. "The Cosmic Role of the Logos, as Conceived from Heraclitus until Eriugena." *Greek Orthodox Theological Review* 59, nos. 1–4 (2014): 13–39.

De Jonge, Marinus. "Christian Influence in the Testaments of the Twelve Patriarchs." In *Studies on the Testaments of the Twelve Patriarchs: Text and Interpretation*, edited by Marinus De Jonge, 193–246. SVTP 3. Leiden, Netherlands: Brill.

———. *Pseudepigrapha of the Old Testament as Part of Christian Literature: The Case of the Testaments of the Twelve Patriarchs and the Greek Life of Adam and Eve*. SVTP 18. Leiden, Netherlands: Brill, 2003.

De Mendieta, Emmanuel Amand. *Mount Athos: The Garden of the Panaghia*. Hakkert: Akademie-Verlag, 1972.

Deutsch, Robert. "Roman Coins Boast 'Judaea Capta.'" *BAR* 36, no. 1 (2010): 51–53.

Dewsnap, Molly. "The Twins and the Scholar: How Two Victorian Sisters and a Rabbi Discovered the Hebrew Text of Ben Sira." *BAR* 22, no. 5 (1996): 54–62.

Dio Cassius. *Roman History.* Vol. 8. Translated by Earnest Cary. LCL 176. Cambridge MA: Cambridge University Press, 1925.

Diodorus Siculus. *Library of History.* Vol. 12. Translated by Francis R. Walton. LCL 423. Cambridge MA: Cambridge University Press, 1967.

DiTommaso, Lorenzo, and Christfried Böttrich, eds. *The Old Testament Apocrypha in the Slavonic Tradition: Continuity and Diversity.* Tübingen, Germany: Mohr Siebeck, 2011.

Dölger, Franz. "Der Heilige Berg Athos und seine Bücherschätze: Archivarbeit auf dem Athos; und Neues vom Berg Athos." In *Paraspora: Aufsatze zum Geschichte, Kultur und Sprache des byzantinischen Reiches,* edited by Franz Dölger, 391–438. Ettal, Germany: Buch Kunstverlag, 1961.

Donalson, Malcolm. *A Translation of Jerome's Chronicon with Historical Commentary.* Lewiston NY: Edwin Mellen, 1996.

Donaldson, Terence L. *Judaism and the Gentiles: Jewish Patterns of Universalism (to 135 CE).* Waco TX: Baylor University Press, 2007.

Downey, Glanville. *Ancient Antioch.* Princeton NJ: Princeton University Press, 1963.

———. *A History of Antioch in Syria: From Seleucus to the Arab Conquest.* Princeton NJ: Princeton University Press, 1961.

Easton, Burton Scott. "Lewis, Agnes Smith, 1843–1926." *ATR* 9, no. 2 (1926): 168.

Edgar, G. C., and A. S. Hunt, eds. *Select Papyri.* Vol. 2. LCL 282. Cambridge MA: Harvard University Press, 1934.

Eisenman, Robert. *James the Brother of Jesus: The Key to Unlocking the Secrets of Early Christianity and the Dead Sea Scrolls.* New York: Viking, 1997.

Elizur, Shulamit. "Two New Leaves of the Hebrew Version of Ben Sira." *DSD* 17 (2010): 13–29.

Elizur, Shulamit, and Michael Rand. "A New Fragment of the Book of Ben Sira." *DSD* 18 (2011): 200–205.

Ellens, J. Harold. *The Ancient Library of Alexandria and Early Christian Theological Development.* Claremont CA: Institute for Antiquity and Christianity, 1993.

Epictetus. *Discourses.* Bks. 1–2. Translated by W. A. Oldfather. LCL 131. Cambridge MA: Harvard University Press, 1925.

Epiphanius. *Panarion Book I.* Translated by. Frank Williams. Leiden, Netherlands: Brill, 2009.

Epstein, Isidore, ed. *Soncino Talmud.* 30 vols. New York: Bloch Publishing, 1990.

Erho, Ted. "New Ethiopic Witnesses to Some Old Testament Pseudepigrapha." *Bulletin of the School of Oriental and African Studies* 76, no. 1 (2013): 75–97.

Eusebius. *Ecclesiastical History*. Vol. 1. Translated by Kirsopp Lake. LCL 153. Cambridge MA: Harvard University Press, 1926.

———. *Ecclesiastical History*. Vol. 2. Translated by J. E. L. Oulton. LCL 265. Cambridge MA: Harvard University Press, 1932.

Fabricius, Johann. *Codex Pseudepigraphus Veteris Testamenti*. Hamburg: Liebezeit, 1713.

Feldman, Louis H. "Financing the Colosseum." *BAR* 27, no. 4 (2001): 20–31, 60–61.

———. *Jew and Gentile in the Ancient World: Attitudes and Interactions from Alexander to Justinian*. Princeton NJ: Princeton University Press, 1993.

Feldman, Louis H., and Meyer Reinhold, eds. *Jewish Life and Thought among Greeks and Romans: Primary Readings*. Minneapolis: Fortress, 1996.

Feldman, Louis H., James L. Kugel, and Lawrence H. Schiffman, eds. *Outside the Bible: Ancient Jewish Writings Related to Scripture*. Philadelphia: Jewish Publication Society, 2013.

Fine, Steven. *Art, History and the Historiography of Judaism in Roman Antiquity*. BRLJ 34. Leiden, Netherlands: Brill, 2013.

Finkbeiner, Walter E., Philip C. Ursell, and Richard L. Davis, eds. *Autopsy Pathology: A Manual and Atlas*. 3rd ed. Philadelphia: Elsevier, 2016.

Firkovich, Abraham. *Avnei Zikkaron*. Odessa: M. Beilinson, 1872.

Flesher, Paul V. M., and Bruce D. Chilton. *The Targums: A Critical Introduction*. Waco TX: Baylor University Press, 2011.

Flusser, David. *Judaism of the Second Temple Period*. Translated by Azzan Yadin. 2 vols. Grand Rapids MI: Eerdmans, 2007.

Friedlander, Gerald, trans. *Pirke de-Rabbi Eliezer*. New York: Hermon Press, 1965.

Frishman, Judith. "'And Abraham had Faith:' But in What? Ephrem and the Rabbis on Abraham and God's Blessings." In *The Exegetical Encounter between Jews and Christians in Late Antiquity*, edited by Emmanouela Grypeou and Helen Spurling, 163–80. Leiden, Netherlands: Brill, 2008.

Gafni, Isaiah M. "Josephus and 1 Maccabees." In *Josephus, the Bible, and History*, edited by Louis H. Feldman and Gohei Hata, 116–31. Detroit: Wayne State University Press, 1989.

Gibson, Margaret Dunlop. *How the Codex Was Found: A Narrative of Two Visits to Sinai from Mrs. Lewis's Journals, 1892–1893*. Brighton UK: Alpha Press, 1999.

Ginzberg, Louis. *An Unknown Jewish Sect*. New York: Jewish Theological Seminary of America Press, 1970.

Glickman, Mark. *Sacred Treasure: The Cairo Genizah*. Woodstock VT: Jewish Lights Press, 2011.

Goitein, Shlomo Dov. *A Mediterranean Society: The Jewish Communities of the Arab World as Portrayed in the Documents of the Cairo Genizah*. 5 vols. Berkeley: University of California Press, 1967.

Golb, Norman. "Who Hid the Dead Sea Scrolls?" *BA* 48, no. 2 (1985): 68–82.

Goodman, Martin, ed. *Jews in a Graeco-Roman World*. Oxford: Clarendon Press, 1998.

———. *Rome and Jerusalem: The Clash of Ancient Civilizations*. New York: Alfred A. Knopf, 2007.

Graetz, Heinrich. "The Last Chapter of Zechariah." *JQR* 3 (1891): 208–19.

Green, Peter. *Alexander to Actium: The Historical Evolution of the Hellenistic Age*. Berkeley: University of California Press, 1990.

Gruen, Erich S. *Diaspora: Jews Amidst Greeks and Romans*. Cambridge MA: Harvard University Press, 2002.

———. *Heritage and Hellenism: The Reinvention of Jewish Tradition*. Berkeley CA: University of California Press, 2002.

Halbertal, Moshe. *People of the Book: Canon, Meaning, and Authority*. Cambridge MA: Harvard University Press, 1997.

Haran, Menahem. "Book-Scrolls at the Beginning of the Second Temple Period: The Transition From Papyrus to Skins." *Hebrew Union College Annual* 54 (1983): 111–22.

Harviainen, Tapani. "Abraham Firkovich." In *Karaite Judaism: A Guide to its History and Literary Sources*, edited by Meira Pollack, 875–92. Leiden, Netherlands: Brill, 2003.

———. "Abraham Firkovich, the Aleppo Codex, and Its Dedication." In *Jewish Studies at the Turn of the Twentieth Century*. Vol. 1, *Biblical, Rabbinical, and Medieval Studies*, edited by Judit Targarona Borrás and Angel Sáenz-Badillos, 131–36. Leiden, Netherlands: Brill, 1999.

Hoffman, Adina, and Peter Cole. *Sacred Trash: The Lost and Found World of the Cairo Geniza*. New York: Schocken, 2011.

Hollander, Harm W. *Joseph as an Ethical Model in the Testaments of the Twelve Patriarchs*. Leiden, Netherlands: Brill, 1981.

Horbury, William. *Jewish War under Trajan and Hadrian*. New York: Cambridge University Press, 2014.

Horbury, William, and David Noy, eds. *Jewish Inscriptions of Graeco-Roman Egypt*. Cambridge: Cambridge University Press, 1992.

Humbert, J.-B., and A. Chambon. *The Excavations of Khirbet Qumran and Ain Feshka IB: Synthesis of Roland de Vaux's Field Notes*. Translated by S. Pfann. NTOASA 1B. Fribourg: Editions Universitaires, 2003.

Hurst, L. D. "Did Qumran Expect Two Messiahs?" *BBR* 9 (1999): 157–80.

Jaffee, Martin S. *Torah in the Mouth: Writing and Oral Tradition in Palestinian Judaism 200 BCE–400 CE*. Oxford: Oxford University, 2001.

Japhet, Sara. *The Ideology of the Book of Chronicles and Its Place in Biblical Thought*. Translated by Anna Barber. Frankfurt am Main: Peter Lang, 1989.

Jefferson, Rebecca J. W. "The Cairo Genizah Unearthed: The Excavations Conducted by the Count d'Hulst on Behalf of the Bodleian Library and Their Significance for Genizah History." In 'From a Sacred Source:' Genizah Studies in Honour of Stefan C. Reif, edited by Ben Outhwaite and Siam Bhayro, 171–99. Leiden, Netherlands: Brill, 2010.

Jeremias, Joachim. Jesus' Promise to the Nations. Philadelphia: Fortress, 1982.

———. Jesus and the Message of the New Testament. Minneapolis: Fortress Press, 2002.

Josephus. Jewish Antiquities. Vol. 1, bks. 1–3. Translated by H. St. J. Thackeray. LCL 242. Cambridge MA: Harvard University Press, 1930.

———. Jewish Antiquities. Vol. 4, bks. 9–11. Translated by Ralph Marcus. LCL 326. Cambridge MA: Harvard University Press, 1937.

———. Jewish Antiquities. Vol. 5, bks. 12–13. Translated by Ralph Marcus. LCL 365. Cambridge MA: Harvard University Press, 1943.

———. Jewish Antiquities. Vol. 6, bks. 14–15. Translated by Ralph Marcus. LCL 489. Cambridge MA: Harvard University Press, 1943.

———. Jewish Antiquities. Vol. 7, bks. 16–17. Translated by Ralph Marcus and Allen Wikgren. LCL 410. Cambridge MA: Harvard University Press, 1963.

———. Jewish Antiquities. Vol. 8, bks. 18–19. Edited by Louis H. Feldman. LCL 433. Cambridge MA: Harvard University Press, 1965.

———. Jewish Antiquities. Vol. 20, bk. 20. Edited by Louis H. Feldman. LCL 456. Cambridge MA: Harvard University Press, 1965.

———. The Jewish War. Vol. 1, bks. 1–2. Translated by H. St. J. Thackeray. LCL 203. Cambridge MA: Harvard University Press, 1927.

———. The Jewish War. Vol. 2, bks. 3–4. Translated by H. St. J. Thackeray. LCL 487. Cambridge MA: Harvard University Press, 1927.

———. The Jewish War. Vol. 3, bks. 5–7. Translated by H. St. J. Thackeray. LCL 210. Cambridge MA: Harvard University Press, 1928.

———. The Life. Against Apion. Translated by H. St. J. Thackeray. LCL 186. Cambridge MA: Harvard University Press, 1926.

Joslyn-Siemiatkoski, Daniel. Christian Memories of the Maccabean Martyrs. New York: Palgrave, 2009.

JPS Hebrew-English TANAKH. 2nd ed. Philadelphia: Jewish Publication Society, 1999.

Juvenal. Juvenal and Persius. Translated by Susanna Morton Braund. LCL 91. Cambridge MA: Harvard University Press, 2004.

Kahana, Menahem. "The Tannaitic Midrashim." In The Cambridge Genizah Collections: Their Contents and Significance, edited by Stefan C. Reif and Shulamit Reif, 59–73. Cambridge: Cambridge University Press, 2002.

Kahle, Paul. The Cairo Geniza. Oxford: Blackwell, 1959.

Kalman, Jason. Hebrew Union College and the Dead Sea Scrolls. Cincinnati OH: Hebrew Union College, 2012.

————. "Optimistic, Even with the Negatives: The Hebrew Union College-Jewish Institute of Religion and the Dead Sea Scrolls 1948–1993." *AJAJ* 61 (2009): 1–114.

Kamesar, Adam. "The Church Fathers and Rabbinic Midrash." In *Encyclopedia of Midrash*, edited by Jacob Neusner and Alan J. Avery-Peck, 1:20–40. Leiden, Netherlands: Brill, 2005.

————. "The Evolution of the Narrative Aggada in Greek and Latin Patristic Literature." *JTS* 45 (1994): 37–71.

Kamil, Murad. *Catalogue of all Manuscripts in the Monastery of St. Catharine on Mount Sinai*. Wiesbaden: Otto Harrassowitz, 1970.

Kasher, Aryeh. *The Jews in Hellenistic and Roman Egypt: The Struggle for Equal Rights*. Tübingen, Germany: Mohr, 1985.

Katzman, Avi. "Chief Dead Sea Scroll Editor Denounces Judaism, Israel; Claims He's Seen Four More Scrolls Found by Bedouin." *BAR* 17, no. 1 (1991): 64–65, 70, 72.

King, Karen L. *What Is Gnosticism?* Cambridge MA: Harvard University Press, 2003.

Klawans, Jonathan. *Josephus and Theologies of Ancient Judaism*. Oxford: Oxford University Press, 2013.

Knohl, Israel. *The Messiah before Jesus: The Suffering Servant of the Dead Sea Scrolls*. Berkeley: University of California Press, 2000.

Kondoleon, Christine. "The City of Antioch: An Introduction." In *Antioch: The Lost Ancient City*, edited by Christine Kondoleon, 3–11. Princeton NJ: Princeton University Press, 2000.

Kottsieper, Ingo. "'Look, Son, What Nadab Did to Ahikaros . . .' The Aramaic Ahiqar Tradition and Its Relationship to the Book of Tobit." In *Dynamics of Language and Exegesis at Qumran*, edited by Devorah Dimant and Reinhard Gregor Kratz, 145–67. Tübingen, Germany: Mohn Siebeck, 2009.

Kraeling, C. H. "The Jewish Community at Antioch." *JBL* 51 (1932): 130–60.

Kraemer, Ross Shepard. *When Aseneth Met Joseph: A Late Antique Tale of the Biblical Patriarch and His Egyptian Wife, Reconsidered*. Oxford: Oxford University Press, 1998.

Kraft, Robert A. "Tiberius Julius Alexander and the Crisis in Alexandria According to Josephus." In *Of Scribes and Scrolls: Studies on the Hebrew Bible, Intertestamental Judaism, and Christian Origins*, edited by Harold W. Attridge, John J. Collins, and Thomas H. Tobin, 175–84. Lanham MD: University Press of America, 1990.

Kugel, James L. *In Potiphar's House: The Interpretive Life of Biblical Texts*. San Francisco: Harper, 1990.

————. "How Old is the 'Aramaic Levi Document?'" *DSD* 14, no. 3 (2007): 291–312.

————. "On the Interpolations in the 'Book of Jubilees.'" *RevQ* 24, no. 2 (1009): 215–72.

————. "Reuben's Sin with Bilhah in the Testament of Reuben." In *Pomegranates and Golden Bells: Studies in Biblical, Jewish, and Near Eastern Ritual, Law, and Literature in Honor of Jacob Milgrom*, edited by David P. Wright, David Noel Freedman, and Avi Hurvitz, 525–54. Winona Lake IN: Eisenbrauns, 1995.

———. *A Walk through Jubilees: Studies in the Book of Jubilees and the World of Its Creation*. Leiden, Netherlands: Brill, 2012.

Laertius, Diogenes. *Lives of Eminent Philosophers*. Vol. 2. Translated by R. D. Hicks. LCL 185. Cambridge MA: Harvard University Press, 1925.

Lambros, Spyridon. *Catalogue of the Greek Manuscripts on Mount Athos*. 2 vols. London: C. J. Clay and Sons, 1895, 1900.

Larsson, Gerhard. "The Chronology of the Pentateuch: A Comparison of the MT and LXX." *JBL* 102, no. 3 (1983): 401–9.

Leiman, Sid Z., ed. *The Canon and Masorah of the Hebrew Bible: An Introductory Reader*. New York: Ktav, 1974.

———. *The Canonization of Hebrew Literature: The Talmudic and Midrashic Evidence*. Hamden CT: Archon Books, 1976.

———. "The Scroll of Fasts: The Ninth of Tebeth," *JQR* 74, no. 2 (1983): 174–95.

Levine, Étan. "The Syriac Version of Genesis IV:1–16." *VT* 26, no. 1 (1976): 70–78.

Levine, Lee I. *The Ancient Synagogue: The First Thousand Years*. New Haven CT: Yale University Press, 2000.

———. *Jerusalem: Portrait of the City in the Second Temple Period (538 BCE–70 CE)*. Philadelphia: Jewish Publication Society, 2002.

———. *Judaism and Hellenism in Antiquity: Conflict or Confluence?* Peabody MA: Hendrickson, 1999.

———. "The Second Temple Synagogue: The Formative Years." In *The Synagogue in Late Antiquity*, edited by Lee I. Levine, 7–32. Philadelphia: ASOR, 1987.

Lewis, Agnes Smith, and Margaret Dunlop Gibson. *In the Shadow of Sinai: Stories of Travel and Biblical Research*. Brighton: Alpha Press, 1999.

Lim, Timothy H. *The Formation of the Jewish Canon*. New Haven CT: Yale University Press, 2013.

———. "Intellectual Property and the Dead Sea Scrolls." *DSD* 9, no. 2 (2002): 187–98.

Lindenberger, James M. *The Aramaic Proverbs of Ahiqar*. Baltimore: Johns Hopkins University Press, 1983.

Lorein, G. W., and E. van Staalduine-Sulman. "A Song of David for Each Day: The Provenance of the 'Songs of David.'" *Revue de Qumran* 22, no. 1 (2005): 33–59.

Louth, Andrew, Marco Conti, and Thomas C. Oden, eds. *Genesis 1–11*. ACCSOT 1. Downers Grove IL: InterVarsity Press, 2001.

Magness, Jodi. *The Archaeology of Qumran and the Dead Sea Scrolls*. Grand Rapids MI: Eerdmans, 2002.

———. "The Arch of Titus and the Fate of the God of Israel." *JJS* 59 no. 2 (2008): 202–17.

————, ed. *Debating Qumran: Collected Essays on Its Archaeology*. ISACR 4. Leuven: Peeters, 2004.

Malalas, John. *The Chronicle of John Malalas*. Books 8–18. Translated by Matthew Spinka. Chicago: University of Chicago Press, 1940.

Mansfeld, Jaap. "Zeno on the Unity of Philosophy." *Phronesis* 48, no. 2 (2003): 116–31.

Maori, Yeshayahu. "Methodological Criteria for Distinguishing Between Variant *Vorlage* and Exegesis in the Peshitta Pentateuch." In *The Peshitta as a Translation: Papers Read at the Second Peshitta Symposium Held at Leiden 19–21 August 1993*, edited by Peter B. Dirksen and Arie van der Kooij, 103–28. Leiden, Netherlands: Brill, 1995.

Martial. *Epigrams*. Vol. 2, bks. 6–19. Translated by D. R. Shackleton Bailey. LCL 95. Cambridge MA: Harvard University Press, 1993.

Mason, Steve. "Essenes and Lurking Spartans in Josephus' *Judean War*: From Story to History." In *Making History: Josephus and Historical Method*, edited by Zuleika Rogers, 219–61. JSJSup 110. Leiden, Netherlands: Brill, 2006.

————. *Flavius Josephus: Life of Josephus*. Leiden, Netherlands: Brill, 2003.

————. "Josephus." In *The Eerdmans Dictionary of Early Judaism*, edited by John J. Collins and Daniel C. Harlow, 828–32. Grand Rapids MI: Eerdmans, 2010.

————. "Will the Real Josephus Please Stand Up?" *BAR* 23, no. 5 (1997): 58–68.

Maximus, Valerius. *Memorable Doings and Sayings*. Books 1–5. Translated by D. R. Shackleton Bailey. LCL 492. Cambridge MA: Harvard University Press, 2000.

Mazar, Benjamin. "Jerusalem in the Biblical Period." In *Jerusalem Revealed: Archaeology in the Holy City, 1968–1974*, edited by Yigael Yadin, 1–8. Jerusalem: Israel Exploration Society, 1975.

McKnight, Scot. *A Light among the Gentiles: Jewish Missionary Activity in the Second Temple Period*. Minneapolis: Fortress, 1991.

Meridel, Holland. "Robert Curzon, Traveller and Book Collector." *Bulletin of the John Rylands University Library* 65, no. 2 (1983): 123–57.

Milik, Jósef T. "Tefillin, Mezuzot et Targums." *DJD*. Vol. 6, *Qumran Cave 4, vol. 2*, 33–85. Oxford: Clarendon Press, 1977.

Milne, H. J. M., and T. C. Skeat. *Scribes and Correctors of the Codex Sinaiticus*. London: British Museum, 1938.

Modrzejewski, Joseph. *The Jews of Egypt: From Rameses II to Emperor Hadrian*. Philadelphia: Jewish Publication Society, 1995.

Moore, Stewart A. *With Walls of Iron: Jewish Ethnic Identity and Relations in Hellenistic Egypt*. JSJSup 171. Leiden, Netherlands: Brill, 2015.

Mucznik, Sonia, and Asher Ovadiah. "*Deisidaimonia, Superstitio*, and *Religio*: Graeco-Roman, Jewish and Early Christian Concepts." *LA* 64 (2014): 417–40.

Murphy, Frederick J. *Pseudo-Philo: Rewriting the Bible*. New York: Oxford University Press, 1993.

Narinskaya, Elena. *Ephrem, a 'Jewish' Sage: A Comparison of the Exegetical Writings of St. Ephrem the Syrian and Jewish Traditions*. EEMT 7. Turnhout, Belgium: Brepols, 2010.

Netzer, Ehud. *The Architecture of Herod, the Great Builder*. Tübingen, Germany: Mohr Siebeck, 2006.

Newsom, Carol A. "Sectually Explicit" Literature from Qumran." In *The Hebrew Bible and Its Interpreters*, edited by William H. Propp, Baruch Halpern, and David Noel Freedman, 167–187. Winona Lake IN: Eisenbrauns, 1990.

Newsom, Carol A., and Eileen Schuller, et al. DJD. Vol. 11, *Qumran Cave 4, vol. 6: Poetical and Liturgical Texts, part 1*. Oxford: Clarendon Press, 1998.

Niehoff, Maren R. *Jewish Exegesis and Homeric Scholarship in Alexandria*. Cambridge: Cambridge University Press, 2011.

Orosius, Paulus. *The Seven Books of History against the Pagans*. Translated by Roy J. Deferrari. FOTC 50. Washington DC: Catholic University of America Press, 1964.

Outhwaite, Ben. "The Hebrew Manuscript Collection of Cambridge University Library." *European Judaism: A Journal for the New Europe* 41, no. 2 (2008): 37–38.

Parker, D. C. *Codex Sinaiticus: The Story of the World's Oldest Bible*. Peabody MA: Hendrickson, 2010.

Pattie, T. S. "The Codex Sinaiticus." *British Library Journal* 3, no. 1 (1977): 1–6.

Peterson, Michael D. "Tischendorf and the *Codex Sinaiticus*: The Saga Continues." In *The Church and the Library: Studies in Honor of Rev. Dr. George C. Papademetriou*, edited by Dean Papademetriou and Andrew J. Sopko, 75–92. Boston: Somerset Hall Press, 2015.

Petronius. *Satyricon. Apocolocyntosis*. Translated by Michael Heseltine and W. H. D. Rouse. LCL 15. Cambridge MA: Harvard University Press, 1913.

Philo. *Every Good Man Is Free. On the Contemplative Life. On the Eternity of the World. Against Flaccus. Hypothetica. On Providence*. Translated by F. H. Colson. LCL 363. Cambridge MA: Harvard University Press, 1941.

———. *On Abraham. On Joseph. On the Life of Moses*. Translated by F. H. Colson. LCL 289. Cambridge MA: Harvard University Press, 1935.

———. *On the Confusion of Tongues. On the Migration of Abraham. Who Is the Heir of Divine Things? On Mating with the Preliminary Studies*. Translated by F. H. Colson. LCL 261. Cambridge MA: Harvard University Press, 1932.

———. *On the Embassy to Gaius. General Indexes*. Translated by F. H. Colson. LCL 379. Cambridge MA: Harvard University Press, 1962.

———. *Questions on Genesis*. Translated by Ralph Marcus. LCL 380. Cambridge MA: Harvard University Press, 1953.

Pietersma, Albert. *The Apocryphon of Jannes and Jambres the Magicians*. Leiden, Netherlands: Brill, 1994.

Pliny. *Natural History*. Vol. 2, bks. 3–7. Translated by H. Rackham. LCL 352. Cambridge MA: Harvard University Press, 1942.

———. *Natural History*. Vol. 8, bks. 28–32. Translated by W. H. S. Jones. LCL 418. Cambridge MA: Harvard University Press, 1963.

Plutarch. *Lives*. Vol. 9. Translated by B. Perrin. LCL 101. Cambridge MA: Harvard University Press, 1920.

———. *Moralia*. Vol. 2. Translated by Frank Cole Babbitt. LCL 222. Cambridge MA: Harvard University Press, 1928.

———. *Moralia*. Vol. 4. Translated by Frank Cole Babbitt. LCL 305. Cambridge MA: Harvard University Press, 1936.

Porter, Stanley E. *Constantine Tischendorf: The Life and Work of a 19th Century Bible Hunter*. New York: T&T Clark, 2015.

———. "Hero or Thief? Constantine Tischendorf Turns Two Hundred." *BAR* 41, no. 5 (2015): 45–53, 66.

Price, Whigham A. *The Ladies of Castlebrae*. Gloucester UK: Alan Sutton Press, 1985.

Pucci Ben Zeev, Miriam. *Jewish Rights in the Roman World: The Greek and Roman Documents Quoted by Josephus Flavius*. Tübingen, Germany: Mohr Siebeck, 1998.

Regev, Eyal. "Were the Priests All the Same? Qumranic Halakhah in Comparison with Sadducean Halakha." *DSD* 12, no. 2 (2005): 158–88.

Reif, Stefan C. "The Damascus Document from the Cairo Genizah: Its Discovery, Early Study and Historical Significance." In *The Damascus Document: A Centennial of Discovery: Proceedings of the Third International Symposium of the Orion Center for the Study of the Dead Sea Scrolls and Associated Literature, 4–8 February, 1998*, edited by Joseph M. Baumgarten, Esther G. Chazon, and Avital Pinnick, 109–31. Leiden, Netherlands: Brill, 2000.

———. "Giblews, Jews and Genizah Views." *JJS* 4, no. 2 (2004): 332–46.

———. *A Jewish Archive from Old Cairo: The History of Cambridge University's Genizah Collection*. Richmond UK: Curzon, 2000.

Ritter, Bradley. *Judeans in the Greek Cities of the Roman Empire*. JSJSup 170. Leiden, Netherlands: Brill, 2015.

Robinson, James M., ed. *The Nag Hammadi Library: The Definitive Translation of the Gnostic Scriptures Complete in One Volume*. San Francisco: Harper, 1990.

Robinson, Thomas M. "The Cosmic Role of the Logos, as Conceived from Heraclitus until Eriugena." *Greek Orthodox Theological Review* 59, nos. 1–4 (2014): 13–39.

———. "Heraclitus and Plato on the Language of the Real." *The Monist* 74, no. 4 (1991): 481–90.

Rosenthal, David, ed. *The Cairo Geniza Collection in Geneva: Catalogue and Studies*. Jerusalem: Magnes Press, 2010.

Rouwhorst, Gerard. "Jewish Liturgical Traditions in Early Syriac Christianity." *Vigilae Christianae* 51, no. 1 (1997): 72–93.

Runesson, Anders, Donald D. Binder, and Birger Olsson, eds. *The Ancient Synagogue from Its Origins to 200 CE*. Leiden, Netherlands: Brill, 2008.

Sanders, Edward Parish. *Judaism: Practice and Belief: 63 BCE–66 CE*. London: SCM Press, 1992.

Sandmel, Samuel. *Philo of Alexandria: An Introduction*. New York: Oxford University Press, 1979.

Saphir, Joseph. *Even Sapir*. Lyck: Rudolph Siebert, 1866.

Sarris, Nikolas. "The Discovery of a New Fragment from the Codex Sinaiticus." *Bulletin of the Saint Catherine's Foundation* (2010): 1.

Schäfer, Peter. *Judeophobia: Attitudes toward the Jews in the Ancient World*. Cambridge MA: Harvard University Press, 1997.

———. *The Origins of Jewish Mysticism*. Princeton NJ: Princeton University Press, 2009.

Schechter, Solomon. *Avot de-Rabbi Nathan*. Vienna: Knöppfelmacher Press. 1887.

———, ed. *Documents of Jewish Sectaries: Fragments of a Zadokite Work; Fragments of the Book of the Commandments of Anan*. 2 vols. Cambridge: Cambridge University Press, 1910.

———. "A Fragment of the Original Text of Ecclesiasticus." *The Expositor* 5, no. 4 (1896): 1–15.

———. *Studies in Judaism*. Vol. 2. Philadelphia: Jewish Publication Society, 1908.

Schechter, Solomon, and Charles Taylor. *The Wisdom of Ben Sira, Portions of the Book of Ecclesiasticus*. Cambridge: Cambridge University Press, 1899.

Schiffman, Lawrence. "From the Cairo Genizah to Qumran: The Influence of the Zadokite Fragments on the Study of the Qumran Scrolls." In *The Dead Sea Scrolls: Texts and Context*, edited by Charlotte Hempel, 451–66. Leiden, Netherlands: Brill, 2010.

———. "Halakha and Sectarianism in the Dead Sea Scrolls." In *The Dead Sea Scrolls in Their Historical Context*, edited by Timothy H. Lim, 123–42. Edinburgh: T&T Clark, 2000.

———. "The Place of 4QMMT in the Corpus of Qumran Manuscripts." In *Reading 4QMMT*, edited by M. J. Bernstein and J. Kampen, 81–98. SBL Symposium Series. Atlanta GA: Scholars Press, 1996.

———. *Reclaiming the Dead Sea Scrolls: The History of Judaism, the Background of Christianity, and Lost Library of Qumran*. New York: Doubleday, 1994.

———. "Second Temple Literature and the Cairo Genizah." *Proceedings of the American Academy for Jewish Research* 63 (1997–2001): 137–61.

———. "A Short History of the Dead Sea Scrolls and What They Tell Us." *BAR* 41, no. 3 (2015): 44–53.

Schmelzer, Menachem. "One Hundred Years of Genizah Discovery and Research: The American Share." *Judaica Librarianship* 11, nos. 1–2 (2003): 56–61.

Schoene, Alfred, ed. *Eusebius: Chronicorum Canonum.* Dublin: Weidmann, 1867.

Schofield, Alison. *From Qumran to the Yaḥad: A New Paradigm of Textual Development for the Community Rule.* Leiden, Netherlands: Brill, 2009.

Schwartz, Daniel R. *Agrippa I: The Last King of Judaea.* Tübingen, Germany: Mohr Siebeck, 1990.

———. "Philo, His Life and Times." In *The Cambridge Companion to Philo*, edited by Adam Kamesar, 9–31. Cambridge: Cambridge University Press, 2009.

———. *Reading the First Century: On Reading Josephus and Studying Jewish History of the First Century.* WUNT 1:300. Tübingen, Germany: Mohr Siebeck, 2013.

———, ed. *Was 70 CE a Watershed in Jewish History? On Jews and Judaism before and after the Destruction of the Second Temple.* Leiden, Netherlands: Brill, 2011.

Seidman, Gertrud. "The Rev. Greville John Chester and 'The Ashmolean Museum as a Home for Archaeology in Oxford.'" *Bulletin of the History of Archaeology* 16, no. 1 (2006): 27–33.

Segal, Michael. *The Book of Jubilees: Rewritten Bible, Redaction, Ideology, and Theology.* JSJSup 117. Leiden, Netherlands: Brill, 2007.

Segal, Michael, Emanuel Tov, William Brent Seales, Clifford Seth Parker, Penina Shor, Yosef Porath, and Ada Yardeni. "An Early Leviticus Scroll from En-Gedi: Preliminary Publication." *Textus* 26 (2016): 1–30.

Seneca. *Epistles.* Vol. 1. Translated by Richard M. Gummere. LCL 75. Cambridge MA: Harvard University Press, 1917.

———. *Epistles.* Vol. 2. Translated by Richard M. Gummere. LCL 76. Cambridge MA: Harvard University Press, 1920.

Ševĉenko, Ihor. "New Documents on Constantine Tischendorf and the *Codex Sinaiticus.*" *Scriptorium* 18, no. 1 (1964): 55–80.

Shanks, Hershel. *Freeing the Dead Sea Scrolls and Other Adventures of an Archaeology Outsider.* London: Continuum, 2010.

———. "Intellectual Property Law and the Scholar: Cases I Have Known." In *On Scrolls, Artefacts, and Intellectual Property*, edited by Timothy Lim, Hector MacQueen, and Calum Carmichael, 63–73. JSPSup 38; Sheffield UK: Sheffield Academic Press, 2001.

Simon-Shoshan, Moshe. "The Tasks of the Translators: The Rabbis, the Septuagint, and the Cultural Politics of Translation." *Prooftexts* 27, no. 1 (2007): 1–39.

Simkovich, Malka Z. "Greek Influence on the Composition of 2 Maccabees." *JSJ* 42, no. 3 (2011): 293–310.

———. *The Making of Jewish Universalism: From Exile to Alexandria.* Lanham MD: Rowman and Littlefield, 2017.

Sly, Dorothy. *Philo's Alexandria*. London: Routledge, 1996.

Smallwood, E. Mary. "Palestine c. A. D. 115–118." *Historia: Zeitschrift für Alte Geschichte* 11, no. 4 (1962): 500–510.

Smith, Agnes Lewis. *Light on the Four Gospels: From the Sinai Palimpsest*. London: Williams and Norgate, 1913.

Soskice, Janet M. *The Sisters of Sinai: How Two Lady Adventurers Discovered the Hidden Gospels*. New York: Knopf, 2009.

Sotiris, Kadas. *Mount Athos: An Illustrated Guide to the Monasteries and Their History*. Athens: Ekdotike Athenon, 1980.

Speake, Graham. *Mount Athos: Renewal in Paradise*. New Haven CT: Yale University Press, 2002.

Spiridon, Lambros P. *Catalogue of the Greek Manuscripts on Mount Athos*. 2 vols. New York: Macmillan, 1895, 1900.

Stern, Menahem. *Greek and Latin Authors on Jews and Judaism*. 3 vols. Jerusalem: Israel Academy of Sciences and Humanities, 1974–1984.

Stone, Michael E. *Apocrypha, Pseudepigrapha, and Armenian Studies: Collected Papers*. Paris: Peeters, 2006.

Stuckenbruck, Loren T. "Messianic Ideas in the Apocalyptic and Related Literature of Early Judaism." In *Messiah in the Old and New Testaments*, edited by Stanley E. Porter, 90–113. Grand Rapids MI: Eerdmans, 2007.

Suetonius. *Lives of the Caesars*. Vol. 2. Translated by J. C. Rolfe. LCL 38. Cambridge MA: Harvard University Press, 1914.

Sukenik, Eliezer L. *The Dead Sea Scrolls of the Hebrew University*. Jerusalem: Magnes, 1955.

Tacitus. *The Histories; The Annals*. Translated by Clifford H. Moore. LCL 292. Cambridge MA: Harvard University Press, 1969.

Talmon, Shemaryahu. *Masada*. Vol. 6, *The Yigael Yadin Excavation, 1963–1965*. Jerusalem: Israel Exploration Society, 1999.

Taylor, Joan E., and Philip R. Davies. "The So-Called Therapeutae of 'De Vita Contemplativa': Identity and Character." *Harvard Theological Review* 91 no. 1 (1998): 3–24.

Tcherikover, Victor A. "Jewish Apologetic Literature Reconsidered." *Eos* 48 (1956): 169–93.

Tcherikover, Victor A., and Alexander Fuks. *Corpus Papyrorum Judaicarum*. 2 vols. Cambridge MA: Harvard University Press, 1957–1960.

Tepper, Yigal, and Yotam Tepper. "Archaeological Views: Walking Roads." *BAR* 42, no. 1 (2016): 20, 62.

Thiering, Barbara E. *Jesus and the Riddle of the Dead Sea Scrolls: Unlocking the Secrets of His Life Story*. San Francisco: Harper, 1992.

Tischendorf, Constantin. *Codex Sinaiticus: The Ancient Biblical Manuscript Now in the British Museum. Tischendorf's Story and Argument Related by Himself.* 8th ed. London: Lutterworth, 1923.

Trever, John C. *The Dead Sea Scrolls—A Personal Account.* Grand Rapids MI: Eerdmans, 1979.

———. *The Untold Story of Qumran.* Westwood NJ: F. H. Revell, 1965.

Van der Horst, Peter W., ed. *The Sentences of Pseudo-Phocylides: With Introduction and Commentary by P. W. van der Horst.* SVTP 4. Leiden, Netherlands: Brill, 1978.

VanderKam, James C. *The Dead Sea Scrolls Today.* Grand Rapids MI: Eerdmans, 1994.

VanderKam, James, and Peter Flint. *The Meaning of the Dead Sea Scrolls: Their Significance for Understanding the Bible, Judaism, Jesus and Christianity.* San Francisco: Harper, 2002.

Vermes, Geza. *The Complete Dead Sea Scrolls in English.* Rev. ed. London: Penguin, 2004.

———. *The Resurrection: History and Myth.* New York: Doubleday, 2008.

Von Arnim, Hans. *Stoicorum Veterum Fragmenta.* 3 vols. Berlin: De Gruyter, 1903.

Von Harnack, Adolf. *New Testament Studies.* Translated by J. R. Wilkinson. CTL 20. New York: Putnam, 1907.

Wasserstein, Abraham, and David J. Wasserstein. *The Legend of the Septuagint: From Classical Antiquity to Today.* Cambridge: Cambridge University Press, 2006.

Waterfield, Robin. *Dividing the Spoils: The War for Alexander the Great's Empire.* Oxford: Oxford University Press, 2011.

Weiss-Rosmarin, Trude. "Shlomo Dov Goitein—Scholar Extraordinary." *Judaism* 33, no. 3 (1984): 309–17.

Wills, Lawrence M. *The Jewish Novel in the Ancient World.* Ithaca NY: Cornell University Press, 1995.

Wright, Benjamin G. *The Letter of Aristeas: 'Aristeas to Philocrates' or 'On the Translation of the Law of the Jews.'* CEJL 8. Berlin: De Gruyter, 2015.

Yadin, Yigael. *The Excavations of Masada, 1963/64.* IEJ 15, nos. 1–2. Jerusalem: Israel Exploration Society, 1965.

———. *The Scroll of the War of the Sons of Light against the Sons of Darkness.* Oxford: Oxford University Press, 1962.

———. *Tefillin from Qumran.* Jerusalem: Israel Exploration Society, 1969.

———. "Tefillin (Phylacteries) from Qumran (XQPhyl 1–4)." *Eretz Israel* 9 (1969): 60–83 [Hebrew].

Yerushalmi, Yosef Hayim. *Zakhor: Jewish History and Jewish Memory.* Seattle: University of Washington Press, 1982.

Yonge, Charles D., trans. *The Works of Philo: Complete and Unabridged.* 11th ed. Peabody MA: Hendrickson, 2011.

Yoshiko Reed, Annette. "The Construction and Subversion of Patriarchal Perfection: Abraham and Exemplarity in Philo, Josephus, and the *Testament of Abraham*." *JSJ* 40, no. 2 (2009): 185–212.

———. "The Modern Invention of 'Old Testament Pseudepigrapha.'" *JTS* 60, no. 2 (2009): 403–36.

Zeitlin, Solomon. "Scholarship and the Hoax of the Recent Discoveries." *JQR* 39, no. 4 (1949): 337–63.

Zetterholm, Magnus. "Antioch." In *The Eerdmans Dictionary of Early Judaism*, edited by John J. Collins and Daniel C. Harlow, 336–38. Grand Rapids MI: Eerdmans, 2010.

GENERAL INDEX

Diaspora, xxiii, 94–95, 98, 107, 173–74, 187, 198, 243

dietary laws, xv, xvii, xix, 63, 75, 94, 96, 109–12, 119, 121, 129, 131, 146, 171, 178, 187, 194, 253, 272

Dio Chrysostom, 158

Dionysios son of Theon, 102

Discoveries in the Judaean Desert, 44–46, 48

Domitian, 81, 105, 191, 193

Donceel, Robert, 51

Donceel Voûte, Pauline, 51

Doris, 72

Dorner, Dalia, 47

Drusus, 74

Duhm, Bernhard, 7–8

earthquake, 122

École Biblique et Archéologique Français, 43–44, 51

Egypt, 3, 5–6, 12, 19, 22, 39, 61–63, 72, 93–94, 100, 105–8, 110, 112, 141, 195, 203, 226–27, 234–36, 251–52, 261, 268; magicians, 260; people, 91–93, 97, 110, 133, 228, 237, 253, 261, 268

Egypt Exploration Fund, 12

Ein Gedi, 52

Eisenman, Robert, 46–48

Eleazar (high priest in the Letter of Aristeas), 141

Eleazar (Pharisaic opponent of John Hyrcanus), 148

Elephantine, 93–94

Elijah, 215

Enoch, 35, 62–63

Epicureans, 195

Esau, 107, 218–19, 223, 225, 253

Essenes, 18, 145–48, 151, 155–58, 165–66, 170–71, 189, 195

Esther, 243, 245, 249, 257

Ethiopia, 36–37, 39, 54; Bible, 38; church, 36–38; monasteries, 36–38

Ethiopic Manuscript Imaging Project, 38

Ethiopic Monastic Manuscript Library, 38

Ethnarch, 94–95

Europe, 98, 129

Eusebius, 105–6, 240

Eve. *See* Hava

exemplum, 137

exile, xv, 7, 93, 173, 223, 241

Ezekiel the Tragedian, 111–12, 239–40

Ezra, xiv–xv

Fabricius, Johann Albert, xx–xxi

Felix, 189

Festival of Weeks, 76, 149, 181, 223

Firkovich, Abraham, 10, 14

Fiscus Judaicus, 84, 105

Flaccus, Aulus Avilius, 95, 100–101, 132

Flaccus, Lucius Valerius, 97

Flavian dynasty, 81

Frederick Augustus II, 22

Friedberg Genizah Project, 15

Gabriel, 267

Gad, 252–53

Gaius Caligula, 73, 99–102, 132, 139

Galba, 83

Galilee, 71, 73, 196

Gamaliel, 83, 167, 216–17

Garden of Eden, 179, 264

Gaul, 73

Gaza, 68

Ge'ez (Ethiopic), 36–38

George Fox University, 37

Gerousia, 95

Gessius Florus, 77–78

Getty Museum, 29

Gibeah, 59

Gibson, James Young, 3
Gibson, Margaret Dunlop, 3–5, 16
Gihon, 59
Goitein, Shlomo Dov, 12–13
Google, 49
Great Lavra Monastery, 30–31
Greece, 3, 29–30, 39, 62; culture, 65, 96,
    112, 125, 131–32, 134, 194, 198, 246, 272;
    language, xiii, xix, 4, 16, 22, 27, 29–30,
    35, 87–88, 95, 109–10, 112, 130, 141, 159,
    184, 190, 204, 208–11, 216, 235, 241,
    243, 250, 260–61; literature, 271; peo-
    ple, 91–93, 95, 103–4, 109, 116–17, 121,
    155–56, 234, 258; philosophy, 131–32,
    135, 140, 142; rule, 129; stylistics, xix,
    95, 199, 239; Ptolemaic, 64, 123, 129;
    Syrian, xxv, 64–67, 123, 165, 184, 257

Habakkuk, 42, 246
Hades, 254
Hadrian, 84–85, 106–7
Hagar, 180
halakha (Jewish law), xv, xxvi, 18, 50, 86
Haman, 240, 247
Hananiah, 244
Hanukkah, 257
Harvard University, 44
Hasideans, 165
Hasidic Judaism, 4
Hasmoneans, xviii, 64, 68–72, 77, 145–
    47; rebellion, xxv, 64–67, 87, 257–58
Hava, 210–11, 263
Haverford College, 38
Hebrew, xix, 4–5, 7–8, 16–17, 35, 39, 47, 53,
    87–88, 109–10, 112, 140–41, 150, 159, 178,
    184, 204, 207–11, 213, 216, 235, 243, 246
Hebrew Union College, 46, 48
Hebrew University of Jerusalem, 13,
    42–43, 45, 48

Hebron, 59
Heliodorus, 228
Heliopolis, 93
Heraclitis, 135
Hermes, 235
Herod, 71–74, 86, 156
Herodium, 73
Herod Philip, 73
Hexapla, 15–16, 210
Hillel, Rabbi, xv, 152
Hinzinger, Claus, 44
holidays, Jewish, 76, 96, 112, 131, 171,
    182–83, 187, 208, 223; Greek and
    Roman, 66, 96, 117, 129–30, 178–79
Holofernes, 255–57
Homer, 92, 111, 250
Huntington Library, 48
Hussein, King, 44
Hyrcania, 61
Hyrcanus, John, 148, 152
Hyrcanus I, 71
Hyrcanus II, 70–71

idol worship, 60, 75, 223, 244–55
Idumeans, 70–71, 74, 79
Institut de Paris, 14
Isaac, 136, 178, 181, 218, 225, 253
Isaiah, 124
Ish-bosheth, 177
Ishmael, 180, 253; Ishmaelites, 34
Isis, 92
Islam, 219
Israel Antiquities Authority, 46–52
Israelite kingdom, 60
Issachar, 253

Jacob (biblical patriarch), 19, 33, 60, 107,
    122, 136, 178, 181–82, 218, 224, 253
Jacob (Judas's son), 75

Levi, Israel, 14

Levites, 160

Lewis, Agnes Smith, 3–5, 16, 26, 40

Lewis, Samuel Savage, 3

Logos, 135–36

Lucas (Lukuas), 105–6

Lusius Quietus, 105–6

Lydda, 105

Lysimachus, 62

Lystra, 120

Maccabees. *See* Hasmoneans

Macedonia, 62–63, 93, 129

Malalas, John, 115, 118

Madan, Falconer, 12

Manetho, 210

Manoog, Charles, 43

Mar Athanasius Samuel, 42–43

Mariamne, 71–72

Marquette University, 35

Masada, 17, 66, 73, 157, 167–68, 192

Masoretic text, 18, 53, 207

Mastema, 258, 261–62

mathematics, 112, 131, 195

Mattathias, 64–65, 67, 165

Men of the Great Assembly, xviii, 150, 206

Menahem, Essene, 156

Menelaus, 67

menorah, 35, 81

Merkel, David, 52

Mesopotamia, 106

Messiah, 74–75, 84–85, 119, 123, 184, 214, 217–18, 261, 268–69

Metropolitan Museum of Art, 28–29

Michael, 229–30, 260, 262, 265–68

Midian, 261

midrash, xxvi, 132, 138–39, 154, 180–81

Mikva. *See* ritual immersion

Milik, Józef, 44

Mishael, 244

Moab, 85

Montefiore, Claude, 4

Mordecai, 228, 240, 245, 247–49, 257

Moses, xvi, 67, 111, 138, 150, 176, 179, 205, 228, 234–40, 254–55, 261, 267–68

Mosseri Collection, 14

Mosseri, Jacques, 14

Mount Athos, xiii, 29–34, 37, 39–40, 53

Mynas, Mynoides, 32

Nabataea, 70

Nahor, 182

Naphtali, 252–53

Nasri Ohan, 42

National Library of Israel, 38

National Library of Russia, 10, 14, 19, 24–25, 30, 33, 35

Natural Law, 139

Nebuchadnezzar, 63, 173, 257

Nehemiah, xiv–xv

Nero, 83, 103, 189–90, 192, 261

Nicanor, 192

Nile, 91, 93, 203

Noahide laws, 75

Octavian. *See* Augustus

Onqelos, 217–19

Ohan, Nasri, 42

Onias III, xxvii, 66–67

Oral Law, xiv, xxvi, 18, 68, 70, 146, 150–51, 154, 164

Origen, 15–16, 210

Orlinsky, Harry, 43

Orlov, Andrei, 35

Orontes River, 115

Orpheus, 234

Ostraca, 93–94

Otho, 83

Palestine, 3, 5–6, 9

Palestine Archeological Museum, 43, 48, 51

palimpsest, 15, 22, 26, 29

Panayotov, Alex, xxi–xxii

Papyri, 3, 27, 93–94, 102–3, 172, 203

Parthians, 71

Passover, 76–77, 145, 149, 176, 181, 215

Patriarch, xviii, 83

Paul, xvi, 88, 119–20

Paulus Orosius, 106

Pentephres, 252

Perea, 71

Persia, 61, 93, 174, 215, 258; Persians, 93, 248; culture, 272; Empire, xv, 61–62; king, 260; language, 39

Peshitta, 210–13

Peter, 74, 119–20

Pharisees, 18, 68–71, 73–74, 86, 100, 145–54, 164, 166–67, 171–72, 189, 195

Pharaoh, 112, 226–27, 240, 251–52, 254–55

Pharos, 109

Philip of Macedonia, 62

Philo of Alexandria, xiii, xxii, 92, 94–95, 98–102, 105, 109–10, 131–40, 142–43, 156–57, 169, 195, 198, 228, 235, 256

Phylacteries, 41, 51–52

Pickwoad, Nicholas, 28, 39–40

pilgrimage, 76

Piyyut, 15

Plato, 92, 137, 139–40

platonic philosophers, 136

Pliny the Elder, 157, 254

Poimenidou, Maria, 31

Pompey, 70–71, 87, 106, 184

Poppea, 190

Porath, Yosef, 52

Potiphar, 251

Potiphar's wife, 233

priesthood, 19, 67, 83, 148, 160–61, 164, 173, 180, 189, 232, 235, 246; high priesthood, 66, 68, 70–71, 79, 118, 165, 167

Princeton University, 14

Ptolemaic Kingdom, 62–64, 91–93

Ptolemy I Soter, 62–63, 91, 93, 195

Ptolemy II Philadelphus, 63, 108–9, 140–42, 209

Purim, 257

Pythagoreans, 195

Qimron, Elisha, 45–47

Quintus Marcius Turbo, 105

Qumran, xiii, xxiv, 19, 37, 41, 43–45, 49–53, 157–64, 168, 207, 217, 268

Rabbis, xvi, xviii, xxvi, 13, 68, 96, 172, 197, 207, 219; community, 206, 272; Judaism, 50, 52, 55, 86, 273; literature, xvii, 4, 16–18, 36, 69, 74, 80, 107; period, xiv–xv, xviii, xxiii, 35, 63, 109, 204; tradition, 7, 20, 82–83, 110, 265

Rachel, 253

Raguel, 239

Rebecca, 181–82, 218, 224–25

Rehoboam, 59–60

Reif, Stefan, 13

Religio, 98

resurrection, 70, 111, 131, 150–51, 154–55, 266–67, 269

Reuben, 231, 253

ritual immersion, 161

ritual purity, 49–50, 161, 163–64, 171

Robinson, James, 46–47

Rockefeller Museum. *See* Palestine Archeological Museum

Rome, 36, 100–102, 105, 118, 121; culture, xv, 74, 96, 112, 125, 194, 234, 272;

Empire, xvi, 26, 66, 68, 70–89, 91–101, 105, 107, 117–18, 122, 124, 132, 166–68, 184, 189–93, 218–19, 261, 272; forum, 81; historians, 196; legions, 104; people, 72, 110, 121, 198, 242; Senate, 97

Sabbath, xv, xvii, xix, 78–79, 92, 94, 96, 109–12, 129, 131, 133–35, 146, 165, 170–71, 178, 180–83, 187, 194–95, 199, 208, 216, 253, 272
sabbatical year, 80
Saddok. *See* Zadok (member of Josephus's "fourth philosophy")
Sadducees, 18, 70, 79, 86, 146–55, 164–66, 171, 189, 195
Saint Petersburg, 23–24, 35
Salahi, Faidi, 42
Salome, sister of Herod, 72–73
Salome Alexandra, 68–70, 152
Samael, 258, 264–65
Samaritans, 18, 164
Saphir, Jacob, 9–10
Sarah, 137–38, 181, 226–27, 240
Sarris, Nikolas, 27–28
Satan, 211–13, 258–60
Saul, 59, 177, 235
Scaurus, 70
Schechter, Mathilde, 6
Schechter, Solomon, 4–12, 16–17, 26, 40, 164
Schiffman, Lawrence, 164
Scriptoria, 21
Seales, Brent, 52
Sebastos, 73
Seleucid Kingdom, 62–64
Seleucus I Nicator, 62, 116–17
Seleucus IV, 66
Septuagint, xix–xx, xxiii, 4, 15, 63, 108–10, 131–32, 138, 140, 198, 209–10, 243, 246

Shanks, Hershel, 46–47
Shehem, 59
Shlomo Itzchaki, Rabbi (Rashi), 219–20
Shor, Pnina, 52
showbread, 81
Sicarii, 166–67
Silk Road, 38
Simeon, 253
Simeon (son of Judas), 75
Simeon II (father of Onias III), xxvii
Simonides, 193
Sinaites, Father Justin, 28–29
Sisera, 256
Skehan, Patrick, 44
Slavonic, 34–35
slavery, 63, 80, 83, 91, 93, 142, 145, 179, 191–93
Smith, John, 3
Society of Biblical Literature, 47
Socrates, 137
Solomon, 59, 207, 262
St. Athanasios, 30
St. Catherine's Monastery, xiii, 4, 21–30, 37, 39–40, 53
St. Mark's Monastery, 42
Starcky, Jean, 44
Stoicism, 95–96, 147
Stoic philosophers, 135–36, 156, 195
Strabo, 94
Strugnell, John, 44–47
Stuckenbruck, Loren, 36–37
Suetonius, 105
Sukenik, Eliezer, 42–43
Sukkot. *See* Tabernacles
Sulzberger, Meir, 5–6
Superstitio, 98
Suriel, 267
Susanna, 63, 243–44
Symmachus, 15

synagogues, xxi, xxiii, 6, 15, 52–53, 61, 78, 116, 125, 149, 216; at Alexandria, 92, 94, 100, 108, 112; at Antioch, 116–18, 125; at Daphne, 119, 125

Synesius, 158

Syria, 62, 118, 123–24

Syria Palestina, 85

Syriac, 3–4, 26–27, 124, 184, 204, 210–11, 215

Syriac Sinaiticus, 4–5, 26–28

Syrian wars, 64

Ta'amireh Tribe, 41

Tabernacles, xv, 68, 74, 76, 149, 181, 215, 223

Talmud, xxvi, 6, 11, 13, 256

Targum, 211, 215–20

taxes, 60, 71, 78, 84, 96, 105, 166, 193–94

Taylor-Schechter Genizah Collection, 13–14, 49

Temple, Jerusalem, xvi, 24, 34, 36, 59, 61, 65–68, 70–71, 73–83, 86–89, 97–99, 101, 105, 118, 125, 132, 141, 148–51, 153–54, 167, 169, 173, 180, 184–85, 205–6, 215, 241–42, 268–69; at Elephantine, 93–94; at Leontopolis, Persian, 246–47; Roman, 81, 105

Tepper, Yigal, 76

Tepper, Yotam, 76

tetrarchy, 73

theater, 66, 82, 115, 122

Theodotion, 16

Therapeutae, 169–71

Thrace, 62

Tiberius, 74, 98–101

Tiberius Julius Alexander, 77, 104–5

Tiglath-Pileser III, 60

Tischendorf, Constantin, 21–26, 32, 39–40

Titus, 77, 79, 116–17, 192–93

Torah, xvii, 18, 52–54, 69, 74, 109, 134–35, 139, 146, 148, 150, 152–53; scroll, 109, 203

Toth, Michael, 29

Tov, Emanuel, 46, 49

Trajan, 105–7

Turkey, 115

University of Athens, 27

University of Berlin, 4

University of Cambridge, 4, 9–10, 13–16

University of Frankfurt, 12

University of Oxford, 11–12, 16

University of Pennsylvania, 14

Uriah, 174

Uriel, 267

Uspensky, Porphyrius, 26, 33

Vatican, 35–36, 54

Ventidius Cumanus, 77

Vermes, Geza, 221

Vespasian, 78–79, 81–84, 105, 107, 116, 169, 190–192, 195, 261

victories, 81

Villemain, Abel-Francois, 32

Vitellius, 83

Wacholder, Ben Zion, 46

War of Quietus, 105

Wellhausen, Julius, 7–8

Westminster College, 16

Wise, Michael, 48

Yadin, Yigael, 42, 45, 52, 161

Yannai, 15–16

Yehoshua, 83

Yerushalmi, Yosef Hayim, 197

INDEX BY PASSAGE

This index comprises categories that are arranged with an eye toward chronology. Some categories in this index include texts whose dates of composition are widely disputed.